Lecture Notes in Computer Science 12223

More information about this series at http://www.springer.com/series/7410

Clémentine Maurice · Leyla Bilge ·
Gianluca Stringhini · Nuno Neves (Eds.)

Detection of Intrusions
and Malware, and
Vulnerability Assessment

17th International Conference, DIMVA 2020
Lisbon, Portugal, June 24–26, 2020
Proceedings

 Springer

Editors
Clémentine Maurice
Univ Rennes, CNRS, IRISA
Rennes, France

Leyla Bilge
NortonLifeLock Research Group
Biot, France

Gianluca Stringhini
Department of Electrical and Computer
Engineering
Boston University
Boston, MA, USA

Nuno Neves
Department of Informatics
University of Lisboa
Lisbon, Portugal

ISSN 0302-9743   ISSN 1611-3349   (electronic)
Lecture Notes in Computer Science
ISBN 978-3-030-52682-5   ISBN 978-3-030-52683-2   (eBook)
https://doi.org/10.1007/978-3-030-52683-2

LNCS Sublibrary: SL4 – Security and Cryptology

This Springer imprint is published by the registered company Springer Nature Switzerland AG
The registered company address is: Gewerbestrasse 11, 6330 Cham, Switzerland

Preface

On behalf of the Program Committee, it is our pleasure to present the proceedings of the 17th International Conference on Detection of Intrusions and Malware and Vulnerability Assessment (DIMVA 2020), which took place virtually due to the COVID-19 pandemic, June 24–26, 2020. Since 2004, DIMVA has been bringing together leading researchers and practitioners from academia, industry, and government to present and discuss novel security research in the broader areas of intrusion detection, malware analysis, and vulnerability assessment. DIMVA is organized by the Special Interest Group – Security, Intrusion Detection, and Response (SIDAR) – of the German Informatics Society (GI).

This year, DIMVA received 45 valid submissions from academic and industrial organizations from more than 60 different institutions across 21 countries. Each submission was carefully reviewed by at least three Program Committee members or external experts. The submissions were evaluated on the basis of scientific novelty, importance to the field, and technical quality. The final selection of papers was decided by Program Committee members during online discussions. The Program Committee selected 13 full papers for presentation at the conference and publication in these proceedings, resulting in an acceptance rate of 28.9%. The accepted papers present novel ideas, techniques, and applications in important areas of computer security, including Web security, malware analysis and defense, security of industrial systems and cyber physical systems, attack mitigation, network security, and software security.

A successful conference is the result of the joint effort of many people. We would like to express our appreciation to the Program Committee members and external reviewers for the time spent reviewing papers, participating in the online discussion, and shepherding some of the papers to ensure the highest quality possible. We also deeply thank the members of the Organizing Committee for their hard work in making DIMVA 2020 such a successful event. We are wholeheartedly thankful to our sponsors ERNW, Siemens, and Springer for generously supporting DIMVA 2020. We also thank Springer for publishing these proceedings as part of their LNCS series and the DIMVA Steering Committee for their continuous support and assistance.

Finally, DIMVA 2020 would not have been possible without the authors who submitted their work and presented their contributions, as well as the attendees. We would like to thank them all, and we look forward to their future contributions to DIMVA.

June 2020

Clémentine Maurice
Leyla Bilge
Gianluca Stringhini
Nuno Neves

Organization

DIMVA was organized by the Special Interest Group – Security, Intrusion Detection, and Response (SIDAR) – of the German Informatics Society (GI).

Organizing Committee

General Chair
Nuno Neves   FCUL, University of Lisbon, Portugal

Program Chair
Clémentine Maurice   CNRS, IRISA, France

Program Co-chair
Leyla Bilge   NortonLifeLock Research Group, France

Publications Chair
Gianluca Stringhini   Boston University, USA

Publicity Chair
Pedro Ferreira   FCUL, University of Lisbon, Portugal

Sponsor Chair
Thomas Schreck   University of Applied Sciences, Germany

Local Arrangements Chair
Ibéria Medeiros   FCUL, University of Lisbon, Portugal

Steering Committee (Chairs)

Ulrich Flegel   Infineon Technologies AG, Germany
Michael Meier   University of Bonn and Fraunhofer FKIE, Germany

Steering Committee

Magnus Almgren   Chalmers University of Technology, Sweden
Sébastien Bardin   CEA, France
Gregory Blanc   Télécom SudParis, France
Herbert Bos   Vrije Universiteit Amsterdam, The Netherlands
Danilo M. Bruschi   Università degli Studi di Milano, Italy

Roland Bueschkes	RWE AG, Germany
Juan Caballero	IMDEA Software Institute, Spain
Lorenzo Cavallaro	King's College London, UK
Hervé Debar	Télécom SudParis, France
Sven Dietrich	City University of New York, USA
Cristiano Giuffrida	Vrije Universiteit Amsterdam, The Netherlands
Bernhard Haemmerli	Acris GmbH and HSLU Lucerne, Switzerland
Thorsten Holz	Ruhr-Universität Bochum, Germany
Marko Jahnke	CSIRT, German Federal Authority, Germany
Klaus Julisch	Deloitte, Switzerland
Christian Kreibich	ICSI, USA
Christopher Kruegel	UC Santa Barbara, USA
Pavel Laskov	University of Liechtenstein, Liechtenstein
Federico Maggi	Trend Micro Research, Italy
Roberto Perdisci	University of Georgia and Georgia Institute of Technology, USA
Michalis Polychronakis	Stony Brook University, USA
Konrad Rieck	TU Braunschweig, Germany
Jean-Pierre Seifert	Technical University Berlin, Germany
Robin Sommer	ICSI/LBNL, USA
Urko Zurutuza	Mondragon University, Spain

Program Committee

Magnus Almgren	Chalmers University of Technology, Sweden
Giovanni Appruzzese	University of Modena and Reggia Emilia, Italy
Elias Athanasopoulos	University of Cyprus, Cyprus
Davide Balzarotti	Eurecom, France
Sébastien Bardin	CEA LIST, France
Gregory Blanc	Télécom SudParis, Institut Polytechnique de Paris, France
Herbert Bos	Vrije Universiteit Amsterdam, The Netherlands
Juan Caballero	IMDEA Software Institute, Spain
Lucas Davi	University of Duisburg-Essen, Germany
Sven Dietrich	City University of New York, USA
Ulrich Flegel	Infineon Technologies AG, Germany
Aurélien Francillon	Eurecom, France
Yanick Fratantonio	Eurecom, France
Mariano Graziano	Cisco Talos, USA
Daniel Gruss	Graz University of Technology, Austria
Christophe Hauser	University of Southern California, USA
Alexandros Kapravelos	North Carolina State University, USA
Vasileios Kemerlis	Brown University, USA
Erik van der Kouwe	Vrije Universiteit Amsterdam, The Netherlands
Christian Kreibich	Corelight, USA
Anil Kurmus	IBM Research, Switzerland

Pierre Laperdrix   CNRS, Lille University, France
Martina Lindorfer   TU Wien, Austria
Michael Meier   University of Bonn and Fraunhofer FKIE, Germany
Marius Muench   Vrije Universiteit Amsterdam, The Netherlands
Nick Nikiforakis   Stony Brook University, USA
Yossi Oren   Ben-Gurion University, Israel
Giancarlo Pelegrino   CISPA Helmholtz Center for Information Security,
                                 Germany
Fabio Pierazzi   King's College London, UK
Michalis Polychronakis   Stony Brook University, USA
Georgios Portokalidis   Stevens Institute of Technology, USA
Thomas Schreck   Munich University of Applied Sciences, Germany
Michael Schwarz   Graz University of Technology, Austria
Deborah Shands   SRI International, USA
Seungwon Shin   KAIST, South Korea
Yan Shoshitaishvili   Arizona State University, USA
Gianluca Stringhini   Boston University, USA
Juan Tapiador   Universidad Carlos III, Spain
Sam Thomas   University of Birmingham, UK
Mathy Vanhoef   New York University Abu Dhabi, UAE
Pierre-Antoine Vervier   Symantec Research Labs, USA

Additional Reviewers

Babak Amin Azad   Stony Brook University, USA
Volker Baier   TÜV-Süd Sec-IT, Germany
Tobias Cloosters   University of Duisburg-Essen, Germany
Yaakov Cohen   Ben-Gurion University, Israel
Shaked Delarea   Ben-Gurion University, Israel
Vitaly Dyadyuk   Ben-Gurion University, Israel
Sergej Epp   Palo Alto Networks, Germany
Jens-Rene Giesen   University of Duisburg-Essen, Germany
Gibran Gomez   IMDEA Software Institute, Spain
Brian Kondracki   Stony Brook University, USA
Tomer Laor   Ben-Gurion University, Israel
Tapti Palit   Stony Brook University, USA
Sebastian Poeplau   Eurecom, France
Merve Sahin   SAP Security Research, France
Giada Stivala   CISPA Helmholtz Center for Information Security,
                                 Germany
Soheil Khodayari   CISPA Helmholtz Center for Information Security,
                                 Germany
Avinash Sudhodanan   IMDEA Software Institute, Spain
Sebastian Surminski   University of Duisburg-Essen, Germany

Sponsors

Contents

Detection and Containment

Vulnerability Discovery and Analysis

Automated CPE Labeling of CVE Summaries with Machine Learning

Emil Wåreus[1,2](✉) and Martin Hell[2](✉)

[1] Debricked AB, Malmö, Sweden
[2] Department of Electrical and Information Technology,
Lund University, Lund, Sweden
{emil.wareus,martin.hell}@eit.lth.se

Abstract. Open Source Security and Dependency Vulnerability Management (DVM) has become a more vital part of the software security stack in recent years as modern software tend to be more dependent on open source libraries. The largest open source of vulnerabilities is the National Vulnerability Database (NVD), which supplies developers with machine-readable vulnerabilities. However, sometimes Common Vulnerabilities and Exposures (CVE) have not been labeled with a Common Platform Enumeration (CPE) -version, -product and -vendor. This makes it very hard to automatically discover these vulnerabilities from import statements in dependency files. We, therefore, propose an automatic process of matching CVE summaries with CPEs through the machine learning task called Named Entity Recognition (NER). Our proposed model achieves an F-measure of 0.86 with a precision of 0.857 and a recall of 0.865, outperforming previous research for automated CPE-labeling of CVEs.

Keywords: Machine learning · Open source · Vulnerabilities · CVE · CPE

1 Introduction

In almost all software development today, using open source and third-party components is crucial for its success. It is beneficial to the quality, security, functionality, and development efficiency. However, at the same time, it increases the exposure to vulnerabilities in code developed by third parties. To maintain control over the security of the developed software, the maintainers need to continuously monitor if vulnerabilities have been introduced or found in these third-party dependencies. This is commonly done with Dependency Vulnerability Management (DVM) tools that automate the process of Software Composition Analysis (SCA), and matches used software components with known vulnerabilities.

The main source of vulnerabilities is the National Vulnerability Database (NVD) [15]. These vulnerabilities have a unique Common Vulnerabilities and Exposures (CVE) identifier. The list of such identifiers is maintained by Mitre

© Springer Nature Switzerland AG 2020
C. Maurice et al. (Eds.): DIMVA 2020, LNCS 12223, pp. 3–22, 2020.
https://doi.org/10.1007/978-3-030-52683-2_1

and includes a short summary of the vulnerability. In the last few years, around 30–50 new vulnerabilities have been given a CVE identifier and been recorded in NVD each day. Combining this with the fact that software projects can have thousands of dependencies, including transitive dependencies, it is clear that the process of identifying new vulnerabilities must be automated.

NIST security professionals take the CVEs as they are published by Mitre and link one or more Common Platform Enumerations (CPE) [14] to each CVE. These CPEs are used to specify which software and versions are vulnerable. NIST also adds other pieces of information, such as a CVSS score, and thus maintains a rich database of information about published vulnerabilities.

While the summary, as recorded in the original identifier provided by Mitre, often includes information regarding which product and versions are affected, the list of CPEs formalizes this information and provides it in a standardized, and machine-readable, format. Thus, the CPE is a crucial addition to the CVE information when vulnerability identification and assessment are being automated.

Unfortunately, far from all CVEs maintained in the NVD database are correctly linked to CPEs. Moreover, as reported in [4], there is a notable time-lag from the first CVE disclosure to the addition of CPEs to the vulnerability. In 2018, the median time to correctly assign the CPE metadata was 35 days. The manual effort performed in the analysis of CVEs is not limited to only assigning CPEs in this 35 day period, but we are only interested in the CPEs in our current experiments. As soon as the CVE is known (or even before), exploits are developed and attacks can be found in the wild. Thus, such a time-lag can leave a software system vulnerable to attacks since automated tools are not able to correctly inform developers and users of these vulnerabilities.

In this paper, we use Natural Language Processing (NLP), or more specifically, Named Entity Recognition (NER), to automatically build a CPE, or list of CPEs, from the summary text. We build a model inspired by [12]. As input to the model, we use word and character level embeddings, casing-features, and a security lexicon of common CPEs. The model itself consists of a Bidirectional Long-Short-Term Memory (BLSTM) network together with a Conditional Random Field (CRF) to determine the labels. Using such NLP algorithms, we achieve unprecedented performance, with an F-measure of 0.8604, recall of 0.8637, and precision of 0.8571.

The paper is organized as follows. In Sect. 2 we give a brief background on the vulnerability data of interest and Natural Language Processing. In Sect. 3 we present the dataset that we use and its corresponding labels. In Sect. 4 we frame the problem and determine how we evaluate our results. Section 5 presents our model, the features, and some theory for the model. Then, we present and discuss our results in Sect. 6. Related work is described in Sect. 7 and the paper is concluded in Sect. 8.

2   Background

2.1   Vulnerability Data

A new vulnerability is often reported as a CVE. The list of CVEs is maintained by Mitre and each entry contains a unique CVE number, a short summary, and at least one external reference [20]. The CVE summary typically includes the affected product and versions. An example of the ShellShock CVE-2014-6271 is given below.

> GNU Bash through 4.3 processes trailing strings after function definitions in the values of environment variables, which allows remote attackers to execute arbitrary code via a crafted environment, as demonstrated by vectors involving the ForceCommand feature in OpenSSH sshd, the mod_cgi and mod_cgid modules in the Apache HTTP Server, scripts executed by unspecified DHCP clients, and other situations in which setting the environment occurs across a privilege boundary from Bash execution, aka "ShellShock."

This information is then used by NVD, adding, among other things, a CVSS score, and a list of CPEs. The CVSS score provided by NIST is environment independent, but useful when assessing the severity of the vulnerability. The CPE provides a standardized string for defining which product and versions are affected by the vulnerability.

The current version of CPE is 2.3. The format is specified in [14], and is given by the string

```
cpe:2.3:part:vendor:product:version:update:edition:
language:sw_edition:target_sw:target_hw:other
```

The first part defines that it is a CPE and its version. Then, *part* can be one of h for hardware, a for application and o for operating system. The following fields are used to uniquely specify the component by defining *vendor*, the name of the *product*, the product *version* etc. It is common to use the fields up to and including version, even though, as can be seen, further details about the component can be defined. An example, as can be found in CVE-2014-6271, is given by

```
cpe:2.3:a:gnu:bash:4.3:*:*:*:*:*:*:*
```

NVD also provides a JSON feed with CVE data for each vulnerability. This feed supports additional fields for defining ranges of versions that are vulnerable. This feed provides a more efficient representation if there are many versions affected. This feed is further detailed in Sect. 3.

NVD consists of around 130 000 vulnerabilities (early 2020). The summary is given immediately when the CVE is published since it is required by Mitre, while the CPE is later added by NVD. The discrepancy differs between different CVEs, but an analysis in [4] reported that, in 2018, the median to correctly assign CPE data was 35 days.

2.2   Natural Language Processing and Named Entity Recognition

Natural Language Processing (NLP) is the task to make computers understand linguistics, usually with the support of machine learning. Within NLP, tasks such as machine translation, document classification, question answering systems, automatic summary generation, and speech recognition are common [10]. One of the main advantages of using machine learning for NLP is that the algorithms may gain a contextual semantic understanding of text where classifications are not dependent on a single word, but rather a complex sequence of words that can completely alter the meaning of the document. This may be beneficial to our system, as new CPEs that have not been seen before in the NVD database may be correctly classified from the CVE-summary through a contextual understanding of the document.

Named Entity Recognition (NER), or sequence labeling, is the NLP task of classifying each word in a sequence. One of the most common benchmarks in NER is the CoNLL-2003 dataset [21], where the task is to label words with ether person-, organization-, or location-names. NER is an important task within NLP, as a system needs to understand what category a word or sub-sequence belongs to truly understand the contextual meaning of the document.

3   Data and Labels

To successfully create machine learning models, it is necessary to collect data to train it. The goal for the model is to learn the general underlying structure of the problem through training on that data, which acts as a representation of that problem. This data is referred to as the *dataset*. Our dataset consists of historical vulnerabilities with already determined CPEs. These can be retrieved using the NVD data feed. Each entry in the dataset have the following features:

- **cveId:** The unique identifier and name for each CVE.
- **updatedAt:** The date and time of the last update from NVD for this particular CVE.
- **summary:** A text description of the CVE, often naming the vulnerable software, including product, vendor, and version.
- **cweName:** The Common Weakness Enumerator.
- **cpes:** A list of CPEs linked to this particular CVE. Each CPE contains:
  - *vendor:* The vendor of the product or software.
  - *product:* Name of the software.
  - *version:* An exact statement of a single vulnerable version.
  - *versionStartExcluding:* All versions are vulnerable after (excluding) this version.
  - *versionStartIncluding:* All versions are vulnerable after (including) this version.
  - *versionEndExcluding:* All versions are vulnerable before (excluding) this version.

- *versionEndIncluding:* All versions are vulnerable before (including) this version.

Our analysis concludes that 81.9% of all CPEs from CVEs in NVD only specifies one of the following fields: *version, versionStartExcluding, versionStartIncluding, versionEndExcluding,* and *versionEndIncluding.* About 14.5% have no version range specified, and 3.6% have exactly two version ranges specified. Figure 1 illustrates how a CVE-CPE link can be structured.

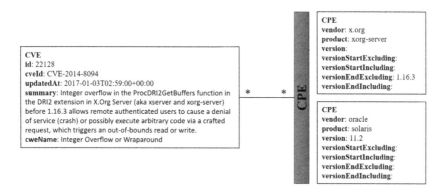

Fig. 1. Overview of the relationship between a CVE and multiple CPEs.

As seen in Fig. 1, some of the product and vendor strings can be found in the summary. The version can also be found in the summary but is dependent on the context of the summary to determine if other versions are vulnerable (in this case all versions before version 1.16.3). In this paper, only the summary is regarded as input features, the CPE-list as the labels, and all other data is disregarded in the model. Naturally, all CPEs may not be possible to link to the summary through text models as there is no occurrence of the product or vendor in the paragraph. This is shown in Fig. 1, as Oracle Solaris is not mentioned in the paragraph, but is considered vulnerable from the context that X.Org xorg-server is vulnerable. In our analysis, we find that about 59% of CPEs can be mapped with regex methods to its CVE summary, and for 27% of the CVEs, all corresponding CPEs can be mapped to its summary. To map a CPE to a CVE-summary, each single word/version-string in the CPE must be matched to a word in the summary disregarding casing and special characters. Multi-word labels must be matched in the correct order, and up to 5 intermediate words are disregarded.

A sequence word labeling model requires a label for each word in the sentence. There are eight labels to consider in the CPEs provided by NVD: *vendor, product, version, versionStartExcluding, versionStartIncluding, versionEndExcluding, verisonEndIncluding,* and *O* (which denotes the none-label). Some vendors or products consist of multiple words, which need to be accurately predicted by the model. To denote this, labels are split into B- and I-labels where B denotes a start of a label, and I denote the word following the previous B or I labeled words. A part of an example sentence, taken from the CVE summary in Fig. 1, can be seen in Table 1.

Table 1. Example of labeled sentence.

Text:	extension	in	X.Org	Server	before	1.16.3		allows	remote	authenticated
Label:	O		O	B-product	I-product	O	B-versionEndExcluding	O	O	O

4   Problem Statement and Evaluation

The high-level problem we try to solve is one of determining what software and what versions are described in a document. This could be limited to mapping each document to already existing CPEs in the available CPE-list [16]. We choose not to do this because the available CPE-list is deficient as it is lacking entries for many products. Analyzing all available CPEs mentioned in CVEs, about 60% of those are only mentioned once. Thus, the probability of a new CVE describing a new, none existent, CPE is high. Therefore, we decide to allow our system to create new CPEs, in terms of finding software that has not been mentioned in any existing CPE list yet. A completely successful NER-predicted CVE-summary from our test-data will let us reconstruct all corresponding CPEs correctly, while the model may create new CPEs on new CVE-summaries.

To determine success, we measure our system as conventional NER-model. Over each predicted sequence we calculated the *precision*

$$precision = \frac{\sum true\_positive}{\sum true\_positive + \sum false\_positive}, \tag{1}$$

recall

$$recall = \frac{\sum true\_positive}{\sum true\_positive + \sum false\_negative}, \tag{2}$$

and their harmonic mean *F1*

$$F1 = 2 \cdot \frac{precision \cdot recall}{precision + recall}, \tag{3}$$

and remove every correctly predicted O-label from the measurements as it greatly inflates the result. We also measure the overall *accuracy* of the model as the number of completely correctly NER-predicted CVE-summaries divided by the total number of summaries in that particular dataset. A hold-out strategy is implemented to measure these metrics, with a training set to train the model on, a validation set to optimize the model during development, and a testing set to test the final result.

The final model is intended to be used in DVM-tools to provide an estimation of CPEs that are associated with a CVE. This estimated association is provided with no or very little time-lag, which may prevent "one day"-vulnerabilities. The time-lag was further discussed in Sect. 1. Furthermore, additional CPEs could be provided to older CVEs that have been incorrectly labeled with the wrong CPEs or are missing some CPE associations.

5   Modeling

In this section, the feature engineering and machine learning model is described. The model is inspired by the work of [2] and [12] in the context of generic NER, where the contribution was to feed the text-data into multiple input sequences to capture different levels of semantics in the text. In brief, words are converted to vector representations [13] to embed contextual semantic meaning in its vector values. Additional word level and character level features are engineered to capture variations, such as word level numerical saturation, casing, and commonly used CPE-products and -vendors. These features are fed into a recurrent Bidirectional Long Short-term Memory (BLSTM) network to perform sequence labeling. Dropout [19] is used to regularize the model after concatenated embeddings, after the recurrent layer, and within the case-feature layer. This model was chosen as it presented a superior performance on the specific task of CPE-labeling compared to other common architectures, such as BERT [3]. The model is also suitable, as domain knowledge can easily be embedded through feature engineering. An overview of the architecture is presented in Fig. 2.

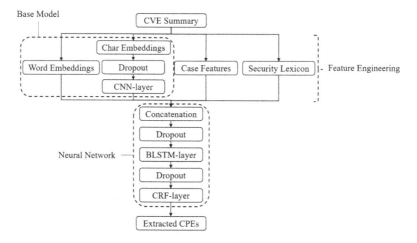

Fig. 2. Overview of the model architecture and data pipeline.

5.1   Feature Engineering

This subsection will discuss the four parallel input layers used in the feature engineering part of our model as seen in Fig. 2. These are word level embeddings, character level embeddings, word level case-features, and a word level lexicon of known statements. The word and character level embeddings are regarded as part of the *base model*, and case and lexicon features are regarded as optional/experimental features to the model. The output features are concatenated into an information rich sequential matrix that is fed into a neural network described in Sect. 5.2.

Word Level Embeddings. Each word is transformed into a 50, 100, 200, or 300 dimensional numerical vector to represent the semantics of that word with Glove embeddings [18]. These embeddings are pre-trained on a large set of Wikipedia articles and consists of a vocabulary of 400 000 words. This language model serves as a good starting point for our experiments, as they are well documented and tested, which enables us to look into other variables in the modeling. These embeddings are not tuned during training and missing words from the vocabulary are assigned a default randomly generated vector.

Character Level Features. To extract character level features for each word, we employ a three-stage process of embedding on character level, applying a one-dimensional convolution (CNN-layer), and extracting the final word-features with a max-pooling layer. The embeddings are randomly initialized and tuned during training. Dropout is applied to prevent the model from overfitting. The employed CNN-layer has a filter-size of 30 and a kernel-size of 3. A max-operation is done over each filter, so each word outputs a character-feature vector of shape (1, 30), and for the whole word-sequence a shape of (word-sequence-length, 30). Character level features enable the model to learn new words through decoding of character-sequences, and can thereby give similar output-values to insignificant variations of very similar character sequences. As our text-domain (security) is quite different from the pre-trained word level embeddings (Wikipedia), the character level embeddings enable our model to learn security-related semantics.

Word Level Case Features. In the task to find versions, products, and vendors, casing and other word-properties may be important to determine the label of that particular word. For instance, it is common that products' and vendors' names are capitalized. The version label contains a high concentration of character level digits, but may also contain mid-word punctuation and special characters. Table 2 shows the different case-features, which are fed into random-uniformly initialized trainable embeddings with the same dimension as the number of cases.

Security Lexicon. To embed domain knowledge into the system, a security-lexicon is built. The labels *product* and *vendor* are included in the lexicon features. The lexicon is constructed from the complete set of CVEs from the NVD database consisting of about 130 000 vulnerabilities describing about 50 000 different products, excluding all CVEs in the validation and test dataset. Each entry into the lexicon can describe one of three entities, *product*, *vendor*, and

Table 2. Number of entries in security lexicon

Case	Property
Numeric	Integer fraction = 1.0
Mostly numeric	Integer fraction > 0.5
Contains numeric	Integer fraction ≤ 0.5
All lower	All lower case
All upper	All upper case
Initial upper	First character upper case
Default	All other cases

product and vendor. Some product/vendor names exist both as products and vendors, which explains this separate feature. The total number of entries in the lexicon can be seen in Table 3.

Table 3. Number of entries in security lexicon

Feature	Number of entries
Product	8513
Vendor	3097
Product and vendor	1005

When constructing the security lexicon, only common CPE-products and -vendors are added to the lexicon. The cutoff was set to the top 80% of the most common products and vendors to avoid CPEs with very few mentions. As seen in Fig. 3, the accumulated product mentions are heavily skewed towards products with very few mentions. This distribution may discourage the use of a lexicon-feature and increase the importance of case-features and contextual understanding of the model, as the probability of new CVE-summaries containing already existing CPEs has historically been low.

5.2 Neural Network

The input layer of the model consists of some or all features described in Sect. 5.1. The outputs of these features are all considered as embeddings that can be concatenated into a high-dimensional feature-map considering multiple characteristics of the input sequence. These concatenated embeddings are then fed into a neural network for sequence classification. The network architecture is inspired by [12], where the embeddings are fed into a Bidirectional Long Short-term Memory (BLSTM) layer and labels are decoded in a Conditional Random Field (CRF).

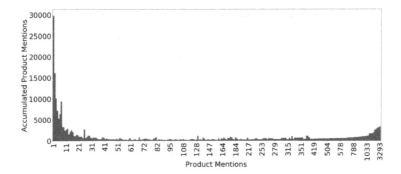

Fig. 3. Accumulated mentions of product over the number of mentions of a product. The X-axis denotes the number of mentions of individual CPE-product and the Y-axis denotes the number of accumulated mentions of products with X-mentions. The mean of the distribution is 4.69 mentions per product and the median is 1 mention per product.

BLSTM-Layer. The LSTM [7] neural network unit is a type of recurrent layer that has theoretically strong capabilities to capture long-distance dependencies in sequential data. In text-data, recurrent models are capable of capturing contextual semantics in the data, and correctly model the sequential variations and dependencies of that text data. Conventional recurrent units suffer from problems such as the vanishing and exploding gradient [1,17] which disables these networks to be effective on some tasks. The LSTM unit handles these complications by an internal architecture consisting of an *input gate, output gate, forget gate*, and a *cell state*. An overview of the LSTM cell can be seen in Fig. 4.

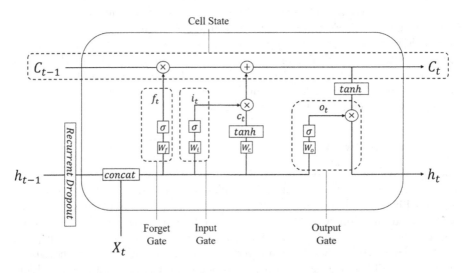

Fig. 4. Long Short Term Memory cell. The input gate, output gate, forget gate, and cell state are marked in dotted lines.

In the figure, X_t denotes the t'th embedded input word to the LSTM cell and h represents the hidden state. The variable h_{t-1} is the output from the previous LSTM cell and h_t serves as the output prediction from this LSTM cell for the t'th word in the sequence. C denotes the cell state, which passes the memories of the already processed sequence to the LSTM cell. The forget gate is a nested neural network with a sigmoid activation function that scales the previous hidden state sequence between 0 and 1, where a low output value for a particular part of the sequence denotes that word should be forgotten. The output from the forget gate f_t is derived through

$$f_t = \sigma(W_f \times concat(h_{t-1}, X_t) + b_f), \tag{4}$$

where W_f and b_f are the trainable weights. The activation function σ is derived through

$$\sigma(x) = \frac{1}{1 + e^{-x}}. \tag{5}$$

The input gate values are derived similar to Eq. (4),

$$i_t = \sigma(W_i \times concat(h_{t-1}, X_t) + b_i), \tag{6}$$

where W_i and b_i are trainable weights as well. Similarly to Eq. (4), the sigmoid in Eq. (6) normalizes the input values and previous hidden state between 0 and 1, which corresponds to their relative importance in this particular time step t. This layer is responsible to decide what new data should be added to the cell state. To calculate the cell state, the input and previous hidden state is passed through the following equation

$$\hat{c}_t = tanh(W_c \times concat(h_{t-1}, X_t) + b_c), \tag{7}$$

to calculate the actual information that the input at step t brings. W_c and b_c are trainable weights. The $tanh$ function normalizes the input between -1.0 and 1.0 through the following equation

$$tanh(x) = \frac{e^x - e^{-x}}{e^x + e^{-x}}. \tag{8}$$

The relative importance is calculated for X and h and applied to the output from Eq. (7), which together with the forget gate forms the cell state through

$$C_t = f_t \times C_{t-1} + i_t \times \hat{c}_t, \tag{9}$$

where C_{t-1} is the previous cell state. To calculate the output from a particular part of the sequence, which corresponds to the hidden state h_t, the input X_t and h_{t-1} are passed through an output gate. This gate decides what information should be passed to the next hidden state and output as a sequence prediction. The output gate is derived through

$$\hat{o}_t = \sigma(W_o \times concat(h_{t-1}, X_t) + b_o), \tag{10}$$

where W_o and b_o are trainable weights and the current hidden state is calculated through

$$h_t = \hat{o}_t \times tanh(C_t). \tag{11}$$

The output is passed to the next layer of the model, and is a matrix of shape [*batch_size, sequence_length, weight_shape*], where the *batch_size* is the number of parallel input examples fed to the model, *sequence_length* is length of the sentence, and *weight_shape* is a user set parameter that decides the number of weights used in the four nested neural networks.

To make this LSTM layer bidirectional [6], one simply use two separate, but identical, LSTM layers that pass over the input sequence in one direction each. The output is then concatenated. The output is regularized with dropout [19].

The reason for using a BLSTM is that an LSTM cell does not know anything about the future sequence $t+1, t+2, \ldots$, which may be contextually valuable. For instance, when classifying a version, a part of the sequence may be "[..] vulnerable version 1.3.4 and earlier". A BLSTM can capture the semantic meaning of "and earlier", and correctly classifies this as *versionEndIncluding*.

CRF-Layer. As shown in the architectural overview in Fig. 2, the output from the BLSTM is fed to a Conditional Random Field (CRF) [8] layer. The benefits of a CRF layer is statistically correlated label determination when assigning a class to a word in a sequence. For instance, the probability of a word being labeled with *I-product* increases if the previous word has been labeled with *B-product*. With CRF, labels are assigned jointly to reflect a final prediction for all entities in the sequence that make sense together. This is done through conditional probabilities and global normalization of a random field model.

Consider the output sequence of the BLSTM-layer $\mathbf{h} = \{\mathbf{h}_1, \mathbf{h}_2, \mathbf{h}_i, ..., \mathbf{h}_N\}$, where $\mathbf{h}_i$ denotes the numerical vector output from the BLSTM-layer corresponding to the i'th word from the CVE-summary word sequences of length N. The label sequence $\mathbf{y} = \{y_1, y_2, y_i, ..., y_N\}$ denotes each corresponding labels to the CVE-summary word sequence, where y_i denotes the predicted label for the i'th word. $Y(\mathbf{h})$ denotes the universe of all possible labels for $\mathbf{h}$. The conditional random field describes the conditional probability of label y_i in respect to input h_i and surrounding labels $y_{v \neq i} = y_{v \sim i}$, where $\sim$ denotes v as close to i, as $p(y_i|h_i, y_v, v \sim i)$ over all possible label sequences.

To determine the probability, a layer of weights $\mathbf{W}$ and biases $\mathbf{b}$ are used as

$$p(\mathbf{y}|\mathbf{h}; \mathbf{W}, \mathbf{b}) = \frac{\prod_{i=1}^{n} \gamma_i(y_{i-1}, y_i, \mathbf{h}_i)}{\sum_{y^* \in Y(\mathbf{h})} \prod_{i=1}^{n} \gamma_i(y_{i-1}^*, y_i^*, \mathbf{h}_i)}, \tag{12}$$

where

$$\gamma_i(y', y, \mathbf{h}_i) = exp(\mathbf{W}_{y',y}^T \mathbf{h}_i + \mathbf{b}_{y',y}). \tag{13}$$

The weights are trained through gradient descent and the Adam optimizer [11], as the rest of the model. The output of the CRF-layer is decoded from the highest conditional probability over the full sequence and serves as the output of the model.

6   Results and Discussion

6.1   Training

To train the model a dataset of 15190 CVEs from NVD was used, with an evaluation set of 3798 entries and a test set of 4748 entries. The test and evaluation split was done randomly. Experiments were conducted on whether to do a time-split instead of the dataset to prevent look-ahead bias but resulted in an insignificant performance change. The model was optimized with Bayesian hyperparameter optimization [9] over the following hyperparameters:

- The *learning rate* is a parameter that scales how much each weight should be updated in each gradient descent step [11].
- The *number of cells in the LSTM-layers* determines the size of the weight matrices W_f, W_i, W_{of}, and W_c, and their corresponding biases.
- Whether the *casing features* should be used.
- Whether the *lexicon features* should be used.
- The dimension of *word level embeddings* of pre-trained vectors.
- The dimension of *character level embeddings* of randomly initialized vectors.
- The *Dropout*-rate before and after the BLSTM-layer, and inside the char-features.
- The *Recurrent dropout*-rate in the LSTM-cells which determines the dropout rate of previous hidden state h_{t-1}.

The training was performed on NVIDIA TESLA K80 GPU and it took about 4–6 h to train the model once. In total, it took about 30 h to do the full training sweep on 16 K80s for 80 training iterations with different hyperparameter settings. This amounts to about 20 GPU-days. The parameter search space can be seen in Table 4. The Adam optimizer [11] was used to update the trainable parameters in the model and early stopping to reduce the risk of overfitting.

Table 4. Hyperparameters search space and parameters used for best result.

Hyperparameter	Optimal value	Search space
Learning rate	0.00113	0.0001 to 0.01
LSTM cells	305	100 to 400
Use casing	True	True or False
Use lexicon	False	True or False
Word embedding dimension	100	50, 100, 200, or 300
Character embedding dimension	119	10 to 120
Dropout	0.2106	0.2 to 0.8
Recurrent dropout	0.2486	0.2 to 0.8

6.2   Main Results

In Table 5 the results are presented for the different model configurations. It is clear that the security lexicon did not provide any significant signal to improve the model. The word level casing feature proved beneficial to the performance with a significant improvement over the base model. The best performance on the test set was attained without the lexicon features and with casing features with an F-measure of 0.8604, a precision of 0.8571, and a recall of 0.8637. It is also clear that the same model had the best performance on the validation set, but we can see some indications of overfitting to the training-set as the F-measure, recall, and precision are much higher. This may indicate that additional performance could be gained with more aggressive regularization techniques. The fully combined model had much worse performance on the training set and similar performance on the test and validation set. This may indicate that further training and hyperparameter optimization could increase the performance of this model and enable it to surpass the other options.

Table 5. Results of the four training cases

Model	Test set			Validation set			Training set		
	F1	Precision	Recall	F1	Precision	Recall	F1	Precision	Recall
Base model	0.8499	0.8437	0.8562	0.8435	0.8379	0.8491	0.9498	0.9404	0.9595
+ lexicon	0.8554	**0.8604**	0.8505	0.8493	0.8570	0.8418	0.9986	0.9983	0.9989
+ case	**0.8604**	0.8571	0.8637	0.8533	0.8536	0.8530	0.9963	0.9952	0.9973
+ lexicon + case	0.8574	0.8505	**0.8645**	0.8527	0.8482	0.8572	0.9422	0.9336	0.9510

An example of the output can be seen in CVE-2018-11761, where *"In Apache Tika 0.1 to 1.18, the XML parsers were not configured to limit entity expansion. They were therefore vulnerable to an entity expansion vulnerability which can lead to a denial of service attack."* is correctly parsed to **vendor**: *apache*, **product**: *tika*, **versionStartIncluding**: *0.1*, **versionEndIncluding**: *1.18* by the model. This example was in the test set, and is therefore never seen by the algorithm during training.

6.3   Performance over CPE-product, -vendor, and -version

At a more granular level shown in Table 6, we can observe the performance of each label on the test set, as well as the number of instances of each label in the test set *Label Count* and the number of predicted instances *Prediction Count*. We can see that some classes perform better than others. The F-measure is high for B-vendor, B-product, and B-version, as well as I-product. It is clear that there is a correlation between Label Count and all performance scores, which makes sense for this type of model as neural networks tend to be very data-hungry. In Fig. 6 labels with more examples in the dataset clearly have higher performance than less common labels. There seems to be a cutoff at approximately 300 examples to have an F-measure above 0.8. We can also observe that the performance for multi-word labels are worse, as the scores for I-labels are lower. To further increase the performance on I-labeled entries, it may be beneficial to create n-grams features in the lexicon or collect additional data for those particular cases. Figure 5 visualizes the results from Table 6. The model achieves a similar distribution over each label, which is visualized in Fig. 7.

Table 6. Granular test results from model with case features and without lexicon. Scores are over each possible label for the model. Label Count describes how many instances of that particular label is present in the test set, and Prediction Count describes how many predictions the model produces for a particular label.

Label	F1	Recall	Precision	Prediction count	Label count
B-versionEndIncluding	0.7817	0.7817	0.7817	875	875
B-version	0.8573	0.8618	0.8527	2655	2627
B-versionStartIncluding	0.7415	0.7238	0.76	100	105
B-product	0.8711	0.8774	0.8649	4840	4771
O	0.9935	0.9931	0.9938	184649	184768
B-versionEndExcluding	0.7987	0.7922	0.8053	303	308
B-vendor	0.9126	0.8951	0.9308	2715	2823
I-version	0.4396	0.3509	0.5882	34	57
B-versionStartExcluding	0	0	0	2	1
I-product	0.8549	0.8812	0.8302	3787	3568
I-vendor	0.5714	0.5	0.6667	111	148
I-versionEndExcluding	0	0	0	0	1
I-versionEndIncluding	0.2581	0.16	0.6667	6	25
I-versionStartExcluding	0	0	0	0	0
I-versionStartIncluding	0	0	0	0	0

6.4   Feature Analysis

The lexicon features did not provide any significant performance gains together with or compared to the case-features. It is possible that the case features better captured characteristics of the vendor and product labels since those are commonly capitalized in some manner, rather than over-relying on a fairly static memory of common labels. This result is in line with the distribution of products shown in Fig. 3, as 60% of all products NVD are mentioned only once. Other papers, such as [4] and [5] use keyword-based systems or features targeting narrow properties of the vendor- and product label. These systems are not taking the context of the sequence into consideration when performing classification, which we believe is the main reason why we achieve significantly better results.

With a contextually aware classification, our system is able to find new CPEs that have never been seen before by NVD in any CVEs. This is highly desirable in a system to automatically extract CPEs from CVEs due to the distribution in Fig. 3.

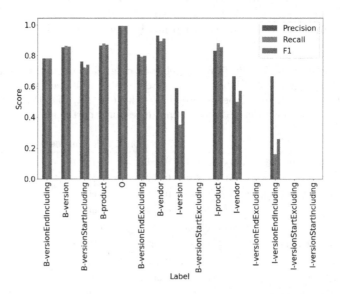

Fig. 5. Precision, F-measure, and Recall over each possible class for the model with case-features and without lexicon-features.

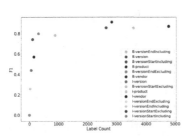

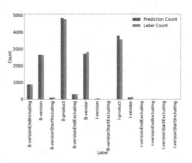

Fig. 6. Scatter plot over Label Count and F1-score for each class (excluding 'O'). This plot indicates that there seems to be a minimum amount of examples in each class to achieve an F1-score above .8 at approximately 300.

Fig. 7. Label and Prediction count for each class in the test dataset. Note that the 'O'-label is removed for this visualization.

6.5   Increasing Performance on Rare Labels

Our dataset consists of about roughly 20% of all available CVEs NVD, which may limit our results. This particular subset was chosen as over 90% of all CPE-version, -product, and -vendor strings for all CPEs paired with a CVE could be found in the summary through regular expression. Stronger regular expressions could increase the number of training examples, and further increase the performance of the system. To increase the performance in the more challenging task of classifying multi-word labels, an overweight to these cases could be provided to the training data, or the model could be pre-trained on a larger high-quality data set such as CoNLL 2003 [21].

6.6   Error Analysis

The overall accuracy of the system of correctly labeling every CPE in each CVE is 0.6744, measured as the full CVE-summary being correctly NER-annotated by the system. If the system only regards pursuing vendor and product classification, the accuracy would increase to 0.7772, which is more comparable to earlier research as they do not always search for version ranges in the summary. The distribution of the number of errors in all sequences that were incorrect is visualized in Fig. 8, where the accumulated error for sequences with up to 3 errors stands for about 80% of the miss-classified summaries. Looking further into what types of errors the model makes, Fig. 9 visualizes in total about 90% of all miss-classifications. In the top four spots, regarding about 40% of the error are bad predictions on the product label, with the I-label scoring higher than the B-label. This strengthens the hypothesis that the system needs improvement to better find multi-word labels. The top two mistakes contribute to a lower precision, as it incorrectly finds a CPE-product where there is none, and error three and four contributes to a lower recall as products are miss-classified as a O-words.

7   Related Research

Other research has tried more extensive engineering of text-features to extract CPEs from the CVE-summary published by NVD. In [5] the authors mine the target product, vendor, and version from the summary by tokenization of each word much like our case-feature and lexicon-feature to discover punctuation, capitalization, and commonly used vendors/products. They also generate snippets (sequence of tokens) to cover multi-word labels through engineered rules based on the feature vector. Multiple token-sequences can then be grouped into a CPE (vendor-product-version link) based on rules, such as that all version tokens that are within 6 tokens of a product token are assigned to that product token. The context of each version is analyzed to determine the version type (before/after, including/excluding). The authors achieve an F-measure of 0.70 (precision: 0.71, recall: 0.69), which we significantly outperforms as we attain an F-measure of 0.86 (precision: 0.857, recall: 0.864).

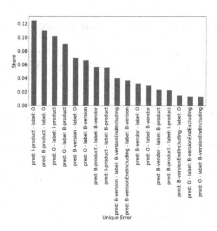

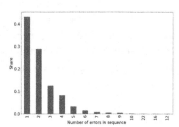

Fig. 8. Distribution of number of miss-classifications in a sequence over all miss-classifications.

Fig. 9. Common miss-classifications made by the system. This explains about 90% of the error.

A similar system of finding CPEs to "one day"-vulnerabilities was proposed in [4], where the authors use a key-word based technique with TF-IDF to find the probability of each word being assigned to a certain sub-class within a CPE. The output of the model is an ordered list of words with a high probability of being a relevant word in a CPE. The authors results may not be comparable to our research, as their system is not intended for automated use and needs explainability. Although, to make a fair comparison we compare their results of the precision of the top predicted word in each ordered list, which is just below 0.6. Our system achieves a higher precision of 0.857. Still, their research indicates that a TF-IDF implementation of a lexicon feature could provide additional performance to our system in terms of finding already mentioned products and vendors.

The model is largely based upon [12], which combined engineered features, a BLSTM-network and a CRF-layer to perform NER on the CoNLL 2003 [21] dataset. They achieve an F-measure score as high as 0.9121, which to our knowledge held the state-of-the-art during some time in 2016. Results from different datasets are not comparable, as the quality and the general challenge of each dataset may be different. Other, more recent, implementations of state-of-the-art NLP-models were implemented in our research such as BERT [3], but with a significant decrease in performance compared to our model.

8   Conclusion

Our research concludes that it is possible to automate CPE-labeling of CVEs with machine learning with high precision and recall, in regards to the CPEs that are actually mentioned in the CVE-summary. Our model is able to find CPE-products, -vendors, and -versions with an F-measure 0.8604 (precision:

0.8571, recall: 0.8637) through NER-tagging, and completely reconstruct all corresponding CPEs in 67.44% of CVE-summaries. This system enables DVM-tools to automatically and without time-lag get an estimate of some CPEs a particular CVE describes and thereby reduce the risk of becoming a victim of a "one day"-vulnerability. Additionally, CPEs may also be found in incorrectly labeled CVEs or from vulnerabilities from other sources, such as forums, email-threads, or RSS-feeds. To our knowledge, our results establish a new state-of-the-art in extracting CPEs from CVE-summaries.

The system could be further developed by embedding knowledge of the available universe of CPEs into the results of the prediction so that each estimated CPE could be pared to one or multiple existing CPEs. A TF-IDF or n-grams implementation of the security lexicon feature, as in [4], could also improve the performance of the system, possibly also taking advantage of a security-lexicon, which in our case brings no noteworthy additional performance.

Acknowledgements. This work was financially supported by the Swedish Foundation for Strategic Research, grant RIT17-0035.

References

1. Bengio, Y., Simard, P., Frasconi, P.: Learning long-term dependencies with gradient descent is difficult. IEEE Trans. Neural Networks **5**(2), 157–166 (1994)
2. Chiu, J.P., Nichols, E.: Named entity recognition with bidirectional LSTM-CNNs. Trans. Assoc. Comput. Linguist. **4**, 357–370 (2016). https://www.aclweb.org/anthology/Q16-1026
3. Devlin, J., Chang, M., Lee, K., Toutanova, K.: BERT: pre-training of deep bidirectional transformers for language understanding. CoRR abs/1810.04805 (2018). http://arxiv.org/abs/1810.04805
4. Elbaz, C., Rilling, L., Morin, C.: Automated keyword extraction from "one-day" vulnerabilities at disclosure. Research Report RR-9299, Inria Rennes - Bretagne Atlantique, November 2019. https://hal.inria.fr/hal-02362062
5. Glanz, L., Schmidt, S., Wollny, S., Hermann, B.: A vulnerability's lifetime: enhancing version information in CVE databases. In: Proceedings of the 15th International Conference on Knowledge Technologies and Data-Driven Business, i-KNOW 2015. Association for Computing Machinery, New York (2015)
6. Graves, A., Schmidhuber, J.: Framewise phoneme classification with bidirectional LSTM networks. In: Proceedings of the 2005 IEEE International Joint Conference on Neural Networks, vol. 4, pp. 2047–2052, July 2005
7. Hochreiter, S., Schmidhuber, J.: Long short-term memory. Neural Comput. **9**, 1735–1780 (1997)
8. John Lafferty, A.M., Pereira, F.C.: Conditional Random Fields: Probabilistic Models for Segmenting and Labeling Sequence Data, pp. 282–289, June 2001
9. Kaul, P., Golovin, D., Kochanski, G.: Google Cloud, August 2017. https://cloud.google.com/blog/products/gcp/hyperparameter-tuning-cloud-machine-learning-engine-using-bayesian-optimization
10. Khurana, D., Koli, A., Khatter, K., Singh, S.: Natural Language Processing: State of The Art, Current Trends and Challenges (2017). http://arxiv.org/abs/1708.05148

11. Kingma, D., Ba, J.: Adam: a method for stochastic optimization. In: International Conference on Learning Representations, December 2014
12. Ma, X., Hovy, E.: End-to-end sequence labeling via bi-directional LSTM-CNNs-CRF. In: Proceedings of the 54th Annual Meeting of the Association for Computational Linguistics (Volume 1: Long Papers), Berlin, Germany, pp. 1064–1074. Association for Computational Linguistics, August 2016
13. Mikolov, T., Chen, K., Corrado, G., Dean, J.: Efficient estimation of word representations in vector space. In: Proceedings of Workshop at ICLR 2013, January 2013
14. NIST, National Institute of Standards and Technology: Common Platform Enumeration: Naming Specification, Version 2.3, NIST Interagency Report 7695 (2011)
15. NIST, National Institute of Standards and Technology: National Vulnerability Database (2019). https://nvd.nist.gov
16. NIST, National Institute of Standards and Technology: Official Common Platform Enumeration (CPE) Dictionary (2020). https://nvd.nist.gov/products/cpe
17. Pascanu, R., Mikolov, T., Bengio, Y.: Understanding the exploding gradient problem. CoRR abs/1211.5063 (2012). http://arxiv.org/abs/1211.5063
18. Pennington, J., Socher, R., Manning, C.: Glove: global vectors for word representation. In: Proceedings of the 2014 Conference on Empirical Methods in Natural Language Processing (EMNLP), Doha, Qatar, pp. 1532–1543. Association for Computational Linguistics, October 2014. https://www.aclweb.org/anthology/D14-1162
19. Srivastava, N., Hinton, G., Krizhevsky, A., Sutskever, I., Salakhutdinov, R.: Dropout: a simple way to prevent neural networks from overfitting. J. Mach. Learn. Res. **15**, 1929–1958 (2014). http://jmlr.org/papers/v15/srivastava14a.html
20. The MITRE Corporation: Common Vulnerabilities and Exposures (2019). https://cve.mitre.org
21. Tjong Kim Sang, E.F., De Meulder, F.: Introduction to the CoNLL-2003 shared task: language-independent named entity recognition. In: Proceedings of the Seventh Conference on Natural Language Learning at HLT-NAACL 2003 - Volume 4, CONLL 2003, USA, pp. 142–147. Association for Computational Linguistics (2003)

Backstabber's Knife Collection: A Review of Open Source Software Supply Chain Attacks

Marc Ohm[1(✉)], Henrik Plate[2], Arnold Sykosch[1,3], and Michael Meier[1,3]

[1] Institute for Computer Science 4, University of Bonn,
Endenicher Allee 19A, 53115, Bonn, Germany
{ohm,sykosch,mm}@cs.uni-bonn.de
[2] SAP Security Research, SAP Labs France, 805 Av. Maurice Donat,
06250, Mougins, France
henrik.plate@sap.com
[3] Department for Cyber Security, Fraunhofer FKIE,
Zanderstraße 5, 53177, Bonn, Germany

Abstract. A software supply chain attack is characterized by the injection of malicious code into a software package in order to compromise dependent systems further down the chain. Recent years saw a number of supply chain attacks that leverage the increasing use of open source during software development, which is facilitated by dependency managers that automatically resolve, download and install hundreds of open source packages throughout the software life cycle. Even though many approaches for detection and discovery of vulnerable packages exist, no prior work has focused on malicious packages. This paper presents a dataset as well as analysis of 174 malicious software packages that were used in real-world attacks on open source software supply chains and which were distributed via the popular package repositories npm, PyPI, and RubyGems. Those packages, dating from November 2015 to November 2019, were manually collected and analyzed. This work is meant to facilitate the future development of preventive and detective safeguards by open source and research communities.

Keywords: Application security · Malware · Software supply chain

1 Introduction

In general, software supply chain attacks aim to inject malicious code into a software product. Frequently, attackers tamper with the end product of a given vendor such that it carries a valid digital signature, as it is signed by the respective vendor, and may be obtained by end-users through trusted distribution channels, e.g. download or update sites.

A prominent example of such supply chain attacks is NotPetya, a ransomware concealed in a malicious update of a popular Ukrainian accounting software [8]. In 2017, NotPetya targeted Ukrainian companies but also hit global corporations, causing damage worth billions of dollars and is said to be one of the most

© Springer Nature Switzerland AG 2020
C. Maurice et al. (Eds.): DIMVA 2020, LNCS 12223, pp. 23–43, 2020.
https://doi.org/10.1007/978-3-030-52683-2_2

devastating cyberattacks known today [30]. In the same year, a malicious version of CCleaner, a popular maintenance tool for Microsoft Windows systems, was downloadable from the vendor's official website, and remained undetected for more than a month. During this period it was downloaded around 2.3 million times [27]. Another flavor of supply chain attacks aims at injecting the malicious code into a dependency of a software vendor's product. This attack vector was already predicted by Elias Levy in 2003 [29], and recent years saw a number of real-world attacks following that scheme. Such attacks become possible, because modern software projects commonly depend on multiple open source packages, which themselves introduce numerous transitive dependencies [2]. Such attacks abuse the developers' trust in the authenticity and integrity of packages hosted on commonly used servers and their adoption of automated build systems that encourage this practice [1].

A single open source package may be required by several thousands of open source software projects [23], which makes open source packages a very attractive target for software supply chain attacks. A recent attack on the npm package `event-stream` demonstrates the potential reach of such attacks: The alleged attacker was granted ownership of a prominent npm package simply by asking the original developer to take over its maintenance. At that time, `event-stream` was used by another 1,600 packages, and was on average downloaded 1.5 million times a week [22]. Open source software supply chain attacks are comparable to the problem of vulnerable open source packages which may pass their vulnerability to dependent software projects. This is known as one of the OWASP Top-10 application security risks [31]. However, in case of supply chain attacks, malicious code is deliberately injected and attackers employ obfuscation and evasion techniques to avoid detection by humans or program analysis tools.

The main contribution of this paper is the collection, categorization, and manual analysis of a dataset with malicious code from 174 packages that were used for real-world attacks on open source software supply chains between 2015 and 2019.

The remainder of the paper is structured as follows: Sect. 2 summarizes related work and Sect. 3 outlines the methodology used for the main contributions of this paper. Section 4 presents the necessary background on supply chain attacks, in particular two attack trees developed both on the basis of the dataset and by reviewing and investigating potential attacks and actual weaknesses of open source ecosystems. That is followed by Sect. 5, presenting the analysis and categorization of the actual code of 174 malicious packages observed in the wild. Section 6 summarizes and concludes the paper.

2   Related Work

Related work mostly covers *vulnerable* packages, which contain design flaws or code errors that are accidentally introduced, without bad intention but through negligence, and which may pose a potential security risk. In contrast to that, *malicious* packages contain design flaws or code errors that have been implemented selectively, with caution and the intention to be exploited or triggered at later times in the software life cycle. Technically, malicious code and vulnerable code may look identical, the main difference lies in the intention of the developer (or lack thereof) and, in some cases, the use of evasion or obfuscation techniques to hinder the detection of such code.

Malicious and vulnerable packages reside in the same ecosystem and live through the same software life cycle. As such, related works that investigate package reuse in open source ecosystems in general, or the impact and spread of vulnerable packages in particular, also apply to malicious packages.

Decan, Mens, and Constantinou [13] leveraged security reports in order to examine how and when vulnerabilities in npm software packages are discovered and fixed. In order to assess the effect on other packages hosted on npm, a dependency graph was used. The key findings are that nearly half of the packages inherited vulnerabilities from other packages, and that version pinning to vulnerable and outdated packages are the main cause for such inherited vulnerabilities, even if fixes are available.

Zimmermann, Staicu, Tenny, and Pradel [40] were able to verify these findings and provide mitigation techniques. Highly popular packages and highly active developers were identified as single point of failures. Thus, the authors propose to raise developer awareness through training as well as automated code analysis.

Pfretzschner and Othmane [32] proposed a system to identify software supply chain attacks in npm packages by static code analysis. The tool is able to detect four kinds of attacks: Leakage of global variables, manipulation of global variables, local function manipulation, and dependency-tree manipulation. However, the authors failed to identify real-world examples of these attacks for evaluation.

Garrett, Ferreira, Jia, Sunshine, and Kästner [18] proposed anomaly detection through unsupervised learning in order to identify suspicious package updates. For that purpose they collected over 700,000 packages from npm and normal behavior was inferred from 1,500 randomly selected packages. The system reported 539 suspicious updates per week reducing manually inspection by 89%.

Jukka Ruohonen [33] examined vulnerable Python packages regarding their CVSS (Common Vulnerability Scoring System) score and the respective weakness according to CWE (Common Weakness Enumeration). An auto regressive model was used to calculate how likely a new release is vulnerable based on previous releases' vulnerability. It was found that the prediction of this event is difficult despite good statistical performance. However, the supply chain of a package was not taken into consideration.

While related work mostly focused on *vulnerable* packages and impact assessment with regard to *specific open source ecosystems*, especially Node.js (npm), this work considers *malicious* packages *across several ecosystems*.

3   Methodology

It is important to distinguish between vulnerable and malicious packages. As said, *vulnerable* packages may contain design flaws or code errors that are accidentally introduced, without bad intention but through negligence, and which may pose a potential security risk. According to the Cambridge Dictionary *malicious* means "**intended** to cause damage to a computer system, or to steal private information from a computer system". Technically, malicious and vulnerable coding can be similar or even identical, thus, the main difference lies in the attacker's intention.

The main contribution of this paper is a dataset of malicious packages used in real-world attacks and their analysis. The analysis is detailed in Sect. 5 and comprises the subset of malicious packages used in real-world attacks for which the actual malicious code could be obtained (typically a compressed archive). Compilation took place between July 2nd and August 2nd, 2019 and was updated on 27th of January 2020. The dataset covers the programming languages JavaScript with its package repository npm, Java (Maven Central), Python (PyPI), PHP (Packagist) and Ruby (RubyGems), which are the most popular languages according to newly created GitHub repositories in 2018 [17].

During that time, the vulnerability database Snyk[1], security advisories[2,3,4], and research blogs (e.g. [3,4]) were reviewed to identify malicious packages and possible attack vectors. Only packages that are explicitly labeled as malicious are considered. Leaving out packages labeled as vulnerable might lead to missing some malicious packages. However, manually reviewing all vulnerable packages to find intention and hence prove maliciousness is infeasible. Likewise, the development of an automatized procedure is out of scope for this work but definitely desirable for future work.

Nonetheless, parts of the collection are automatized. This way no packages should be missed because of negligence or fatigue. A parser for the Snyk database is utilized to extract names, affected versions, and disclosure dates of packages listed as malicious. In the next step the publication of malicious versions of a package are dated according to Libraries.io[5], a service that monitors package releases across all major package repositories. Advisories and public incident reports are used to date the public disclosure of the malicious package.

Malicious packages are typically not available anymore on standard package repositories of the respective programming language, e.g. npm or PyPI. Thus, the script tries to download the affected version of a package from a PyPI[6], RubyGems[7], or npm[8] mirror. Failed attempts are manually checked for availability.

Collected packages are statically analyzed in a manual fashion. The package's metadata like name and publication/disclose date are analyzed to find out how it were injected into the ecosystem and how long it was available. The location of the suspicious code is found by manually looking through the package's code.

---

[1] https://snyk.io.

[2] https://www.npmjs.com/advisories.

[3] https://github.com/rubysec/rubygems-advisories.

[4] https://github.com/pypa/warehouse.

[5] https://libraries.io.

[6] https://nero-mirror.stanford.edu.

[7] https://mirror.auckland.ac.nz.

[8] https://registry.npm.taobao.org.

In-depth analysis is carried out to verify the maliciousness as well as to reveal the trigger and condition for malicious behavior, what its objective and targeted operating system (OS) is, and whether obfuscation was employed.

4   Background: Supply Chain Attacks

This background section starts with a high-level introduction of activities and systems related to open source software development projects in Sect. 4.1. Furthermore, different attack vectors for software supply chains will be presented with the help of two attack trees. In general, attack trees allow for a systematic description of attacks against any kind of system [34]. The root node of a given tree thereby corresponds to the attacker's top-level goal, and child nodes represent alternative ways to achieve it. The top-level goals of the attack trees presented in Sects. 4.2 and 4.3 are to inject malicious code into the software supply chain, thus, into a dependency of a development project, and to trigger that malicious code in different circumstances.

4.1   Open Source Development Projects

In a typical development environment as visualized in Fig. 1, *Maintainers* are members of a development project who administer the depicted systems, provide, review and approve contributions, or define and trigger build processes. Open source projects also receive code contributions from *contributors*, which may be reviewed and merged into the project's code base by maintainers. The *build process* ingests the source code and other resources of a project, and has the goal to produce software artifacts. These artifacts are subsequently published such that they become available to end-users and other development projects, either through to distribution platforms like app stores such that they may be consumed by end-users or to *package repositories* for other development projects.

The project resources reside in a *version control system* (VCS), e.g. Git, and are copied to the local file system of the *build system*. Among those resources is a declaration of direct dependencies, which is analyzed at the start of the build process by a *dependency manager* in order to establish the complete dependency tree with all direct and transitive dependencies. As all of them are required during the build, for instance, at compile time or during test execution, they are downloaded (pulled) from *package repositories* such as PyPI[9] for Python, npm[10] for Node.js, or Maven Central[11] for Java.

Such project environments are subject to numerous trust boundaries, and many threats target the respective data flows, data stores and processes. Managing those threats may be challenging even when considering only the environment of a single software project. When considering supply chains with dozens or hundreds of dependencies, it is important to notice that such an environment

---

[9] https://pypi.org.
[10] https://www.npmjs.com.
[11] https://search.maven.org/.

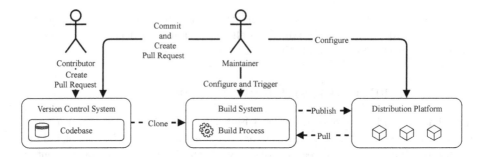

Fig. 1. High-level development and build activities.

exists for every single dependency, making it obvious that the combined attack surface of such projects is considerably larger than that of software entirely developed in-house.

Taking the perspective of attackers, malevolent actors have the intention to compromise the security of the build or runtime environment of software projects through the infection of one or more upstream open source packages, each one of which is developed in environments comparable to Fig. 1. How to reach this goal is described in the following sections by means of two attack trees that provide a structured overview about attack paths to inject a malicious code into dependency trees of downstream users and to trigger its execution at different times or under different conditions.

4.2   Injection of Malicious Code

The attack tree illustrated by Fig. 2 is an extension and refinement of the graph presented by Pfretzschner and Othmane [32], and has as top-level goal to inject malicious code into the dependency tree of downstream packages. Thus, the goal is satisfied once a package with malicious code is available on a distribution platform, e.g. package repository, and it became a direct or transitive dependency of one or more other packages.

To inject a package into dependency trees an attacker may follow two possible strategies, he may either *infect an existing package* or submit a *new package*.

Obviously, developing and publishing a new rogue package using a name that is not used by anybody else avoids interference with other legitimate project maintainers. However, such a package has to be discovered and referenced by downstream users in order to end up in the dependency trees of victim packages. This may be achieved using a name similar to existing package names (*typosquatting*) [3,4,14,15,35,36], or by developing and promoting a *trojan horse* [12]. An attacker might also use the opportunity to reuse the identifier of an existing project, package, or user account withdrawn by its original and legitimate maintainer (*use after free*) [10].

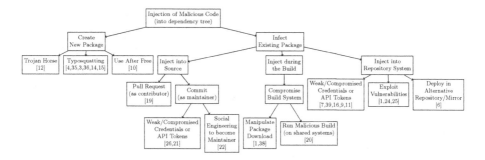

Fig. 2. Attack tree to inject malicious code into dependency trees.

The second strategy is to infect an *existing package* that already has users, contributors and maintainers. The attacker might choose packages for different reasons, e.g. a significant number or specific group of downstream users. Once the attacker chooses a package to infect, the malicious code may be injected *into the sources*, *during the build*, or *into the package repository*.

Open source projects live and strive through community contributions. Thus, attackers can mimic benign project contributors. For instance, an attacker may pretend to solve an existing issue by *creating a pull request* (PR) with a bug fix or a seemingly useful feature or dependency [19]. The latter could be used to create a dependency on an attacker-controller package created from scratch using the techniques described beforehand. In any case, this PR has to be approved and merged into the main code branch by a legitimate project maintainer. Alternatively, an attacker may *commit* malicious code into the project's code base all by himself by using *weak or compromised credentials* or security-sensitive API tokens [21,26]. Furthermore, attackers may become maintainer themselves through *social engineering* [22]. In all cases, no matter how the malicious code has been added to the sources, it will become part of an official package during the next release build—regardless where that build happens. Compared to attacks on build systems and package repositories, malicious code in VCS is more accessible to manual or automated reviews of commits or entire repositories.

The *compromise of build systems* typically entails tampering with resources used throughout the build process, e.g. compilers, build plugins or network services such as proxies or DNS servers. Such resources may be compromised if the build system, be it a developer's work station or a dedicated build server, is subject to vulnerabilities, or if insecure communication channels are such that attackers can *manipulate the package download* from repositories [1,38]. The release builds of the targeted package may also run on a shared build system and thus used by multiple projects [20]. Depending on the setup, such build processes may not run in isolation, hence resources such as package caches or build plugins are shared between the builds of different projects. In this case, an attacker may compromise shared resources during a *malicious build* of a project under his control such that the targeted project is compromised at a later point in time.

Even popular package repositories are still subject to simple but severe security vulnerabilities. While all the other attack vectors seek to inject malicious code into a single package, the *exploit of vulnerabilities* in package repositories themselves puts the entire repository with all its packages at risk [24,25]. Similar to injecting the code in the sources, the attacker may use *weak or compromised credentials* [7,9,11,16,39] or gain maintainer authorizations through *social engineering* [22] in order to publish malicious versions of legitimate packages.

Further, an attacker may upload malicious package versions to *alternative repositories or repository mirrors* [5,6] that are not provisioned by the original maintainers, and wait for victims pulling dependencies from there. Supposedly, such repositories and mirrors are less popular, and the attack is dependent on the victim's configuration, e.g. the order of repositories queried for dependencies or the use of mirrors.

4.3   Execution of Malicious Code

Once malicious code is present in a project's dependency tree, the attack tree illustrated by Fig. 3 has the top-level goal to trigger the malicious code under different conditions. Such conditions may be used to evade detection and/or target attacks towards specific users and systems.

Malicious code may trigger at different *life cycle phases* of the infected package and its downstream users (c.f. Sect. 5.3). If malicious code is contained in *test cases*, the attack primarily targets the contributors and maintainers of the infected package, which run such tests on their developer work stations and build systems. In many of the recorded attacks, malicious code is contained in *install scripts*, which are automatically executed during package installation by downstream users or their dependency managers. Such install scripts exist for Python and Node.js, and may be used to perform pre- or post-installation activities. Malicious code in install scripts puts the contributors and maintainers of downstream packages as well as their end users at risk. Malicious code may also be triggered at *runtime* of downstream packages, which requires that it is invoked as part of the regular control flow of the victim package. In Python, this may be achieved by including malicious code in __init__.py, which is invoked through *import* statements. In JavaScript, this may be achieved by monkey-patching (modifying) existing methods. The specifics of individual programming languages, package managers, etc. may easily be covered by refining this goal.

Independent of the life cycle phase, the execution of malicious behavior may always trigger (unconditioned) or only if certain conditions are met (*conditional execution*). As for any other malware, conditioned execution complicates the dynamic detection of malicious open source packages, since the respective conditions may not be known, understood or met in sandbox environments. Conditioning the execution on the *application state* is a common means to evade detection, e.g. in test environments or dedicated malware analysis sandboxes. Again, the specifics of individual build systems may be covered by respective sub goals, e.g. the presence of Jenkins environment variables indicates that malicious code is

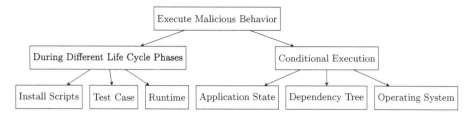

Fig. 3. Attack tree to execute malicious code.

triggered during a build rather than in a production environment. Moreover, conditions may be related to a specific victim package, e.g. check a specific application state such as the balance of a crypto wallet [22]. Heavy reuse of open source packages may lead to a malicious package ending up in the dependency tree of many downstream packages. If only certain packages are of interest to attackers, they may condition the code execution on the nodes of a given *dependency tree* at hand [22]. Furthermore, the *operating system* used may serve as condition.

5   Description of the Dataset

The dataset contains 174 packages and was compiled according to our methodology as described in Sect. 3. A total number of 469 malicious packages could be identified. Additionally, 59 packages were found that could be identified as proof of concept (published by researchers) and hence are excluded from further examination. Eventually, we were able to obtain at least one affected version for 174 packages. The rate of successful downloads of malicious packages for npm is 109/374 (29.14%), for PyPI 28/44 (63.64%), for RubyGems 37/41 (90.24%), and for Maven Central 0/10 (0.00%). All statements and statistics below refers to the set of downloaded packages as it is infeasible to infer characteristics from unobserved packages.

5.1   Composition and Structure

The dataset consists of 62.6% packages published on npm and hence are written for Node.js in JavaScript. The remaining packages were published via PyPI (16.1%, Python) and via RubyGems (21.3%, Ruby). Unfortunately, a malicious Java package targeting Android developers could not be downloaded. For PHP, we were not able to identify any malicious package at all.

The complete dataset is available for free on GitHub[12]. However, access will be granted on justified request only due to ethical reasons. The dataset is structured as follows: *package-manager/package-name/version/package.file*.

Malicious packages are grouped by their originating package manager on the first level. Further, multiple affected versions of one package are grouped

---

[12] https://dasfreak.github.io/Backstabbers-Knife-Collection.

under the respective package's name. As example for the affected version of the well-known case of event-stream it is: *npm/event-stream/3.3.6/event-stream-3.3.6.tgz.*

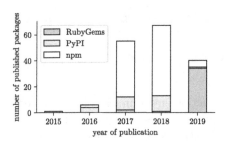
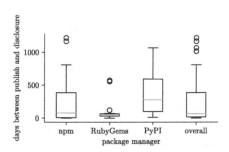

Fig. 4. Publication dates of collected packages.

Fig. 5. Temporal distance between date of publication and disclosure.

5.2 Temporal Aspects

Figure 4 visualizes the publication dates of the collected packages which range from November 2015 to November 2019. The publication and disclosure dates are identified according to the upload time of the package and the publication date of the corresponding advisory identifying the respective version as malicious (cf. Sect. 3). A trend for an increasing number of published malicious packages is apparent. While malicious packages for PyPI are known to date back to 2015 and since then are increasing, npm gained a massive amount of malicious packages in 2017. Malicious packages on RubyGems experienced a boom in 2019.

Note that there are more incidents in total than Fig. 4 references, as it does not include reported malicious packages that we could not obtain. PyPI and npm show an ever-increasing trend as they can easily be used to spread malicious code due to their package managers' ability to execute arbitrary code on installation (c.f. Sect. 5.3). In contrast to that, RubyGems does not allow code execution on install but seems to be targeted more often in recent attacks. This might be due to PyPI's and npm's increasing efforts to hinder attackers from abusing their package repositories and managers, respectively.

Figure 5 shows that **on average a malicious package is available for 209 days** ($min = -1, max = 1,216, \sigma = 258, \tilde{x} = 67$) before being publicly reported. A minimum of -1 days was reached for *npm/eslint-config-airbnb-standard/2.1.1* which was affected by *npm/eslint-scope/3.7.2.* Even though the infection of *npm/eslint-scope/3.7.2* was known, the package was still in use due to the developers' re-packaging strategy, i.e. the infected version was hard copied into the source of *npm/eslint-config-airbnb-standard/2.1.1.* The maximum of $1,216$ days was reached by *npm/rpc-websocket/0.7.7* which took over an abandoned package and went undetected for a long period.

In general this shows that packages tend to be available for a longer period. While PyPI has the highest average online time, that period varies the most for npm, and RubyGems tends to detect malicious packages more timely.

5.3 Trigger of Malicious Behavior

Malicious behavior of a package may be triggered at different points of interaction with the package. Most typically, a package may be installed, tested, or executed. A separation per package repository is visualized in Fig. 6.

It is apparent that **most malicious packages (56%) start their routines on installation**, which might be due to poor handling of arbitrary code during install. This can be triggered by the package repositories' install command, e.g. npm install <package>, which invokes code as defined in the package's definition, e.g. package.json and setup.py. This code might be arbitrary to do whatever is necessary to install the package, e.g. download additional files. It is by far the easiest way for attackers to effectively activate their malicious code and hence used frequently. This seems very common for malicious packages on PyPI. The difference for nmp and PyPI might stem from npm packages having more dependencies than a typical Python package [37] which might lead to more malicious packages targeting other dependent package on runtime like in the case of event-stream [22].

In contrast, Ruby does not implement such install logic and hence no packages for that case exist in Ruby. Consequentially, all found packages on RubyGems use runtime as trigger, often targeting Ruby on Rails, a server-side web application framework. Overall, 43% of the packages expose their malicious behavior during the program's runtime, i.e. when invoked from another function.

For 1% of the packages the test routines are used as trigger. Invoking the test routine of *npm/ladder-text-js/1.0.0* would execute sudo rm -rf /* which, if successful, deletes all the user's files. Note that this observation might not generalize due to the low number of found packages using this technique.

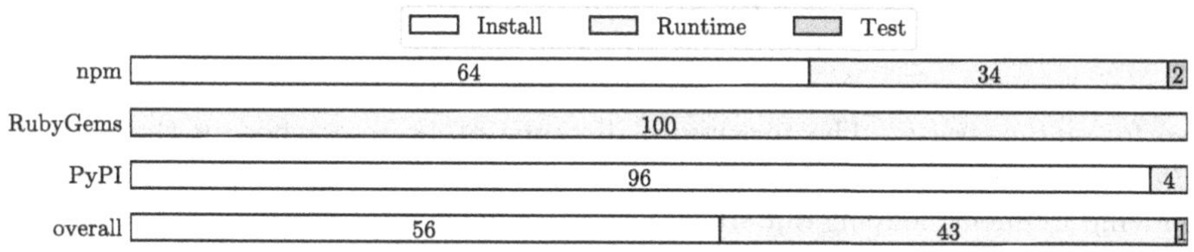

Fig. 6. Trigger of malicious behavior separated per package repository and overall.

5.4 Conditional Execution

As seen in Fig. 7, **41% of the packages check for a condition before triggering further execution**. This may depend on the application's state, e.g. check whether the main application is in production

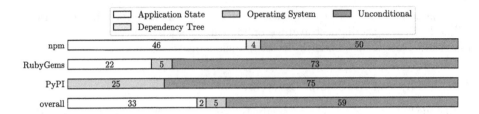

Fig. 7. Ratio of conditional and unconditional execution per package repository and overall.

mode (e.g. *RubyGems/paranoid2/1.1.6*), resolvability of a domain name (e.g. *npm/logsymbles/2.2.0*), or the amount contained in a crypto wallet (e.g. *npm/flatmap-stream/0.1.1*). This may be done to find profitable targets and evade sandboxing (dynamic analysis).

Other techniques are to check whether another package is present in the dependency tree (e.g. *npm/load-from-cwd-or-npm/3.0.2*) or whether the package is executed on a certain OS (e.g. *PyPI/libpeshka/0.6*). This is done to either target another package or because the malicious functions rely on OS characteristics and functions.

The majority of packages published on PyPI and RubyGems execute unconditionally. For npm the ratio of conditional and unconditional execution is nearly equal. However, packages from PyPI seem not to use Application State as condition which might be due to Python not being used on server-side – unlike npm and Ruby (on Rails) – very often.

5.5   Injection of Malicious Package

In Fig. 8 it is apparent that **most (61%) malicious packages mimic existing packages' names via typosquatting**. A deeper analysis of that phenomenon revealed that the Levenshtein distance of an average typosquatting package to its target is 2.3 ($min = 0, max = 11, \sigma = 2.05, \tilde{x} = 1.0$). In some cases the typosquatting target is available from another package repository, e.g. the Linux package repository `apt` under the exact same name. This is for instance the case for *python-sqlite*. The maximum distance of 11 is reached in the case of *pythonkafka* which targeted *kafka-python*. Common techniques are adding or removing hyphens, leaving out single letters, or exchange of letters that are often mistyped. A word that is targeted exceptionally often is "color" or, respectively, its British English counterpart: "colour". Typosquatting is already proven to be a highly effective technique to infect large numbers of victims in short time [36].

The second most common injection method was the infection of an existing package. This may often be achieved with *compromised credentials* for the repository system (e.g. *npm/eslint-scope/3.7.2*). In most cases, the exact infection technique could not be determined in retrospect. This is because the related source is often removed from the version control system or no further details about the injection are made public. Hence, these packages are listed as *infect existing package*. This technique requires more work from the attackers point of view as he has to take over a developer's/publisher's account first. Once that is accomplished, an update containing malicious content can easily reach numerous users as they are already using that package and depend on its functionality. It is especially dangerous if no version pinning is used and dependencies are updated automatically.

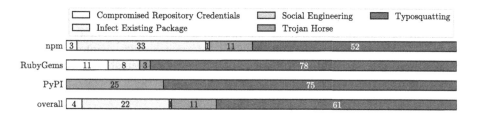

Fig. 8. Injection technique used to introduce the malicious package into a package per package repository and overall.

Another injection technique is to create a new package which consist of nothing but the malicious package to which we refer to as *trojan horse*. No meaningful typo-squatting targets were found for these packages. These packages might have been around as preparation for further attacks to be used in conjunction with an infected existing package or standalone.

5.6 Primary Objective

As shown in Fig. 9, **most packages aim at data exfiltration**. Commonly, the data of interest is the content of /etc/passwd, ~/.ssh/*, ~/.npmrc, or ~/.bash_history. Furthermore, malicious packages try to exfiltrate environment variables (which might contain access tokens) and general system information. Another popular target (7 reported packages, 3 of them available in our dataset) is the token for the voice and text chat application Discord. A Discord user's account may be linked to credit card information and thus be used for financial fraudulence. Exfiltrated data – especially access tokens – may be used for further attacks and spreading of the malicious code [28]. Credit card information may be used for financial fraud.

Moreover, 34% of the packages function as dropper to download second stage payload. Another 5% open a backdoor, i.e. reverse shell, to a remote server and await further instructions. This category will turn victims into zombies that can be controlled by the attacker, e.g. for DDoS attacks. 3% aim to cause a denial of service by exhausting resources through fork bombs and file deletion (e.g. *npm/destroyer-of-worlds/1.0.0*) or breaking functionality of other packages (e.g. *npm/load-from-cwd-or-npm/3.0.2*). This only yields gain for an attacker if a competing party is attacked. Only 3% have financial gain as primary objective by for instance running a cryptominer in the background (e.g. *npm/hooka-tools/1.0.0*) or stealing cryptocurrency directly (e.g. *pip/colourama/0.1.6*). In addition, combinations of the above mentioned objectives might occur.

5.7 Targeted Operating System

In order to identify the targeted OS, the source code was manually analyzed for hints which may be as explicit as an if–then construct like `if platform.system() is 'Windows'` as used in e.g. *PyPI/openvc/1.0.0* or implicit by relying on resources only available on certain OS. These resources may be for instance files containing sensible information like `.bashrc` etc. (cf. Sect. 5.6, *npm/font-scrubber/1.2.2*) or executables like `/bin/sh` (e.g. *npm/rpc-websocket/0.7.11*).

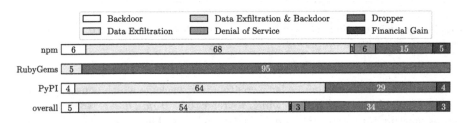

Fig. 9. Primary objective of the malicious package per package repository and overall.

The analysis of the packages for their targeted OS as shown in Fig. 10 revealed that **most packages (53%) are agnostic, i.e. do not rely on OS-specific functions**. The analysis was done on the initial visible code of the package and thus the targeted OS of the second stage payload remains unknown. However, Unix-like systems seem to be targeted more often than Windows and macOS. This might be due to Unix-like systems being used as build environments and hence more valuable data like access tokens (c.f. Sect. 5.6) may be accessible.

There is only one known case of macOS being the target in which the package *npm/angluar-cli/0.0.1* performs a denial of service attack on the McAfee virus scanner for macOS by deleting and modifying its files.

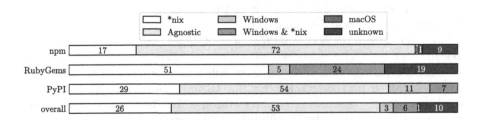

Fig. 10. Targeted operating system per package repository and overall.

5.8   Obfuscation

Malicious actors often try to disguise the presence of their code, i.e. hindering its detection by sight. Noticeable in Fig. 11 is that **nearly the half of the packages (49%) employ some kind of obfuscation**. Most often a different encoding (Base64 or Hex) is used to disguise the presence of malicious functions or suspicious variables such as domain names. This is an easy and effective way to go since most languages have these capabilities on-board without external dependencies.

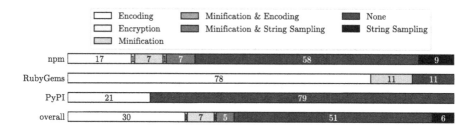

Fig. 11. Employed obfuscation technique per package repository and overall.

A technique often used by benign packages to compress source code and thus save bandwidth is minification. However, this is a welcome opportunity for malicious actors to sneak in extra code which is unreadable for humans (e.g. *npm/tensorplow/1.0.0*). Another way to hide variables is to use string sampling. This requires a seemingly random string which is used to rebuild meaningful strings by picking letter by letter (e.g. *npm/ember-power-timepicker/1.0.8*).

In one case the malicious functions are hidden by encryption. The package *npm/flatmap-stream/0.1.1* leverages AES256 with the short description of the targeted package as decryption key. That way, the malicious behavior is solely exposed when used by the targeted package. Furthermore, combinations of the above mentioned techniques exist.

5.9   Clusters

In order to infer on the presence of attack campaigns, all packages were analyzed for reuse of malicious code or dependency relationships. The malicious code snippets that were manually identified were compared visually for similarity. This way, **it was possible to identify 21 clusters** for which at least two packages either have similar malicious code in common, or an attacker-controlled package depends on another one with the actual malicious code. In total, 157 of the 174 packages (90%) belong to a cluster. On average a cluster comprises 7.28 packages ($min = 2, max = 36, \sigma = 8.96, \tilde{x} = 3$).

A cross comparison of publications dates of packages within one cluster revealed that the average temporal distance between publications is 42 days,

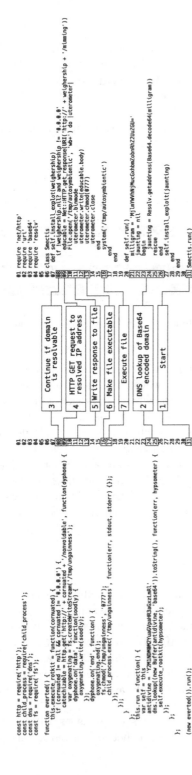

Fig. 12. Comparison and explanation of two malicious packages: *npm/jqeury/3.3.1* on the left; *RubyGems/active-support/5.2.0* on the right. The code was found in `ext/trellislike/unflaming/waffling/extconf.rb` and `package/src/data/var/everted.js`, respectively. Names of classes, variables, and function are randomly picked from an English dictionary (different for each package of the cluster). After instantiation (1), a DNS lookup (2) for an obfuscated (Base64) domain is started. Both snippet contain code for conditional execution. If the lookup is either empty or the non-routable meta-address 0.0.0.0 (3), the execution of malicious code is skipped. This may be seen as evasion technique as it may be the case for sandboxed environments as used for dynamic malware analysis. However, if the domain can be resolved, a HTTP GET request is send (4). The response is written to new a file located in `/tmp` (5, 6), and executed (7).

6:50:18 (min = 1:29:40, max = 353 days, 11:17:02, σ = 78 days, 0:43:10, $\tilde{x}$ = 7 days, 15:24:51). The biggest cluster was formed around the `crossenv` case [35] counting 36 packages published with an average temporal distance of 5.98 days. It was published in two waves, 11 packages within 15 min on 19th of July 2017 and another 25 packages within 30 min on 1st of August 2017.

The cluster having publication dates that are 353 days apart consists of the two packages *PyPI/jeilyfish/0.7.0* and *PyPI/python3-dateutil/2.9.1*. The first was published on 12/11/18 12:26 AM and contained code that download a script to steal SSH and GPG Keys from Windows machines. It went undetected for a long time until the second package was published on 11/29/19 11:43 AM which did not contain malicious code itself but referenced the first package. The cluster was reported and deleted on 12/12/19 05:53 PM.

While most clusters solely contain packages from one package repository, it was possible to find a cluster that mainly contained packages from npm but also *RubyGems/active-support/5.2.0* from RubyGems. This means that attack campaigns exist or at least techniques flow across multiple package repositories.

5.10   Code Review of Two Malicious Packages

For vivid illustration, *npm/jqeury/3.3.1* (left) and *RubyGems/active-support/5.2.0* (right) will be discussed in Fig. 12. They both belong to the same cluster according to our manual assessment of code similarity, even though they were published on different repositories.

6   Discussion and Conclusions

From an attacker's point of view, package repositories represent a reliable and scalable malware distribution channel. We were able to create the first manually curated dataset of malicious open source packages that have been used in real-world attacks. It consists of 174 malicious packages (62.6% npm, 16.1% PyPI, 21.3% RubyGems) ranging from November 2015 to November 2019. Manual analysis revealed that most packages (56%) trigger their malicious behavior on installation, and 41% use further conditions to determine whether to run or not. More than half of the packages (61%) leverage typosquatting to inject themselves into the ecosystem, and data exfiltration is the most common goal (55%). The packages typically are agnostic to operating systems (53%), and often employ obfuscations (49%) to hide themselves. Finally, we were able to detect multiple clusters of malicious packages through reused code even across different programming languages. The dataset provides insight and is available for free to facilitate research in the area of prevention, detection, and mitigation of software supply chain attacks.

However, there are some limitations. Our dataset is highly biased towards malicious packages that are written in JavaScript for Node.js and published on npm which is due to npm's enormous size and popularity. Unfortunately, we were not able to obtain malicious packages for Java (Maven Central) and PHP

(Packagist). Furthermore, roughly 34% of the malicious packages are droppers with the goal to download a second stage payload, which might not be available anymore. One might notice that we listed the deployment in alternative repository or mirrors as injection method but downloaded most of the packages from such sources. While it is possible that these packages have been altered to be malicious, the package's presence in our dataset is still valid as the package would be malicious is both cases. Furthermore, the "intended" maliciousness according to the advisories was verified through manual analysis. Leaving out packages labeled as vulnerable might lead to missing some malicious packages. However, automated detection of maliciousness is out of scope of this work but up for future work. One possible approach for applying the lessons learned from our manual code review could be to identify common control or data flow patterns in malicious code, e.g., silenced exceptions, and search for their presence in other packages.

Our analysis shows that it is important to make use of already available security means. To tackle the most prominent trigger – arbitrary code execution during installation – package managers need to be reworked. Python, for instance, already offers Python Wheels,[13] which avoids code execution during installation. We offer two recommendations for dealing with existing infected packages. For maintainers, multi-factor authentication and strong passwords should be mandatory. Developers should use version pinning. However, the version needs to be chosen absolute, i.e. no automated security patches or bug fixes (minor updates) which again may be counterproductive when it comes to vulnerabilities. Typosquatting packages are already being frequently purged by common package repositories but nonetheless make it through often. General awareness of developers and more stringent rules from the package repositories may help against that type of attack.

However, now that a dataset exists it is possible to use proven malicious packages as seeds in order to find more related cases (c.f. Sect. 5.9). In this context, the manually curated and labeled dataset allows for supervised learning approaches that support the automated and repository-wide search for malicious packages. Moreover, with regard to existing and new mitigation strategies, the presented dataset may pose as a benchmark. Last, acknowledging the importance of a comprehensive and up-to-date dataset, it will be necessary to continue its curation – contributions are welcome.

Acknowlegements. This work is funded under the SPARTA project, which has received funding from the European Union's Horizon 2020 research and innovation programme under grant agreement No. 830892.

---

[13] https://pythonwheels.com/.

References

1. Chess, B., Lee, F.D.Q., West, J.: Attacking the build through cross-build injection: how your build process can open the gates to a trojan horse. https://www.fortify.com/downloads2/public/fortify_attacking_the_build.pdf (2007). Accessed 06 Mar 2019
2. Baker, G.: Keep your dependencies secure and up-to-date with GitHub and Dependabot (2019). https://github.blog/2019-01-31-keep-your-dependencies-secure-and-up-to-date-with-github-and-dependabot/. Accessed 08 Oct 2019
3. Bertus: Cryptocurrency clipboard hijacker discovered in PyPi repository (2018). https://medium.com/@bertusk/cryptocurrency-clipboard-hijacker-discovered-in-pypi-repository-b66b8a534a8. Accessed 09 Mar 2019
4. Bertus: Discord token stealer discovered in PyPi repository (2019). https://medium.com/@bertusk/discord-token-stealer-discovered-in-pypi-repository-e65ed9c3de06. Accessed 02 July 2019
5. Bintray: Malicious packages reported in JCenter (2017). https://status.bintray.com/incidents/w4dfr0rpznkt. Accessed 14 Mar 2019
6. Braun, M.: A confusing dependency (2018). https://blog.autsoft.hu/a-confusing-dependency/. Accessed 14 Mar 2019
7. ChALkeR: Gathering weak npm credentials (2017). https://github.com/ChALkeR/notes/blob/master/Gathering-weak-npm-credentials.md. Accessed 10 Mar 2019
8. Cimpanu, C.: Petya ransomware outbreak originated in Ukraine via tainted accounting software (2017). https://www.bleepingcomputer.com/news/security/petya-ransomware-outbreak-originated-in-ukraine-via-tainted-accounting-software/. Accessed 24 Feb 2019
9. Cimpanu, C.: Backdoored python library caught stealing SSH credentials (2018). https://www.bleepingcomputer.com/news/security/backdoored-python-library-caught-stealing-ssh-credentials/. Accessed 10 Mar 2019
10. Claburn, T.: You can resurrect any deleted GitHub account name (2018). https://www.theregister.co.uk/2018/02/10/github_account_name_reuse/. Accessed 06 Mar 2019
11. Coe, B.E.: A core contributor to the conventional-changelog ecosystem had their npm credentials compromised (2018). https://github.com/conventional-changelog/conventional-changelog/issues/282#issuecomment-365367804. Accessed 17 Feb 2020
12. Constantin, L.: Npm attackers sneak a backdoor into node.js deployments through dependencies (2018). https://thenewstack.io/npm-attackers-sneak-a-backdoor-into-node-js-deployments-through-dependencies/. Accessed 06 Mar 2019
13. Decan, A., Mens, T., Constantinou, E.: On the impact of security vulnerabilities in the npm package dependency network. In: 2018 IEEE/ACM 15th International Conference on Mining Software Repositories (MSR), pp. 181–191. IEEE (2018)
14. Denbraver, H.: Malicious packages found to be typo-squatting in python package index (2019). https://snyk.io/blog/malicious-packages-found-to-be-typo-squatting-in-pypi/. Accessed 17 Feb 2020
15. Dunn, J.E.: Pypi python repository hit by typosquatting sneak attack (2017). https://nakedsecurity.sophos.com/2017/09/19/pypi-python-repository-hit-by-typosquatting-sneak-attack/. Accessed 17 Feb 2020
16. Edge, J.: A backdoor in a popular ruby gem (2019). https://lwn.net/Articles/785386/. Accessed 17 Feb 2020

17. Elliott, T.: The state of the octoverse: top programming languages of 2018, November 2018. https://github.blog/2018-11-15-state-of-the-octoverse-top-programming-languages/. Accessed 30 Sept 2019

18. Garrett, K., Ferreira, G., Jia, L., Sunshine, J., Kästner, C.: Detecting suspicious package updates. In: Proceedings of the 41st International Conference on Software Engineering: New Ideas and Emerging Results, pp. 13–16. IEEE Press (2019)

19. Gilbertson, D.: I'm harvesting credit card numbers and passwords from your site. Here's how (2018). https://hackernoon.com/im-harvesting-credit-card-numbers-and-passwords-from-your-site-here-s-how-9a8cb347c5b5. Accessed 09 Nov 2018

20. Gruhn, V., Hannebauer, C., John, C.: Security of public continuous integration services. In: Proceedings of the 9th International Symposium on Open Collaboration, WikiSym 2013, pp. 15:1–15:10. ACM, New York (2013)

21. Holmes, E.: How I gained commit access to homebrew in 30 minutes (2018). https://medium.com/@vesirin/how-i-gained-commit-access-to-homebrew-in-30-minutes-2ae314df03ab. Accessed 06 Mar 2019

22. II, T.H.: Compromised npm package: event-stream (2018). https://medium.com/intrinsic/compromised-npm-package-event-stream-d47d08605502. Accessed 06 Mar 2019

23. Janaszek, M.: State of package.json dependencies (2018). https://medium.com/warsawjs/state-of-package-json-dependencies-de99828b6c3f. Accessed 08 Oct 2019

24. Justicz, M.: Remote code execution on rubygems.org (2017). https://justi.cz/security/2017/10/07/rubygems-org-rce.html. Accessed 06 Mar 2019

25. Justicz, M.: Remote code execution on packagist.org (2018). https://justi.cz/security/2018/08/28/packagist-org-rce.html. Accessed 7 Oct 2019

26. Khandelwal, S.: Password-guessing was used to hack Gentoo Linux Github account (2019). https://thehackernews.com/2018/07/github-hacking-gentoo-linux.html. Accessed 07 Oct 2019

27. Khandelwal, S.: CCleaner attack timeline - here's how hackers infected 2.3 million PCs (2018). https://thehackernews.com/2018/04/ccleaner-malware-attack.html. Accessed 24 Feb 2019

28. Kuizinas, G.: State of package.json dependencies (2017). https://medium.com/@gajus/distributing-a-self-replicating-malicious-code-using-npm-cf2bf3209293. Accessed 14 Apr 2020

29. Levy, E.: Poisoning the software supply chain. IEEE Secur. Priv. 1(3), 70–73 (2003)

30. Ng, A.: Us: Russia's NotPetya the most destructive cyberattack ever (2018). https://www.cnet.com/news/uk-said-russia-is-behind-destructive-2017-cyberattack-in-ukraine/. Accessed 25 Feb 2019

31. OWASP: Owasp top 10: the ten most critical web application security risks (2017). https://www.owasp.org/images/7/72/OWASP_Top_10-2017_%28en%29.pdf.pdf. Accessed 06 Mar 2019

32. Pfretzschner, B., ben Othmane, L.: Identification of dependency-based attacks on node.js. In: Proceedings of the 12th International Conference on Availability, Reliability and Security, p. 68. ACM (2017)

33. Ruohonen, J.: An empirical analysis of vulnerabilities in python packages for web applications. In: 2018 9th International Workshop on Empirical Software Engineering in Practice (IWESEP), pp. 25–30. IEEE (2018)

34. Schneier, B.: Attack trees, December 1999. https://www.schneier.com/academic/archives/1999/12/attack_trees.html. Accessed 14 Apr 2020

35. Spring, T.: Attackers use typo-squatting to steal npm credentials (2017). https://threatpost.com/attackers-use-typo-squatting-to-steal-npm-credentials/127235/. Accessed 06 Mar 2019

36. Tschacher, N.P.: Typosquatting in programming language package managers. Master's thesis, Universität Hamburg, Fachbereich Informatik (2016)
37. Vaidya, R.K., De Carli, L., Davidson, D., Rastogi, V.: Security issues in language-based sofware ecosystems. arXiv preprint arXiv:1903.02613 (2019)
38. Veytsman, M.: How to take over the computer of any Java (or Clojure or Scala) developer (2014). http://blog.ontoillogical.com/blog/2014/07/28/how-to-take-over-any-java-developer/. Accessed 14 Mar 2019
39. Zhu, H., Mills, B.: Postmortem for malicious packages published on july 12th, 2018 (2018). https://eslint.org/blog/2018/07/postmortem-for-malicious-package-publishes. Accessed 07 Oct 2019
40. Zimmermann, M., Staicu, C.A., Tenny, C., Pradel, M.: Small world with high risks: a study of security threats in the npm ecosystem. arXiv preprint arXiv:1902.09217 (2019)

Putting Attacks in Context: A Building Automation Testbed for Impact Assessment from the Victim's Perspective

Herson Esquivel-Vargas[1]([⊠]), Marco Caselli[2], Geert Jan Laanstra[1], and Andreas Peter[1]

[1] University of Twente, Enschede, The Netherlands
{h.esquivelvargas,g.j.laanstra,a.peter}@utwente.nl
[2] Siemens AG, Munich, Germany
marco.caselli@siemens.com

Abstract. Cybersecurity research relies on the reproducibility and deep understanding of attacks to devise appropriate solutions. Different kinds of testbeds are typically used to systematically execute attacks and evaluate defenses. Testbeds are widely used to demonstrate Building Automation and Control System (BACS) attacks and defenses, considered too risky to be executed on real infrastructures. However, those testbeds implement arbitrary configurations of building services that do not resemble real-world deployments. In this work, we present the first BACS testbed specially designed to assess the impact of cyberattacks from the victim's perspective. It features general purpose building services such as illumination, ventilation, and temperature control, whose configuration is easily adapted to emulate the requirements of real-world locations. In this way, the context added to our testbed allows us to better understand the impact of BACS attacks through concrete and realistic scenarios. Moreover, by analyzing different configurations of the BACS (i.e., contexts), we found out that identical attacks may have dramatically different impacts. Thus, reinforcing our view on the relevance of adding context to BACS testbeds.

1 Introduction

Cyber Physical Systems (CPSs) refer to a variety of applications where computer systems interact with physical aspects of the world [22]. Those physical aspects include variables such as speed, temperature, and pressure, whose automated control has proved crucial in many industries. The building automation industry is one of them, where physical variables are controlled through building services such as heating, ventilation, and air conditioning. The interconnection and centralized management of building services is achieved through Building Automation and Control Systems (BACSs).

The influence that CPSs exert in the real world has been traditionally regarded as a major security concern. For that reason, the *impact* of CPS

© Springer Nature Switzerland AG 2020
C. Maurice et al. (Eds.): DIMVA 2020, LNCS 12223, pp. 44–64, 2020.
https://doi.org/10.1007/978-3-030-52683-2_3

attacks has been typically measured as the deviation of physical variables from pre-established setpoints [1,14,33]. While such deviations indeed constitute the physical manifestation of an attack, not all of them represent a threat. In fact, several physical changes may naturally occur without noticeable consequences.

Specifically on BACSs, the experience on real-life attacks suggests that the adversaries' goal is typically to leverage the physical capabilities of the system to thwart business processes [8,24]. We deem these attacks as a specialization of physical impact attacks, tailored to drift physical variables beyond a business acceptable threshold (see Fig. 1). Since BACS attacks have a direct effect on organizations' daily operations, we argue that the impact assessment of BACS attacks should be done from the victim's perspective, specifically, the *Business Continuity Impact* (BCI).

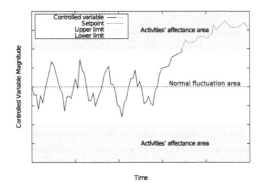

Fig. 1. Controlled variables have limits beyond which the supported activity gets negatively affected. Such limits depend on each specific activity.

From a defensive perspective, BACS attacks must be carefully analyzed by cybersecurity researchers to devise appropriate solutions. The replicability of such attacks is crucial to methodically evaluate defensive approaches. However, attack execution in production infrastructures is risky. To overcome this limitation, testbeds provide a safe experimentation platform that removes the risk of damaging production systems.

Traditional BACS testbeds serve as a demonstration platform for defensive mechanisms [11,13,25] whose capabilities are, in turn, commonly demonstrated in light of two sets of attacks: those that can and cannot be handled by the defensive tool. No context nor special attention to the attacker's goal is needed for such experiments; the focus is placed on the low level details of the attack. Instead, we address the challenge of building the first BACS testbed specialized in the assessment of the BCI of cyberattacks.

The testbed described in this work implements three general building services, namely, illumination, ventilation, and temperature control. Those building services can be reconfigured to fit the requirements of diverse business contexts. Such reconfigurability can hardly be achieved in other kind of CPS testbeds, where one particular scenario is commonly embedded in the hardware itself (e.g., electric grid, water treatment plant, etc.). Leveraging this feature, our testbed allows to reproduce identical attacks on different business contexts and compare their BCI.

Our results show that the context is crucial to properly assess the impact of cyberattacks. The reason being that the BCI is always relative to the victim's use of building services. This insight gets embodied in the testbed by configuring the building services according to the victim's needs. Only then, a context-rich BCI assessment of cyberattacks can be conducted.

Contribution. (i) *A detailed description of the development process of a BACS testbed specialized in the assessment of Business Continuity Impact (BCI) of cyberattacks.* We provide all the engineering materials, custom software, and information sources needed to replicate our testbed.

(ii) *We provide empirical evidence of the context's relevance by exposing remarkably different impacts (BCI) on identical attacks.* Through the implementation of three different emulated environments in our testbed, we provide concrete and realistic examples that show how different organizations under identical attacks suffer the consequences differently.

Organization. Hereafter the paper is organized as follows. The literature review is presented in Sect. 2. We elaborate on the tight relation between business processes and BACSs in Sect. 3. Section 4 describes the process of creating a testbed for BCI assessment from the victim's perspective, followed by our experiments in Sect. 5. Finally, we present the conclusions of our work in Sect. 6.

2   Related Work and Background

Testbeds. The common objective of all security CPS testbeds is to execute attacks and to evaluate defenses. On top of that, different goals are set which yield different testbed implementations. Not necessarily mutually exclusive, typical testbed goals are demonstration, education, and impact assessment [20,32]. Demonstration testbeds are built to convince stakeholders of the applicability of both offensive and defensive research findings [32]. Education testbeds are skill-development platforms where students, researchers, and practitioners can learn hands-on [2,21]. Finally, impact assessment testbeds use a variety of metrics to quantify the consequences of cyber attacks [1,23,27].

BACS testbeds in particular, have overlooked the relevance of *impact* analyses of cyberattacks to mostly focus on the demonstration of security solutions [11,13,25]. To show the strengths and weaknesses of these tools, they appeal to attack instances to exemplify success and failure cases. Although we acknowledge the illustrative value of such testbeds, the lack of high level context information makes it difficult to recognize the attacks' potential impact in real-world scenarios and to realize the actual value of the proposed defenses. Our testbed addresses this limitation by incorporating context as part of its default operation.

Impact Metrics. Several Industrial Control System (ICS) testbeds have been built to study the *physical impact* of cyberattacks. For instance, a water treatment testbed is used in [33], where the impact is defined as the deviation in the pre-established pH level of the water. In [1], a water distribution testbed is presented where the impact of attacks is measured as the decrease in the supplied water with respect to the normal capacity of the system. Yet another example are the smart-grid testbeds presented in [23,27], where the impact of attacks is measured in terms of voltage (in)stability, generation loss, and load shedding increment.

Other kinds of impact have been analyzed as well. Packet delays have been measured as the impact of communication outages [23], and even the performance decrease after introducing cybersecurity controls has been considered [9].

Most impact metrics do not consider the level of disruption from the organization's perspective. Since the goal of BACSs is to support diverse business processes in organizations, a measure of the business impact of cyberattacks is needed. A BACS BCI metric is described in [12]. In summary, it is based on a methodology that merges business and technical aspects of the BACS. From the technical perspective, this methodology leverages on a graph data structure whose nodes and edges represent BACS components and functional dependencies, respectively. BACS components are then labeled with an initial score that represents their support on business processes. Finally, a centrality measure (called BACRank) is computed on the graph to score BACS components based on their BCI.

Rather than designing a new impact metric, our goal in this project is to build a testbed that works as a BACS reference implementation whose properties (e.g., design, emulated business processes, etc.) are used to instantiate existing BCI metrics.

Attacks. There are two main types of attacks in CPSs: those inherited from the IT domain and the attacks that exploit the physical capabilities of the system. Examples of attacks inherited from the IT domain are packet flooding, packet spoofing, and password attacks [15]. On the other hand, attacks that leverage the physical capabilities of the CPS include triggering alarms, opening/closing valves, blinking lights, etc. [1,29]. IT attacks often serve as a first step towards cyber-physical attacks. The scope of our work is focused on cyber-physical attacks.

Specifically on the BACS domain, different attacks have been described in literature. Many of them targeting BACnet (ISO 16484-5) [3], one of the most popular BACS protocols currently in use [13]. A condensed list of attacks is shown in Table 1.

An attack classification framework is needed to methodically analyze attacks and defenses. The threat intelligence community has developed a number of taxonomies to structure knowledge about cyberattacks. One of such taxonomies is Mitre's ATT&CK framework [31]. This framework describes Tactics, Techniques, and Procedures used by adversaries. *Tactics* are the high-level goals of the attacker, whereas *techniques* refer to the expected actions required to achieve those goals. Finally, the *procedures* describe specific details about how to

Table 1. BACS attacks described in literature.

Protocol	Attack	Reference
MS/TP	DoS via frame desynchronization	[16]
ICMP	DoS via smurf attack	[15]
IP	DoS via packet flooding	[15]
PPP	Backdoor via modem connection	[15]
BACnet	DoS via malformed packet injection	[19]
BACnet	DoS via Initialize-Routing-Table command	[15]
BACnet	DoS via Reinitialize-Device command	[11]
BACnet	Snooping via I-Am-Router-To-Network command	[15]
BACnet	DoS via depletion of CoV subscriptions	[26]
BACnet	Firmware corruption via File object writing	[10]
BACnet	Data manipulation via WriteProperty attack	[19]

instantiate the techniques. Although the ATT&CK framework was initially created for standard IT enterprise environments, an analogous framework for ICSs has been published recently.[1] Since the ICS version of the framework fits more accurately the BACS attacks discussed in this paper, we use it to categorize the type of attacks we aim to study and the concrete instances of attacks executed.

3   Business Processes and BACSs

According to the Information Systems Audit and Control Association (ISACA), a *business process* is a set of inter-related activities that deliver a specific product or service to a customer [17]. Building services play an important role in organizations, supporting the execution of their business processes [12]. However, the configuration of the BACS is different depending on the supported business processes. Each business process location has a set of desired or, in many cases, *required* environmental conditions it must comply with in order to fit its purpose. Ventilation, temperature, illumination, among other conditions, are specified for different locations in diverse documents such as standards, regulations, and best practices guides. Thus, setpoints, thresholds, and control algorithms change depending on the particular setting. Examples of regulated environmental conditions are shown in Table 2, taken from [4–7, 28, 30].

Ventilation requirements are commonly expressed as liters per second (L/s) or cubic feet per minute (CFM). Those requirements are intended to keep the CO_2 level below the specified values. Details on how to convert such measures to CO_2 parts per million (ppm) can be found in Appendix A.

---

[1] https://collaborate.mitre.org/attackics/.

Table 2. Required environmental conditions for diverse business process locations.

Business process	Business process location	Illumination (lux)	Ventilation (CO_2 ppm)	Temperature (°C)
Surgeries	Operating room	[500–600]	≤770	[20–24]
Teaching	Lecture hall	[300–500]	≤1400	[20–27]
Server hosting	Data center	[50–100]	– .	[18–27]
Blood tests	Laboratory	[750–1200]	≤1400	[20–27]
Physical conditioning	Fitness gym	[200–300]	≤880	[20–22]

4   Testbed for Business Continuity Impact Assessment

Current security testbeds in the BACS domain focus on the demonstration of the protection capabilities of defensive tools. Such demonstrations typically compare the set of attacks that the tool can handle with the set of attacks it cannot. While these attack-based demonstrations draw all attention to the technicalities of the attack, no context information is given to illustrate the attack's potential impact in real-world scenarios and the best use cases for the proposed tools. No BACS testbeds up to now, have used contextual information to analyze the impact of cyberattacks.

To fill this gap, the focus of our testbed is the assessment of attacks impact from the business perspective. We refer to such impact as Business Continuity Impact (BCI). Our aim is to analyze attacks that exploit the physical capabilities of the BACS and whose ultimate goal is to hinder business processes in the targeted organization. In this section, we describe the development process of our testbed, covering its requirements, design, and implementation.

4.1   Requirements

Scenarios. The goal of our testbed is to provide a platform to assess the impact of attacks launched against different business scenarios. We define *scenario* as the combination of a business process location (in previous sections regarded as *the context*) and its supporting building services. Our observation, as can be derived from Table 2, is that a reduced subset of core building services can abstractly represent different business process locations. Based on this observation, the requirement for our testbed is to implement automated illumination, ventilation, and temperature control, so it can reproduce the environmental conditions of diverse locations such as those listed in Table 2. Finally, a software tool is needed to reconfigure and adapt these building services to the requirements of different locations.

Attacks. We focus on attacks that take advantage of the physical capabilities of the BACS. According to Mitre's tactics, techniques, and procedures hierarchy, those attacks correspond to the *impair process control* tactic,[2] in which "[t]he adversary is trying to manipulate, disable, or damage physical control processes.". From a high level perspective, the requirement for our testbed is to provide the technical means to reproduce *impair process control* attacks.

Impact Assessment. The required impact assessment metric must consider the business process where the BACS is deployed. In particular, we are concerned with attacks that can affect the normal execution of business processes. Such metric is commonly known as BCI and allows to assess the impact of the attacks launched against our testbed from the business perspective. Since our testbed should be easily reconfigured to emulate different scenarios, the impact metric can be used to compare identical attacks on many of them. The goal of such experiments is to figure out to what extent the context influences the BCI.

To summarize our requirements, Fig. 2 shows the relation between attacks, scenarios, and the impact assessment metric, where $I_{i,j}$ is the BCI of attack i under scenario j.

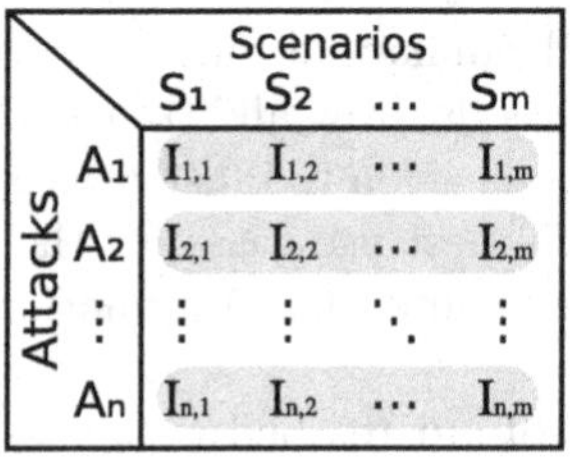

Fig. 2. Summary of our experimental setup requirements: (1) Reproducibility of *impair process control* attacks; (2) Reproducibility of diverse scenarios modeled through building services; and (3) A BCI metric to compare the impact of attacks on multiple scenarios.

4.2   Design

The minimal experimental setup needed to launch attacks and compute the corresponding BCI, must implement one scenario comprised of at least one business process location and one building service. The building service embodies the technical attack surface that will be targeted by the adversary. The business process tunes the impact metric so that its magnitude reflects the consequences of the attack.

Our testbed integrates illumination, ventilation, heating, and cooling as building services. Figure 3 depicts those services as implementations of an abstract *BuildingService*. Whereas each *Scenario* uses one or more *BuildingService*(s),

---

[2] https://collaborate.mitre.org/attackics/index.php/Impair_Process_Control.

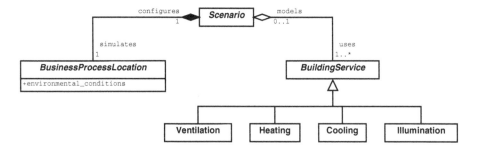

Fig. 3. High level design of our experimental setup.

a *BusinessService* might not necessarily model a *Scenario*. This is how BACS testbeds have been built in the past. It is only by configuring the environmental conditions of a *BusinessProcessLocation* that the overall *Scenario* required to compute the BCI is added to the testbed. From a design perspective, we do not limit the business process locations that can be emulated in our testbed.

The control algorithm differs per building service. Whereas some are activated upon specific time conditions, others require feedback from the environment. The former is known as *open control loop* (see Algorithm 1) and the latter as *closed control loop* (see Algorithm 2). In our testbed, the illumination service is handled by an open control loop. The ventilation and temperature control use closed control loops.

Algorithm 1. Simplified open control loop.

---

  while *True* **do**
    if *time_for_action = True* **then**
      take_action()
    else
      stop_action()
    end if
  end while

Algorithm 2. Simplified closed control loop.

---

  while *True* **do**
    if *controlled_var > upper_limit* **then**
      decrease_controlled_var()
    else if *controlled_var < lower_limit* **then**
      increase_controlled_var()
    end if
  end while

The design of BCI metrics is a complex task beyond the scope of this work. Instead, we use self-evident scenarios whose attacks' BCI can be deduced by domain experts from the business processes' technical requirements. We back up the expert-based assessment with the BCI metric proposed in [12]. We do not design new BCI metrics nor enhance existing ones.

In [12], the components to be assessed are represented as nodes in a graph data structure. The edges of the graph represent dependencies between components. The components' impact scoring is executed in three steps. First, each node is annotated with an initial score that, among other information, considers the relevance of the component from the business perspective. During the second step, the edges are annotated with an estimation of the dependency strength. Finally, after all nodes and edges have been annotated, a graph centrality algorithm (called BACRank) is executed on the graph to assign the final impact score.

The granularity of the components to be assessed depends on the needs of the organization. To simplify our discussion, we use *building services* as high level components to be assessed. This decision reduces the graph size to only three nodes: illumination, ventilation, and temperature control, which includes the heating and cooling services.

4.3   Implementation

Hardware. BACSs comprise diverse components in a 3-layered hierarchical arrangement. At the bottom, there are sensors and actuators, commonly referred to as *field devices*. In the middle, embedded computers in charge of taking inputs from the sensors and sending output signals to the actuators make up the *control layer*. On top, there is a *management layer* which provides unified control and monitoring to BACS administrators.

In our testbed, we use the BACnet communication protocol at the control and management layers [3]. Although at these layers we use software and hardware commonly used in real BACS deployments, at the field level we use smaller actuators than those used in real buildings. This is due to our down-scaled version of building rooms.

We built two physical modules that represent real building rooms. The first module is a *mechanical room* that contains heating and cooling hardware that emulates a building's boiler and chiller, respectively. The second module is a generic *building room* that requires heating and cooling services from the first module. Moreover, it has a thermostat, illumination, and ventilation hardware. The thermostat contains temperature, humidity, occupancy and CO_2 sensors (inputs) and relays to interact with the actuators (outputs). Both modules are physically connected to allow the heat/cold transfer. Figure 4 shows a picture of both physical modules.[3]

---

[3] The 3D CAD designs, schematics of custom electronics, and bill of materials are published in https://www.utwente.nl/en/eemcs/scs/downloads/2020_BACS_testbed/.

Since the illumination service must adapt to different lighting requirements, it is controlled by an *analog output* that regulates the light intensity. The analog output provides a maximum of 20 mA at [0–12] VDC, which is too low to feed the high power LEDs installed in the building room. A customized electronic circuit was designed to dim the lights according to the driving analog output. The other actuators are controlled using *binary outputs* connected to relays. Thus, avoiding the need for additional circuitry.

The cost of the project can be divided in three parts. The structural components, which includes the aluminum base, profiles, plexiglass, among others, have an approximate cost of $700 USD. The BACnet specific hardware and software has an approximate cost of $3.500 USD (see Table 3). Finally, other components including power supplies, actuators, relays, etc. have an approximate cost of $500 USD. After considering outsourced services (e.g., plexiglass laser cutting), the overall cost of the physical components of the testbed is about $5.000 USD. We consider this as reasonable costs for a small testbed and it should allow other research groups to replicate our testbed.

Table 3. BACnet components used in our testbed.

Vendor	Product	BACnet profile	Approximate cost
KMC	BAC-5050	Router	$1.000 USD
KMC	FlexStat BAC-131136CEW	B-ASC	$1.000 USD
MBS	BACeye version 2.1.0.15	B-OWS	$500 USD
Janitza	UMG 604-PRO	B-SA	$1.000 USD

Fig. 4. Testbed modules. The building room (on the right) is physically connected to the mechanical room (on the left) to allow air flow.

Communication. As stated above, the chosen BACS communication protocol is BACnet [3]. The underlying protocols include UDP, IP, ICMP, Ethernet, and

MS/TP. A PPP connection to the Public Switched Telephone Network (PSTN) is also added since it has been documented as an important attack vector for BACS networks [15]. The variety of protocols available provides a considerable attack surface. A network diagram of our testbed is shown in Fig. 5.

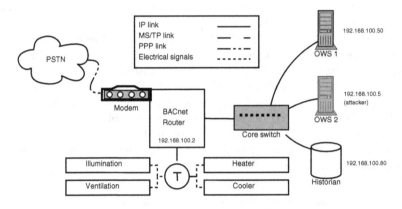

Fig. 5. Network topology (including electrical signals to actuators).

The IP network implements a star topology. The core switch has been configured with a mirroring port to collect all the network traffic exchanged during the experiments.

Software. The most important software applications used in our testbed are BACeye 2.1.0.15 and bacnet-stack 0.8.6.[4] Using bacnet-stack we implement a Linux-based Operator Work Station (OWS 1 in Fig. 5). It runs a custom application developed to quickly reconfigure the testbed to meet the environmental requirements of predefined business process locations.

BACeye runs on a Windows-based OWS, which we assume under control of the attacker (OWS 2 in Fig. 5). Network captures taken during the experiments might show legitimate and malicious traffic from this computer.

The firmware version of the FlexStat controller is R2.1.0.18. The BAC-5050 router runs firmware build R1.8.0.1.

5   Empirical Analysis of BACS Attacks

We execute attacks against the illumination (I), ventilation (V), and temperature control (T) services implemented in our testbed. As specified in our testbed's requirements (Sect. 4.1), the attacks considered is this work correspond to Mitre's *impair process control* tactic. One step down in the ATT&CK hierarchy, there are 11 techniques to implement such tactic. Since we want to replicate the same attack conditions on different scenarios, we chose the *Unauthorized Command*

---

[4] https://sourceforge.net/projects/bacnet/.

Message technique for all the attacks. According to Mitre's website,[5] following this technique "[a]dversaries may send unauthorized command messages to instruct control systems devices to perform actions outside their expected functionality for process control.". Further down in the hierarchy, we also fix the attack *procedure*. We chose one of the attacks listed in Table 1, specifically, data manipulation via the WriteProperty attack [19]. This attack consists of a syntactically valid BACnet message that changes a property in a BACnet object.

To achieve our goal of comparing the BCI of identical attacks on different scenarios, we pick three business process locations from Table 2, namely the operating room, lecture hall, and data center. Those locations are chosen due to their diverse building service requirements. During the experiments, the testbed is configured to fit the environmental conditions defined for each business process location.

The BCI of cyberattacks can be computed in advance by understanding the requirements of business processes on building services. Building services that are essential for business processes will have larger BCI than other services. The impact levels assigned to building services are technically-backed choices made by domain experts. In what follows, we present a short description of such technically-backed choices for each location assessed. A summary is presented in Table 4.

Operating Room. The World Health Organization deems illumination as "one of the major nonstructural elements in a hospital" [35]. While most people would agree that all environmental conditions in operating rooms are important, the severity and immediacy of an attack on the illumination service are key factors to consider it as the highest priority service, above the ventilation and temperature control, both considered of medium impact.

Lecture Hall. The concern for air quality is common in densely occupied indoor spaces [4]. A high concentration of CO_2 (e.g., ≥ 1400 ppm) might lead to illness symptoms such as headaches and dizziness. Moreover, the ventilation is considered a high priority service in lecture halls since it has been shown that improving the air quality increases the students performance [34]. Although illumination and temperature are also relevant, they have been scored as medium impact services.

Data Center. Data centers are extremely sensitive to temperature [6]. Whereas low temperatures increase the chances of electrostatic discharges, high temperatures might damage the servers' hardware, or trigger safety mechanisms to automatically power them off. For those reasons, temperature control is by far considered the most important building service for the continuity of operations in a data center. Data centers do not have ventilation requirements (see Table 2) mainly because servers do not produce CO_2 *in-situ*. Finally, illumination is primarily used to enable video surveillance. For those reasons, the ventilation and illumination are deemed as low impact services.

---

[5] https://collaborate.mitre.org/attackics/index.php/Technique/T855.

Table 4. BCI levels of building service attacks on different contexts. Highlighted in bold font the *high* impact services per location.

Attack	Operating room	Lecture hall	Data center
Illumination	**High**	Medium	Low
Ventilation	Medium	**High**	Low
Temperature	Medium	Medium	**High**

5.1 Attacks

We configured our testbed according to the chosen scenarios to launch three attacks in each of them: turning the illumination off, stopping the ventilation service, and stopping the temperature control service. All attacks are executed against the thermostat FlexStat BAC-131136CEW (BACnet Application-Specific Controller). The specifics of each attack are detailed in Table 5. These attacks do not respond to vulnerabilities particular to the device but to the BACnet protocol itself.[6]

Table 5. Attack procedures against the building controller. Object types and instance numbers provided to ease the analysis of the corresponding pcap files.

No	Attack	BACnet service	Object type	Object instance	Written value
1	Illumination	WriteProperty	Analog output	5	0
2	Ventilation	WriteProperty	Binary output	1	0
3	Temperature	WriteProperty	Binary output	2,1	0

Illumination. The ambient light in the room where the testbed is located is measured in the range of [46, 52] lux. All the illumination experiments start with sensor readings in this range. After approximately 40 samples of ambient light, the illumination service is turned on at the intensity needed to meet the requirements of each specific scenario. Approximately 40 samples later the first attack is executed, which causes the sensor to report the ambient light intensity again, confirming thus the attack. Figure 6 shows the illumination samples collected during our experiments for each scenario.

Ventilation. Unlike lecture halls and operating rooms, data centers do not have CO_2 requirements (see Table 2). Since there are no consequences from the business perspective, we did not execute a ventilation attack on the data center scenario.

---

[6] Network captures of each attack are published in pcap format at https://www.utwente.nl/en/eemcs/scs/downloads/2020_BACS_testbed/.

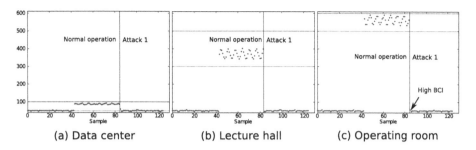

(a) Data center   (b) Lecture hall   (c) Operating room

Fig. 6. Illumination attack on different scenarios. The y-axis represents lux units for all scenarios. Data points collected during the experiment are shown using the "+" character. Dashed lines show the minimum and maximum allowed values.

During the experiments, the ambient CO_2 level is in the range of $[632, 674]$ ppm. For both ventilation attacks we take approximately 10 sensor readings before leaking CO_2 inside the testbed's building room. We use 16 g cylinders of CO_2 commonly found in bike shops to inflate tires. As expected, the CO_2 values increase but are quickly brought back to normal by the ventilation service. Once the CO_2 values are below the threshold, the fan is automatically deactivated which causes the CO_2 level to rise above the maximum limit again. The maximum limit violation triggers the ventilation service a second time. At this point, the attack is executed (i.e., the ventilation is turned off) which causes the CO_2 level to keep increasing. Finally, the CO_2 source depletes its content which drops the sensor readings again. Figure 7 shows the CO_2 level in our testbed during both experiments simulating the lecture hall and operating room locations.

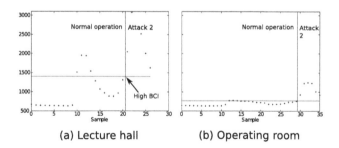

(a) Lecture hall   (b) Operating room

Fig. 7. Ventilation attack on the lecture hall and operating room scenarios. The data center scenario is excluded since it does not have specific CO_2 requirements. The y-axis represents CO_2 ppm units for both scenarios. Data points collected during the experiment are shown using the "+" character. The dashed line shows the maximum allowed values.

Temperature Control. Each experiment starts by recording the ambient temperature of the testbed's *building room*. Afterwards, a source of heat is placed inside the room. For these experiments, three anti-spill aluminum bottles filled with boiling water are used as heat source.

As in the previous experiments, we first let the system react as it was designed to work. Later on, the third attack is executed which turns off both the cooler, physically located in the testbed's *mechanical room*, and the fan, located in the testbed's *building room*. Both devices are controlled from the thermostat by *binary output* object instances 2 and 1, respectively. Although the attack comprises two components, the goal is to increase the temperature regardless of the CO_2 level measured by the ventilation service. Figure 8 shows the temperature plots of our three experiments.

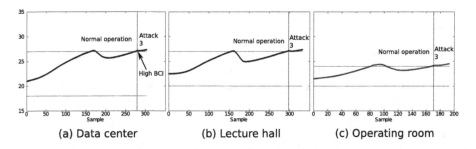

(a) Data center   (b) Lecture hall   (c) Operating room

Fig. 8. Temperature attack on different scenarios. The y-axis represents degrees Celsius for all scenarios. Data points collected during the experiment are shown using the "+" character. Dashed lines show the minimum and maximum allowed values.

5.2 BACRank Scoring

To back up the intuitive BCI of attacks discussed in the previous section, here we follow the methodology described in [12] to measure it. As discussed in Sect. 4.2, the BACS must be modeled as a graph data structure, where the nodes represent the building services implemented: illumination, ventilation, and temperature control.

The edges of the graph model the way in which the BACS is programmed and built. In our testbed, the illumination and ventilation services do not have external dependencies. The temperature control service, on the other hand, depends on the ventilation service to make the heat/cold transfer from the mechanical room to the building room. From the implementation point of view, the strength of such dependency is 100%. A graphical representation of the graph is shown in Fig. 9.

According to [12], each asset m of the BACS is represented as a vertex in the graph, where the granularity of such assets can range from specific data points to entire building services. The initial score given to each vertex (denoted as δ) at time t is defined as:

$$\delta(m,t) = \begin{cases} \max_{1 \leq i \leq n}(\beta(p_i) \cdot \gamma(s_j, p_i)) & \text{if } \text{time}(p_i, t) = \text{time}(m, t) = 1, \\ 0 & \text{otherwise,} \end{cases}$$

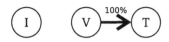

Fig. 9. Graph used to compute the BCI of the illumination (I), ventilation (V), and temperature control (T).

where function β returns the Business Impact Analysis (BIA) [18] score of business process p_i, out of n business processes in the organization. Moreover, function γ encodes how relevant building service s_j (of which m is part) is to business process p_i. Finally, *time* is a binary function that is overloaded to take as input a business process or a BACS asset. $time(p_i, t) = 1$ means that business process p_i is running at time t, and $time(m, t) = 1$ means that asset m is needed at time t.

Three components of the δ function are simplified when using the BACRank methodology in our testbed:

Assets. Unlike [12], that considers software modules as the assets to evaluate, we use building services as coarse grained assets. This decision simplifies our discussion while preserving all the properties of the original methodology.

Business Processes. Since we consider only one business process per organization (i.e., hospital→operating room, hosting company→data center, and university→lecture hall), subscripts are not needed for business processes. Furthermore, since BIA scores of different organizations are not comparable, we assume each business process to have identical values for β.

Time. We assume that all building services and business processes are needed/active at the time of the assessment.

These changes lead to a simplified version of the original function:

$$\delta(s_j) = \gamma(s_j, p).$$

Thus, it is clear that the initial scoring of each building service is a function of the business process p. Table 6 specifies the initial scores of the building services implemented in our testbed. Moreover, it contains the final BCI score of each service and, consequently, of the attacks targeting them. Details on how to compute the BACRank score are described in [12]. A brief summary is also provided in Appendix B.

Table 6. Initial and BCI scores of the implemented building services. Highlighted in bold font the BCI values considered *high* in Table 4.

Location	$\delta(I)$	$\delta(V)$	$\delta(T)$	BCI(I)	BCI(V)	BCI(T)
Operating room	1.0	0.5	0.5	**1.0**	1.0	0.5
Lecture hall	0.5	1.0	0.5	0.3	**1.0**	0.3
Data center	0.1	0.1	1.0	0.1	1.0	**1.0**

The BACRank-based BCI score is normalized in the range [0–1] per organization. By comparing the BCI scores from Table 6 with the BCI scores from Table 4, it is possible to observe a match in the most important building services. That is not the case for some services previously considered of *medium* or *low* impact. This is because in addition to business aspects, BACRank considers technical aspects omitted in the first assessment. The BACRank-based BCI tends to increase the ventilation service score because other building service (i.e., temperature control) as a strong dependency on it.

6   Conclusion

We have presented the first BACS security testbed focused on the assessment of Business Continuity Impact (BCI) of cyberattacks. The unique feature of our testbed is its capability to reconfigure the implemented building services to fit the requirements of different business process locations. Its BACS design and emulated business processes are used to instantiate existing BCI metrics, which shed light on the impact of identical attacks on different scenarios. We have made available all the materials needed for other research groups to replicate our testbed and experiments.

The hardware of our testbed is essentially similar to the hardware found in existing testbeds. In the same way that we abstractly represent business processes as specific configurations of the BACS, existing testbeds could incorporate context by configuring their building services to fit the needs of business processes of choice. Regardless of the original purpose of their testbed (e.g., education, demonstration, etc.), the addition of context would enable them to analyze attacks from the victim's perspective.

Although simple BCI assessments could be done independently of a physical testbed, more sophisticated BCI metrics require additional information such as the BACS design. In these cases, the BACS design of the testbed could be used as an input of the BCI metric. We have presented both kinds of assessments in this work. The development of new BCI metrics was beyond our scope.

Using our testbed, we showed that the addition of context is required to properly assess the BCI of BACS attacks. More than a requirement, such context is a crucial aspect that can swing an attack evaluation from high impact (e.g., illumination in an operating room) to low impact (e.g., the same illumination attack in a data center).

A key aspect of our BCI assessments is that the impact scores are linked to the targeted *physical variables* (and their corresponding building services) but not to the attack procedures. This approach decouples our reasoning about cyberattacks from the low level details of their implementation. The impact materializes only after the variable crosses a predefined threshold, whatever the means.

The selection of security controls should be based on the concept of *risk*, commonly defined as the product of impact and probability of attacks. By identifying the impact of physical variables on business processes, it is possible to make a better assessment of the defensive tools needed to protect the business continuity. This aspect is typically overlooked by current BACS testbeds focused on the demonstration of security solutions.

As future work, we will use the context added to our testbed to experiment with context-aware intrusion detection systems. Moreover, we will address the execution of automated attacks as an optimization problem that tries to maximize the impact in each particular scenario.

Acknowledgments. This work is partially funded by the Costa Rica Institute of Technology.

A   Ventilation Rate

The ventilation rate Q, commonly measured in liters per second (L/s), is computed using Eq. 1, where:

- G is the CO_2 generation rate per person (assumed 0.005 L/s).
- C_i is the acceptable indoor CO_2 concentration, measured in parts per million (ppm) and is different per business process location.
- C_a is the ambient CO_2 concentration (assumed 350 ppm).

$$Q = \frac{G}{(C_i - C_a)} \tag{1}$$

The CO_2 values in Table 2 refer to the C_i parameter, which can be obtained rearranging Eq. 1, given Q.

B   BACRank Centrality Measure

The BACRank centrality measure is defined as:

$$\text{BACRank}(m, t; i) = \begin{cases} \delta(m, t), \text{ at iteration } i = 0, \\ \delta(m, t) + \sum_{n \in N^+(m)} \text{BACRank}(n, t; i - 1) \cdot w(e_{m,n}), \text{ for } i > 0. \end{cases}$$

The BACRank score measures the BCI of node m at time t through several iterations i. At iteration 0, each node in the graph gets as score the initial value assigned by the δ function (see Sect. 5.2). For all the following iterations, node m gets as score the initial value δ plus a contribution from the nodes that depend on m. We call this set $N^+(m)$. The contribution consists on a fraction of current BACRank score of all nodes $n \in N^+(m)$. The fraction of the transferred score depends on the weight of the edge (denoted w) between nodes m and n. After a number of iterations, depending on the complexity of the graph, the BACRank score converges for all nodes in the graph. This is then considered the final BCI score of each *element* in the BACS.

References

1. Ahmed, C.M., Palleti, V.R., Mathur, A.P.: WADI: a water distribution testbed for research in the design of secure cyber physical systems. In: Proceedings of the 3rd International Workshop on Cyber-Physical Systems for Smart Water Networks, CySWATER@CPSWeek 2017, Pittsburgh, Pennsylvania, USA, 21 April 2017, pp. 25–28 (2017). https://doi.org/10.1145/3055366.3055375

2. Almgren, M., et al.: RICS-el: building a national testbed for research and training on SCADA security (short paper). In: Critical Information Infrastructures Security - 13th International Conference, CRITIS 2018, Kaunas, Lithuania, 24–26 September 2018, Revised Selected Papers, pp. 219–225 (2018). https://doi.org/10.1007/978-3-030-05849-4_17

3. ANSI/ASHRAE STANDARD 135–2016: A Data Communication Protocol for Building Automation and Control Networks (2016)

4. ANSI/ASHRAE STANDARD 62.1-2016: Ventilation for Acceptable Indoor Air Quality (2016)

5. ANSI/ASHRAE/ASHE STANDARD 170–2017: Ventilation of Health Care Facilities (2017)

6. ANSI/TIA: ANSI/TIA-492-A Telecommunications Infrastructure Standard for Data Centers (2012)

7. ANSI/TIA: ANSI/TIA-569-C Telecommunications Pathways and Spaces (2012)

8. Bilefsky, D.: Hackers use new tactic at Austrian hotel: locking the doors. https://www.nytimes.com/2017/01/30/world/europe/hotel-austria-bitcoin-ransom.html. Accessed 22 Oct 2019

9. Candell, R., Stouffer, K., Anand, D.: A cybersecurity testbed for industrial control systems. In: Proceedings of the 2014 Process Control and Safety Symposium (2014)

10. Chipkin: The 18 Attack Types Using the Vulnerabilities of BACnet. https://store.chipkin.com/articles/the-18-attack-types-using-the-vulnerabilities-of-bacnet. Accessed 10 Sept 2019

11. Esquivel-Vargas, H., Caselli, M., Peter, A.: Automatic deployment of specification-based intrusion detection in the BACnet protocol. In: Proceedings of the 2017 Workshop on Cyber-Physical Systems Security and PrivaCy, Dallas, TX, USA, 3 November 2017, pp. 25–36 (2017). https://doi.org/10.1145/3140241.3140244

12. Esquivel-Vargas, H., Caselli, M., Tews, E., Bucur, D., Peter, A.: BACRank: ranking building automation and control system components by business continuity impact. In: Computer Safety, Reliability, and Security - 38th International Conference, SAFECOMP 2019, Turku, Finland, 11–13 September 2019, Proceedings, pp. 183–199 (2019). https://doi.org/10.1007/978-3-030-26601-1_13

13. Fauri, D., Kapsalakis, M., dos Santos, D.R., Costante, E., den Hartog, J., Etalle, S.: Role inference + anomaly detection = situational awareness in BACnet networks. In: Detection of Intrusions and Malware, and Vulnerability Assessment - 16th International Conference, DIMVA 2019, Gothenburg, Sweden, 19–20 June 2019, Proceedings, pp. 461–481 (2019). https://doi.org/10.1007/978-3-030-22038-9_22

14. Hadziosmanovic, D., Sommer, R., Zambon, E., Hartel, P.H.: Through the eye of the PLC: semantic security monitoring for industrial processes. In: Proceedings of the 30th Annual Computer Security Applications Conference, ACSAC 2014, New Orleans, LA, USA, 8–12 December 2014, pp. 126–135 (2014). https://doi.org/10.1145/2664243.2664277

15. Holmberg, D., Evans, D.: BACnet wide area network security threat assessment. US Department of Commerce, National Institute of Standards and Technology (2003)
16. HVACR control: Attack BACnet MSTP by frame desynchronization. http://www.hvacrcontrol.com/attack-bacnet-mstp-by-frame-desynchronization/. Accessed 13 Sept 2019
17. ISACA: Cybersecurity fundamentals glossary (2018). https://www.isaca.org/Knowledge-Center/Documents/Glossary/glossary.pdf
18. ISO 27031:2011: Information technology -Security techniques- Guidelines for information and communication technology readiness for business continuity (2011)
19. Kaur, J., Tonejc, J., Wendzel, S., Meier, M.: Securing BACnet's pitfalls. In: ICT Systems Security and Privacy Protection - 30th IFIP TC 11 International Conference, SEC 2015, Hamburg, Germany, 26–28 May 2015, Proceedings, pp. 616–629 (2015). https://doi.org/10.1007/978-3-319-18467-8_41
20. Kavallieratos, G., Katsikas, S.K., Gkioulos, V.: Towards a cyber-physical range. In: Proceedings of the 5th on Cyber-Physical System Security Workshop, pp. 25–34. ACM (2019)
21. Kim, J., Kim, K., Jang, M.: Cyber-physical battlefield platform for large-scale cybersecurity exercises. In: 11th International Conference on Cyber Conflict, CyCon 2019, Tallinn, Estonia, 28–31 May 2019, pp. 1–19 (2019). https://doi.org/10.23919/CYCON.2019.8756901
22. Lee, E.A.: Cyber physical systems: design challenges. In: 11th IEEE International Symposium on Object-Oriented Real-Time Distributed Computing (ISORC 2008), 5–7 May 2008, Orlando, Florida, USA, pp. 363–369. IEEE Computer Society (2008). https://doi.org/10.1109/ISORC.2008.25
23. Liu, R., Vellaithurai, C., Biswas, S.S., Gamage, T.T., Srivastava, A.K.: Analyzing the cyber-physical impact of cyber events on the power grid. IEEE Trans. Smart Grid 6(5), 2444–2453 (2015). https://doi.org/10.1109/TSG.2015.2432013
24. Metropolitan.fi: DDoS attack halts heating in Finland amidst winter. https://metropolitan.fi/entry/ddos-attack-halts-heating-in-finland-amidst-winter. Accessed 22 Oct 2019
25. Pan, Z., Hariri, S., Pacheco, J.: Context aware intrusion detection for building automation systems. Comput. Secur. 85, 181–201 (2019). https://doi.org/10.1016/j.cose.2019.04.011
26. Peacock, M., Johnstone, M.N., Valli, C.: Security issues with BACnet value handling. In: Proceedings of the 3rd International Conference on Information Systems Security and Privacy, ICISSP 2017, Porto, Portugal, 19–21 February 2017, pp. 546–552 (2017). https://doi.org/10.5220/0006263405460552
27. Poudel, S., Ni, Z., Malla, N.: Real-time cyber physical system testbed for power system security and control. Int. J. Electr. Power Energy Syst. 90, 124–133 (2017)
28. Rea, M.: The IESNA Lighting Handbook: Reference & Application. Illuminating Engineering Society of North America, New York (2000)
29. Ronen, E., Shamir, A.: Extended functionality attacks on IoT devices: the case of smart lights. In: IEEE European Symposium on Security and Privacy, EuroS&P 2016, Saarbrücken, Germany, 21–24 March 2016, pp. 3–12 (2016). https://doi.org/10.1109/EuroSP.2016.13
30. Sanders, M.: ACSM's Health/Fitness Facilities Standards and Guidelines. Human Kinetics, Champaign (2019)
31. Strom, B.E., Applebaum, A., Miller, D.P., Nickels, K.C., Pennington, A.G., Thomas, C.B.: Mitre ATT&CK^{TM}: design and philosophy. Technical report (2018)

32. Tippenhauer, N.O.: Design and realization of testbeds for security research in the industrial internet of things. In: Alcaraz, C. (ed.) Security and Privacy Trends in the Industrial Internet of Things. ASTSA, pp. 287–310. Springer, Cham (2019). https://doi.org/10.1007/978-3-030-12330-7_14
33. Urbina, D.I., et al.: Limiting the impact of stealthy attacks on industrial control systems. In: Proceedings of the 2016 ACM SIGSAC Conference on Computer and Communications Security, Vienna, Austria, 24–28 October 2016, pp. 1092–1105 (2016). https://doi.org/10.1145/2976749.2978388
34. Wargocki, P.: Improving indoor air quality improves the performance of office work and school work (2008)
35. World Health Organization and others: Hospital safety index: Guide for evaluators (2015)

Attacks

Fast and Furious: Outrunning Windows Kernel Notification Routines from User-Mode

Pierre Ciholas[1]([⊠]), Jose Miguel Such[2]([⊠]), Angelos K. Marnerides[1]([⊠]), Benjamin Green[1]([⊠]), Jiajie Zhang[1]([⊠]), and Utz Roedig[3]([⊠])

[1] Lancaster University, Lancaster, UK
{p.ciholas,angelos.marnerides,j.zhang41}@lancaster.ac.uk
[2] King's College London, London, UK
jose.such@kcl.ac.uk
[3] University College Cork, Cork, Ireland
u.roedig@cs.ucc.ie

Abstract. Modern Operating Systems (OSs) enable user processes to obtain full access control over other processes initiated by the same user. In scenarios of sensitive security processes (e.g., antivirus software), protection schemes are enforced at the kernel level such as to confront arbitrary user processes overtaking with malicious intent. Within the Windows family of OSs, the kernel driver is notified via dedicated routines for user-mode processes that require protection. In such cases the kernel driver establishes a callback mechanism triggered whenever a handle request for the original user-mode process is initiated by a different user process. Subsequently, the kernel driver performs a selective permission removal process (e.g., read access to the process memory) prior to passing a handle to the requesting process. In this paper we are the first to demonstrate a fundamental user-mode process access control vulnerability, existing in Windows 7 up to the most recent Windows 10 OSs. We show that a user-mode process can indeed obtain a fully privileged access handle *before* the kernel driver is notified, thus prior to the callback mechanism establishment. Our study shows that this flaw can be exploited by a method to (i) disable the anti-malware suite Symantec Endpoint Protection; (ii) overtake VirtualBox protected processes; (iii) circumvent two major video game anti-cheat protection solutions, BattlEye and EasyAntiCheat. Finally we provide recommendations on how to address the discovered vulnerability.

1 Introduction

Process isolation acts as a core OS security function, prohibiting user interaction with processes that do not belong to them. Hence, the OS prevents access to process memory, and does not allow interference with process execution. Nonetheless, interaction is possible if two processes are owned by the same user. Whilst both processes have the same owner, interaction is not considered as a security

© Springer Nature Switzerland AG 2020
C. Maurice et al. (Eds.): DIMVA 2020, LNCS 12223, pp. 67–88, 2020.
https://doi.org/10.1007/978-3-030-52683-2_4

risk as in reality many processes require such interaction to fulfill their tasks. For instance, a debugger must be able to attach itself to another process to control it and access its process memory. In fact, OSs provide Application Program Interface (API) functions to support such interactions. Namely, Linux provides the *ptrace* system call to observe and control another process whereas Windows provides the *OpenProcess* system call to obtain process handles that can then be used to interact with other API functions (e.g., *ReadProcessMemory*).

Regardless of the usefulness derived from the interaction between various user-mode processes, there exist situations where such functionality needs to be controlled. For example, on a desktop computer all User Interface (UI)-dependent processes initiated by the user have access to each other. Unavoidably, if the user accidentally executes a piece of malware, the resulted spawned process is able to access and control all other processes belonging to the same user. Consequently, the malware can deploy a range of operations on other processes, including suspending or terminating the process, or reading and modifying its memory. Under this simple access take over, malware would therefore be in a position to access a banking application and read credit card details, or suspend execution of anti-virus software processes running as the current user.

The Windows OS family contains kernel API functions for modules (drivers) to protect security sensitive processes such as anti-virus software. As currently implemented in Windows OSs, the kernel driver is notified when a user-mode process requiring protection starts. Subsequently, the kernel driver registers a callback procedure in memory, triggered every time another process requests a handle on the protected process. The kernel driver is set up to intercept system calls such as *OpenProcess*, and selectively remove permissions (e.g. read access to the process memory) before passing the handle to the requesting process. Subsequently, the caller obtains a process handle with reduced capabilities that prevent security critical forms of process interaction. In general, the kernel driver feature is widely used in Windows OS to protect critical processes. For instance, anti-virus software utilises the aforementioned feature to prevent malware from disabling anti-virus processes; Virtual Machines (VMs) use it to enforce appropriate isolation preventing access to security critical kernel functions exposed by their drivers from other processes; anti-cheat software uses this feature to prevent cheaters from obtaining access to the game process.

In this paper we show that the previously described protection method can be circumvented, highlighting a fundamental issue within the Windows OSs. We argue that this discovery is not a traditional vulnerability that could be fixed with a simple patch, but rather a core OS security design flaw. Through this work, we demonstrate that arbitrary user-mode processes can obtain fully privileged handles before the kernel driver instruments a callback protection procedure. Consequently, user-mode processes can outrun notification routines destined for the kernel protection driver of the newly created processes. This vulnerability has been acknowledged by Microsoft (see Sect. 6.5); however, Microsoft argues that the issue should be addressed by individual software developers, as addressing it on a kernel level would lead to backward compatibility issues.

The contributions of our work are:

- *Outrunning Kernel Notifications:* we introduce how kernel notification routines can be outrun by an unprivileged user-mode process.
- *Example Exploits:* we show how the flaw can be exploited to (i) disable the anti-malware suite Symantec Endpoint Protection; (ii) take control of Virtual-Box protected processes; (iii) circumvent the two major video game anti-cheat protection software solutions, BattlEye and EasyAntiCheat.
- *Mitigating the Flaw by Design:* we recommend that user-mode functions taking a Process identifier (PID) as a parameter should not be able to do so with incomplete initialisation since kernel routines are triggered post initialisation. Although, Microsoft does not plan to implement such functionality as it would create compatibility issues.
- *Handle Invalidation Procedure*: we indicate that on spawn detection of the protected process, the kernel driver could initiate immediate termination, thus invalidating any handle that might have been obtained by exploiting the discovered vulnerability. The driver can then respawn the process from kernel-space and set up callback protection without delay. However, the proposed procedure has limitations and cannot be used in all cases.

The remainder of this paper is structured as follows: Sect. 2 focuses on the required background knowledge to understand the identified vulnerability, associated exploits, and their impact. Section 3 discusses the discovered vulnerability and two example exploits applying alternate exploitation methods. Section 4 demonstrates the vulnerability and our two exploits over three case studies. Related work is presented in Sect. 5, followed by a discussion in Sect. 6 detailing how we discovered the vulnerability, its consequences, and possible solutions. We conclude and summarise the paper in Sect. 7.

2 Background

One of the many roles an OS has, is to enable processes to execute concurrently, securely isolated, with sufficient guarantees that they will not disrupt each other or the overall system. However, in some cases processes require interaction to fulfill their tasks, and must request authorisation to do so from the OS. Traditionally, on Microsoft Windows OSs the function *OpenProcess* is used to request a handle on a target process; the obtained handle represents authorisation.

A handle has a set of privileges [1] allowing it to be used for specific operations. For instance, a process handle may permit the creation of child processes and new threads, duplication of handles, querying of information, setting of quotas as well as suspension, resumption and termination of the process. Moreover, a handle can permit the creation of virtual memory operations, reading and writing of the process virtual memory, and synchronisation with a given target process. Many of these aforementioned privileges can be used to alter adjacent processes, it may therefore be important to apply restrictions. Examples of processes where privilege limitation is necessary include anti-malware software,

software using drivers exposing sensitive kernel functions, banking and point of sale applications, and multiplayer video game processes.

Access to processes can be limited by executing them as different users. However, if processes are executed under the same user, control can be challenging to implement, as by default a user has full access to all of his processes. In addition, processes running as administrator can also access user processes. Microsoft provides a standard method to implement such protection using specialised kernel API functions, to limit handle privileges obtained for a process running as the same user or higher privileged users. To the best of our knowledge, this is the only officially advised method to implement such a security mechanism.

A kernel driver uses the kernel API function *PsSetCreateProcessNotifyRoutine/Ex* to receive notification of new processes. When a new handle on a process is requested, a callback previously registered with *ObRegisterCallbacks* is triggered, and the kernel process can apply filters to limit the privileges of this handle. Thus, fine-grained access control amongst processes owned by the same user or more privileged users can be implemented. This is an important feature, as on a Windows OS most processes run under the user logged into the GUI of the system. This includes processes of security critical applications.

2.1 Notification Routines

To implement process protection, the kernel driver must be notified of new processes in the system. The driver registers a *create process notify routine* using *PsSetCreateProcessNotifyRoutine/Ex* providing a pointer to one of its functions that will be executed when a new process is created or terminated. The pseudo-code in Listing 1.1 depicts the key instructions.

```
1  NTSTATUS DriverEntry(PDRIVER_OBJECT DriverObject,
       PUNICODE_STRING RegistryPath) {
2    PsSetCreateProcessNotifyRoutine(
       ProtectionDriverFindProtected, FALSE);
3  }
4
5  NTSTATUS ProtectionDriverFindProtected(HANDLE ParentId,
       HANDLE ProcessId, BOOLEAN Create) {
6    // Code executed at process creation
7  }
```

Listing 1.1. Key steps to register a notify routine

In the *DriverEntry* function, the kernel driver calls *PsSetCreateProcessNotifyRoutine* with *ProtectionDriverFindProtected* as a parameter. This instructs the kernel to execute the driver's function *ProtectionDriverFindProtected* when new processes are created or terminated. The kernel passes parameters to this function: (i) a HANDLE to the parent process, (ii) a HANDLE to the new process, and (iii) a BOOLEAN indicating if the process was started or terminated. Now that the driver is notified of any new processes, it can be decided in *ProtectionDriverFindProtected* if a process requires protection, and what type of protection to apply. For example, protection might be applied to processes matching a specific image name or signature.

Figure 1 shows the sequence of events when a new process is created. In this diagram, process A starts process B. For example, process A could be *explorer.exe* used to find and then double click on an application to start process B. The parent process (process A) in this example uses *CreateProcess* to create process B, however, the same sequence of events occurs if another function is used to create process B (e.g. *CreateProcessAsUser*, *ShellExecute*, or *system*).

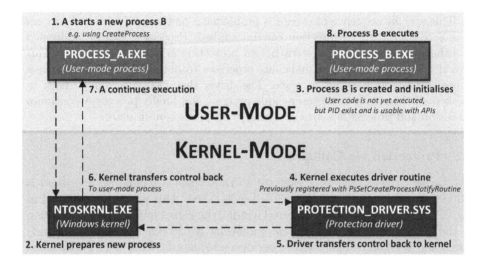

Fig. 1. Creating a new process with a driver's process create notify routine

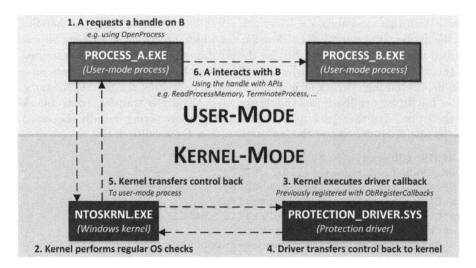

Fig. 2. Handle request with a driver having set up callbacks protection

The kernel performs various checks and operations to prepare process B for execution. Amongst these operations, the kernel creates memory structures describing the new process, such as *KPROCESS* or *EPROCESS*, and attributes a unique PID to the new process, making it reachable with other API functions taking a PID as a parameter, including *OpenProcess*. The kernel then looks at the registered *create process notify routines*, and transfers execution to the drivers having registered one. In our example, control is then passed to our kernel driver, and its *ProtectionDriverFindProtected* function is executed. The code in this function first checks whether protection should be applied, then applies it if necessary.

This specific sequence of events is problematic as the newly created process B is accessible before protection can be applied. Process B can be addressed by other processes in the system before protection is applied in Step 4. This provides a time window for malicious processes to obtain a handle on process B before protection is put in place. The driver then transfers control back to the kernel, then back to the user-mode process, and finally process A continues execution and process B starts executing with protection in place.

2.2 Protection via Callback

The kernel driver registers a callback so that when a handle on a process is requested, a function in the kernel driver is called. This process is depicted in Fig. 2. Before delivering the requested handle, the kernel first transfers execution to the driver, and passes parameters allowing it to retrieve relevant information about the handle operation to perform adequate filtering. This information includes whether the handle is newly created or duplicated, whether it is a kernel handle or not, a pointer to the target process or thread, a pointer to the object type, and a pointer to a memory structure describing operation-specific parameters. With this mechanism, a driver can apply fine grained filtering on handles to the process it protects. The decision on which processes to protect is performed when the driver is notified on the creation of new processes as described in the previous section. The driver can, for example, remove specific rights on a handle, preventing operations including reading or writing the process memory. After the driver's callback function is executed, the driver transfers control back to the kernel, and then back to the user-mode process having initially requested the handle. Listing 2 shows the key steps to register a callback.

```
1 PVOID pCbHandle = NULL;
2 OB_OPERATION_REGISTRATION obCbOp;
3 OB_CALLBACK_REGISTRATION obCbReg;
4 obCbOp.ObjectType = PsProcessType;
5 obCbOp.Operations |= OB_OPERATION_HANDLE_CREATE;
6 obCbOp.PreOperation = PreCbOp;
7 obCbReg.OperationRegistration = &obCbOp;
8 ObRegisterCallbacks(&obCbReg, &pCbHandle);
9 OB_PREOP_CALLBACK_STATUS PreCbOp(PVOID RegistrationContext,
      POB_PRE_OPERATION_INFORMATION OperationInformation) {
```

```
10        // Code executed at handle request
11  }
```

Listing 1.2. Key steps to set up callbacks protection

To register a callback, we initialise and fill the required memory structures, specifying that we want our callback to be triggered when a handle is requested on processes. We set our callback to be executed when a new handle is created with the flag *OB_OPERATION_HANDLE_CREATE*, and supply a pointer to the function to be executed. Finally we register the callback by calling *ObRegisterCallbacks*.

3   Vulnerability

A vulnerability arises from an insecure time period during new process creation. In this initial phase the process is initialised by performing all of the operations required prior to the execution of the program. Among these operations, the OS kernel internal memory structures describing this new process are created, and the process is given a unique PID, enabling API functions taking a PID as a parameter, including *OpenProcess*. This insecure time period is present between stage 2 and 4, as shown in Fig. 1. During initialisation, any driver designed to apply protection has not yet received notification that a new process has been created, and therefore no protection can be applied, while the process is already reachable from API functions. Figure 3 shows a simplified time-line of these events.

Fig. 3. Time-line of a newly spawned process

Exploiting this insecure period of time is therefore possible if one can (i) know that a newly process has spawned and (ii) know its PID, before the initialisation completes. We have discovered two different methods to accomplish this and exploit the vulnerability.

The First Method is Based on Registering a Job Object on the Parent Process of the Target Process. A job object allows groups of processes to be managed as a unit. Job objects are namable, securable, sharable objects that control attributes of the processes associated with them [2,3]. We noticed that job objects allow a process to be notified of a new child process with its PID directly after it starts, before the initialisation phase completes, and before the driver is notified and applies any protection. Our exploit can then simply call *OpenProcess* to obtain a fully privileged process handle before protection is applied. We named this first exploit *hFromJob*, since it gives a fully privileged handle (h) using a job object (FromJob), following the Hungarian naming convention that Microsoft traditionally uses.

The Second Method Uses Aggressive PID Guessing. We simply start several threads calling *OpenProcess* on all the possible IDs that the new process could be assigned. A separate thread then analyses all the handles gathered, and stops the exploit once it has obtained a handle to the targeted process. We named this second exploit *hThemAll*, since it obtains a fully privileged handle (h) by attempting to obtain it through all possible PIDs (ThemAll).

3.1 Exploit Using Job Object (hFromJob)

In this first exploit, we create a job object on *explorer.exe* assuming that the target process will spawn as its child process. This configuration is useful as a proof of concept, as it represents starting a process by double-click, the normal procedure a user would adopt to start a new process. This exploit can be adapted to other scenarios by creating a job object on the known parent process. For example, programs started from the command line have *cmd.exe* as parent; the job object should therefore be on this process instead.

The key steps are to create an IO port handle using *CreateIoCompletionPort*, create a handle to the job object with *CreateJobObjectW*, configure the job object with *SetInformationJobObject*, and finally assign the job object to the parent process with *AssignProcessToJobObject*. The exploit process will be notified of new processes being spawned by checking the I/O completion port queue. Therefore, we start a thread on a function that checks the queue as fast as possible, and directly calls *OpenProcess* on any new process. This method outruns kernel process notification routines since the notification from the job object takes place before the end of the initialisation phase. This exploit has the following requirements: (i) the parent process of the targeted process must be known in advance, and (ii) it must be possible to obtain a process handle on the parent with the permissions *PROCESS_SET_QUOTA* and *PROCESS_TERMINATE*. The C++ source code for this exploit can be found on GitHub [4].

3.2 Exploit Using PID Guessing (hThemAll)

An alternative approach is possible. It is feasible to simply predict or "guess" the PID of the target process. To the best of our knowledge, it is not possible to predict with 100% accuracy the PID of the next process to be spawned from usermode, therefore we took advantage of how Windows manages PIDs to narrow the search space for the next PID: (i) Both process IDs and thread IDs are generated in the same namespace, therefore, they cannot overlap [5]; (ii) PIDs & TIDs are always multiples of 4; (iii) Windows attempts to keep process and thread IDs in low numbers.

The exploit starts by listing all currently existing PIDs and TIDs, excluding them as potential PID for our target process to be spawned. We then create several threads attempting to obtain a fully privileged handle on every possible PID as fast as possible. Every new process handle is placed in a list analysed by a separated thread individually. When a handle to the target process is found, the exploit terminates. The C++ source code can also be found on GitHub. [6]

4 Case Studies

We developed our own protection driver following Microsoft's driver developer guidelines. We first use this demonstrator to clearly showcase the vulnerability. Thereafter, we describe how the vulnerability can be exploited to (i) disable the anti-malware suite Symantec Endpoint Protection; (ii) take control of Virtual-Box protected processes; (iii) circumvent the two major video game anti-cheat protection software, BattlEye and EasyAntiCheat. We demonstrate that the vulnerability can be used to bypass protection mechanisms for a wide variety of current applications, highlighting the severity of this issue.

4.1 Bypassing Our Own Protection Driver

Anti-malware solutions, security critical applications, and video game anti-cheat software are not open source and often obfuscate code structure and operations. We decided that our work would benefit from presenting the vulnerability in a context where both attack and target code structure is known. This allows us to precisely pinpoint and clearly describe the vulnerability along with the sequence of events leading to its exploitation. We therefore developed a minimalist kernel driver that installs protection for a specific process that we then target with our exploits; we attempt to obtain a fully privileged handle to the process protected by the kernel driver.

The simplified pseudo-code in Listing 1.3 shows the key steps our driver follows to set up protection. The full code of the driver can be found on GitHub [7].

The driver starts by registering a routine with *PsSetCreateProcessNotify-Routine*, which causes our driver's function *ProtectionDriverFindProtected* to be called whenever a process is created or terminated, as explained in Sect. 2. It then registers a callback by calling the function *ProtectionDriverSetProtection*, which will cause the function *PreCbOp* to be executed when a new handle is requested on a process. This function, not included in the pseudo code for simplicity, fills the required memory structures before calling *ObRegisterCallbacks* as per Microsoft's guidelines [8].

```
1 HANDLE hProtectedPID = NULL;
2 NTSTATUS DriverEntry(PDRIVER_OBJECT DriverObject,
     PUNICODE_STRING RegistryPath) {
3   PsSetCreateProcessNotifyRoutine(
     ProtectionDriverFindProtected, FALSE);
4   RegisterCallback();
5 }
6 NTSTATUS ProtectionDriverFindProtected(HANDLE ParentId,
     HANDLE ProcessId, BOOLEAN Create) {
7   if (IsProtected(ProcessId, "Protected.exe"))
8     hProtectedPID = ProcessId;
9 }
10 OB_PREOP_CALLBACK_STATUS PreCbOp(PVOID RegistrationContext,
     POB_PRE_OPERATION_INFORMATION OperationInformation) {
11   HANDLE TargetProcessId = PsGetProcessId((PEPROCESS)
     OperationInformation->Object);
12   if (TargetProcessId != hProtectedPID)
13     return OB_PREOP_SUCCESS;
14   if (OperationInformation->Operation ==
     OB_OPERATION_HANDLE_CREATE)
15     OperationInformation->Parameters->
     CreateHandleInformation.DesiredAccess &= ~
     PROCESS_TERMINATE;
16 }
```

Listing 1.3. Key steps of the protection driver

The function *ProtectionDriverFindProtected* checks the new process's image name and compares it to the protected process name, then sets the protected process ID in the global variable *hProtectedPID* when found. In our proof of concept driver we protect the latest instance of any process with the image name *Protected.exe*. This first phase allows the driver to find the protected process ID, so the defence mechanism using callbacks can modify future requested handles.

If the requested handle is on the protected process, the function *PreCbOp* removes the permission *PROCESS_TERMINATE* (0x1) as evidence, demonstrating that the handle permissions were successfully edited by our driver. This last phase represents the defence mechanism implemented by our driver.

As an experiment, we first launch a dummy process named *Protected.exe*, and then attempt to obtain a fully privileged handle from another process. This works as intended, obtaining a fully privileged handle and therefore full access to the target process. Next, we load our protection driver, then execute *Protected.exe* and attempt to obtain a fully privileged handle from another process. This results in the acquisition of a handle without *PROCESS_TERMINATE* (0x1) permission. This indicates that our protection driver has successfully protected the process, and removed the permission to terminate it on the handle.

Finally we terminate *Protected.exe* and execute our two exploits (*hFromJob* and *hThemAll*) described in Sect. 3 before executing *Protected.exe*. This time, both our exploits successfully obtain a fully privileged handle, which indicates that the protection was not in place on time to protect the process. This shows that kernel notification routines are slow enough that we can obtain a handle using PID guessing (with exploit *hThemAll*), and that user-mode process notifications obtained from job objects are also faster than kernel notification routines (with *hFromJob*). This allows us to bypass any protection set after *PsSetCreateProcessNotifyRoutine/Ex* by outrunning them from unprivileged user-mode processes; in this specific case we bypassed the callback protection.

We provide a short video demonstrating this experience [9].

4.2 Disabling Anti-malware

In this second case study we use our exploits to obtain a fully privileged handle on the service process of Symantec Endpoint Protection. Symantec anti-malware service, *ccSvcHst.exe*, is spawned as a child of *services.exe* under the user *NT AUTHORITY\SYSTEM*, which spawns another instance of the same binary running under the current user.

When requesting a fully privileged handle on the anti-malware user process using *OpenProcess* with *PROCESS_ALL_ACCESS*, a handle is received but with only the following permissions: Query information, Create processes, VM read, Synchronize, Read control, and Write owner (0x1AF490). This demonstrates that Symantec's driver installs protection to modify the handle permissions on its user-mode processes with *ObRegisterCallbacks*. The driver also needs to be notified of the system process being spawned, which is done with *PsSetCreateProcessNotifyRoutine/Ex*. Thus, the anti-malware appears to use the protection method we described and is therefore potentially vulnerable.

For this experiment our *hFromJob* exploit is not usable, as it requires a handle to the parent process of the target with the permissions *PROCESS_SET_QUOTA* and *PROCESS_TERMINATE* to make use of the API *AssignProcessToJobObject*. The system process *services.exe*, being a protected system process (Protected Process Light (PPL)) means that *OpenProcess* would fail. It should be possible to use this exploit if one bypasses PPL and obtains a sufficiently privileged handle on *services.exe*, however for simplicity we will only use the exploit *hThemAll* for this case study where no additional steps are required.

We begin the experiment by configuring *hThemAll* to look for a handle on a process named *ccSvcHst.exe* using 6 threads. We execute the exploit, then start the service of the anti-virus. Once the user processes have spawned, we used Process Hacker [10] to verify the permissions of our process handle, and observe that we have been granted a fully privileged handle.

With this fully privileged handle it is now possible to tamper with the anti-malware system in a variety of ways. Most anti-malware have watchdog systems restarting the user-mode process if terminated, therefore simply terminating it has little interest, however a very simple workaround is to freeze its threads with the API *NtSuspendProcess*, disabling malware detection alerts to the user, and disrupting its real-time protection capabilities. Since this technique exploits an insecure time period at launch, a piece of malware executing early, i.e. during the boot or user login sequence, could take control of the anti-malware processes from the start. Otherwise the malware could terminate the process using a variety of methods ranging from simply calling TerminateProcess to a denial of service, in which case the anti-malware watchdog would restart a new instance, allowing us to exploit the vulnerability on this newly spawned process. Malware could also simply wait for the process to restart on its own during maintenance and update cycles.

4.3 Bypassing Virtualisation Defences

Virtualisation solutions are complex in that they require device drivers to provide additional functionality at kernel level. They are also required to make these capabilities available to specific user-mode processes. Therefore, virtualisation kernel drivers will often expose potentially sensitive functionality to user-mode processes. For this reason, only the trusted user-mode process of the virtualisation software should be able to access the virtualisation environment's kernel driver. This includes processes running under the same user or a user with higher of privileges. If a privileged handle is obtained on the virtualisation user-mode process, then malware could leverage this handle to obtain access to the kernel driver via the captured user-mode process.

Virtualisation software Virtual Box uses a driver for the protection of its user-mode processes. When a virtual machine is started, another instance of *VirtualBox.exe* is spawned, which has a handle on the driver *VBoxDrvStub* with read and write permissions. The second instance of *VirtualBox.exe* then spawns a thrird instance of *VirtualBox.exe* which is the process running the virtual machine. This process has a handle on the driver *VBoxDrv* with read and write permissions. Both of these processes are protected in such a way that if another process operating under the same user, or a higher privileged user, attempts to obtain a fully privileged handle, the returned handle is modified to only have the access mask 0x131c11 (Query information, VM read, Suspend/resume, Terminate, Synchronize, Delete, Read control).

Through the use of exploits *hThemAll* and *hFromJob*, we can successfully obtain a fully privileged handle on the first instance of *VirtualBox.exe*. This process has a handle on the driver *VBoxDrvStub*, which exposes potentially sensitive kernel functionality. Both exploits successfully provide a fully privileged handle on the second instance of *VirtualBox.exe* that is normally protected. This gives us access to the driver *VBoxDrvStub* that could be leveraged for further exploitation. Interestingly, our exploits do not obtain a fully privileged handle on the third instance of *VirtualBox.exe* protected process. This indicates that this process is either protected, or more likely is *spawned* differently. This latter behaviour could be used as a basis for effective mitigation of the vulnerability. We discuss this later in Sect. 6.

4.4 Bypassing Video Game Anti-cheat Defences

Obtaining access to a game's process allows hackers to manipulate it to gain unfair advantages. Anti-cheat companies offer game developers software to prevent other programs, including programs running at higher privilege levels from gaining access to the game's process using protection drivers. For our use cases, we have experimented on games protected by the two major anti-cheat systems: BattlEye and EasyAntiCheat.

We observe that a lesser privileged handle is obtained despite requesting all privileges on the game process, indicating the use of the vulnerable APIs. Using our two exploits, we successfully obtain a fully privileged handle on games protected by both anti-cheat software solutions.

We have informed anti-cheat software providers of this vulnerability (see Sect. 6), they have now included additional defences. We discuss these additional defences in more detail in Sect. 6. The vulnerability affected a wide variety of internationally recognised anti-cheat protected games with millions of players.

5   Related Work

This section presents other security mechanisms available in Microsoft Windows and evaluate their validity as mitigation. We also present academic work and patents related to the very specific nature of the vulnerability discussed.

5.1   Other Windows Security Mechanisms

Protected Processes: The Protected Process security mechanism was introduced in Windows Vista and has been expanded in later versions with variants including Protected Process Light (PPL). Protected processes differ from regular processes due to the level of access other processes in the system can obtain on them [11]. When a process is protected by this mechanism, other non-protected processes can only obtain handles on it with tightly restricted rights. If it was possible to spawn a process as protected from its initial inception, including the initialisation phase, this could void our exploits. Unfortunately, this security mechanism is only reserved for system use and is not available for third party software developers.

Anti-malware Services Protection: Microsoft provides a complete guide and specialised tools for anti-malware developers, allowing their driver to launch before other boot-start drivers, and therefore ensure that subsequent drivers do not contain malware [12]. This security measure helps protect against malicious drivers, but does not offer any mitigation against the presented attack, since it does not change the order of operations during process creation.

Mandatory Integrity Control (MIC): MIC is a mechanism for controlling access to securable objects [13]. It uses 4 levels of integrity with the labels low, medium, high, and system, preventing lower integrity processes from accessing the resources of higher levels. The MIC security mechanism was introduced in Windows Vista. This could in very specific circumstances mitigate the presented attack. For example, if the exploits were started with the low integrity label, and the target was allocated a medium integrity label, the exploits would fail. However this security mechanism falls short when defending interactions between processes of the same integrity level. Since most processes run within the same level, this cannot be considered a reliable counter-measure. For anti-malware solutions specifically, running their critical processes with a high integrity level should provide protection against the exploits when run with the medium default integrity level.

Protected Mode: The protected mode is based on MIC and was originally created to enhance the security of Microsoft's web browser Internet Explorer [14]. This security feature was designed to limit possible attacks from a compromised Internet Explorer process, by running it with greatly reduced privileges. To the best of our knowledge, it is not possible to run third party programs in protected mode natively. Even if this was possible, as a security mechanism it is designed to restrict a specific process, preventing it from interacting with others, not to prevent access from other processes as the vulnerable APIs targeted in this paper do. This security mechanism is therefore not a viable option.

AppContainer Isolation: When creating a program with AppContainer, the process is executed with extreme limitations, allowing only those features critical to the program operations. This security feature functions in a similar way to other mandatory access control implementations in other operating systems, such as Security-Extended Linux (SELinux) or AppArmor in Linux. All non-required resources are kept out of reach, including other processes, therefore a compromised or malicious process cannot take over the rest of the machine [15]. Files, registry, windows, and network resources are also restricted, and access can be managed with fine granularity if required. Finally, process isolation prevents the AppContainer program from influencing other processes. However, after experimenting with AppContainer ourselves, we were able to restrict a process's access to resources and other processes, but could not restrict other processes from accessing itself. Consequently, we could not use AppContainer as a valid form of mitigation.

5.2   Research Efforts and Patents

A multitude of projects and software make use of kernel notify routines and callbacks. *PsSetCreateProcessNotifyRoutine/Ex* and *ObRegisterCallbacks* are often used for automated malware detection and prevention, or program behavioural analysis which permits the creation of tools for reverse engineering such as Capture presented in [16].

There exist only a few usable methods to monitor the behaviour of a program for which the source code is not available. These methods can be categorised as follows: (i) User level API hooking, (ii) kernel level API hooking, and (iii) Kernel callbacks [16]. User-level API hooking can be easily detected or bypassed by unprivileged programs. For this reason the quasi-totality of reputable anti-malware use solutions in kernel space. Many kernel-mode malware and rootkits made use of kernel level API hooking (e.g. SSDT hooking) to hide their presence and execute malicious code stealthily, consequently Microsoft now defends the kernel with various protections including PatchGuard (also known as Kernel

Patch Protection, KPP). A good example of malware making use of *PsSetCreateProcessNotifyRoutine/Ex* is the Rustock Rootkit and Spam Bot studied and documented in [17]. Due to its potential for abuse, it is no longer possible to enact kernel level API hooking on the modern versions of Windows, leaving only user level API hooking and a set of kernel API functions to implement security.

A presentation on how anti-viruses implement their monitoring, detection, and defences can be found in [18]. As recommended by Microsoft, all 5 of the major anti-viruses investigated in this work make use of the kernel callbacks and routines, including *PsSetCreateProcessNotifyRoutine/Ex* to obtain process creation and termination notifications to then run analysis and mitigations. This makes these anti-viruses vulnerable to the attack presented in this paper. One of the anti-viruses tested in [18] is Norton Security 2015, which is the anti-virus we selected as a use case.

A multitude of academic projects and patents in the field of malware analysis heavily rely on *PsSetCreateProcessNotifyRoutine/Ex*. In [19] a set of monitoring drivers are presented, including a process monitoring driver that uses *PsSetCreateProcessNotifyRoutine* to obtain information on newly created or terminated processes. In [20] the researchers attempted to correlate network traffic with user applications using the vulnerable API. Injecting data flow control object into processes using the same system as in our protection driver (using first *PsSetCreateProcessNotifyRoutine* then *ObRegisterCallbacks*) is presented in [21]. In [22], a system stored on a mass storage device is presented that registers a process notification routine to then hook functions in processes. Two researchers have designed a portable dynamic malware analysis tool following Microsoft recommendations in [23], therefore using the vulnerable *PsSetCreateProcessNotifyRoutine* to monitor process activities. A system aiming at identifying processes responsible for system slow downs making use of process notification routines is presented in [24]. In [25], a method relying on hooking/detouring the execution flow of *PsSetCreateProcessNotifyRoutine/Ex* to prevent malware from de-registering notify routines is presented. Because of their reliance on the vulnerable API, all of these projects could be disrupted or bypassed entirely.

6 Discussion

6.1 Discovery

The vulnerability was discovered whilst investigating how several system processes obtained privileged handles on video games despite active anti-cheat using protection drivers. Three system processes held privileged handles: *csrss.exe* (all privileges), *lsass.exe* (read/write), and *PcaSvc*'s *svchost.exe* (all privileges).

We investigated how *PcaSvc* obtained its handle, and quickly identified that it was accommodated through a normal *OpenProcess* call. We also noticed that if a delay is placed before calling *OpenProcess*, when execution is resumed the handle is modified as intended by the protection driver. This indicated that Windows system processes receive new process notifications before the kernel notification routine are triggered.

To verify this hypothesis, we developed a proof of concept exploit by hooking *OpenProcess* in *PcaSvc*'s process. With this hook, the PID of the new process is passed to another process using shared memory and its execution is resumed using a semaphore, allowing it to call *OpenProcess* and obtain a fully privileged handle. This exploit confirmed that *PcaSvc* was outrunning the kernel process notification routines used by the anti-cheat driver.

By analysing the internals of *PcaSvc*, we discovered that job objects are used to receive notifications. We then created the standalone exploit *hFromJob* replicating *PcaSvc*'s behaviour. Finally, we developed the second exploit *hThemAll*, which affords fewer restrictions and further confirms that the vulnerability emerges from an insecure time period during process initialisation.

6.2   Vulnerability Time Period Measurement

Measuring the vulnerability time period is not easy, since it depends on hardware characteristics such as CPU frequency, number of cores, threads, and also current system state and other parameters hard to fully control. We have conducted all our experiment in a 2.40 GHz mono-core VM on an idle system.

To measure the vulnerability time period we have counted how many fully privileged handles could be retrieved before the protection is set up. We have used the first **non**-fully privileged handle obtained as a sign that the exploitation time window has finished. We have measured using 3 methods: (1) using the *RDTSC* (Read Timestamp Counter) CPU instruction to get a number of CPU cycles, (2) *QueryPerformanceCounter*, which is a Microsoft supplied high resolution time stamp that can be used for time-interval measurements, and (3) *GetTickCount64* which uses the CPU clock to give an interval in milliseconds.

We first modified *hFromJob*, so that when its first fully privileged handle is obtained, it calls a measuring function that keeps calling *OpenProcess* requesting all permissions and verifying if the returned handles correctly has them using *NtQueryObject*. When the first lesser privileged handle is obtained, the measuring function calculates the time difference using the methods listed above. hFromJob successfully obtained between 63 and 105 fully privileged handles during our tests, occuring during 21 to 35 million cycles (from RDSTC), while *QueryPerformanceCounter* returned between 89 and 140 k (with a base frequency of 10 million retrieved with *QueryPerformanceFrequency*). GetTick-Count64 doesn't provide enough accuracy and returned 0 in all our tests, indicating that the vulnerability is faster than its accuracy (Microsoft estimates this accuracy to be between 10 and 16 ms). Using the RDTSC readings, the vulnerability time period was measured to be between 8.75 and 14.5 ms, while using the readings of the performance counter the vulnerability time period is measured between 8.9 and 14 ms.

hThemAll is harder to measure, since we use a set of threads blindly attempting to get handles and a control thread looking for our target. By configuring the exploit to be extremely aggressive and using up most of the system resources by using 16 threads for exploitation we notice that many more (thousands) fully privileged handles are obtained. Since the resources that should be used to initialise the process are redirected to the exploit, the vulnerability time period is extended due to the initialisation phase being slowed down. We attempted to measure the vulnerability time period with a single-threaded version. Since this exploit does PID guessing, we ran the experiment multiple times aiming at guessing the PID correctly soon to reveal the vulnerability time period. In the best result, *hThemAll* successfully obtained more 218 fully privileged handles before being stopped. This indicates that the vulnerability was present for at least 29 ms.

6.3 Implications

The discovered vulnerability poses the question of how to best implement protections for user-mode processes. Microsoft provides routines to obtain notifications in kernel drivers, however we demonstrated that they can be outrun by user-mode processes. Therefore a malicious process can outrun and consequently bypass any protections set up following reception of such notifications, simply through execution prior to its target. The protection can also be defeated after the target has been started if it can be forcibly restarted (e.g. by terminating it or crashing it).

The identified vulnerability allows outrunning thread notification routines set up with *PsSetCreateThreadNotifyRoutine/Ex*, and load image notification routines set up with *PsSetLoadImageNotifyRoutine*. Since writing to the process memory is possible with the process handle, a malicious program can force the execution of any code with a simple detour or hook within the context of the target process before any notification routine is triggered.

The most severe consequences of this vulnerability are for anti-malware solutions. Due to the fact that a process with malicious intent can interact with other processes before the routines trigger, it is feasible to fully modify and control them before protection has been applied. Malware can, for example, execute malicious code within the context of another process, or hijack the process completely with techniques such as process hollowing [26]. As demonstrated, if malware can be started early enough, or can force the user-mode process of the anti-virus to restart. Thus malware can control, disable, or prevent it from alerting the user of any present threats.

We argue that applications requiring exposure of sensitive kernel mode functions to their user-mode process, such as virtualisation software, are also at risk. These applications limit access to their user-mode processes obtaining a handle on the driver, thus preventing other processes from using these critical kernel functions. If an external process gains access to the permitted user-mode process possessing a valid handle on the driver, it can then can be exploited as demonstrated by our Virtual Box use case.

In general, a number of applications with high security requirements may be at risk; examples include other virtualisation and anti-malware software, but also banking applications or point-of-sales systems. In the latter two examples, applications store security-critical information (e.g. full credit card details) in memory which could be retrieved with memory scanning.

While Microsoft does not explicitly promotes *PsSetCreateProcessNotifyRoutine/Ex* to set up this security mechanism, it is to the best of our knowledge required to set up such protection. The different case studies of real-world software presented in this paper confirms this to an extent.

Setting up this protection solely with callbacks is possible, however it is not possible to retrieve information on the process requesting the handle. Consequently, all handles get their permissions modified, including handles for Windows system processes such as *csrss* or *lsass* which either respectively prevent the new process to initialise and run or create various instability and/or crashes. This worryingly indicates that the operating system itself requires the behaviour leading to the vulnerability to function correctly, making patching even more challenging for the kernel developers.

Because the timeline of the different notifications and triggers are not documented, developers may have written vulnerable code by wrongly assuming that kernel notifications should trigger before user-mode notifications, which is not precised on Microsoft API documentation. It is our opinion that kernel notifications should always trigger before user-mode following the protection rings hierarchy.

We thoroughly tested this vulnerability through the case studies discussed in Sect. 4 on Windows 10 x64 and Windows 7 x64 up to date as of November 2019. Furthermore, we hypothesise the vulnerability is most likely present in other Windows versions including Windows 8, all Windows editions and architectures included.

6.4   Responsible Disclosure

We first disclosed the vulnerability to Microsoft in July 2018 following their guidelines [27]. The formal disclosure provided a description of the vulnerability, the code of both exploits [4,6], and the protection driver [7], along with the compiled binaries to allow for the recreation of our experiments. Moreover, we provided a video of the vulnerability in action [9]. The response from Microsoft was produced almost a year after our disclosure and is provided in Sect. 6.5.

In parallel, we also disclosed this vulnerability to the remaining stakeholders from our case studies. In fact, after disclosing our finding to anti-cheat companies, we noticed that they implemented new countermeasures aiming at preventing the exploitation of this vulnerability. Our analysis shows that the affected anti-cheat companies developed a procedure that terminates the first instance of the game launched, then respawns it from kernel space to obtain the handle instantly and set up the callback without delay. This behaviour appears similar to our observations with VirtualBox. Such a solution is sub-optimal for a number of reasons. Overall, a malicious program can still briefly obtain a fully privileged handle on the first instance. Moreover, it is not applicable for all programs. Since this solution requires forceful termination of the protected process, and subsequent respawning from kernel-space, some applications may not function correctly after such an operation. Furthermore, in order to implement this solution, developers are required to have a signed kernel mode driver, this is not common for most developers. Note however that this solution should be applicable on the use cases previously presented in Sect. 4.

We have also identified the development of an additional defence and detection mechanism that implements a periodic walk-through of the handle table for all running processes. The goal of this mechanisms is to search for open handles on protected processes. Thus, if a handle to a protected process is found, the implemented procedure modifies the granted permissions. It is unclear how anti-cheat companies implement such a process, since it requires using undocumented kernel functions and memory structures to do Direct Kernel Object Modification (DKOM), which is discouraged by Microsoft.

6.5   Microsoft's Response

Microsoft replied to our responsible disclosure and have acknowledged the vulnerability. Unfortunately, Microsoft *"will not be addressing this scenario for in market operating systems via a security update"*. The response decision extends further stating that Microsoft's *"assessment considers this scenario to be a defense in depth against third party products"*. Finally Microsoft acknowledges that fixing this vulnerability *"for in market OS's would potentially result in significant application compatibility issues"*. Microsoft also gave us permission to publicly disclose this vulnerability.

In our opinion, fixing this vulnerability would require changes to the functions themselves, including the parameters they take. Eventually, such an approach would most likely not be retro-compatible and cause problems. However, a new function could be made available with a new name, most likely with the suffix *Ex* or *Ex2* as per Microsoft's tradition, with a security notice placed on the older functions indicating that a newer, more secure function is available as it has been done many times in the past for other vulnerable functions.

In order to efficiently address the discovered vulnerability, the affected kernel function must be modified. Ironically this is made impossible by default due to various security mechanisms preventing any kernel modifications such as Kernel Patch Protection (KPP, also known as PatchGuard). Unfortunately, without Microsoft upgrading the kernel API functions, this vulnerability cannot be adequately fixed in all circumstances. Nonetheless, in the next section we explore possible solutions that, while they will not be able to remove the vulnerability, could significantly mitigate it without requiring kernel modifications.

6.6   Possible Solutions

The most appropriate solution would be to modify the kernel so that user-mode functions taking a PID as a parameter either instantly fails or, more elegantly, get delayed until the process finishes its initialisation, and the kernel routines trigger. This solution can only be implemented by Microsoft.

A solution could be to use notification routines allowing notification of the process to protect being spawned, but then directly terminating the process and spawning it again from kernel space using a function that immediately returns either the PID or a handle, such as *ZwCreateProcess*. This appears to be the solution anti-cheat softwares have set up following our disclosure, and how VirtualBox is spawning the virtual machine's *VirtualBox.exe* dedicated process. This solution is effective but requires a signed kernel driver, which most developers do not have and comes at a cost, in addition to the expertise required for its implementation. It may also be inapplicable in many scenarios, especially if attempting to protect third party processes that are not designed to be forcibly terminated then restarted in a different way. Fortunately, the software in our use cases satisfy these requirements and can implement this solution.

Based on our reverse engineering, anti-cheat software appears to have implemented an additional mitigation in addition to the aforementioned solution. They periodically scan the object table of all processes running on the system, and if a handle to the protected process is found the permissions are then edited accordingly to the desired filtering rules. This is not in our opinion a viable solution, as our exploits would still obtain privileged handles and could use them for a brief moment which is sufficient to tamper with the process. This mitigation also requires the use undocumented internal kernel functions and memory structures, as well as Direct Kernel Object Modification (DKOM) which are highly discouraged by Microsoft. Note that while this solution doesn't fully protect against the vulnerability, it allows detection of exploitation.

It is possible to set up a handle permission filter using callbacks without being notified of newly spawned processes, and therefore without using the vulnerable API functions. Using this method, all handles are filtered and have their permissions modified. Unfortunately, in this case even Window's vital systems processes such as *csrss.exe* have their handle permissions modified, which prevent the protected process to execute correctly. Quite ironically, it seems that Windows itself makes use of this insecure time period to operate correctly. This may be prevented if the driver could collect information about the process requesting the handle from within the callback function, and let Windows system processes acquire unmodified handles, along with possible other white-listed processes. Unfortunately, with the current kernel callback functions it is not possible to retrieve such information, making this solution impossible. Microsoft could implement this solution without compatibility issues by modifying the kernel memory structure *POB_PRE_OPERATION_INFORMATION* to include information about the requesting process. Alternatively, Microsoft could modify the kernel callback API functions, to have an additional parameter allowing for the retrieval of this information, however this would unavoidably lead to compatibility issues due to function parameters and memory structures changes.

7   Conclusions

In this paper we introduce a fundamental security design flaw within the Microsoft Windows OSs. We demonstrated the feasibility of outrunning

Windows kernel process notification routines from unprivileged user-mode processes. Thus, effectively bypassing any protection set in kernel mode following notification routines. Consequently, Microsoft's standard method of protecting user processes via a kernel driver is ineffective. We verified our work on current Windows 7 x64 and Windows 10 x64 up to date up to date as of November 2019.

In order to validate our findings, we implemented our own protection driver and assessed its features. Our findings highlight that the discovered vulnerability can be exploited to bypass protection built for sensitive and widely used applications. We have assessed and demonstrated the aforementioned property by studying the behaviour of the (i) Symantec Endpoint Protection anti-malware suite; (ii) virtualisation environments such as VirtualBox; (iii) anti cheat protection software such as BattlEye and EasyAntiCheat. In addition, solutions to address the vulnerability were presented, namely to change the Windows API for handle requests, respawning the protected process from kernel space to immediately set up protection, scanning object tables system-wide for detection and protection, and providing sufficient information to callback driver functions to avoid using routines.

We disclosed the vulnerability to Microsoft. Microsoft acknowledged the problem but decided against a OS patch. As shown, in response to our work application developers have reacted and implemented unique fixes to their applications. However, we feel that this is an inefficient strategy as the solutions are incomplete, different from case to case, and have to be re-designed for each situation. A comprehensive solution in the form of an OS update from Microsoft would effectively mitigate this vulnerability, however there would be an undesirable cost from a compatibility perspective. Maybe this work serves as a well documented example where security improvements cannot be easily balanced with other industry requirements.

We have made the source code of every binary discussed in this paper publicly available on GitHub [4,6] so developers can assess if their solutions are vulnerable, and attempt to implement additional security on a minimalist protection driver [7] before adding it to their products. A compiled version is also available for quick testing and experimenting. Finally we made a video showing the API functioning normally, then the effects of our exploits [9].

Overall, we argued that the discovered vulnerability is not caused by a simple development bug, but rather a fundamental security flaw deeply ingrained in the OS core design, laying the foundations for a new generation of OS-level attacks.

References

1. Microsoft. Msdn, process security and access rights. https://msdn.microsoft.com/en-us/library/windows/desktop/ms684880(v=vs.85).aspx
2. Russinovich, M.E., Solomon, D.A., Yosifovich, P., Ionescu, A.: Windows Internals, 7th edn. Microsoft Press, Redmond (2018)
3. Microsoft. Msdn, about processes and threads. https://docs.microsoft.com/en-us/windows/desktop/procthread/about-processes-and-threads

4. Anonymous. Github, hfromjob exploit. https://github.com/Anonymous-3ab41c/FastAndFurious/blob/master/hFromJob.cpp
5. Margosis, A., Russinovich, M.E.: Troubleshoot with the Windows Sysinternals Tools. Microsoft Press, Redmond (2018)
6. Anonymous. Github, hthemall exploit. https://github.com/Anonymous-3ab41c/FastAndFurious/blob/master/hThemAll.cpp
7. Anonymous. Github, protectiondriver. https://github.com/Anonymous-3ab41c/FastAndFurious/blob/master/ProtectionDriver.c
8. Microsoft. Msdn, obregistercallbacks function. https://docs.microsoft.com/en-us/windows-hardware/drivers/ddi/content/wdm/nf-wdm-obregistercallbacks
9. Anonymous. Youtube, outrunning windows kernel notification routines from user-mode. https://youtu.be/dp_GqDfUUxA
10. Liu, W.J.: (wj32). Process hacker. https://processhacker.sourceforge.io/
11. Microsoft. Protected processes. http://download.microsoft.com/download/a/f/7/af7777e5-7dcd-4800-8a0a-b18336565f5b/process_Vista.doc
12. Microsoft. Early launch antimalware. https://docs.microsoft.com/en-us/windows-hardware/drivers/install/early-launch-antimalware
13. Microsoft. Mandatory integrity control. https://docs.microsoft.com/en-us/windows/desktop/secauthz/mandatory-integrity-control
14. Microsoft. Understanding and working in protected mode internet explorer. https://technet.microsoft.com/en-us/windows/bb250462(v=vs.60)
15. Microsoft. Appcontainer isolation. https://docs.microsoft.com/en-us/windows/desktop/SecAuthZ/appcontainer-isolation
16. Seifert, C., Steenson, R., Welch, I., Komisarczuk, P., Endicott-Popovsky, B.: Capture-a behavioral analysis tool for applications and documents. Digit. Invest. **4**, 23–30 (2007)
17. Chiang, K., Lloyd, L.: A case study of the rustock rootkit and spam bot. HotBots **7**, 10 (2007)
18. Liang, S.C.: Understanding behavioural detection of antivirus (2016)
19. Jeong, H.C., Im, C.T., Oh, J.H.: Malware auto-analysis system and method using kernel callback mechanism, US Patent App. 12/942,700, 29 March 2012
20. Liu, Z., Chen, P.: Improved method of packet filtering. In: Proceedings, The 2009 International Symposium on Web Information Systems and Applications (WISA 2009), p. 294. Academy Publisher (2009)
21. Perez, D.S., Balinsky, H., Simske, S.J.: Injection of data flow control objects into application processes, US Patent App. 14/917,839, November 24 2016
22. Aussel, J.-D.: Portable mass storage device with hooking process, US Patent App. 12/667,196, 22 July 2010
23. Pektaş, A., Acarman, T.: Portable dynamic malware analysis with an improved scalability and automatisation. In: Kurzynski, M., Wozniak, M., Burduk, R. (eds.) CORES 2017. AISC, vol. 578, pp. 211–220. Springer, Cham (2018). https://doi.org/10.1007/978-3-319-59162-9_22
24. Shochat, E., Elkind, D.: Real time monitoring of computer for determining speed of various processes, US Patent 8,307,246, 6 November 2012
25. Teller, T., Segal, A.: Method of defending a computer from malware, US Patent 9,536,090, 3 January 2017
26. Leitch, J.: Process hollowing (2013)
27. Microsoft. Microsoft, report an issue faq. https://www.microsoft.com/en-us/msrc/faqs-report-an-issue

HAEPG: An Automatic Multi-hop Exploitation Generation Framework

Zixuan Zhao[1,2,3,4], Yan Wang[1,2,3,4], and Xiaorui Gong[1,2,3,4]($\boxtimes$)

[1] School of Cyber Security, University of Chinese Academy of Sciences,
Beijing, China
[2] Key Laboratory of Network Assessment Technology, Beijing, China
[3] Beijing Key Laboratory of Network Security and Protection Technology,
Beijing, China
[4] Institute of Information Engineering, Chinese Academy of Sciences, Beijing, China
{zhaozixuan,wangyan,gongxiaorui}@iie.ac.cn

Abstract. Automatic exploit generation for heap vulnerabilities is an
open challenge. Current studies require a sensitive pointer on the heap to
hijack the control flow and pay little attention to vulnerabilities with limited capabilities. In this paper, we propose HAEPG, an automatic exploit
framework that can utilize known exploitation techniques to guide exploit
generation. We implemented a prototype of HAEPG based on the symbolic
execution engine S2E [15] and provided four exploitation techniques for
it as prior knowledge. HAEPG takes crashing inputs, programs, and prior
knowledge as input, and generates exploits for vulnerabilities with limited capabilities by abusing heap allocator's internal functionalities.

We evaluated HAEPG with 24 CTF programs, and the results show that
HAEPG is able to accurately reason about the type of vulnerability for 21
(87.5%) of them, and generate exploits that spawn a shell for 16 (66.7%)
of them. All the exploits could bypass NX [25] and Full RELRO [28]
security mechanisms.

Keywords: Automatic exploit generation · Heap vulnerability ·
Symbolic execution

1 Introduction

Automated exploit generation (AEG) is becoming an important method in
vulnerability-centric attacks and defenses. Software vendors use it to evaluate
the severity of security vulnerabilities more quickly and allocate appropriate
resources to fix critical vulnerabilities. Defenders learn from synthetic exploits
to generate Intrusion Detection System rules and block potential attacks.

Most AEG solutions [12,13,20,23,26] usually only support stack-related or
format string vulnerabilities, which are rare in modern systems [2]. Due to the
complexity of heap allocator functions, only a few existing solutions can generate
exploits for heap-based vulnerabilities. These solutions have different approaches.

© Springer Nature Switzerland AG 2020
C. Maurice et al. (Eds.): DIMVA 2020, LNCS 12223, pp. 89–109, 2020.
https://doi.org/10.1007/978-3-030-52683-2_5

For instance, Revery [30] applies a layout-oriented fuzzing and control-flow stitching solution to explore exploitable states in paths derived from vulnerability points. Gollum [22] employs a custom heap allocator to create exploitable heap layouts and a fuzzing technique based on prior work [21] to solve the heap manipulation problem. SLAKE [14] uses a static-dynamic hybrid analysis to search for useful kernel objects and manipulates heap layout by adjusting the free list in the slab.

All these solutions corrupt a sensitive pointer (e.g., VTable pointer) and derive an attacker-controlled memory-write or indirect call, which means that the presence of a sensitive pointer is key to hijack the control flow. In this case, once the heap layout is well arranged, an attacker creates an exploit primitive with only one operation, i.e., triggering the vulnerability, and we call it single-hop exploitation. However, not all vulnerabilities can be exploited using simple single-hop techniques. For example, with an off-by-one error [11], it is infeasible to fully control any sensitive pointer by merely triggering the vulnerability, let alone overwriting the instruction pointer to an arbitrary value. To solve this issue, the following challenges need to be addressed:

Challenge 1: Exploring the Power of Heap Vulnerabilities with Limited Capabilities. To exploit vulnerabilities with limited capabilities, an attacker needs to manipulate the heap layout and abuse the heap allocator's internal functionalities to create several intermediate hops, expand the range of corruptible memory with the help of the hops, and eventually derive an arbitrary memory-write or indirect call. We call these techniques multi-hop exploitation. Some solutions [19,32] aim to discover such techniques for heap allocators. However, they can not apply the techniques to programs with heap-based vulnerabilities automatically. To the best of our knowledge, existing AEG solutions paid very little attention to it.

Challenge 2: Modeling Heap Interactions Between Programs and Heap Allocators. To conduct multi-hop exploitation, AEG solutions have to craft inputs and drive victim programs to allocate and deallocate objects of a specific size or write specific data to heap objects. However, programs typically do not expose any direct interfaces for users to interact with their heap allocators. Therefore, AEG solutions have to recognize heap interactions and assemble them in a particular way to generate exploits.

Our Solution. In this paper, we propose HAEPG to address the challenges above. Given a program with heap-based vulnerabilities and crashing inputs, it attempts to achieve the execution of arbitrary code through multi-hop exploitation.

HAEPG abstracts machine-level instructions and function calls interacting with the heap allocator as heap interactions. It relies on the fact that most programs distribute functions with function dispatchers (e.g., event handling and connection processing loops) and extracts the paths that make up such dispatchers. Then, HAEPG applies hybrid techniques to locate and analyze heap interactions and infer dependencies between different interactions and paths.

After this, HAEPG collects runtime information in programs when executing crashing inputs. It inspects vulnerable objects and analyzes the type of memory corruption as well as the size of corrupted data.

Furthermore, we studied manual multi-hop exploitation techniques for heap vulnerabilities. These techniques usually abuse the heap allocator's internal functionalities and improve the vulnerabilities' capability by carefully crafted heap interaction sequences. We designed a templating language to abstract known multi-hop exploitation techniques as exploit templates. HAEPG uses them to achieve an arbitrary execution and generate end-to-end exploits.

We built a prototype of HAEPG based on the symbolic execution engine S2E [15] and wrote templates for four exploitation techniques of ptmalloc [4], the standard allocator of glibc, and evaluated it on 24 programs from well known Capture The Flag (CTF) competitions. The results show that HAEPG is able to accurately reason about the type of vulnerability for 21 (87.5%) of them, and generate exploits that spawn a shell for 16 (66.7%) of them.

2   Motivational Example

In this section, we give an example to illustrate multi-hop exploitation and reveal problems AEG solutions encounter when handling the example.

The Vulnerability. The example is running on a GNU/Linux system with an unmodified version of glibc.. As shown in Fig. 1, the program has three functions, i.e., *addItem*, *removeItem*, *editItem*, which are used to allocate an object, release an object, and modify an object. There is a poison-null-byte error [16] at Line 22, but it only corrupts the meta-data between heap objects, while the content of the heap objects remains unaltered.

Multi-hop Exploitation. The example in Fig. 1 shows the exploitation via the unsafe unlink technique [9]. We first allocate three heap objects A, B, and C. The pointer that the program used to access object B is stored in BSS. Then, we trigger the vulnerability in object A to shrink the object B's size, as shown in *state 3*, and forge a fake chunk in object A in *state 4*. The fake chunk is well arranged to bypass sanity checks and leads to an arbitrary write primitive in *state 6* after releasing object B in *state 5*. Finally, we corrupt a function pointer with the arbitrary write primitive and hijack the control flow.

These states can be categorized as follows:

- **Initial state:** State when the program starts running, e.g., *state 1*.
- **Preparation state:** State when the program manipulates memory layouts for exploitation before the corruption happens, e.g., *state 2*.
- **Corrupting state:** State when triggering the vulnerability, e.g., *state 3*.
- **Intermediate state:** State that the program would go through for reaching an exploitable state from the initial state, e.g., *state 4-5*.
- **Exploitable state:** State with an exploit primitive for exploitation, e.g., *state 6* and *7*.

```
1. void addItem(){
2.    int size = read_int();
3.    size_list[index] = size;
4.    heap_list[index] = malloc(size);
5.    if(!heap_list[index])
6.        puts("malloc error");
7.    return;
8. }
9. void removeItem(){
10.    if(heap_list[index]){
11.        free(heap_list[index]);
12.        heap_list[index] = 0;
13.    }
14.    if(size_list[index])
15.        size_list[index] = -1;
16. }
17. void editItem(){
18.    for(int i = 0; i < size_list[index]; i++){
19.        read(0, heap_list[index] + i, 1);
20.        if(!heap_list[index][i])
21.            break;
22.    }
23.    heap_list[index][size_list[index]] = NULL;
24. }
25. void main(){
26.    while(True){
27.        index = readInst();
28.        choice = readInst();
29.        switch(choice){
30.            case 1: addItem(); break;
31.            case 2: removeItem(); break;
32.            case 3: editItem(); break;
33.        }
34.    }
35. }
```

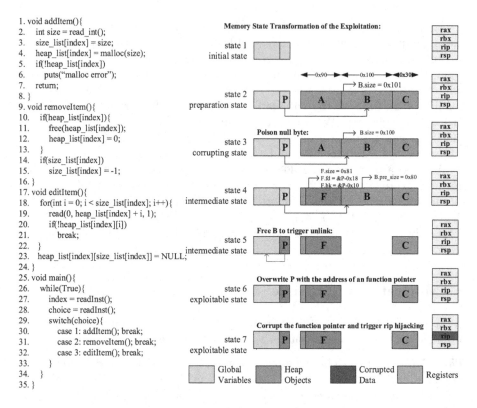

Fig. 1. An example of poison-null-byte

It is easy for modern fuzzing tools [10,33] to generate crashing inputs for the vulnerability. However, most of the AEG solutions could not handle this case because there is no direct exploit primitive upon crash of the program. For instance, the auto-exploit kit framework Mechanical Phish [26], which is developed by Shellphish and came third in DARPA CGC [17], could only detect the vulnerability and generate no exploit for the example, because Mechanical Phish requires a controllable pointer for injecting shellcodes or rop-chains. The solution Revery [30] could find the corrupting *state 3*. However, it has no capabilities for bypassing the heap allocator's sanity checks and enhancing the vulnerability's capability, and thus could not turn the vulnerability into an exploit.

3   Methodology

Figure 2 shows an overview of HAEPG. It takes programs and crashing inputs as input, and templates for the guidance of exploitation. HAEPG first models heap interactions of the target program with function paths and heap primitives. It extracts function paths from the program using static analysis, and dynamically tracks instructions and function calls of the function paths interacting with the heap allocator during runtime and records relations of different heap interactions.

Then, HAEPG runs the program with the crashing input to retrieve information about the vulnerability, including its type and the scale of corrupted data. We designed a templating language for templating widely used exploitation techniques. Each template contains the necessary information for guiding the exploitation. HAEPG filters applicable exploit templates by checking if the heap allocator and the program meets the templates' requirements. It attempts to generate an attack sequence and cyclically assesses and corrects the sequence until the program reaches an exploitable state, or the analysis exceeds a configurable upper bound for generation attempts (e.g., 20 times).

Finally, HAEPG uses the generated exploit primitive to corrupt the instruction pointer for transferring control flow to one-gadget [18]. One-gadgets are code fragments inside glibc that invokes "/bin/sh" without any arguments, effectively spawning a shell for the attacker. Once HAEPG detects a shell process is created in the target program, it solves the path and data constraints collected when executing the attack sequence and generates an exploit input.

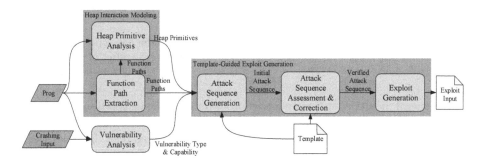

Fig. 2. Overview of HAEPG

3.1 Heap Interaction Modeling

Function Path Extraction. A function dispatcher is a code structure that is widely used in programs for function distribution, and usually implemented as if-else or switch-case structure wrapped in a loop. Programs cyclically receive instructions at the loop entry and execute corresponding functions. We define the basic block sequences from the loop entry to the loop exit as function paths, which have the following properties:

- **Atomicity:** Function paths are indivisible at runtime. A program cannot execute half of a function path and then jump to other function paths. The structure of the function dispatcher has determined that each function path must be executed entirely before executing others.

- **Reentrant:** Function paths have the same entrance and exit. When it reaches the exit of the function path, the program returns to the entrance and chooses the next function path according to instructions. Thus a program can execute a function path several times through proper instructions.

To extract function paths, `HAEPG` first generates a control-flow graph of the target program and marks the loops containing the function calls of heap allocations or deallocations as candidate function dispatchers. If the loop body of the function dispatcher is a switch-case statement, `HAEPG` will search for the basic block with several successors and extract the path of each successor as a function path. Otherwise, the loop body could be a sequence of nested if-else statements. `HAEPG` will traverse the loop backward the starting from the end of the loop body and check the number of each basic block's precedents during the traversal. The first basic block, which has a large number of precedents, e.g., more than 5, would be marked as the merge point of all dispatched functions, and we extract all paths from the loop entry to this block as function paths.

Heap Primitive Analysis. Heap primitives model the interactions between programs and heap allocators. We distinguish between the following three types and their attributes:[1]

Allocation	**Deallocation**	**Edit**
size: the size of allocation	*addr*: the address to be	*base*: the base of edit address
addr: the address returned	released	*offset*: the offset of edit address
by the heap allocator		*data*: the data to be written

In general, heap primitives are these program machine instructions: (1) function calls interacting with the heap allocator, such as malloc, calloc, free, etc. (2) function calls with heap pointers as arguments, such as read, fgets, etc. (3) memory-write instructions with heap objects as the destination address.

To analyze heap primitives, `HAEPG` executes function paths using symbolic execution. It symbolizes all input bytes and tracks instructions and the calling of APIs interacting with the heap region. `HAEPG` only records instructions and the calling of the APIs in the target program as heap primitives and ignores shared libraries, because tracking both the target program and the shared libraries would increase performance overhead. If any attribute of heap primitives are symbolic, `HAEPG` will solve and record the range of it without concretizing it. To reason about the relationship between heap primitives, `HAEPG` associates a globally unique taint tag for each heap pointer returned by an allocation and identifies primitives that operated on a tainted pointer.

3.2 Vulnerability Analysis

We obtain crashing inputs with AFL [33] and analyze the vulnerability's capability by detecting violations of memory usage. `HAEPG` dynamically executes the

---

[1] Note that we only model the basic interaction types. Heap allocators can have other types of interactions (e.g., realloc), which are outside the scope of this paper.

crashing inputs and taints return pointer of allocations similarly to the heap primitive analysis. Additionally, it propagates the tag to the pointed memory object's bytes. We further add annotations about a heap object's status to the tags: Initially, tags are uninitialized, and instructions writing to the object will change the status to busy while instructions releasing the object will change it to free. Furthermore, HAEPG records the size of corresponding objects for tags. If any instruction accesses the heap memory, we could get the pointer's tag ptag and the pointed object's memory tag mtag, together with the statuses and sizes of them. Before changing the statuses of them, HAEPG checks if any of the violation rules shown in Table 1 is triggered.

Table 1. List of vulnerability types, trigger options, and violation rules

Vulnerability type	Trigger operation	Violation rule
Double free	Free a heap chunk	mtag.status == free or ptag.status == free
Use After Free	Store n bytes of data in memory address [base + off] (base and off are the base and offset of addressing)	mtag.status == free or ptag.status == free
Overflow		n + off >ptag.size
Poison Null Byte		n + off == ptag.size + 1 and the last byte of data is null byte
Off by One		n + off == ptag.size + 1

If a violation rule is triggered, HAEPG will record the scale of corrupted data, such as the range of overflowed bytes or the size of the vulnerable chunk.

3.3 Template-Guided Exploit Generation

In this section, we will illustrate our method of exploit generation. We bring existing exploitation techniques as prior knowledge of constructing memory states and reaching exploitable states into HAEPG. Moreover, instead of hard-coding exploitation techniques into HAEPG, we developed a templating language to describe exploitation techniques. The method of dynamic interpreting templates and constructing attack sequences provides flexibility and extendability to HAEPG.

Templates. The procedure of applying exploitation techniques is program-sensitive, as even slight changes in the target program result in need of vastly different exploitation strategies. Thus we collect constant and essential components of exploitation techniques and abstract them as templates, which give information over the following components:

- **Backbone Primitives Sequence:** The order of heap primitives, which used to trigger the vulnerability and abuse internal functionalities of heap allocators, remains constant. For example, cyclically releasing a heap chunk in the fastbin attack to gain an arbitrary allocation from a double-free vulnerability [5]. We refer to such heap primitives as a backbone primitives sequence.
- **Layout Constraints:** Intermediate states of the multi-hop exploitation may need to meet certain constraints. For example, an unsafe unlink attack requires the victim chunk to be allocated in unsortedbin size, and the fake chunk to be adjacent to the victim chunk. We refer to such constraints as layout constraints.
- **Requirements:** To use an exploitation technique, the program has to meet some requirements. For example, the program must have the ability to allocate objects in fastbin size for fastbin attack.

These components indicate how to construct memory states to reach an exploitable state in multi-hop exploitation and constraints that memory states should satisfy. Likewise, each template consists of three parts, including requirements of using the template, backbone primitives, and layout constraints. We will introduce the templating language we used to abstract exploitation techniques in Sect. 4.3.

Attack Sequence Generation. Attack sequence generation is closely tied to the provided templates. Firstly, HAEPG checks if the target program meets the specified requirements, such as the vulnerability type and the glibc version. If the program passed these checks, HAEPG will select this template for the next steps; otherwise, it will try other templates.

Next, HAEPG traverses the backbone primitives of the template. It scans all function paths to find the ones containing the backbone primitives, and combines these function paths together with their heap primitives as an attack sequence.

We designed the following two methods to execute an attack sequence:

- **Heap Simulator:** The simulator is an independent binary that uses the same heap allocator as the target program (i.e., ptmalloc for our prototype). We use it to execute the heap primitives of the attack sequence and simulate the intermediate states of the target program.
- **Symbolic Execution:** We let the target program execute function paths of the attack sequence and associate heap primitives as data constraints with the interrelated memory data and registers in S2E (e.g., transform the size of allocations to data constraints of malloc/calloc's first argument).

Attack Sequence Assessment and Correction. HAEPG assesses the attack sequence according to the layout constraints of the template. It dynamically executes the target program and the attack sequence and records heap layouts at runtime. Then, it extracts the address of each essential heap object, the real size of them, and the address where the object pointers are stored, etc. With this information, once precedent backbone primitives of a memory state are finished,

HAEPG will check if the current heap layout meets the layout constraints, including the distance of heap objects and the status of them.

To improve performance, HAEPG first uses the heap simulator for a quick assessment. Only after the attack sequence passed the assessment, HAEPG will use S2E for an accurate assessment.

If the layout constraints are met, the program will enter an exploitable state, and HAEPG would attempt to generate an exploit. Otherwise, HAEPG will find the conflicting heap layout. Then, HAEPG will infer the reason for the conflict and attempt to correct it. In general, the reasons for the conflict are as follows:

1. Heap chunk A should be free but it is busy or uninitialized;
2. Heap chunk A and B must be adjacent but there are other busy chunks between them;
3. Heap chunk A and B must be adjacent but the adjacent chunk of A is free.

For the first case, HAEPG inserts a path into the attack sequence to release the chunk A. For the second case, HAEPG tries to insert paths to release all chunks in the middle of chunk A and B. If chunks cannot be released, HAEPG would allocate a heap chunk with the same size as chunk A before the allocation of it to get a new heap layout, which might lead to a satisfying heap layout. The third case is generally caused by extra heap chunks of the freelist which make chunk B gets allocated on a wrong slot, and HAEPG fills extra chunks by allocating chunks with the same size as B. Finally, HAEPG generates a new attack sequence and repeats the assessment and correction until it finds an attack sequence that leads to an exploitable memory state (i.e., a state matching the layout constraints).

Exploit Generation. Once the attack sequence passed the assessment, HAEPG executes it using symbolic execution and detect exploit primitives by tracking instructions of the target program and checking if symbolic data is present in one of the following locations: (1) the content and target address for memory-write instructions and function calls; (2) the head pointer of one of the bins; (3) the target address for indirect calls/jumps; (4) the value of function pointers of the program and glibc (e.g., GOT and *malloc_hook*).

Based on the location of symbolic data, HAEPG can use one of the following exploit primitives to derive an exploit input:

- **Arbitrary Execution (AX):** If the target address of indirect calls is symbolic, or any function pointer is symbolic, HAEPG could corrupt the instruction pointer to an arbitrary value. In this case, HAEPG uses a one-gadget [18] as the target address. Note that each one-gadget has individual memory and register constraints that need to be satisfied. Hence, HAEPG will check the related memory and registers when the instruction pointer is corrupted and pick a proper one-gadget for exploitation.
- **Arbitrary Write (AW):** If the value and the target address of any memory-write instructions or function calls are symbolic, HAEPG can write arbitrary data to an arbitrary location. HAEPG leverages it to overwrite a function pointer of the GOT or glibc (glibc is preferred if Full RELRO [28] is enabled)

and exercises a function path that calls the corrupted function pointer, which transforms the exploit primitive to an arbitrary execution.

- **Arbitrary Allocation (AA):** If the head pointer of a bin is symbolic, HAEPG can allocate a chunk at an arbitrary location. However, this primitive has different constraints based on the type of bin. For tcache, the allocator does not check the meta-data of the allocated chunk, so we treat the primitive as an arbitrary write primitive; For fastbin, the allocator checks the consistency of chunk size, so an attacker has to find or construct a fake meta-data to bypass the sanity check. Fortunately, there are some data in glibc which is suitable for bypassing the sanity check and transforming the exploit primitive to an arbitrary execution[2].

After corrupting the instruction pointer with a one-gadget, HAEPG will hook the APIs for process generation (e.g. execve). Once HAEPG detects an invokation of these APIs with the argument of bash's path, it solves constraints collected when executing the attack sequence and generates an exploit input.

4   Implementation

4.1   Static Analysis

Control Flow Graph Construction. As discussed by Shoshitaishvili et al. [27], it is very challenging to recover an accurate CFG for programs due to indirect calls. Since CFG generation is not a contribution of this paper, we only focus on programs with no recursion and indirect calls. We developed a simple CFG generation program for HAEPG's prototype, which constructs the CFG by extracting jump targets of basic blocks in the disassembly using static analysis. It is sufficient for our evaluation set.

Redundant Function Path Simplification. Since a function path is a sequence of basic blocks, branches create a new function path for each branch target. As we use dynamic analysis to infer the dependencies between function paths, a large number of function paths increases HAEPG's performance overhead. As we only focus on heap interactions, most of the function paths are redundant for HAEPG because heap interactions of them are the same or similar, which will cause dynamic analysis to do repetitive work. Besides, some function paths should be dropped because they are not related to exploitation. We simplify function paths with the following methods:

- **Merging:** We construct the CFG for the branch in Line 14 to Line 16 in Fig. 1, as shown in Fig. 3.a. To reduce the impact of branches on the number of paths, we extract an API call sequence from the paths and mark the

---

[2] For example, the function pointers nearby *malloc_hook* in glibc, which could be mistaken as valid meta-data by the allocator. We could directly overwrite *malloc_hook* and hijack the instruction pointer by allocating a chunk on it.

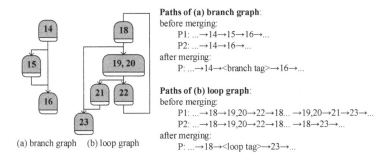

Paths of (a) branch graph:
before merging:
    P1: ...→14→15→16→...
    P2: ...→14→16→...
after merging:
    P: ...→14→<branch tag>→16→...

Paths of (b) loop graph:
before merging:
    P1: ...→18→19,20→22→18... →19,20→21→23→...
    P2: ...→18→19,20→22→18... →18→23→...
after merging:
    P: ...→18→<loop tag>→23→...

(a) branch graph   (b) loop graph

Fig. 3. Two types of structure to be optimized

branch with a `branch tag` if the API call sequence does not contain heap interactions.

A loop can have more than one exit, and the extra exits increase the number of function paths. We take the loop of $func3$ in Fig. 1 as an example, and the CFG is shown in Fig. 3.b. The loop has two exits, i.e., Line 21 and 23. Since Line 23 is the successor of Line 21, we regard Line 23 as the only exit of the loop and replace the loop with a ¡to merge function paths exiting from Line 21 or 23 into one.

- **Pruning:** Programs check functions' return values and perform different operations if they indicate the failure of function execution. Such operations are usually organized with conditional branches, which also increase the number of function paths. As exploiting the failure of function calls usually depends on programs rather than heap allocators, we consider them out of scope for `HAEPG`. We discard those paths as irrelevant and filter them out using a lightweight taint analysis for functions' return values.

4.2 Dependency of Function Paths

`HAEPG` may fail to execute function paths because program variables do not meet path constraints in symbolic execution. In this case, `HAEPG` executes other function paths first, which set the program variables correctly. We refer to these variables as reliant variables, and the latter function paths are the dominant paths of the formers. For example, we assume that function path $FP1$ is the sequence of line number 27-29-30-5-7 in Fig. 1, and $FP2$ is 27-29-31-10-11-14-15 (we only take the line number of branches). `HAEPG` would fail to jump to Line 11 from Line 10 when executing $FP2$ without executing $FP1$ first because the value of $heap\_list[index]$ does not meet $FP2$'s path constraints. In this case, $heap\_list[index]$ is the reliant variable of $FP2$, and $FP1$ is the dominant path of $FP2$.

    `HAEPG` has to find all dominant paths for such function paths to avoid missing heap primitives in them. It first dynamically executes function paths and records the following information: (1) new values that the function path used to overwrite or update the original reliant values; (2) constraints not being satisfied and

Listing 1. Template of unsafe unlink

```
1   RQMT: Include(UNSORTEDBIN, hmodel.malloc_sizes) and
2         Include(vuln.type, ["Off-by-One", "Poison-Null-Byte", "Overflow"])
      ↪ and
3         VersionLower(allocator.ver, "2.26")
4   EXEC: vul_ptr = Allocation(size = (0x80 + RANDNUMB * 0x10 + 8), tag = vul.
      ↪ vul_tag)
5         vic_ptr = Allocation(size = (0xf0 + RANDNUMB * 0x100))
6         sep_ptr = Allocation(size = RANDNUMB)
7   SATS: adjacent(vul_ptr, vic_ptr) == True and adjacent (vic_ptr, topchunk)
      ↪ == False
8   EXEC: vul_data = h64(0) + h64(vul_ptr.size - 8 + 1) + h64(vul_ptr.base - 0
      ↪ x18) + h64(vul_ptr.base - 0x10) + RANDBYTE * (vul_ptr.size - 0x28)
      ↪ + h64(vic_ptr.size & (~8)) + "00"
9         Edit(base = vul_ptr, offset = 0, data = vul_data)
10  SATS: vul_ptr.chunk.fd == 0 and
11        vul_ptr.chunk.bk == (vul_ptr.chunk.raw_size - 0x10) and
12        vic_ptr.chunk.pre_size == (vic_ptr.chunk.bk - 1) and
13        vic_ptr.chunk.raw_size & 1 == 0
14  EXEC: Deallocation(vic_ptr)
15  EXEC: Edit(base = vul_ptr.base - 0x18, offset = 0, data = "A" * 0x20)
```

causing termination of states in symbolic execution. HAEPG infers expected values
of reliant variables by solving these constraints and finds function paths that can
set reliant variables correctly (i.e., the dominant paths).

4.3   Templating Engine

Templating Language. Our templating language describes exploitation techniques via requirements, backbone primitives, and layout constraints. We mark
them in the template with labels *RQMT*, *EXEC*, and *SATS*, as shown in
Listing 1. The language provides users with functions and objects to describe
exploitation techniques, and Table 2 shows the central components of the language.

We employ the following methods to concretize the attributes of the heap
primitives of attack sequences:

- **Direct Calculation:** HAEPG determines some of the attributes of heap primitives based on the range of them and the template, such as the size of an
  allocation. It solves these attributes when constructing the attack sequence.
  We refer to it as direct calculation.
- **Lazy Calculation:** Some of the attributes of heap primitives could only be
  determined at runtime, such as *vul_ptr.chunk*, *vul_ptr.base*, and the data of
  edit at Line 7 in Listing 1. They remain unsolved when the attack sequence
  is constructed. HAEPG collects runtime information and solves these attributes
  during the execution. We refer to it as lazy calculation.

Note that the Allocation function returns a *HeapChunk* object whose
member variables represent meta-data's fields, the user payload, and the address

where the heap pointer is stored. A user does not need to initialize these member variables because HAEPG would automatically initialize them using lazy calculation. Listing 1 shows the template of unsafe unlink. It intuitively describes the exploitation of Fig. 1 showcased in.

When generating attack sequences, the backbone primitives from the same *EXEC* label are out of order, and HAEPG simulates the changes of reliant variables and sorts backbone primitives on the premise that reliant variables meet the expectation of function paths.

Heap Simulator. The main part of the simulator is a loop that wraps the three heap primitive functions described in Sect. 3.1. It takes heap primitives as the input and executes the corresponding functions to simulate the heap interactions of the target program. After finishing the execution of each function, the simulator will output its heap layout. HAEPG uses the simulator to simulate the memory states of the target program.

5   Evaluation

To evaluate the effectiveness of HAEPG, we implemented a prototype of HAEPG and assessed it with 24 programs CTF challenges, and all of them can be found in ctftime.org [1], pwnable.tw [7], and github.com [3]. We selected programs based on the following criteria: (1) programs must have at least one heap vulnerability, and vulnerabilities are diverse; (2) programs with higher scores are preferred. In general, challenges with higher scores are more difficult. Most selected challenges have higher scores than the median score for their CTF game, and 4 of them have the highest score in the exploitation category. We wrote templates for four common heap exploitation techniques: fastbin attack [5], unsafe unlink [9], house of force [6], and tcache poisoning [8], which are applicable to a significant amount of CTF challenges. However, some challenges are not shipped with their respective glibc, and we provided default glibc for them (2.27 for those whose intended solution involves tcache and 2.24 for others)[3]. The result shows that HAEPG can generate exploits for most of them.

All programs are tested in Ubuntu18.04, with Intel(R) Xeon(R) Gold 6154 CPU @ 3.00GHz*24 and 512GB RAM. We enabled NX [25] and disabled ASLR [24] for all programs. We disabled ASLR because bypassing ASLR it is an orthogonal problem out of the scope of this paper.

5.1   Effectiveness

Table 3 shows the result of our evaluation. It contains details of programs, such as names and CTF competitions. Moreover, it shows the glibc version, the vulnerability type that HAEPG identified, and whether HAEPG could generate an exploit

---

[3] We provided ld.so for different versions of glibc, and changed the absolute paths of ld.so and libc.so to relative paths for all test cases. In this way, we were able to load arbitrary ld.so and libc.so on our evaluation system.

Table 2. List of function and variables provided by the templating language

Types	Name	Description
Object	vuln	vulnerability information, including vulnerability type and capability (for example, overflowed data size)
	hmodel	heap interaction model, including function paths and their heap primitives
	allocator	the allocator, including the version information
Type	HeapChunk	value returned by Allocation
Function	Include	check if two parameters are inclusive
	Allocation	allocation primitive
	Deallocation	deallocation primitive
	Edit	edit primitive
	Adjacent	check if two heap objects are adjacent in heap layout
	Distance	return the distance of two heap objects

for them. As a result, HAEPG accurately reasons about the type of vulnerability for 21 (87.5%) programs successfully and generate working exploits for 16 (66.7%) of them. Moreover, we bypassed Full RELRO [28] by corrupting the function pointers in glibc (e.g., *malloc_hook*) instead of GOT.

We also evaluated Revery [30] and Mechanical Phish [26] as a comparison, and none of them could generate exploits for these programs. Revery found corrupting states for these challenges. It reached unlink states for challenges that could be exploited with unsafe unlink (the results of them are marked with "*" in Table 3). However, Revery could not generate complete exploits because it uses fuzzing to explore the memory state space. Unfortunately, this is insufficient to forge fake chunks. Mechanical Phish found crashing states for these challenges with Driller [29], but it could not generate exploits because there was no pointer corrupted with symbolic bytes. Hence, Mechanical Phish could not hijack the instruction pointer or inject shellcodes/rop-chains.

5.2   Performance

To evaluate the performance of HAEPG, we recorded the time HAEPG spent for heap interaction modeling and exploit generation, as shown in Fig. 4. With the help of merging and pruning, HAEPG reduced the number of function paths significantly, and the total time for exploit generation of most programs is less than 400 s. The program with the most function paths without simplification is *airCraft*, which has 4284 function paths. Heap interaction modeling of this program without simplification took more than 10 h, while after removing the redundant function paths, it only left 6 of them and took 344 s for modeling. Besides, programs with complex algorithms, such as *note3*, which has a sophisticated bitwise algorithm, require a lot of analysis time due to complex constraints that need more time for solving.

Table 3. List of CTF pwn programs evaluated with `HAEPG`

Exp. Tech.	Name	CTF	Glibc ver.	Vul. type	Exp. prim.	Exp. gen.	Revery	M. Phish
Fastbin Attack	CaNaKMgF Remastered	ASIS CTF 2017	2.23	Double Free	AA	✔	✗	✗
	halconyheap	TJCTF 2019	2.23	Double Free	AA	✔	✗	✗
	stringer	RCTF 2018	2.23	Double Free	AA	✔	✗	✗
	secretgarden	Pwnable.tw	2.23	Double Free	AA	✔	✗	✗
	babyheap	Fireshell CTF 2019	2.24	UAF	AA	✔	✗	✗
	aircraft	RCTF 2017	2.24	UAF	AA	✗	✗	✗
Unsafe Unlink	stkof	HITCON 2014	2.23	Overflow	AW	✔	✗*	✗
	simple_note	Tokyo Westerns 2017	2.24	Off by One	AW	✔	✗*	✗
	fb	AliCTF 2016	2.24	Poison Null Byte	AW	✔	✗*	✗
	note3	ZCTF 2016	2.19	Overflow	AW	✔	✗*	✗
House of Force	gryffindor	InCTF 2017	2.23	Overflow	AX	✔	✗	✗
	bamboobox	NTU-CTF-2017	2.24	Overflow	AX	✔	✗	✗
Tcache Poisoning	three	BCTF 2018	2.27	UAF	AA	✔	✗	✗
	penpal world	RedpwnCTF 2019	2.27	UAF	AA	✔	✗	✗
	one	SECCON CTF 2019	2.27	Double Free	AA	✔	✗	✗
	girlfriend	StarCTF 2019	2.27	Double Free	AA	✔	✗	✗
	zero to hero	PicoCTF2019	2.27	Double Free	AA	✔	✗	✗
–	house_of_atum	BCTF 2018	2.27	UAF	–	✗	✗	✗
–	iz_heap_lv2	ISITDTU CTF 2019	2.27	Off by One	–	✗	✗	✗
–	schmaltz	InCTF 2019	2.28	Double Free	–	✗	✗	✗
–	children_tcache	HITCON 2018	2.27	Poison Null Byte	-	✗	✗	✗
-	Auir	CSAW CTF 2017	2.23	–	–	✗	✗	✗
–	Secret Note V2	HITCON 2018	2.23	–	–	✗	✗	✗
–	Car_Market	ASIS CTF 2016	2.23	–	–	✗	✗	✗

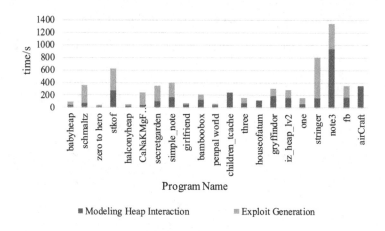

Fig. 4. Time intervals of modeling heap interaction and exploit generation

5.3   A Multi-hop Exploitation Case Study

We take *stkof* as an example and show how HAEPG automatically generates an exploit for a CTF challenge. The binary has three critical functions in *stkof*, *do_alloc*, *do_dealloc*, and *do_edit*, which are used for allocating, deallocating, and modifying heap chunks, respectively. An overflow in the *do_edit* function allows an attacker to write an arbitrary amount of data past the bounds of a chunk. Based on the vulnerability's capability, HAEPG used the template of unsafe unlink (as shown in Listing 1) for exploitation.

As shown in Fig. 5, HAEPG first generated *Attack Sequence 1* based on the unsafe unlink template. The template required the *vul_ptr* and *vic_ptr* to be adjacent when triggering the vulnerability. However, the glibc created *stdout_buffer* between the *vul_ptr* and *vic_ptr* unexpectedly when initializing io streams (HAEPG did not capture it because it only tracked heap interactions in *stkof* and ignored shared libraries). Thus HAEPG attempted to fix the heap layout by releasing the *stdout_buffer* first. Since *stdout_buffer* was generated by glibc, there is no function path that can release it. Hence, HAEPG tried to create a new heap layout. It constructed *Attack Sequence 2* by inserting a function path with an allocation primitive. HAEPG used the primitive to allocate a chunk *ph_ptr* in the same size as *vul_ptr*. The *ph_ptr* is allocated at *vul_ptr*'s original address and forced the *vul_ptr* and *vic_ptr* to be allocated at higher addresses, and they are adjacent to each other as desired. Now, the meta-data of *vic_ptr* can be corrupted through the overflowing from *vul_ptr*. Through the last deallocation, the heap allocator finally unlinked the fake chunk inside *vul_ptr* and caused an arbitrary write primitive. HAEPG corrupted *malloc_hook* with a one-gadget pointer via this primitive and hijacked the instruction pointer by inserting the function path of *do_alloc* into the *Attack Sequence* 2. When a shell was spawned, HAEPG generated the exploit input in S2E.

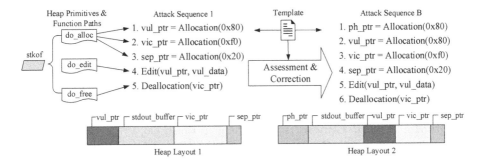

Fig. 5. Heap primitives to exploit *stkof*

5.4   Failed Cases

Failed on Exploit Generation: HAEPG corrupted a forward pointer of fastbin for *airCraft*. However, exploiting the AA primitive derived from fastbin attack requires a fake meta-data which is valid for size 0x88 in this case. HAEPG could not find such a primitive to store the illegal heap object, so it could not construct an exploitable state. To exploit the challenge, an attacker has to forge a fake chunk on the global data region in advance, which is beyond HAEPG's ability.

HAEPG failed on *house_of_atum* because the program only provides two heap objects for use at the same time, which are not sufficient for existing templates. The intended way is to confuse the tcache list and fastbin list.

Missing Capable Templates: HAEPG relies on templates for exploit generation, which means it can only handle the cases that are exploitable with existing templates, and can not use unknown exploitation techniques by itself. For instance, HAEPG can not handle *children_tcache*, *iz_heap_lv2*, and *schmaltz* because they are not exploitable with the provided templates. The intended solutions for *children_tcache*, *iz_heap_lv2* are to overlap heap objects by corrupting heap meta-data and triggering consolidation. As to *schmaltz*, the intended solution is to put a chunk in two different tcache lists and then corrupt the link pointer of it to get an AA primitive.

We downgraded the glibc version for them for further tests. HAEPG successfully generated exploit inputs for *iz_heap_lv2* and *schmaltz* with the templates of unsafe unlink and tcache poisoning. HAEPG could not solve *children_tcache* because the program only provides one chance to write for each object, which is not sufficient for provided templates.

Failed on Vulnerability Detection: Since HAEPG tracked heap interactions at the object level, it failed to detect memory corruptions in some cases. For instance, the challenge *Car_Market* has a buffer overflow inside objects, i.e., it will corrupt the adjacent data fields rather than adjacent objects. A more fine-grained method is needed to handle this case.

Failed on Program Analysis: HAEPG could not analyze sophisticated programs, such as *SecretNoteV2*, which has an AES encryption algorithm, and

Auir, which is an obfuscated program. As HAEPG relies on symbolic execution, these programs generated a large number of complex constraints and states, resulting in path/state explosion.

6   Related Work

Automatic Exploit Generation. Mechanical Phish [26] is a cyber reasoning system developed by the Shellphish team for DARPA's CGC [17]. It finds PoCs of vulnerabilities using Driller [29] and reproducing crashing states in Angr [27]. Then, it checks if input data corrupts write pointers or the instruction pointer at crashing points. If so, it will create shellcodes or rop-chains for exploitation. In the end, it solves data constraints and generates exploit inputs.

Revery [30] is an automatic exploit generation tool for heap-based vulnerabilities. It employs taint analysis and shadow memory to detect memory corruption in crashing inputs. Moreover, it searches for exploitable points using a layout-oriented fuzzing technique. In the end, Revery generates exploits by stitching the diverging paths and crashing paths together. As shown in Sect. 5, Revery failed on the evaluation set because the fuzzing technique that Revery used to explore exploitable points is not capable of multi-hop exploitation.

FUZE [31] is a novel framework to automate the process of kernel UAF exploitation. It analyzes and evaluates system calls which are valuable and useful for kernel UAF exploitation using kernel fuzzing and symbolic execution. Then, it leveraged dynamic tracing and SMT solver to guide the heap layout manipulation. The authors used 15 real-world vulnerabilities to demonstrate that FUZE could not only escalate kernel UAF exploitability but also diversify working exploits.

SLAKE [14] is a solution to exploit vulnerabilities in the Linux kernel. It uses a static-dynamic hybrid analysis to search for objects and syscalls which are useful for kernel exploitation. Then, SLAKE models the capability of vulnerability and matching the capability with corresponding objects. To exploit the vulnerability, SLAKE chooses the method of exploitation based on the vulnerability type and manipulates heap layouts by adjusting the free list in the slab.

Gollum [22] is the first approach to automatic exploit generation for heap overflows in interpreters. It employs a custom heap allocator SHAPESHIFTER to generate exploitable heap layouts and utilizes a genetic algorithm to find heap interaction sequences that can lead to the target heap layouts. If Gollum reaches the target heap layouts, it corrupts the function pointers of victim objects by triggering heap overflows. Like HAEPG, Gollum corrupts the instruction pointer with one-gadgets to generate exploits.

The solutions above which toward interpreter or kernel explore the heap state space with the knowledge of language grammars or kernel syscalls. However, there is no such standard input protocol for applications as each application parses inputs differently. Our method modeled heap interactions in the dimension of the program path, and the result showed the potency of it.

Besides, these solutions assume there is a sensitive pointer which could be overwritten by merely heap layout manipulation and triggering vulnerabilities. As we discussed before, the premise does not always hold for some vulnerabilities and applications, which makes exploitation harder. Our method could effectively solve this problem, and this is the main advantage of our method over others.

Moreover, instead of encoding existing exploitation techniques into HAEPG, we developed a templating language to abstract them. A user could write their templates without the need to know the internal details of HAEPG. The solutions mentioned above have no such interface.

Heap Exploitation Techniques Discovery. Heaphopper [19] is an automated approach to analyze the exploitability of heap implementations in the presence of memory corruption. It takes the binary library of heap implementation, a list of transactions (e.g., malloc and free), the maximum number of transactions that an attacker can perform, and a list of security properties as input. Heaphopper generates lists of transactions by enumerating permutations of the transactions and generate C files and compiled programs for them. Then, it executes these programs and tracks the memory states of them. If any program leads to states violating the security properties, Heaphopper will take the C file of it as output.

ARCHEAP [32] uses fuzzing rather than symbolic execution to discover new heap exploitation techniques. It generates test cases by mutating and synthesizing heap operations and attack capabilities, and checks whether the generated test cases can be potentially used to construct exploitation primitives, such as arbitrary write or overlapped chunks. As a result, ARCHEAP discovered five previously unknown exploitation primitives in ptmalloc and found several exploitation techniques against jemalloc, tcmalloc, and even custom heap allocators.

The solutions above focus on exploit techniques discovery rather than application, so they are usually used for heap allocator's security assessment. Our solution can generate exploits using known exploit techniques, but it can not make use of unknown exploit techniques.

7   Discussion

HAEPG is dedicated to automating the process of multi-hop exploitation for heap-based vulnerabilities. However, it has the following limitations:

- HAEPG could not analyze sophisticated programs or real-world programs. First, the static analysis which HAEPG used to extract CFG is not good at handling indirect calls/jumps. Second, symbolic execution's drawbacks make HAEPG only applicable to small programs. Third, a significant amount of real-world programs uses multi-threading or multi-processing, which brings additional challenges to the program analysis techniques used by HAEPG.
- HAEPG is fundamentally incomplete because it only searches for specific memory states based on existing templates rather than exploring the whole memory state space, which means HAEPG could not generate exploits with exploitation techniques where no template is given.

– HAEPG is implemented for ptmalloc and can not generate exploits for programs using other allocators for now. To adapt HAEPG to other heap allocators, we have to change the codes of parsing heap objects, the strategy of heap layout manipulation, and the codes of detecting and leveraging exploit primitives. We leave it as future work.

8   Conclusion

In this paper, we proposed an automatic exploit generation solution HAEPG for heap vulnerabilities, which uses hybrid techniques to build the heap interaction model and navigate the multi-hop exploitation. HAEPG could generate complex exploits that abuse heap allocator's internal functionalities and enhance the vulnerabilities' capability step by step, which previously could only be completed manually. We evaluated HAEPG with CTF challenges, and the result showed the effectiveness of HAEPG. In the end, we believe that HAEPG improves the state-of-the-art of automated exploit generation and provides useful building blocks for solving remaining challenges in the field.

References

1. Ctftime. https://ctftime.org/. Accessed 2020
2. Cve details. https://www.cvedetails.com/. Accessed 2019
3. Github. https://github.com/. Accessed 2020
4. The gnu c library (glibc). https://www.gnu.org/software/libc/. Accessed 2019
5. Heap exploitation - fastbin attack. https://0x00sec.org/t/heap-exploitation-fastbin-attack/3627. Accessed 2019
6. The malloc maleficarum glibc malloc exploitation techniques. https://dl.packetstormsecurity.net/papers/attack/MallocMaleficarum.txt. Accessed 2020
7. Pwnable.tw. https://pwnable.tw/. Accessed 2020
8. tcache_poisoning.c. https://github.com/shellphish/how2heap/blob/master/glibc_2.26/tcache_poisoning.c. Accessed 2019
9. Unlink exploit. https://heap-exploitation.dhavalkapil.com/attacks/unlink_exploit.html. Accessed 2019
10. Honggfuzz: A general-purpose, easy-to-use fuzzer with interesting analysis options (2017). https://github.com/google/honggfuzz. Accessed 2020
11. Cwe-193: Off-by-one error (2019). https://cwe.mitre.org/data/definitions/193.html. Accessed 2019
12. Avgerinos, T., Cha, S.K., Hao, B.L.T., Brumley, D.: AEG: Automatic exploit generation. In: 18th Network and Distributed System Security Symposium (2011)
13. Cha, S.K., Avgerinos, T., Rebert, A., Brumley, D.: Unleashing mayhem on binary code. In: 2012 IEEE Symposium on Security and Privacy. IEEE (2012)
14. Chen, Y., Xing, X.: Slake: facilitating slab manipulation for exploiting vulnerabilities in the Linux kernel. In: 2019 ACM SIGSAC Conference on Computer and Communications Security. ACM (2019)
15. Chipounov, V., Kuznetsov, V., Candea, G.: S2e: a platform for in-vivo multi-path analysis of software systems. In: ACM SIGARCH Computer Architecture News, vol. 39. ACM (2011)

16. cwe.mitre.org: Cwe-626: Null byte interaction error (poison null byte). https://cwe.mitre.org/data/definitions/626.html. Accessed 2019
17. DARPA: Cyber grand challenge. https://www.cybergrandchallenge.com/. Accessed 2019
18. david942j@217: [project] the one-gadget in glibc. https://david942j.blogspot.com/2017/02/project-one-gadget-in-glibc.html. Accessed 2019
19. Eckert, M., Bianchi, A., Wang, R., Shoshitaishvili, Y., Kruegel, C., Vigna, G.: Heaphopper: bringing bounded model checking to heap implementation security. In: 27th USENIX Security Symposium (USENIX Security 18) (2018)
20. Heelan, S.: Automatic generation of control flow hijacking exploits for software vulnerabilities. Ph.D. thesis, University of Oxford (2009)
21. Heelan, S., Melham, T., Kroening, D.: Automatic heap layout manipulation for exploitation. In: 27th USENIX Security Symposium (USENIX Security 18) (2018)
22. Heelan, S., Melham, T., Kroening, D.: Gollum: Modular and greybox exploit generation for heap overflows in interpreters. In: 2019 ACM SIGSAC Conference on Computer and Communications Security. ACM (2019)
23. Huang, S.K., Huang, M.H., Huang, P.Y., Lai, C.W., Lu, H.L., Leong, W.M.: Crax: software crash analysis for automatic exploit generation by modeling attacks as symbolic continuations. In: 2012 IEEE Sixth International Conference on Software Security and Reliability. IEEE (2012)
24. PaX-Team: Pax address space layout randomization. https://pax.grsecurity.net/docs/aslr.txt. Accessed 2019
25. PaX-Team: Pax non-executable pages design & implementation. https://pax.grsecurity.net/docs/noexec.txt. Accessed 2019
26. Shoshitaishvili, Y., et al.: Mechanical phish: Resilient autonomous hacking. In: 2018 IEEE Symposium on Security and Privacy (2018)
27. Shoshitaishvili, Y., et al.: Sok: (state of) the art of war: Offensive techniques in binary analysis. In: 2016 IEEE Symposium on Security and Privacy. IEEE (2016)
28. Sidhpurwala, H.: Hardening elf binaries using relocation read-only (relro). https://www.redhat.com/en/blog/hardening-elf-binaries-using-relocation-read-only-relro. Accessed 2019
29. Stephens, N., et al.: Driller: augmenting fuzzing through selective symbolic execution. In: 23th Network and Distributed System Security Symposium, vol. 16 (2016)
30. Wang, Y., et al.: Revery: From proof-of-concept to exploitable. In: 2018 ACM SIGSAC Conference on Computer and Communications Security. ACM (2018)
31. Wu, W., Chen, Y., Xu, J., Xing, X., Gong, X., Zou, W.: Fuze: towards facilitating exploit generation for kernel use-after-free vulnerabilities. In: 27th USENIX Security Symposium (USENIX Security 18) (2018)
32. Yun, I., Kapil, D., Kim, T.: Automatic techniques to systematically discover new heap exploitation primitives. arXiv preprint arXiv:1903.00503 (2019)
33. Zalewski, M.: American fuzzy lop (2017). https://lcamtuf.coredump.cx/afl/

Understanding Android VoIP Security: A System-Level Vulnerability Assessment

En He[1], Daoyuan Wu[2(✉)], and Robert H. Deng[3]

[1] OPPO ZIWU Cyber Security Lab, Shenzhen, China
heeeeen@gmail.com
[2] The Chinese University of Hong Kong, Hong Kong, China
dywu@ie.cuhk.edu.hk
[3] Singapore Management University, Singapore, Singapore
robertdeng@smu.edu.sg

Abstract. VoIP is a class of new technologies that deliver voice calls over the packet-switched networks, which surpasses the legacy circuit-switched telecom telephony. Android provides the native support of VoIP, including the recent VoLTE and VoWiFi standards. While prior works have analyzed the weaknesses of VoIP network infrastructure and the privacy concerns of third-party VoIP apps, no efforts were attempted to investigate the (in)security of Android's VoIP integration at the system level. In this paper, we first demystify Android VoIP's protocol stack and all its four attack surfaces. We then propose a novel vulnerability assessment approach that assembles on-device Intent/API fuzzing, network-side packet fuzzing, and targeted code auditing. By testing Android from version 7.0 to the recent 9.0, we have discovered 8 zero-day Android VoIP vulnerabilities, all of which were confirmed by Google with bug bounty awards. The security consequences are serious, including denying voice calls, caller ID spoofing, unauthorized call operations, and remote code execution. To mitigate these vulnerabilities and further improve Android VoIP security, we uncover a new root cause that requires developers' attention during their design and implementation.

1 Introduction

VoIP is a class of new technologies that deliver voice calls over the packet-switched networks, instead of the legacy circuit-switched telecom networks, i.e., the so-called Public Switched Telephone Network (PSTN). By transmitting the voice data over the Internet, VoIP offers clear benefits over the PSTN calling service, including improved quality of service, high-fidelity codecs, and lower monetary costs. As a result, network operators are actively promoting VoIP to modern Android smartphones [1–3], with the latest VoLTE (Voice over LTE) and VoWiFi (or Wi-Fi Calling) schemes being deployed.

Existing works on Android VoIP security, however, are far from comprehensive. They focused either on the weaknesses of VoIP network infrastructure, e.g., the insecure deployment of VoIP protocols at the network service providers' side,

C. Maurice et al. (Eds.): DIMVA 2020, LNCS 12223, pp. 110–131, 2020.
https://doi.org/10.1007/978-3-030-52683-2_6

or on the privacy concerns of third-party VoIP apps. Notably, Li et al. [4] and Kim et al. [5] discovered multiple vulnerabilities in VoLTE's both control- and data-plane functions, and Xie et al. [6] uncovered four vulnerabilities in operational Wi-Fi calling services. Regarding Android VoIP's client-side security, only the privacy risks of some VoIP apps were tested [7,8], e.g., whether their traffic are encrypted with SSL/TLS. It is thus unclear whether Android's VoIP integration at the operating system level are secure or not.

In this paper, we conduct the first study to systematically analyze Android VoIP's (in)security at the system level. Our study begins with a demystification of Android VoIP's protocol stack and its attack surfaces. Specifically, we study VoIP-related Android system code to identify VoIP components and their implementations, including SIP (Session Initiation Protocol) via the `nist-sip` library, SDP (Session Description Protocol) via `gov.nist.javax.sdp`, RTP (Real-time Transport Protocol) via `librtp-jni.so`, codecs via `libstagefright`, and SIP user agent via the system phone and dialer apps. Furthermore, we identify all the four potential attack surfaces that allow physical, local, remote, and nearby attacks against Android VoIP.

With these components and their attack surfaces in mind, we propose a novel vulnerability assessment approach that assembles on-device Intent/API fuzzing, network-side packet fuzzing, and targeted code auditing. First, we perform Android Intent and system API fuzzing to comprehensively fuzz the local surface. Second, we set up a unique VoIP testbed to perform three protocol fuzzings that mutate different fields in SIP, SDP, and RTP protocols either directly from a user agent or through a Man-In-The-Middle proxy. Lastly, we combine automatic fuzzing tests with targeted code auditing, including log-driven and protocol specification based auditing, to eventually determine vulnerabilities.

By periodically fuzzing VoIP components on the recent Android OS from version 7.0 to 9.0 over two years, we have discovered a total of nine zero-day vulnerabilities, eight of which are system vulnerabilities and have been confirmed by Google with bug bounty awards. Two-thirds of these vulnerabilities can be exploited by a network-side adversary, which suggests that Android VoIP's major risks come from the remote and nearby attack surfaces. Moreover, six of nine vulnerabilities' severity levels were rated by Google Android security team as high or critical (the most two serious levels), which implies that most of Android VoIP vulnerabilities are serious. The incurred security consequences include denying voice calls, caller ID spoofing, unauthorized call operations, and remote code execution. Furthermore, we uncover a new root cause, incompatible processing between VoIP and PSTN calls, that leads to six VoIP vulnerabilities and requires developers' extra attention in their future design and implementation.

To summarize, we have made the following contributions in this paper:

- The first demystification of Android VoIP's protocol stack and all its four attack surfaces (Sect. 3);
- A novel approach that assembles on-device Intent/API fuzzing, network-side packet fuzzing, and targeted code auditing (Sect. 4);

– New and comprehensive vulnerability assessment results, with nine zero-day
  vulnerabilities analyzed and their root causes uncovered (Sect. 5 and Sect. 6).

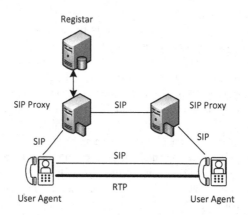

Fig. 1. A typical network infrastructure of SIP.

2   Background

Before presenting our work, we first introduce the necessary background on VoIP
and Android in this section.

2.1   VoIP Background

Android VoIP mainly uses the SIP (Session Initiation Protocol) protocol, which
was drafted by IETF in RFC 3261 [9]. As a VoIP signaling protocol, SIP provides a mechanism for one or more participants to create, modify, and terminate
sessions. Fig. 1 presents a typical network infrastructure of SIP, which consists
of the following components:

– User Agent (UA): A SIP user agent is a logical network node of SIP, which is
  responsible for creating, sending, and receiving SIP messages and maintains
  a SIP session.
– Proxy Server: A SIP proxy server helps deliver SIP messages between different
  user agents. It can also perform routing control and check the integrity of SIP
  messages.
– Registrar Server: A SIP registrar server is used for accepting SIP REGISTER
  requests from user agents, and places the location information it receives in
  those requests.

Similar to HTTP, SIP is a text-based protocol. It employs SDP (Session Description Protocol) to describe session contents. A typical SIP message can be an INVITE, REGISTER, OPTIONS, BYE, or CANCEL request. One important field in the SIP header is the SIP URI (Unified Resource Identifier), which represents the sender or receiver address. A SIP URI is in this format: `sip:user_name@server_ip_address`, e.g., `sip:anonymous@192.168.8.151`.

A SIP call involves three phases: the initial signaling phase, the conversation phase, and the end signaling phase. The INVITE and BYE requests are used in the two signaling phases. During the conversation phase, two calling parties exchange audio/video streams using the codecs that are negotiated via RTP (Real Transmission Protocol) [10].

2.2   Android Background

On Android, each application, no matter a system or a third-party app, runs in its own app sandbox [11]. Different apps communicate with each other through a new IPC (Inter-Process Communication) channel called Binder-based *Intent*. Each app has its own private data and requires permissions to access system's resources. For example, systems VoIP apps have the `RECORD_AUDIO` and `CALL_PRIVILEGES` permissions.

There are four kinds of Android components, including the user interface based `Activity`, the long-running `Service`, the event-triggered `Broadcast Receiver`, and the database-like `Content Provider`. Although the Intent-based inter-component communication (ICC [12]) enables flexible code and data sharing across different components, it also brings a widely spreading threat called *component hijacking* [13,14]. By sending a crafted (malicious) Intent message to an *exported* component that reserves dangerous permissions or sensitive data, an adversary could misuse the permissions [15,16], manipulate private data [13,17]. In this paper, besides system-level vulnerabilities, we also uncover one component hijacking vulnerability in a popular VoIP application.

3   Demystifying Android VoIP

In this section, we demystify Android VoIP's implementation and all its four attack surfaces. To the best of our knowledge, we are the first to give this demystification.

3.1   Android VoIP's Protocol Stack

By studying Android's source code, we are able to depict its implementation of VoIP protocol at different layers. Figure 2 highlights Android VoIP's protocol stack in the gray color. Starting from the bottom layer, the stack consists of the following components:

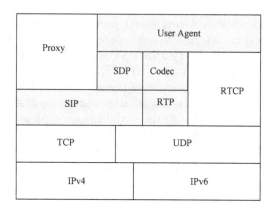

Fig. 2. Android's integration of VoIP protocol stack.

- *SIP (Session Initiation Protocol):* Android's SIP implementation directly uses the `nist-sip` library, which was developed by National Institute of Science of Technology (NIST). It is a purely Java based SIP implementation, and provides API classes (e.g., `SipSession` and `SipProfile`) via the `android.net.sip` package.
- *SDP (Session Description Protocol):* Similar to SIP, Android's SDP also uses the NIST implementation (`gov.nist.javax.sdp`), and provides a hidden API class called `SdpSessionDescription`.
- *RTP (Real-time Transport Protocol):* Android implements RTP in a C/C++ dynamic link library called `librtp-jni.so`. It also provides a few API classes via the `android.net.rtp` package.
- *Audio or Video Codec:* Android VoIP supports only a handful of codecs, including PCM (Pulse-Code Modulation) type A and type U codec, AMR (Adaptive Multi-Rate) codec, and GSM EFR (Enhanced Full Rate) codec. Supporting these codecs relies on `libstagefright`.
- *SIP UA (User Agent):* Android VoIP implements its UA into the system phone app (`com.android.phone`). It is a high-privilege app under the Linux user group of `radio`. Hence, it can not only access typical phone-related permissions (e.g., accessing user contacts and making a phone call) but also low-level resources in the Telephone Manager and Radio Interface Layer (RIL). Additionally, displaying VoIP caller numbers is handled by the system dialer app (`com.android.dialer`).

It is worth noting that these VoIP components are not isolated in Android. Indeed, a VoIP session on Android always initiates from the SIP UA and goes through all those protocol and codec components. As a result, by targeting at the system phone and dialer apps, we can trigger Android VoIP's code flows and test the entire Android VoIP components.

3.2 Android VoIP's Attack Surfaces

Figure 3 shows all the potential surfaces that Android VoIP could be attacked:

- *Physical Attack Surface:* If an adversary could physically access a victim user's phone, he is able to set the phone's VoIP configuration without the authorization, causing a security breach. Although such attack is rare, it still needs to be considered, as we will demonstrate in Sect. 5.
- *Local Attack Surface:* Since the system phone app is a privileged app, it can access not only permission-protected resources but also system interfaces in Telephone Manager and Radio Interface Layer (RIL). An on-device malicious app thus can attack the phone app via the IPC communication to obtain VoIP-related privileges.
- *Remote Attack Surface:* Since the phone needs to communicate with outside via IP and mobile communication, it brings another attack surface. Specifically, a network-side adversary can send crafted payloads in SIP/SDP/RTP packets to exploit Android VoIP components remotely, causing remote denial of service and code execution.
- *Nearby Attack Surface:* With the popularity of HFP (Hand-Free Profile) devices, a user may use a Bluetooth earphone or a Bluetooth car kit during her VoIP call. These nearby Bluetooth devices bring a new attack surface. On one hand, the malicious payload in VoIP traffic may reach to the system Bluetooth components. On the other hand, the malicious traffic from Bluetooth devices may also attack VoIP components.

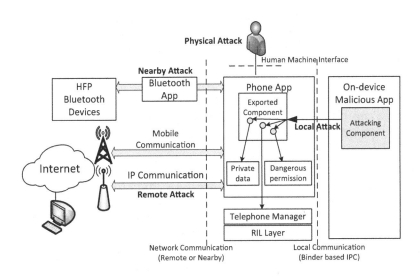

Fig. 3. Android VoIP's four attack surfaces: physical, local, remote, and nearby.

4 Methodology

After understanding Android's VoIP integration and its attack surfaces, we propose a novel approach to systematically assessing Android VoIP's vulnerabilities. In this approach, we first automatically test Android VoIP components via on-device and network-side fuzzing, and further combine them with targeted code auditing to eventually determine vulnerabilities. In this section, we present these three modules, among which network-side packet fuzzing is the most special one.

4.1 On-Device Intent/API Fuzzing

To comprehensively fuzz the local surface of Android VoIP components, we perform both Android Intent fuzzing and system API fuzzing. Specifically, Intent fuzzing aims to test exported components in VoIP system apps, while system API fuzzing tries to discover unprotected VoIP system service interfaces. In this subsection, we first introduce the fuzzing framework before present its two detailed fuzzing methods.

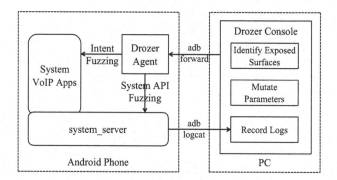

Fig. 4. The on-device fuzzing framework, with not only the conventional Intent fuzzing but also the creative system API fuzzing based on Java reflection.

On-Device Fuzzing Framework. As shown in Fig. 4, we develop an on-device fuzzing framework based on Drozer [18]. We use a drozer console on PC to control the fuzzing process on a test phone via its drozer agent. We deliver fuzzing commands through Android's `adb forward` command and receive fuzzing logs through the `adb logcat` command. For both Intent and system API fuzzing, we perform these three steps: identifying exposed surfaces, mutating parameters, and recording logs.

On-Device Intent Fuzzing. In the Intent fuzzing, exposed surfaces are VoIP apps' `exported` components that can be accessed by any other third-party apps on the same phone. We identify these exported components by analyzing component information in the app's `AndroidManifest.xml` file. To mutate Intent parameters, we try both empty (i.e., `null`) parameters and the parameters that satisfy a component's `data` schemes (e.g., `content://` and `vk.voip`).

On-Device System API Fuzzing. In the system API fuzzing, exposed surfaces are those unprotected system service interfaces. We identify them by using Java reflection to invoke Android `ServiceManager`'s `listServices` function, which can list not only all the available system service interfaces but also their accepted parameter types. We then launch targeted fuzzing against these exposed service interfaces according to their parameter types.

4.2   Network-Side Packet Fuzzing

To test Android VoIP's network components, we need to launch network-side packet fuzzing. In this subsection, we first introduce our testbed for network-side fuzzing, and then present three protocol fuzzing and two fuzzing modes.

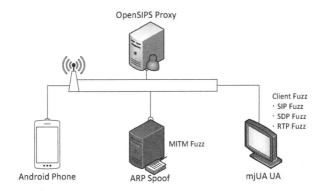

Fig. 5. Our testbed for network-side fuzzing.

Setting up the Testbed. Figure 5 shows the architecture of our testbed for network-side fuzzing, where an Android phone acts as the victim user and a mjSIP-based User Agent mimics the adversary. Note that mjSIP [19] is a command-line based SIP UA implementation with flexible options. Additionally, we use OpenSIPS [20] to establish a SIP proxy server, and connect all these three parties in the same Wi-Fi network.

Fuzzing Different Protocols. We leverage mjSIP (`uac.sh`) to fuzz all the three protocols in the Android VoIP stack (see Sect. 3), namely SIP, SDP, and RTP fuzzing. Listing 1.1 shows the mjUA commands used in our three fuzzing methods. Additionally, we install an AutoAnswer app in the Android phone to automate the entire fuzzing process.

- *SIP Fuzzing:* In this fuzzing, we mutate the user name and server name in a SIP URI name. For example, we can use a long SIP name to launch

Listing 1.1. A list of the mjUA commands used in our fuzzing.

```
$ ./uac.sh -h
  -f <file>: specifies a configuration file (sdp fuzzing)
  -c <call_to>: config the victim SIP URI
  -y <secs>: could be used as fuzz interval time
  --display-name <str>: display name (sip fuzzing)
  --user <user> : user name (sip fuzzing)
  --send-file <file> the specified audio file (rtp fuzzing)
```

Listing 1.2. The media description we leverage for SDP fuzzing.

```
# Media descriptors:
# One or more 'media' (or 'media_desc') parameters specify for each media:
    media type, port, and protocol/codec.
# Zero or more 'media_spec' params can be used to specify attributes: codec
    name, sample rate, and frame size.
# Examples:
#   media=audio 4000 rtp/avp
#   media_spec=audio 0 PCMU 8000 160
#   media_spec=audio 8 PCMA 8000 160
#   media_spec=audio 101 G726-32 8000 80
#   media_spec=audio 102 G726-24 8000 60
#   media=video 3002 rtp/avp
#   media_spec=video 101
```

the fuzzing: `$./uac.sh --user <long_SIP_name>`. Additionally, we can also change the display SIP name using the `display-name` option, as shown in Listing 1.1.

- *SDP Fuzzing:* In this fuzzing, we mutate different fields in the SDP's media description. We launch the SDP fuzzing by preparing variants of a mjSIP configuration file: `$./uac.sh -f configFile.cfg`. The media format of this configuration file is listed in Listing 1.2. Specifically, we can change the "media" and "media_spec" parameters in multiple ways. For example, we can use different media type, port, and protocol/codec for the "media" parameter and specify different media attributes for the "media_spec" parameter.

- *RTP Fuzzing:* To fuzz RTP codecs, we generate `PCMU/PCMA/AMR/GSM-EFR` codec corpuses and send them to the Android phone one by one via mjUA's `send-file` option. The detailed fuzzing code is shown in Fig. 6. Specifically, we first prepare a seed file called `sample-gsm-8000.gsm`, and use this seed file to randomly generate different audio files (`fuzz_$i.tone`).

Direct Fuzzing and MITM Fuzzing. As shown in Fig. 5, we provide two fuzzing modes: direct fuzzing from the UA and MITM (Man-In-The-Middle) fuzzing. To enable the MITM fuzzing, we leverage this Ethercap [21] command to perform an ARP spoof for constructing a transparent proxy: `sudo ettercap -T -V hex -F rtpfuzz.ef -M arp /192.168.8.152// /192.168.8.191//`. With such a MITM proxy, it is convenient for us to leverage existing VoIP traffic for mutation. For example, we can mutate RTP headers by setting an Ethercap filter, which can specify which packet to filter and how to manipulate. The mutated new packets will be then forwarded to the Android phone.

```
1 ⏸!/bin/bash
2
3 ITER=$1
4 SEED=fuzztone/sample-gsm-8000.gsm
5
6 for i in $(seq $ITER)
7 do
8    # cat $SEED | radamsa -m bf,br,sr -p bu > fuzztone/fuzz_$i.tone
9    echo $i
10   ./uac.sh --send-file fuzztone/fuzz_$i.tone -f fuzz_config/amr.cfg --send-only
11   # ./uac.sh --send-file blankfile -f fuzz_config/amr.cfg --send-only
12   adb shell log -p e -t fuzzrtp fuzz_$i
13   adb logcat -c
14   declare -i i=i+1
15 done
16
```

Fig. 6. A code illustration of our RTP/Codec fuzzing.

4.3   Targeted Code Auditing

To eventually determine vulnerabilities, it is necessary to launch manual code auditing after the automatic fuzzing. In this subsection, we propose two *targeted* code auditing methods that leverage fuzzing logs and protocol specification to reduce manual efforts.

Table 1. Zero-day Android VoIP vulnerabilities discovered in our work.

Discovery method	ID	CVE/AID	Attack vector	Vulnerable entry component	Affected Android	Severity level	Security consequence
On-device Fuzzing	V1	H1-#386144	Local	com.vkontakte.android	All	Low	Triggering a call without user's consent
	V2	CVE-2017-11042	Local	org.codeaurora.ims	≤ 7.1.2	Moderate	Unauthorized setting of call transfer
Network-side Fuzzing	V3	A-31823540-1	Remote	com.android.dialer	≤ 7.1.1	High	Undeniable VoIP call spam
	V4	CVE-2017-0394	Remote	com.android.phone	≤ 7.1.1	High	Remote DoS once accepting a call
	V5	CVE-2018-9475	Remote[a]	com.android.bluetooth	≤ 9.0	Critical	Remote code execution due to overflow
	V6	CVE-2019-9311	Remote[a]	com.android.bluetooth	≤ 9.0	Moderate	Remote DoS once receiving a call
Code Auditing	V7	CVE-2016-6763	Physical	com.android.phone	≤ 7.0	High	Sensitive data leak; Permanent DoS
	V8	A-31823540-2	Remote	com.android.dialer	≤ 7.1.1	High	Caller ID spoofing
	V9	A-32623587	Remote	com.android.dialer	≤ 7.1.1	High	Caller ID spoofing

[a] These two remote vulnerabilities could be triggered only when the phone is connected with a *nearby* Bluetooth HFP device.

Log-Driven Auditing. Both on-device and network-side generate a number of fuzzing logs. We thus leverage them for a log-driven code auditing. Specifically, for a process crash produced by our fuzzing, we can collect either a Java exception for Java components (e.g., `IllegalStateException: Reject SDP: no suitable codecs`) or a fault status for native code (e.g., `pid: 8112, tid: 8161, name, XXX, signal 11 (SIG SEGV), fault addr: YYY`). Moreover, we can obtain the detailed location where the code encounters an error, e.g., `createAnswer(SipAudioCall.java:805)` and `libbluetooth_jni.so(clccRes- ponseNative+30)`. We then use these code locations to driven our auditing.

Protocol Specification Based Auditing. PSTN and VoIP protocols have some specifications that we can leverage for a targeted auditing. For example, special attributes, e.g., the call transfer splitting character "&" and the phone number prefix "phone-context", in PSTN may have different behaviors in VoIP, which we will illustrate later. We then leverage this kind of protocol specification differences for an efficient auditing.

5 Evaluation

In this section, we present our results of fuzzing VoIP components on the recent Android OS from version 7.0 to 9.0. Since this is a periodic fuzzing effort (i.e., not a single experiment) over a period of around two years, we focus on reporting our findings in this paper. As shown in Table 1, we have discovered a total of nine zero-day vulnerabilities, eight of which are system vulnerabilities and have been confirmed by Google with bug bounty awards. Table 1 lists the meta information of these vulnerabilities, including the entry components where vulnerabilities can be triggered from, the severity level rated by Google Android Security team, and the corresponding security consequence.

5.1 Vulnerabilities Discovered via On-Device Fuzzing

By performing on-device fuzzing, we find that Android VoIP generally protects its local attack surface, with only one vulnerability discovered by the system API fuzzing and no vulnerable component identified by the Intent fuzzing. To also demonstrate the effectiveness of our Intent fuzzing, we test and identify a VoIP vulnerability in a very popular app called VK[1], which has cumulatively over 100 million installs on Google Play.

V1: Maliciously Triggering a VoIP call in the VK App. The VK app (version 5.13) was identified by us to contain an exported component, `LinkRedirActivity`, which accepts an Intent with the `content://` scheme and with the `vk.voip` data type. Surprisingly, `LinkRedirActivity` would directly make a VoIP call to a VK user account specified by the `vk.voip` data. As a

---

[1] https://play.google.com/store/apps/details?id=com.vkontakte.android.

result, an on-device malicious app can send a crafted Intent to trigger a VoIP call without user's consent and even when the phone screen is turned off. More seriously, the victim user could be eavesdropped if the callee VK account was set to an account under the attacker's control, the idea of which is similar to the login CSRF (Cross-Site Request Forgery) [22] attack in web security. To patch this vulnerability, VK added a user confirmation dialog before `LinkRedirActivity` can make any VoIP call.

V2: Unauthorized Call Transfer in the IMS Interface. Android has a system service called QtilMS, which is for IMS (IP Multimedia Subsystem) related functionality and implemented by Qualcomm. However, our system API fuzzing found that QtilMS exposed two VoIP APIs, `SendCallTransfer Request` and `SendCallForwardUncondTimer`, to any third-party app. Normally, these two system APIs are only accessible to those with the `CALL_PRIVILEGES` permission. However, our fuzzing shows that any app without the permission can also invoke the APIs, because no checking is enforced by QtilMS. As a result, an on-device malicious app can misuse those two privileged APIs to set unauthorized call transfer. To mitigate this, Qualcomm added the permission check for the access of those two QtilMS APIs.

5.2 Vulnerabilities Discovered via Network-Side Fuzzing

Compared to the on-device fuzzing, our network-side fuzzing discovered more VoIP vulnerabilities, as shown in Table 1. This suggests that Android VoIP's major risks come from the remote and nearby attack surfaces. In this subsection, we first introduce two vulnerabilities that can be exploited remotely, and then present another two vulnerabilities that involve the nearby Bluetooth-based HFP (Hands-Free Profile) devices.

V3: Undeniable VoIP Call Spam Due to Long SIP Name. We discovered this vulnerability through a SIP fuzzing test using the long SIP name: `$./uac.sh --user <long_SIP_name> <victim's sip account>`. As shown in Fig. 7, the callee user's VoIP phone interface could be filled up by the very long SIP name, e.g., 1,043 characters in our test case. In this scenario, the victim user cannot answer or reject a call, because no button is shown up. If the adversary frequently launches this undeniable VoIP call spam, the victim has to disable the network connection or shutdown her phone. We call this kind of denial of service attack "VoIP call bomb", as similar to SMS bomb [23]. To defend against this attack, Google restricts the length of SIP user name.

V4: Remote DoS in Telephony Once Accepting a Call. We discovered this vulnerability through the SDP fuzzing using a malformed configuration file: `$./uac.sh -f malformed.cfg`. As shown in Fig. 8, it can crash the victim's phone process once she accepts the call, causing a remote DoS (denial of service). Our fuzzing identified two weaknesses in the affected Telephony module, either of which could be exploited for the attack. One way is to use a codec that is not in the supported codec list (see Sect. 3.1). For example, if we add

Fig. 7. A demo of exploiting V3.   **Fig. 8.** A demo of exploiting V4.

"media_spec=audio 102 G726-24 8000 60" into the malformed.cfg file, the phone process crashes with an illegal state exception "Reject SDP: no suitable codecs". The other way is to use the invalid SDP description. For example, if we add "media=AAAA 4000" into the malformed.cfg file, the phone process crashes with an illegal SDP argument exception. To patch these weaknesses, Google added exception catch statements for those two unhandled exceptions.

The Model of Bluetooth-Involved VoIP Vulnerabilities. As shown in Table 1, the V5 and V6 vulnerabilities could be triggered only when the phone is connected with a nearby Bluetooth device. Hence, we first explain the model of these Bluetooth-involved VoIP vulnerabilities before presenting their specific weaknesses. Figure 9 depicts such a vulnerability model. Specifically, mobile phone acts as an AG (Audio Gateway) in the HFP (Hands-Free Profile) communication, and Bluetooth earphone or Bluetooth car kit is the HF (Hand Free) device. When a remote attacker makes a VoIP call to a phone connected with a HF device, the HF device will query all the call information (e.g., caller number) from the phone via HFP's AT+CLCC command. As a result, the VoIP call input will be delivered to `libbluetooth-jni` for processing. A vulnerability could happen if it cannot process an unexpected VoIP call input (e.g., a long user name), because Bluetooth may consider only the traditional, instead of VoIP, phone call.

V5: Remote Code Execution Due to Stack Buffer Overflow. Both V5 and V6 suffer from the unexpected long user name (or caller number) in a VoIP call. For V5, the vulnerable code locates in the function of preparing CLCC response, as shown in Listing 1.3. It tries to return the caller number in the

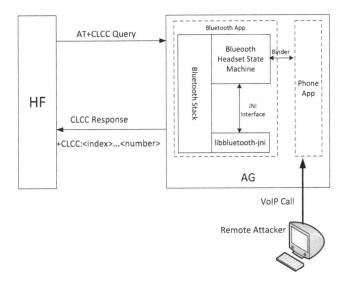

Fig. 9. A model of Bluetooth-involved VoIP vulnerabilities.

Listing 1.3. The vulnerable code of stack buffer overflow in V5.

```
bt_status_t HeadsetInterface::ClccResponse(...) {
  ...
  if (number) {
    size_t rem_bytes = sizeof(ag_res.str) - res_strlen;
    char dialnum[sizeof(ag_res.str)]; //length is 513 bytes
    size_t newidx = 0;
    if (type == ADDRTYPE_INTERNATIONAL && *number != '+')
      dialnum[newidx++] = '+';
  }

  for (size_t i = 0; number[i] != 0; i++) {
    if (utl_isdialchar(number[i]))
      dialnum[newidx++] = number[i]; //Overflow when > 513
  }
  ...
}
```

CLCC response, but uses only a 513-byte array (`dialnum`) to store it. A stack buffer overflow thus happens when a caller number with more than 513 bytes is inputted. This vulnerability allows an adversary to overwrite the return address of the `ClccResponse` function, causing remote code execution. For example, the adversary can launch the exploit using this command: `$./uac.sh --user $(python -c 'print ''8''*1055')`.

V6: Remote DoS in Bluetooth Once Receiving a Call. This vulnerability is similar to V5, but it is triggered when the call state changes, i.e., `BTHF_CALL_INCOMING` in Listing 1.4. In this example, developers also did not expect the long caller number in a VoIP call. Specifically, the return value of the first `snprintf` statement can be greater than `sizeof(ag_res.str)`'s 513 bytes. Since the `sizeof(ag_res.str)-xx` variable now is an unsigned negative

Listing 1.4. The vulnerable code of integer underflow in V6.

```
case BTHF_CALL_STATE_INCOMING:
  if (num_active || num_held)
    res = BTA_AG_CALL_WAIT_RES;
  else
    res = BTA_AG_IN_CALL_RES;

  if (number) {
    int xx = 0;
    // number (xx) might be longer than sizeof(ag_res.str)
    xx = snprintf(ag_res.str, sizeof(ag_res.str), "\"+%s\""
          ,number);
    ag_res.num = type;
    if (res == BTA_AG_CALL_WAIT_RES)
      snprintf(&ag_res.str[xx], sizeof(ag_res.str)-xx,",%d"
          ,type); //a negative value becomes a large integer
  }
  break;
```

number, it becomes a very large positive integer, which eventually triggers the `abort` checking statement and causes remote DoS. Compared to the DoS in V4, triggering DoS in V6 requires a Bluetooth device connected, but just needs to receive, rather than answer, a call.

To patch V5 and V6, Google restricted the length of caller number inputted in the Bluetooth module.

5.3   Vulnerabilities Discovered via Code Auditing

In this subsection, we present the vulnerabilities that are dedicatedly discovered by our targeted code auditing. Specifically, we are able to use protocol specification based auditing to discover these vulnerabilities, since their root causes are the inconsistency between VoIP's specification and Android's traditional phone call processing.

V7: Data Leak and Permanent DoS Due to Path Traversal. In this vulnerability, we exploit the inconsistency between SIP URI and Android/Linux file directory. Specifically, SIP URI treats ".." and "/" as normal characters, whereas they are special characters in the Android's file name convention. As a result, a path traversal vulnerability appears in the code shown in Listing 1.5. The directory that contains the serialized ".pobj" SIP profile file is named in this format: "sip_user@server_ip", e.g., "alice@171.11.160.202". An attacker thus can misuse these two names to manipulate the path of `mProfileDirectory`. For example, by physically setting "sip_user" and "server_ip" in the format of Fig. 10(a), `mProfileDirectory` becomes "/data/data/com.android.phone/files/alice/@SomeSite/../../../../../../sdcard/" and leaks the sensitive SIP profile file to the public SD card. A permanent DoS could also happen

Listing 1.5. Simplified vulnerable code of path traversal in V7.

```
File f = new File(mProfileDirectory + p.getProfileName())
File f = new File(new File(root, name), ".pobj")
```

if "server_ip" is set to overwrite another system app's file, e.g., mmssms.db shown in Fig. 10(b). Due to this fake mmssms.db file, the real one cannot be created and thus deny any SMS functionality. Only a factory reset can recover the phone.

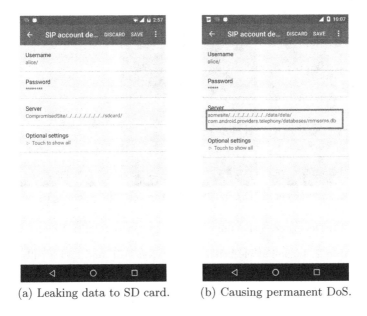

(a) Leaking data to SD card.   (b) Causing permanent DoS.

Fig. 10. Demo screenshots of exploiting the vulnerability V7.

V8: Caller ID Spoofing Due to Mis-parsing "&". The last two vulnerabilities, V8 and V9, are due to the inconsistency between SIP URI and PSTN (Public Switched Telephone Network) number format. In vulnerability V8, it is related to a special character "&" in the caller number. For a caller number with "&", the system dialer app treats the number before "&" as the actual calling number and the number after "&" as the call transfer number, according to PSTN's convention. However, the dialer does not consider an incoming VoIP call and performs the same for a VoIP call number. As a result, an adversary can mimic any phone number by simply adding a "&" character in the end, causing a caller ID spoofing attack. For example, the attacker can mimic the emergency number by setting the SIP name as "911&", as shown in Fig. 11(a). He can also spoof as a contact number of the victim if the attacker knows the number, and the dialer will display the name and profile photo of the spoofed contact, as shown in Fig. 11(b).

V9: Caller ID Spoofing Due to "phone-context". Another inconsistency between SIP URI and PSTN number format is the "phone-context" parameter [24], which can be used to specify the prefix of a phone number. For example, in PSTN's convention, the number "650253000;phone-context=+1" is equivalent

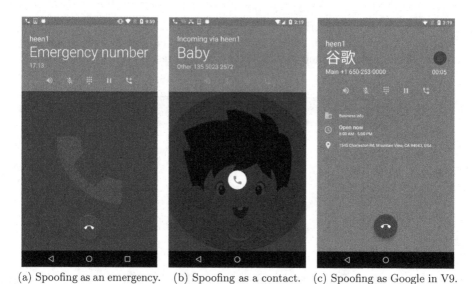

(a) Spoofing as an emergency.   (b) Spoofing as a contact.   (c) Spoofing as Google in V9.

Fig. 11. Demo screenshots of exploiting the vulnerability V8 and V9.

Table 2. Incompatible behaviors between VoIP and PSTN calls.

ID	Attribute	Incompatible behaviors	
V3	Number length	513+ bytes in SIP URI	≤ 513 in PSTN no
V5	Number length	513+ bytes in SIP URI	≤ 513 in PSTN no
V6	Number length	513+ bytes in SIP URI	≤ 513 in PSTN no
V7	".../" character	Part of SIP URI	Parent dir in Linux
V8	"& " character	Part of SIP URI	Call transfer in PSTN
V9	"phone-context"	Part of SIP URI	Prefix for PSTN no

to "+1650253000", where the value of "phone-context" becomes the prefix of the number. However, such convention should not apply to VoIP calls, which is unfortunately ignored by the dialer app. As a result, an adversary can intentionally set the caller number as "650253000;phone-context=+1", and the dialer app will interpret it as "+1650253000" and display it as Google's call, which is clearly presented in Fig. 11(c). Note that such mapping from "+1650253000" to Google is automatically performed by Android's CallerID mechanism [25], which tries to correlate well-known phone numbers or mark spam numbers in the normal scenario. But here it worsens the severity instead.

6   A New Root Cause

Besides the vulnerability-level cause analysis in Sect. 5, we try to uncover the root causes underneath those vulnerabilities. Among the nine vulnerabilities we discovered, three of them have previously known root causes, i.e., no protection of exported components in V1 [13,15], no checking of system APIs in V2 [26,27], and missed error handling in V4 [28]. For the rest of six vulnerabilities, we identify a new root cause that is dedicated to Android VoIP and not known before.

We call this root cause "incompatible processing between VoIP and PSTN calls". Specifically, since both VoIP calls and traditional PSTN calls are handled by the Android telephony system, there exist some incompatible processing behaviors between VoIP and PSTN calls. Such incompatibility is the root cause of six VoIP vulnerabilities we identified, as summarized in Table 2. For example, for the attribute of phone number length, VoIP SIP can use more than 513 bytes, whereas only less than 513 bytes is used in the traditional PSTN phone number. Other examples are the special characters of "../", "&", and "phone-context", which could be treated as a part of the URI in VoIP SIP. But they originally have special meanings in the Linux and PSTN specification, causing incorrect processing in the Android VoIP code. Understanding these incompatible behaviors and other potential incompatibility between VoIP and PSTN calls can help us further improve Android VoIP security. We thus call for VoIP developers' extra attention in their future design and implementation.

7   Related Work

In this section, we present the closely related research on VoIP security, protocol fuzzing, and Android dynamic testing.

VoIP Security. There were some research [29–33] to explore the general security issues of VoIP, e.g., denial of service, eavesdropping, and call hijacking, since over ten years ago. In particular, the VOIPSA organization gave a clear taxonomy [34] of VoIP's threats. Recently, with the high popularity of Android phones and mobile networks, researchers started to investigate the security of VoIP apps and network infrastructure in the real world. They have identified the privacy risks in some VoIP apps [7,8] and infrastructure vulnerabilities in several mobile carriers [4–6]. In particular, both Li et al. [4] and Kim et al. [5] identify a number of serious vulnerabilities in mobile carriers' VoLTE networks, including free data, caller spoofing, over-billing, and denial-of-service. Compared with all these works, we are the first to systematically study the security of system-level VoIP implementation on Android, with 8 zero-day vulnerabilities identified and confirmed by Google.

Protocol Fuzzing. Our network-side fuzzing in Sect. 4.2 belongs to the general category of network protocol fuzzing. In the classical book of *Fuzzing: Brute Force Vulnerability Discovery* [35], the authors explained network protocol fuzzing on both Windows and Unix. Regarding the stateful network protocol fuzzing, SNOOZE [36] and Prospex [37] are two pioneer systems. Auto-Fuzz [38] is an open-source network protocol fuzzing framework. There are also some fuzzers specific to certain protocols, such as for OPC protocol [39] and TLS libraries [40,41]. Moreover, KiF [42] is a dedicated SIP fuzzer that was released in 2007, but unfortunately, it does not apply to Android phones. Very recently, Pham et al. proposed AFLNet [43], a greybox fuzzer based on the popular AFL (American Fuzzy Lop) to specifically fuzz network protocol implementations. In this paper, our network-side fuzzing tool is the first Android VoIP fuzzer for SIP, SDP, and RTP fuzzing.

Android Dynamic Testing. Our on-device fuzzing in Sect. 4.1 is related to the general Android dynamic testing [44–48]. For example, SMV-Hunter [44] and FileCross [45] leveraged Android adb commands to dynamically test Android apps' security vulnerabilities. AppIntent [46], further instrumented Android operating system for the effective dynamic testing of Android apps. Two crowdsourcing apps, UpDroid [47] and NetMon [48], were recently proposed to leverage crowds' user interaction for dynamic app tests in the wild. Besides general Android dynamic testing, the closest work to our Intent fuzzing is IntentFuzzer [49], which also leveraged Drozer for Intent fuzzing. The difference is that our fuzzing targets at VoIP components, instead of the permission-protected components in IntentFuzzer [49]. Additionally, buzzer (Binder Fuzzer) [50] analyzed input validation vulnerabilities associated with Android system services, which is similar to our System API fuzzing except that we use Java reflection to effectively identify service interfaces and their parameters. Furthermore, our on-device fuzzing is an unified framework that performs both Intent and System API fuzzing.

8   Conclusion

In this paper, we conducted the first study to systematically investigate the (in)security of Android's VoIP integration at the system level. We began with a demystification of Android VoIP's protocol stack and all its four attack surfaces. We then proposed a novel vulnerability assessment approach that first employs on-device Intent/API fuzzing and network-side packet fuzzing to automatically test Android VoIP components, and further combines them with targeted code auditing to eventually determine vulnerabilities. By periodically fuzzing VoIP components on the recent Android OS from version 7.0 to 9.0 over two years, we discovered a total of nine zero-day vulnerabilities, two-thirds of which can be exploited by a network-side adversary. These vulnerabilities caused serious security consequences, including denying voice calls, caller ID spoofing, unauthorized call operations, and remote code execution. Finally, we uncovered a new root cause, incompatible processing between VoIP and PSTN calls, that leads to six VoIP vulnerabilities and requires developers' extra attention in their future design and implementation.

References

1. T-Mobile: Android VoLTE settings by T-Mobile Support. https://support.t-mobile.com/docs/DOC-22754 (2019). Accessed
2. G.co.uk: VoLTE support in UK's networks (2019). https://www.4g.co.uk/what-is-volte/. Accessed
3. Summerson, C.: How to Enable Wi-Fi Calling on an Android Phone (2017). https://www.howtogeek.com/234608/how-to-enable-wi-fi-calling-on-an-android-phone/ (released))
4. Li, C.Y., Tu, G.H., Peng, C., Yuan, Z., Li, Y., Lu, S., Wang, X.: Insecurity of voice solution VoLTE in LTE mobile networks. In: Proceedings of the ACM CCS (2015)
5. Kim, H., et al.: Breaking and fixing VoLTE: exploiting hidden data channels and mis-implementations. In: Proceedings of ACM CCS (2015)
6. Xie, T., Tu, G.H., Li, C.Y., Peng, C., Li, J., Zhang, M.: The dark side of operational Wi-Fi calling services. In: Proceedings of the IEEE CNS (2018)
7. Azfar, A., Choo, K.K.R., Liu, L.: Android mobile VoIP apps: a survey and examination of their security and privacy. In: Electronic Commerce Research (2016)
8. Dargahi, T., Dehghantanha, A., Conti, M.: Forensics analysis of Android mobile VoIP apps. In: Contemporary Digital Forensic Investigations of Cloud and Mobile Applications (2017)
9. RFC 3261: SIP: Session Initiation Protocol (2002). https://tools.ietf.org/html/rfc3261 (released)
10. RFC 3550: RTP: A Transport Protocol for Real-Time Applications (2003). https://tools.ietf.org/html/rfc3550 (released)
11. Davi, L., Dmitrienko, A., Sadeghi, A., Winandy, M.: Privilege escalation attacks on Android. In: Proceedings of the Springer ISC (2010)
12. Octeau, D., et al.: Effective inter-component communication mapping in Android with Epicc: an essential step towards holistic security analysis. In: Proceedings of the USENIX Security (2013)
13. Lu, L., Li, Z., Wu, Z., Lee, W., Jiang, G.: CHEX: statically vetting Android apps for component hijacking vulnerabilities. In: Proceedings of the ACM CCS (2012)
14. Wu, D., Cheng, Y., Gao, D., Li, Y., Deng, R.H.: SCLib: a practical and lightweight defense against component hijacking in Android applications. In: Proceedings of the ACM CODASPY (2018)
15. Grace, M., Zhou, Y., Wang, Z., Jiang, X.: Systematic detection of capability leaks in stock Android smartphones. In: Proceedings of the ISOC NDSS (2012)
16. Bugiel, S., Davi, L., Dmitrienko, A., Fischer, T., Sadeghi, A., Shastry, B.: Towards taming privilege-escalation attacks on Android. In: Proceedings of the ISOC NDSS (2012)
17. Wu, D., Chang, R.K.C.: Indirect file leaks in mobile applications. In: Proceedings of the IEEE Mobile Security Technologies (MoST) (2015)
18. Lab, F.S.: Drozer: Comprehensive security and attack framework for Android (2019). https://labs.f-secure.com/tools/drozer/. Accessed
19. mjSIP: Homepage of mjSIP (2019). http://www.mjsip.org/mjua.html. Accessed
20. OpenSIPS: Homepage of OpenSIPS (2019). https://opensips.org/. Accessed
21. Ethercap: Ethercap (2019). https://www.ettercap-project.org/. Accessed
22. Detectify Knowledge Base: Login CSRF (2019). https://support.detectify.com/customer/portal/articles/1969819. Accessed
23. Boyd, J.: What Is an SMS Bomber? (2019). https://www.techwalla.com/articles/what-is-an-sms-bomber (released)

24. RFC 3966: The tel URI for Telephone Numbers (2004). https://tools.ietf.org/html/rfc3966 (released)
25. Google: Use caller ID & spam protection (2019). https://support.google.com/phoneapp/answer/3459196?hl=en. Accessed
26. Shao, Y., Ott, J., Chen, Q.A., Qian, Z., Mao, Z.M.: Kratos: discovering inconsistent security policy enforcement in the Android framework. In: NDSS (2016)
27. Aafer, Y., Huang, J., Sun, Y., Zhang, X., Li, N., Tian, C.: AceDroid: normalizing diverse Android access control checks for inconsistency detection. In: NDSS (2018)
28. Wu, D., Gao, D., Cheng, E.K.T., Cao, Y., Jiang, J., Deng, R.H.: Towards understanding Android system vulnerabilities: techniques and insights. In: Proceedings of the ACM AsiaCCS (2019)
29. Keromytis, A.D.: Voice-over-IP security: Research and practice. In IEEE Security & Privacy (2010)
30. Keromytis, A.D.: A comprehensive survey of voice over IP security research. In IEEE Communications Surveys and Tutorials (2012)
31. Birke, R., Mellia, M., Petracca, M.: Understanding VoIP from backbone measurements. In: Proceedings of the IEEE INFOCOM (2007)
32. McGann, S., Sicker, D.C.: An analysis of security threats and tools in SIP-based VoIP systems. In: Second VoIP Security Workshop (2005)
33. Butcher, D., Li, X., Guo, J.: Security challenge and defense in VoIP infrastructures. In: IEEE Transactions on Systems Man, and Cybernetics (2007)
34. VOIPSA: VoIP Security and Privacy Threat Taxonomy (2005). https://www.voipsa.org/Activities/VOIPSA_Threat_Taxonomy_0.1.pdf (released)
35. Sutton, M., Greene, A., Amini, P.: Fuzzing: Brute force vulnerability discovery (2007)
36. Banks, G., Cova, M., Felmetsger, V., Almeroth, K., Kemmerer, R., Vigna, G.: Snooze: toward a stateful network protocol fuzzer. In: Proceedings of the Springer ISC (2006)
37. Comparetti, P.M., Wondracek, G., Kruegel, C., Kirda, E.: Prospex: protocol specification extraction. In: Proceedings of the IEEE Symposium on Security and Privacy (2009)
38. Gorbunov, S., Rosenbloom, A.: AutoFuzz: automated network protocol fuzzing framework. J. Comput. Sci. Network Secur. **37**, 1152–1162 (2010)
39. Wang, T., Xiong, Q., Gao, H., Peng, Y., Dai, Z., Yi, S.: Design and implementation of fuzzing technology for OPC protocol. In: Proceedings of the International Conference on Intelligent Information Hiding and Multimedia Signal Processing (2013)
40. Ruiter, J., Poll, E.: Protocol state fuzzing of TLS implementations. In: Proceedings of the USENIX Security (2015)
41. Somorovsky, J.: Systematic fuzzing and testing of TLS libraries. In: Proceedings of the ACM CCS (2016)
42. Abdelnur, H.J., State, R., Festor, O.: Kif: A stateful SIP fuzzer. In: Proceedings of the ISOC IPTComm (2007)
43. Pham, V.T., Böhme, M., Roychoudhury, A.: AFLNet: a greybox fuzzer for network protocols. In: Proceedings of the IEEE International Conference on Software Testing, Verification and Validation (Testing Tools Track) (2020)
44. Sounthiraraj, D., Sahs, J., Greenwood, G., Lin, Z., Khan, L.: SMV-Hunter: Large scale, automated detection of SSL/TLS man-in-the-middle vulnerabilities in Android apps. In: Proceedings of the ISOC NDSS (2014)
45. Wu, D., Chang, R.K.C.: Analyzing Android Browser Apps for file:// Vulnerabilities. In: Proceedings of the Springer ISC (2014)

46. Yang, Z., Yang, M., Zhang, Y., Gu, G., Ning, P., Wang, X.: AppIntent: analyzing sensitive data transmission in Android for privacy leakage detection. In: Proceedings of the ACM CCS (2013)
47. Tang, X., Lin, Y., Wu, D., Gao, D.: Towards dynamically monitoring Android applications on non-rooted devices in the wild. In: Proceedings of the ACM WiSec (2018)
48. Wu, D., Gao, D., Chang, R.K.C., He, E., Cheng, E.K.T., Deng, R.H.: Understanding open ports in Android applications: discovery, diagnosis, and security assessment. In: Proceedings of the ISOC NDSS (2019)
49. Yang, K., Zhou, L., Wang, Y., Zhuge, J., Duan, H.: IntentFuzzer: detecting capability leaks of Android applications. In: Proceedings of the ACM AsiaCCS (2014)
50. Cao, C., Gao, N., Liu, P., Xiang, J.: Towards analyzing the input validation vulnerabilities associated with Android system services. In: Proceedings of the ACM ACSAC (2015)

Web Security

Web Runner 2049: Evaluating
Third-Party Anti-bot Services

Babak Amin Azad[1(✉)], Oleksii Starov[2], Pierre Laperdrix[3],
and Nick Nikiforakis[1]

[1] Stony Brook University, Stony Brook, USA
baminazad@cs.stonybrook.edu
[2] Palo Alto Networks, Santa Clara, USA
[3] CNRS, Univ. Lille, Inria, Lille, France

Abstract. Given the ever-increasing number of malicious bots scouring the web, many websites are turning to specialized services that advertise their ability to detect bots and block them. In this paper, we investigate the design and implementation details of commercial anti-bot services in an effort to understand how they operate and whether they can effectively identify and block malicious bots in practice. We analyze the JavaScript code which their clients need to include in their websites and perform a set of gray box and black box analyses of their proprietary back-end logic, by simulating bots utilizing well-known automation tools and popular browsers.

On the positive side, our results show that by relying on browser fingerprinting, more than 75% of protected websites in our dataset, successfully defend against attacks by basic bots built with Python scripts or PhantomJS. At the same time, by using less popular browsers in terms of automation (e.g., Safari on Mac and Chrome on Android) attackers can successfully bypass the protection of up to 82% of protected websites.

Our findings show that the majority of protected websites are prone to bot attacks and the existing anti-bot solutions cannot substantially limit the ability of determined attackers. We have responsibly disclosed our findings with the anti-bot service providers.

1 Introduction

The modern web is home to benign and useful bots, such as, search engine crawlers that provide easy access to information around the web. Yet the same technology that enables benign bots is also utilized by malicious bots which disrupt services, steal business and customer information, and make illicit profits for their operators. Malicious bots are used to automatically find and exploit vulnerabilities on websites (such as outdated and vulnerable Content Management Systems) [15], scrape email addresses and content for sending spam and creating phishing websites, registering thousands of accounts and selling them via underground markets (e.g. for fake followers on social networks [47]) and

© Springer Nature Switzerland AG 2020
C. Maurice et al. (Eds.): DIMVA 2020, LNCS 12223, pp. 135–159, 2020.
https://doi.org/10.1007/978-3-030-52683-2_7

brute forcing login forms with credentials stolen from other websites (known as *credential stuffing*). Some of the recent bot attacks include, ride-sharing companies scraping pricing and vehicle information from their competitors websites [9]. Similarly, the bots targeted the airline industry, causing an increase in the look-to-book ratio which leads to increased fees [11].

According to recent estimates, more than 50% of traffic on the web belongs to bots with more than half of that belonging to malicious ones [19]. In this environment, specialized anti-bot services have emerged which offer bot detection and bot blocking as a service to their clients. Even though these services claim to utilize an impressive array of technologies, their operation and effectiveness in detecting and blocking bots have not been evaluated.

In this paper, we report on the first analysis of 15 popular anti-bot services. We identify the JavaScript code which their clients deploy on their websites and perform a white box analysis of its operation. We observe heavy reliance on browser fingerprinting including recent fingerprinting techniques that fingerprint a system's graphics card, local IP address, and even whether the browser attempts to lie about its identity. To understand whether this extracted information is sufficient to detect and block abusive bots, we utilize six different existing automation tools, ranging from off-the-shelf crawlers, to automated browsers. Through the use of carefully designed experiments, we evaluate the ability of the most popular anti-bot services to stop attacks, such as, content scraping, credential brute forcing, and account hijacking.

Among others, we find that few services are capable of significantly slowing down attackers and that certain unusual crawling tools, such as, an AppleScript-controlled Safari Browser and an ADB-controlled Android smartphone can successfully crawl large numbers of webpages and conduct account attacks. More specifically, at least 68% of our simulated scraping requests were not blocked, and more than 90% of our account takeover attempts were successful with at least one of the tested tools. In addition, for more than half of our target websites, there is at least one tool that enables us to do 1,000 password brute force attempts without getting blocked.

Contrary to our expectations, we discover that having a bot reach websites from a public cloud does not significantly decrease its performance since existing services put more emphasis on browser fingerprints rather than source IP address.

2 Background

Since malicious bots can lie about their identity, prior research has proposed a number of methods for bot detection, including behavior-based detection (based on the premise that bots browse websites differently than real users [24,29]), detection based on accessing content that is invisible for regular users [39,52] and more recently, based on browser fingerprinting [14]. Once a visitor is suspected to be a bot, the website can request the solving of CAPTCHAs, rate-limit the user, or altogether block traffic from the offending IP address.

Even though web developers may try to implement the aforementioned techniques, it is unlikely that the developers of small websites can keep up with the adaptation from the side of the bot authors. In order to keep up with attackers, new businesses have emerged that sell bot-detection services to their clients, similar to anti-DDoS companies which protect their clients against DDoS attacks. Website owners can then integrate these services with their website to block bots without needing to know how a bot was identified. One major benefit of using such services compared to a custom implementation of an anti-bot mechanism, is the threat-information sharing that happens in the background. If bot activity with certain characteristics is detected on website A, website B that is also a client of the same anti-bot service, can get information about this bot and block it immediately at its first interaction.

Anti-bot companies advertise a range of bot-related attacks which they can detect and stop. By analyzing the descriptions of their services, we summarize the attack scenarios performed by malicious bots into the three following categories (these attacks are discussed in more detail in Sect. 5):

- **Account Takeover**, also known as *credential stuffing*, refers to automated login attempts with stolen or leaked credentials to target websites. In this case, attackers may take advantage of users reusing credentials across services and leaked password databases found in underground markets.
- **Credential Brute Force** is another type of account takeover attack. In this scenario, the attacker uses a list of popular passwords against user accounts to break into them.
- **Content Scraping** is an automated attempt to steal proprietary website information, such as product price lists and inventory, to gain a business advantage.

Fig. 1. High-level architecture of anti-bot services

The general structure for anti-bot services is depicted in Fig. 1. We arrived at this architecture by studying the design of multiple anti-bot services and abstracting away service-specific details. When users visit a website protected by an anti-bot service, fingerprinting scripts gather information from their browser and send it directly to the anti-bot service's back-end. Information about how users interact with the website and actions taken, such as, login attempts and viewed pages, are also transmitted to the anti-bot service by the webserver using server-side APIs. Plugins are typically provided for popular content management systems (such as WordPress and Drupal) and integration is also available at the website and webserver layers using provided SDKs. In this architecture, every visitor of the website has a unique identifier which is later used by the webserver to query the anti-bot service and receive a risk score. Depending on the configuration of the website, different thresholds on the risk score can trigger different events, such as, showing a CAPTCHA, limiting the number of requests of suspicious users, or altogether blocking them.

A key component of each service is their *fingerprinting scripts*, which attempt to collect as many signals as possible for distinguishing between human and bot-like behavior. Browser fingerprinting has evolved substantially in the past few years from querying simple JavaScript APIs [20] to the rendering of complex 3D scenes with WebGL [16]. By collecting a range of information about the browser, the operating system and the hardware of a device, anti-bot services can obtain a precise view of the overall browsing system which can be used for detecting bots [14]. Next, such services usually claim to have sophisticated machine learning models on their back-end servers, which are trained to identify bot-related fingerprints on large volumes of data that they observe across their clients. In order to get a complete view of these services, both the coverage of fingerprinting features, as well as the accuracy of their back-end models have to be measured to quantify their effectiveness. Hence, in this study, we perform an analysis of their deployed fingerprinting scripts (Sect. 3), as well as gray box and black box testing of anti-bot back-end models (Sect. 5). Our experiments allow us to not only capture the effectiveness of each anti-bot service in detecting bots, but to also measure how well websites interpret and act upon the risk score reported by each anti-bot service.

3 Analysis of Anti-bot Services

For our analysis, using popular search engines, we searched for phrases such as, "bot detection" and "bot prevention", and compiled a list of 15 popular services in September 2017. Table 1 lists the discovered services ranked according to their number of clients. The process of identifying client websites is described in Sect. 5.

Overall, we see that almost half of the anti-bot services have thousands of client websites with Cloudflare being the most popular service having 13.65% of its clients from the Alexa's top 1 million websites. The number of clients for Cloudflare in Table 1 represents the total number of websites observed using Cloudflare. The numbers are based on "BuiltWith" website statistics, which provides reports on web technologies [10]. Since all other services specialize only in bot protection, we already know that clients that use these services want to defend against bots. Whereas for Cloudflare, there can be various reasons to use

Table 1. Popular anti-bot services

Service	Type	# Clients	Alexa 1M
Cloudflare (G)	Bot attacks	7, 250, 835	13.65%
Sift Science	Bot attacks	18, 733	3.41%
Iovation	Account fraud	14, 280	1.62%
ShieldSquare (G)	Bot attacks	8, 151	1.46%
PerimeterX	Bot attacks	7, 808	1.14%
InfiSecure	Bot attacks	5, 443	0.11%
DataDome (G)	Bot attacks	912	5.48%
ThreatMetrix	Account fraud	628	5.41%
Distil Bot Defense	Bot attacks	484	38.43%
Castle (G)	Account fraud	260	4.62%
Simility	Account fraud	182	2.20%
ThisData	Account fraud	138	1.45%
Kount Access	Account fraud	124	31.45%
Unbotify	Bot attacks	60	3.33%
DupZapper	Account fraud	33	3.03%
Overall	Anti-bot	7, 311, 809	13.56%

their service such as DDOS protection, CDNs, or for adding HTTPS support to a website. Therefore, only a subset of these websites might configure Cloudflare's firewall to block bots.

Services in Table 1 marked with (G) indicate those for which we could acquire an account (trial or paid) without having to talk to a sales representative. For these services, we were able to conduct gray box testing, in addition to the black box testing for all services. Among the services we study, we can distinguish the following two main types:

- **Universal solutions against bot attacks** usually collect fingerprints and user-behavior data from clients using JavaScript and other common browser fingerprinting methods. They also collect information from the web server including the specific actions taken by users, such as, the browsing of a specific page, or the submission of a form.
- **Specific services against account fraud** that focus on the defense against account takeover and credential stuffing attacks. These services make use of both bot detection and anomalous account activity to identify attacks.

All of the anti-bot services listed in Table 1, except Cloudflare, use fingerprinting scripts on their clients' websites to assist them in bot detection. We collected client-side fingerprinting scripts from the 14 anti-bot services that use this technique. Next to beautifying and statically analyzing the JavaScript code, we dynamically executed the scripts in order to inspect the sent payloads and detect what fingerprinting-related APIs they utilize. For that, we used a custom browser extension (following the approach of Lerner et al. [28]) that can intercept browser API calls on a page.

3.1 Fingerprinting and Automation Detection Mechanisms

First, we observed that most services use standard fingerprinting features, such as, screen properties, available fonts, plugins and MIME types. We observed similar features being collected to those reported by Vastel et al. [50]. The particular techniques in extracting these features differ, e.g. some services directly enumerate the `navigator.plugins` object, some simply use the PluginDetect library [7], and others have further custom checks. In comparison, we witness that few services incorporate more recent fingerprinting techniques, such as, Canvas or WebGL fingerprinting that can provide a more accurate view of the system's hardware.

Another finding, supporting the fact that anti-bot scripts attempt to capture obvious signs of web automation, is the variety of checks to detect PhantomJS, Nightmare [2], Selenium, and headless Chrome browsers. Different services use different techniques, such as, printing a stack trace and searching for the "selenium" keyword or probing for the existence of known variables (e.g., `window.callPhantom`). By deploying these checks against our own Selenium installations, we discovered that most of the deployed checks do not work for recent Selenium versions (except the `navigator.webdriver` property which is still present on the Selenium ChromeDriver).

Even though not all services use state-of-the-art fingerprinting techniques, those that do also try to detect inconsistencies in the collected browser fingerprints. For example, the user-agent sent by Selenium can be modified to look like a Firefox browser on Android, or Safari on iOS. The problem is that these modifications can lead to inconsistencies where modified and unmodified attributes cannot possibly belong to the same browsing environment. Three services make use of client-side code to detect such cases of mismatch between attributes.

Table 2. Known fingerprinting libraries

Source library	# Services	Source library	# Services	Source library	# Services
Fingerprintjs2 [4]	4	PluginDetect [7]	3	fonts2.swf [1]	1
FontList.swf [4]	3	Evercookies [3]	1	Modernizr [5]	1

As Table 2 shows, a significant number of anti-bot services rely on existing fingerprinting libraries, such as, the popular Fingerprintjs2 [4]. We also observed services that use other advanced fingerprinting features, including the detection of the local IP address through WebRTC and Flash, as well as the recording of user actions, i.e., mouse moves and clicks. Some collect and send this data only once, whereas others periodically collect and report this information. Finally, we discovered a number of cases where more novel fingerprinting techniques were used, like the recently deprecated Battery status API [38] (Castle), AudioContext fingerprinting (PerimeterX), and even DOM changes to a supplied HTML page with different input fields (ThreatMetrix) which can be used to detect browser extensions [44]. This demonstrates that a small number of anti-bot services are closely following browser-fingerprinting research, and incorporate this research in their products.

A service which includes anti-bot functionality but differs from the rest is Cloudflare [17]. Unlike the evaluated third-party anti-bot services, Cloudflare itself is responsible for all resolutions of their clients' domains. As a result, Cloudflare can detect and block traffic at their servers, without any input from their clients. After analyzing the requests, we observed that Cloudflare does not perform any type of client-side fingerprinting using JavaScript or Flash. Cloudflare mostly relies on IP reputation (historical malicious activity), firewall rules based on HTTP requests, and rate limiting to prevent automated and malicious behavior.

3.2   Anti-bot Service Integration with Websites

As depicted in Fig. 1, anti-bot services communicate the decision (often in the form of a risk score) to their clients upon each request. In this section we present our observations on how risk scores or decisions are communicated to clients and how the websites react to these reports.

Communicating the Raw Risk Score. Services like Cloudflare, directly communicate the score to their clients and let them decide which thresholds to choose when blocking bots (e.g., show a CAPTCHA when risk score is greater than 50).

Communicating the Final Verdict. Services like Castle interpret the risk score internally and communicate the final verdict (Allow, Challenge, or Block) to the client websites through their API. Website administrators can then decide to show a CAPTCHA or notify the user via third-party channels.

Handling Everything in the Background. These services analyze the collected fingerprints and events, redirecting users to CAPTCHAs or block pages. As a result, the whole process of decision making happens in the background and website administrators have no control over it. Occasionally, there are no tunable parameters exposed to administrators which means that false positives have to be communicated and remediated through customer-support channels.

Finally, next to communicating the risk score and decision making, how websites react to bots is also defined by the anti-bot service. Some services have the ability to be deployed inline with the web traffic (e.g., Distil Bot Defense and Cloudflare). In this scenario they can straightforwardly redirect malicious users to CAPTCHAs and block pages. Similarly, the integrated SDK can communicate with the anti-bot service and redirect the detected threats to specific block pages. Lastly, the reaction may be left up to the website developers. In the example of Castle, website developers can decide to block the request or notify the users about the breach.

4   Available Tools for Building Bots

In this section, we introduce the tools that we utilized to evaluate whether the anti-bot services are capable of detecting attackers of different levels of expertise (reflected in the complexity of their tools). We categorize the tools that are available for attackers in three groups, covering multiple levels of complexity:

- **Basic bots:** The least sophisticated approach is based on general-purpose automation tools (e.g., Python Requests and PhantomJS). *Python Requests* scripts are capable of sending GET and POST requests but do not execute JavaScript (these are conceptually similar to utilizing command-line tools, such as, `wget` and `curl`). This is the most basic approach that we expect to be detected by anti-bot services. We also include *PhantomJS* in this category, which was the first easy-to-script, headless, JavaScript-supporting browser [40] and therefore attracted a great deal of abuse [41].
- **Automated Browsers:** The second and more sophisticated category involves using real browsers (e.g., Firefox and Chrome) automated by Selenium. These bots can often be augmented with user-action simulation, such as, mouse moves, floating delays, and page scroll.
- **Less Popular fingerprints:** Anti-bot companies claim to share threat information between their clients. As a result, common tools used to create bots can be detected more effectively. Contrastingly, attackers can incorporate less popular tools to potentially bypass bot detection mechanisms, due to their limited history of malicious activity. To model this approach, we use AppleScript-automated Safari and ADB-automated Chrome on Android.

5   Experimental Setup

To analyze the effectiveness of anti-bot services in terms of preventing bot activity, we utilize a number of real-world attack scenarios. In this section, we describe the categories of our tests, and how we utilize tools from different bot categories presented in Sect. 4. We implement a large number of web automation scripts that can interact with websites at different levels of complexity. Each test is comprised of attack and tool combination and is executed from hosts with IP addresses belonging to our campus and a public cloud. These addresses are picked from a pool of 30 campus IP addresses and 30 cloud IP addresses distributed across 8 geographical regions.

5.1   Gray Box Experiments

For the companies that we could obtain paid or trial accounts, we integrate their SDK with our testing website (a WordPress-based, web application). Under the gray box scenario, we run our tests in a fully controlled environment where we control both the bots as well as the website receiving the bot traffic. By monitoring the administration panel provided by the anti-bot service, we have access to the final decisions to allow or block the traffic. Nevertheless, the machine learning models and decision boundaries used to classify the incoming traffic is still a black box. As such, we call these set of tests, gray box.

1. Test Preparation. Initially, for each "attack category," and "web automation tool," we create scripts to mount the attacks and measure their success. Our tests cover the following categories:

Fig. 2. Screenshot of blocking message from Distil Networks

- **Account Takeover:** In this setup, we create an account on websites utilizing anti-bot services (either our own for gray box testing or third-party websites for black-box testing) from a fixed geographical location, IP address, and browser. We then attempt to automatically login to this account from different geographical locations and IP addresses using our bots. This discrepancy in login location, browser fingerprint, and use of automation tools should, in principle, trigger the account-takeover protection system to prevent the "malicious" login activity or alert the user.
- **Credential Brute Force:** To implement this scenario, we use our web automation tools and try to login with 1,000 invalid credentials. We then measure the number of requests before getting blocked. According to prior work [26,32], at least 4% of passwords created under different password policy schemes can be found in under 1,000 guesses.
- **Content Scraping:** By extracting product list and pricing information from 1,000 pages, we evaluate whether the anti-bot service will block our bots.

2. Test Execution. Each attack script is executed from different IP addresses which we rotate as necessary. The hosts are located on our campus and on Linode (a public cloud provider). The reason for using two different locations is to simulate attackers who have access to premium IP address space that is not associated with crawling activity, versus attackers who can just rent virtual machines on public clouds. We do not perform multiple attacks at the same time to ensure that the detection of one attack does not affect the detection of another.

3. Post-processing of Results. After each test, we inspect the anti-bot administration panel and look for reports of blocked bots based on the IP address we used for each attack.

5.2 Black Box Experiments

Most services require their potential customers to talk to a sales representative, prove their identity as a real business, and go through a series of interactions to acquire and adopt anti-bot services. Since we cannot perform gray box testing for these service, we devised a set of black box experiments.

Data Collection. After compiling our list of anti-bot services that we wish to evaluate, we crawl the web and find websites that adopt these services. Starting with a list of known clients for each anti-bot service (e.g., list of clients on the website of anti-bot services), we analyze their websites to identify unique content, such as, JavaScript files or DOM elements that can be used as a signature to detect more clients of each service. The resulting signatures are then queried in the PublicWWW [8] and NerdyData [6] code-search engines and the results are supplemented with our own crawls of the Alexa top 1 million websites.

Given the number of tests we wish to conduct and that we need website-specific scripts that can fill forms and navigate each website, it is not feasible to evaluate all clients of each service. As such, we decided to focus on a subset of their clients by randomly selecting ten clients for each anti-bot service. We ensure that the selected websites do not exhibit any client-side signs (e.g. JavaScript libraries) that would suggest that they are utilizing any anti-bot service, other than the evaluated ones. We also removed websites which, through experimentation, showed signs of additional, server-side software blocking our requests. This is not a challenge since block pages used by anti-bot services are distinctive (Fig. 2) and HTML tags, URLs, and variable names within the page source point to the anti-bot company.

1. Test Preparation. We target the same attack categories that we discussed in gray box tests. Since we do not have access to the administration panel this time, we devised heuristics to detect being blocked based on the received response.

- **Account Takeover and Credential Brute Force:** We use the same type of scripts that we used in gray box tests. Note that in both experiments we create an account on the target website and only target our own user account during the experiments, for ethical purposes.
- **Content Scraping:** In this attack scenario, we inspect the websites of clients of anti-bot services, and identify content that is a likely target for scraping by malicious crawlers (such as pricing of products and inventory details). We then implement the necessary automation scripts for each website, attempting to scrape 1,000 pages worth of content.

We spent a total of 5 man-months developing automation scripts for all tested websites which could appropriately navigate each website according to our desired tests. Another obstacle that we had to overcome is that, due to the churn of clients of the anti-bot services, we had to often repeat experiments with new randomly sampled websites, as some websites stopped being clients of the services before we were able to finish our experiments.

2. Test Execution. Using the same infrastructure, we run our experiments against selected clients of each service. To generalize our results, in addition to Linode, we ran a set of pilot tests from AWS and did not observe significant differences in the results (5% over 60 tests) showing that the choice between popular and less popular cloud providers does not have significant impact on the final results.

3. Post-processing of Results. After each test, we inspect our logs and screenshots to locate the number of successful attempts each bot made before getting blocked and to make sure any observed blocking is the outcome of fingerprint-related and behavior-related information that these services gather from our bots and correlate with server-side events.

The extracted information consisting of fingerprint, headers and user actions are used by each anti-bot service to come up with a verdict for each user ID, which their client will use to decide whether they should block the current request. Section 6 discusses the results from this step in more detail. In all cases where we received unexpected responses, we manually inspected them to verify that our scripts were indeed blocked. We define "success" and "failure" as follows:

- **Successful content scraping** is defined as our bot loading the content for 1,000 pages on protected websites containing information that would be worth scraping for attackers.
- **Successful account takeover** is defined as our bot being able to login to a target user account from a different location and fingerprint from the actual user's fingerprint used to register and login to the account. The test is considered to have failed when the tool fails to login with explicit (e.g. "You are blocked") or implicit (e.g. "Incorrect credentials") responses.

- **Successful brute forcing** in our experiment is defined as a bot sending 1,000 login attempts with incorrect credentials and then being able to login with correct credentials. We designed this test in a way that simulates an attacker attempting a large number of incorrect credentials before finding the correct one.

For credential brute-forcing experiments, we distinguish the following cases as being blocked: being blocked with an explicit message, receiving a CAPTCHA in order to login, target user account being locked (note that this is always our account), being rate-limited for a considerable amount of time or not being able to login with correct credentials after brute forcing. The last case is based on the observation that some anti-bot services silently increase the risk score when the noisy brute force behavior is observed, and as a result, prevent the bot from logging in even with correct credentials.

5.3 Ethical Considerations

To understand how real anti-bot services detect malicious bots on their client websites, we cannot avoid sending bot-like traffic to public websites. To conduct these experiments in an ethical fashion we took special care when designing them and conducting them. For content scraping, we access content that is considered public, i.e., it is not behind a registration wall. For account takeovers, we only try to log in to our own account on all websites from a location/fingerprint that is different from the one that we utilized to register that account. Lastly, for account brute forcing, we only make login attempts against our own accounts, never trying to log in into the accounts of other users. We provide ample time between requests (in the order of seconds) allowing our requests to be interleaved with regular traffic received by the evaluated popular websites. Our bots behave as humans and therefore never send any maliciously-crafted input to target web applications.

As a result, we are confident that our experiments did not have any negative consequences, neither for the protected websites, nor for the anti-bot services themselves.

6   Analysis of Results

In this section, we describe the results of our bot experiments on our test websites (gray box testing) and on client websites of popular anti-bot services (black box testing). By combining data across both types of experiments, we uncover shortcomings and flaws of these services. Our focus in this section is on the common patterns across the services that will provide an opportunity for the attackers to bypass their protection. As our study is not meant to promote one product over another, we opt to anonymize the names of the anti-bot services.

6.1   Gray Box Testing Results

From the list of anti-bot services that we initially started with, we were able to obtain accounts from four services: Service #3, Service #4, Service #2 (providing generic anti-bot protection) and Service #1 (providing specialized protection against account fraud). For the first two services, installing their WordPress plugins and including the JavaScript file in all of our pages was sufficient to adopt them. After each client request reaches the webserver, these plugins collect the request context including HTTP headers, cookies and IP addresses and report it back to the anti-bot service through their APIs. Conversely, Service #2 protection is enabled by routing website traffic through their servers by changing DNS records. In the case of Service #1, while the JavaScript code sends back information on each page load, we needed to manually call their API upon authentication and report the event. Upon successful authentication, we then have to query their API to receive a verdict (Allow, Challenge, and Block) that defines what action the service recommends. The reaction to these verdicts is also the website developers' responsibility and can vary for each client website (e.g., showing CAPTCHA, or requesting a second factor of authentication).

Gray Box Content Scraping Results. The number of successful content-scraping attempts against the three services which protect against it (Service #3, Service #4, and Service #2) is listed in Table 3. For Service #2, none of our scraping bots was ever blocked, regardless of their location (i.e. Campus vs. Cloud). While further fine-tuning the rate limits might be helpful to block more aggressive bots, as long as bots keep their request number low, they can hide within normal user traffic and remain undetected.

Our results show that Service #3 clearly makes a distinction in its decisions to block bots based on their source IP address. Requests from bots originating from campus IP addresses were strictly more successful, compared to those of Linode datacenters. For Service #4, this observation does not always hold true. While Firefox Stripping (i.e. with fingerprinting script blocked) got worse results when originating from Linode, AppleScript and Mobile scrapers remained undetected. This suggests that Service #3 places more weight on the source IP address in their decision-making model, compared to Service #4. Service #3 trusts IP addresses to the extent that attackers with access to prime IP addresses from outside datacenters (Campus address space, in our case) can scrape content even with trivial tools from the "Basic Bots" category.

Gray Box Account Fraud Results. The account-fraud tests are relevant for all four companies in our gray box experiment. We analyze the results for both account takeover and account brute force tests. The time window of interaction for account takeover is limited to two requests (one to grab the CSRF token and one to login). As a result, features, such as, login history including locations, fingerprint of used devices and fingerprints of bots, are more effective in this scenario compared to behavioral anomaly detection. Table 4 shows the number of successful brute force attempts along with whether the account takeover was successful.

Table 3. Number of successful content scraping attempts (Gray box)

Service	Tool/IP	Python	Phantom JS	Firefox (Stripping)	Chrome	Chrome (Mouse)	Firefox (Mouse)	Safari	Mobile
Service #2	Campus	1000	1000	NA	1000	1000	1000	1000	1000
	Cloud	1000	1000	NA	1000	1000	1000	1000	1000
Service #3	Campus	1000	0	1000	1000	1000	1000	1000	1000
	Cloud	4	0	21	23	7	14	24	23
Service #4	Campus	21	0	1000	0	1	1	1000	1000
	Cloud	3	1	16	0	0	0	1000	1000

Plain Python Outperforms PhantomJS: The first unexpected observation, which is consistent among nearly all tests and anti-bot services, is that PhantomJS has inferior performance to plain Python scripts. For example, all services with client fingerprinting capability block login attempts from PhantomJS. Our hypothesis is that this tool was so much overused by attackers (PhantomJS was the first headless JavaScript-supporting browser) that anti-bot services have enough features to detect it with high confidence. Contrastingly, since Python scripts are not capable of executing JavaScript, anti-bot services give them the benefit of the doubt (e.g. it may be a JavaScript-blocking user) and allow a few requests to go through before taking action.

Safari Breaks into All User Accounts: Interestingly, none of the services block Safari that is automated by Applescript. To our surprise, the risk score reported by Service #1 for Applescript is very low (17/100) even though a real user never logged into the user account with an Apple device or Safari. For comparison, this score is in the range of 70–88 for Selenium and 100 (i.e. maximum risk) for PhantomJS.

Table 4. Number of brute force attempts before getting blocked (Gray box) Checkmarks indicate successful account takeover

Service	Service #1		Service #2		Service #3		Service #4	
Tool	Campus	Cloud	Campus	Cloud	Campus	Cloud	Campus	Cloud
Python	1000 ✔	0 ✘	5 ✔	5 ✔	240 ✔	12 ✔	2 ✔	1000 ✔
PhantomJS	0 ✘	0 ✘	5 ✔	5 ✔	0 ✘	0 ✘	0 ✘	0 ✘
Chrome	0 ✘	0 ✘	5 ✔	5 ✔	250 ✔	23 ✔	0 ✘	0 ✘
Firefox	10 ✘	0 ✘	5 ✔	5 ✔	405 ✔	21 ✔	1 ✔	0 ✘
Safari	1000 ✔	0 ✔	5 ✔	5 ✔	334 ✔	13 ✔	1000 ✔	1000 ✔

Not Executing JavaScript Can Be Helpful: Finally, using Python, our bots were able to successfully log into user accounts both from Campus and Linode IP addresses with a high degree of success. Service #1 was the only exception which returned the verdict of "Challenge" only for Python requests from Linode.

For brute force tests (Table 4), similar to account takeover results, Service #3 shows higher sensitivity to source IP addresses and blocks requests from Linode more aggressively whereas Service #4 does not penalize Python and Safari-based bots. For Service #1, this transition from Campus to Cloud was enough to mark all our login attempts as malicious and increase their risk scores, shifting them to their next verdict category: from Allow to Challenge and from Challenge to Block.

6.2   Overall Content Scraping Results

In this section, we report on six anti-bot services which were either included in our gray box tests or match our criteria for black box tests, that is: (a) provide overall protection against automated attacks/mention content scraping as a covered use case; (b) have a representative sample of at least 10 client websites. We chose distinct websites that use only the corresponding service out of the known anti-bot solutions. Each website was tested against eight different automation tools among three bot categories and each test included the scraping of 1,000 pages.

Table 5 summarizes our results for content scraping from gray box tests and black box tests. The column named "IP sensitivity" indicates whether using IP addresses from Cloud (Linode) rather than Campus makes the service block our bots earlier. If there is more than 50% change (i.e., at least half of the websites that did not block us on campus IPs blocked us from cloud IPs), we consider the service to be highly sensitive to cloud IP addresses and if the change is less than 50%, we say the impact of source IP address is low. Finally if we do not observe a significant difference when moving from Campus to Cloud, we infer that presence/absence of an IP address from a cloud provider, does not have an effect on the blocking decision.

In Tables 5 and 6, partial success is marked with half-filled circles indicating that either some tools within that bot category were not blocked (e.g., PhantomJS was blocked but Python was not), or some websites protected by the same service blocked a tool within a category while others did not. Even though we do not have enough information for a definitive answer, we opine that the partial difference in behavior among clients of the same anti-bot company is the result of different characteristics of their normal traffic and the dynamic nature of the machine learning models.

Basic Bots: Nearly all services with the exception of Service #2 are able to block "basic bots" to some extent. Among them, Service #5 and Service #4 successfully block both Python and PhantomJS consistently on all their clients.

Automated Browsers: Service #4 always detects and blocks automated browsers. While Firefox automated by Selenium goes undetected by Service #5 and Service #7, Selenium Chrome is blocked quickly (in less than 100 requests). Adding page scrolls and mouse moves to our automated browsers only helped with Service #7 which led to scraping 1,000 pages on some clients and getting

Table 5. Service ability to block content scraping by different bots (Gray box and Black box tests) (●: Blocked, ◑: Some automation tools can bypass, ○: Failed to block)

Anti-bot service	Basic bots	Automated browsers	Less popular FPs	Stripping	IP sensitivity
Service #2 (G)	○	○	○	NA	None
Service #3 (G)	◑	○	○	NA	High
Service #4 (G)	●	●	○	●	None
Service #5	●	◑	◑	●	None
Service #6	◑	○	○	NA	None
Service #7	◑	◑	○	●	Low

blocked after around 60 attempts on other clients where we could previously make less than five successful requests.

Less Popular Fingerprints: Applescript-Safari and Chrome on Android are able to bypass the limitations imposed by most anti-bot services. The only exception is Service #5 where some of their clients block Applescript-Safari while others block Chrome on Android. Even the websites that block either of these tools, do so after 300–600 attempts. Compared to basic bots and automated browsers which made less than 10 successful attempts on Service #5 clients, this demonstrates that unpopular, JavaScript-enabled clients can be significantly more successful in evading detection.

Stripping: Stripping refers to blocking fingerprinting JavaScript when scraping content from the websites. None of the services allowed our bots to scrape more pages when client side fingerprints were stripped, and most of the time we got blocked earlier (e.g., in less than 5 attempts on Service #5). Since Service #2, Service #3 and Service #6 either do not perform client-side fingerprinting via JavaScript or do not block our automated browsers, we can not compare their performance when automated browsers are used and fingerprinting scripts are blocked.

Figure 3 generalizes the performance of different scraping bots across all evaluated services. There we can see that, even though the different traffic patterns of different websites lead to noisy results, there are clear patterns that favor some tools over others. For example, when operating either an Android bot or a Firefox-Selenium one with added mouse moves from "premium" address space, attackers can scrape content from the vast majority of sites and services. For cloud tests, we repeated the experiments for the tools that showed better performance from campus IP addresses.

6.3   Overall Account Fraud Results

Here, we present our results for the Account Takeover and Brute Force experiments. We analyzed ten anti-bot services which advertise themselves as general

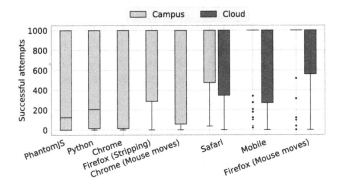

Fig. 3. Performance of content scraping bots

anti-bot or account-fraud protection services and for which we could find at least ten distinct client websites that allowed us to register a new user (a requirement for these experiments). We evaluate these services against five tools by performing a total of 2,800 tests.

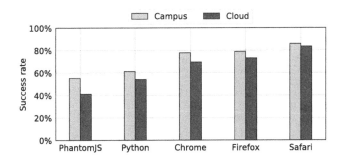

Fig. 4. Performance of account takeover bots

Account Takeover Results. Overall, 2–8% of websites blocked all our account takeover attempts across all bot categories from Campus and Cloud IP addresses respectively. Applescript-Safari was the most successful tool with 82.5% average success rate. Bots based on Safari automated by AppleScript, were able to break into user accounts with unseen fingerprints (Safari browser) and from new IP addresses. Table 6 summarizes our results for gray box and black box tests for account takeover and brute force tests. The results are sobering. By looking at Fig. 4, we observe that because of the absence of a large number of requests to the service during account takeover (attackers have already stolen the credentials and are logging in from a "foreign" environment), most services fail to block the attack. We have already seen that general bot-detection mechanisms fail to block most of the bots right away except basic bots, which also holds true for account takeover attacks. The change in fingerprint and location of the login attempt were not enough to raise an alarm and block the takeover in many of our attempts. As a result, even with the worst-performing bot (i.e. PhantomJS) attackers can successfully conduct an account takeover attack in 40–60% of the time.

Table 6. Service ability to block account takeover by different bots (Gray box and Black box tests) (●: Blocked, ◑: Some automation tools can bypass, ○: Failed to block) Brute force: number of websites without any login rate-limiting

Anti-bot service	Basic bots	Automated browsers	Less popular FPs	Brute force	IP sensitivity
Service #1 (G)	◑	◑	○	6/10	High
Service #2 (G)	○	○	○	0	None
Service #3 (G)	◑	○	○	4/10	High
Service #4 (G)	◑	◑	○	10/10	Low
Service #5	●	●	◑	3/10	High
Service #6	◑	○	○	7/10	Low
Service #7	◑	◑	◑	3/10	Low
Service #8	○	○	○	9/10	None
Service #9	◑	◑	◑	7/10	High
Service #10	●	◑	○	8/10	Low

Credential Brute Force Results. The results for this section are summarized in Table 6. Column "Brute Force" in this table refers to the number of websites on which at least one of our bots was able to perform 1,000 brute force attempts against their login forms. This not only shows the lack of defense from anti-bot services but also signifies that neither the website nor the anti-bot service enforce a hard limit on the number of failed attempts (e.g. by account lockout, CAPTCHA or IP address ban). Lu et al. studied the presence of rate limiting mechanisms on top Alexa websites and already pointed out this lack of protection [30]. Our results support Lu et al.'s findings by showing that, even among the websites that actively seek to protect against bot attacks, 30–100% of them do not enforce any type of login rate limiting.

Among all tested services, Service #5 and Service #7 blocked more categories of bots and enforced rate limits on a wider range of tested clients. For Service #4 and Service #8, almost none of their tested clients enforced rate limiting. Interestingly, simple rate-limiting on POST requests to login pages enforced by Service #2, is sufficient to fully prevent brute force attacks, even without any type of client-side fingerprinting.

Contrary to content-scraping results, different tools from automated browsers and less popular fingerprint categories achieve similar results. However, Safari is still the best performing bot. Orthogonally to the type of bot being used, we observe that most anti-bot services become slightly stricter when the bot is sending authentication requests from Cloud IP addresses. For example, the average number of successful requests by Safari, drops from 564 to 433 after transitioning to cloud. This subtle effect is visible in Fig. 5. More importantly, the hourglass-like distributions of Fig. 5 show that the majority of bruteforce attempts are either blocked in under 400 attempts (the narrow "neck" of the hourglass) or not blocked at all. With the use of more sophisticated tools (right side of the Fig. 5), the number of successful 1,000 bruteforce attempts increases.

When combining account takeover and brute force protection, Service #5, Service #7 and Service #9 block bots across all categories. Yet, specific tools are able to evade detection. On the other end, websites using Service #8 in our dataset did not show any specific pattern of blocking bots (except one website that was enforcing a local rate limit to block brute force attempts).

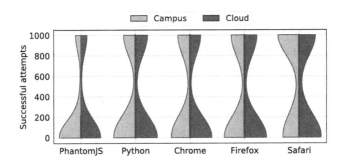

Fig. 5. Performance of brute force bots

7 Discussion

In this paper, we conducted the first, large-scale study of commercial anti-bot services that websites can use to detect and protect their content and their users against malicious bots. Using basic bots as well as popular and less popular automated browsers, in conjunction with different types of IP address space (public clouds vs. campus networks), we evaluated—in an ethical fashion—the ability of ten services to detect and block bots on the websites of their customers. While each service has its own specific strengths and weaknesses (as described in Sect. 5 and Sect. 6), we can still observe common patterns across services. We describe these patterns (and their implications) below:

Variance Across Clients of the Same Service. An unexpected finding of our experiments is that not all clients of the same service block bots in the same way. This could suggest that some services are more sensitive to false positives than others, but it could also suggest misconfigurations from the side of clients of anti-bot services. Our recommendation is that anti-bot services regularly perform bot-based crawling of their own clients and observe whether their own attempts are blocked by their clients. In the cases where blocking is under a configurable threshold, these anti-bot services can reach out to their clients and inquire whether the recorded permissiveness is a conscious choice or merely a misconfiguration.

Browser Fingerprinting. Virtually all services rely, to a certain extent, on browser fingerprinting as part of their bot-detection logic. Browser fingerprinting is a powerful mechanism that can be used either constructively (for authentication) or destructively (for unwanted online tracking) to re-identify users (including attackers). Yet it is also susceptible to evasions when attackers are aware of it. When it comes to advanced attackers who can mix and match bots, constructively using browser fingerprinting is more likely to work in a whitelisting fashion (i.e. is the current user's browsing environment, similar to their past browsing environment?) rather than in a blacklisting fashion (i.e. is the current user's fingerprint matching that of a previously-observed, malicious bot?).

PhantomJS is Universally Recognizable. As we showed in our experiments in Sect. 5, PhantomJS is universally recognizable by anti-bot services and often performs worse than simple bots that do not support JavaScript at all. Even though this is desirable for detecting attackers abusing PhantomJS, academic researchers have also extensively relied on PhantomJS for web-security [37,42, 45,48,51] and web-privacy [13,43] studies. Assuming the increasing adoption of anti-bot services, this means that the results obtained through PhantomJS-related crawling will be decreasingly accurate. In the short term, we recommend that researchers avoid using PhantomJS in favor of newer and more complete crawling tools, such as, headless Chrome and OpenWPM [21]. In the long term, we need both the technical means to evaluate the fingerprintability of crawling frameworks used for research, as well as a discussion between stake-holders on how crawling-based studies should be best conducted.

8   Responsible Disclosure

During this study we observed behaviors that can either be attributed to customer-website misconfigurations of an anti-bot service (i.e. customers do not fully take advantage of the detection capabilities of anti-bot services) or can be blind spots within the detection models of the evaluated services. As such, we contacted 7 services with what we regarded as high-impact misconfigurations or security issues on their client websites in December 2019. During these communications, our goal was to share our findings and obtain more information about the design decisions and details that we could not observe as outsiders. Ultimately, three services (ThreatMetrix, DataDome, and Castle) reached back to us. We have shared the list of vulnerable target websites in our study and our bot scripts with the anti-bot services upon their request and we are in continuous conversation with them. We hope that this information will be used to increase the accuracy and coverage of these services.

9   Related Work

Research-wise, despite its potential for abuse, bot identification has only attracted limited research which, given the adaptations from bot authors, can quickly become dated. Existing attempts to differentiate crawlers from real users rely on differences in their navigational patterns, the percentage of HTTP methods in requests, the types of links requested, and the timing between requests [24,29,46]. These features are then used in supervised machine-learning algorithms trained using ground truth that the authors of each paper were able to procure, typically by manually labeling traffic of one or more webservers to which they had access. Xie et al. propose an offline method for identifying malicious crawlers by searching for clusters of requests towards non-existent resources [52]. Next to ML-based methods, Park et al. [39] investigated the possibility of detecting malicious web crawlers by looking for mouse movement, the loading of Cascading Style Sheets, and the following of an invisible link that is present in the HTML code of a page yet is invisible to regular users. McKenna [31] recently experimented with more types of invisible links and resources but was unable to gauge their effectiveness due to size and duration limitations of their study.

Interestingly, the majority of work on bot detection predates browser fingerprinting despite the latter appearing as early as 2010 [12,13,18,20,21,23,27,36] even though as we showed throughout this paper, *all but one* of the evaluated anti-bot services heavily rely on fingerprinting for identifying bots.

All the prior research that focused on adding new attributes to a fingerprint [22,33,35,44], notably techniques like canvas [34], AudioContext [21] or WebGL [16] fingerprinting, is especially relevant to anti-bot services as it could offer more ways to distinguish a bot from a regular user. Moreover, there exists machine-learning approaches to link fingerprint evolutions over time [49] which could be used to track changes in a bot fingerprint. Relying on fingerprinting techniques, Bursztein et al. proposed Picasso, a tool aimed at identifying inorganic traffic through canvas fingerprinting [14].

Jueckstock et al. introduced VisibleV8, an instrumented Chromium based browser that is capable of monitoring dynamic JavaScript API calls [25]. The authors found that 29% of top 50k Alexa websites probe for artifacts of automated browsing environment but do not evaluate the usage of these artifacts and whether these websites can detect different types of bots in practice. Vastel et al. study the presence of bot-detection artifacts over the Alexa top 10K websites [50]. While they focus on fingerprinting behavior of anti-bot systems, our study systematically evaluates the overall benefits and drawbacks of existing anti-bot approaches as they are deployed in the wild. Moreover, we model real world attack scenarios whereas previous work focused on the fingerprinting surface of browsers and blocking behavior when visiting target websites.

10   Conclusion

In this paper, we reported on the first analysis of anti-bot services for the web. By isolating and analyzing the JavaScript code which the clients of anti-bot services need to utilize, we identified near universal-reliance on browser fingerprinting, including recently-proposed fingerprinting techniques, as well as checks for the consistency of the presented fingerprints. Through large-scale, black box and gray box analyses of each service using off-the-shelf automation tools as well as less-popular automated environments, we quantified the ability of these services to detect and block bots. We discovered that many services perform poorly and browsers that are less commonly automated (i.e Safari on Mac and Chrome on Android) can achieve an overall success rate of 80% during content-scraping attempts. We also discovered that the location of a bot on a public cloud is secondary to its fingerprint and only 4 services are sensitive to the location of source IP address. This allows attackers to launch massive bot campaigns by renting low-cost virtual machines on public data centers.

Overall, our findings suggest that existing services can stop basic bots, but are currently not capable of blocking specialized tools and even the less popular automated browsers, which can bypass the protection of around 75% of content-scraping targets. As such, they cannot substantially limit determined attackers. At the same time, our findings are relevant for all research involving the crawling of websites since websites that utilize anti-bot services may be able to identify the tools used by researchers (such as PhantomJS) and thereby evade accurate analysis.

Acknowledgements. We thank the anonymous reviewers for their helpful feedback. This work was partially supported by a gift from Amazon and the National Science Foundation (NSF) under grants CNS-1813974, CNS-1617902, and CMMI-1842020.

References

1. Panopticlick's fonts2.swf. https://github.com/EFForg/panopticlick-python
2. Nightmare (2014). https://github.com/segmentio/nightmare
3. Evercookie (2017). https://github.com/samyk/evercookie
4. Figerprint2js (2017). https://github.com/Valve/fingerprintjs2
5. Modernizr (2017). https://modernizr.com/
6. Nerdydata: Search engine for source code (2017). https://nerdydata.com
7. PluginDetect (2017). http://www.pinlady.net/PluginDetect/
8. Publicwww: Search engine for source code (2017). https://publicwww.com
9. Uber's Massive Scraping Program Collected Data About Competitors Around The World (2017). https://gizmodo.com/ubers-massive-scraping-program-collected-data-1820887947
10. BuiltWith Technology Lookup (2018). https://builtwith.com/
11. How Bots Are Disrupting Airline Ticket Sales (2019). https://www.eweek.com/enterprise-apps/how-bots-are-disrupting-airline-ticket-sales
12. Acar, G., Eubank, C., Englehardt, S., Juarez, M., Narayanan, A., Diaz, C.: The web never forgets: persistent tracking mechanisms in the wild. In: Proceedings of the 2014 ACM CCS Conference (2014)

13. Acar, G., et al.: FPDetective: dusting the web for fingerprinters. In: Proceedings of the 2013 ACM SIGSAC Conference on Computer & Communications Security, CCS 2013, pp. 1129–1140. ACM, New York (2013)
14. Bursztein, E., Malyshev, A., Pietraszek, T., Thomas, K.: Picasso: lightweight device class fingerprinting for web clients. In: Proceedings of the 6th Workshop on Security and Privacy in Smartphones and Mobile Devices (2016)
15. Canali, D., Balzarotti, D.: Behind the scenes of online attacks: an analysis of exploitation behaviors on the web. In: 20th Annual Network & Distributed System Security Symposium (NDSS 2013) (2013). https://hal.archives-ouvertes.fr/hal-00799082
16. Cao, Y., Li, S., Wijmans, E.: (Cross-)browser fingerprinting via OS and hardware level features. In: 24nd Annual Network and Distributed System Security Symposium, NDSS (2017)
17. Cloudflare: The web performance & security company. https://www.cloudflare.com
18. Das, A., Acar, G., Borisov, N., Pradeep, A.: The web's sixth sense: a study of scripts accessing smartphone sensors. In: Proceedings of the 2018 ACM SIGSAC Conference on Computer and Communications Security, pp. 1515–1532. ACM (2018)
19. DistilNetworks: Bad Bot Report (2018). https://resources.distilnetworks.com/travel/2018-bad-bot-report
20. Eckersley, P.: How unique is your web browser? In: Atallah, M.J., Hopper, N.J. (eds.) PETS 2010. LNCS, vol. 6205, pp. 1–18. Springer, Heidelberg (2010). https://doi.org/10.1007/978-3-642-14527-8_1
21. Englehardt, S., Narayanan, A.: Online tracking: a 1-million-site measurement and analysis. In: Proceedings of the 2016 ACM SIGSAC Conference on Computer and Communications Security, CCS 2016, pp. 1388–1401. ACM, New York (2016)
22. Fifield, D., Egelman, S.: Fingerprinting web users through font metrics. In: Proceedings of the 19th International Conference on Financial Cryptography and Data Security (2015)
23. Gómez-Boix, A., Laperdrix, P., Baudry, B.: Hiding in the crowd: an analysis of the effectiveness of browser fingerprinting at large scale. In: WWW 2018: The 2018 Web Conference, April 2018
24. Jacob, G., Kirda, E., Kruegel, C., Vigna, G.: PUBCRAWL: protecting users and businesses from crawlers. In: USENIX Security Symposium, pp. 507–522 (2012)
25. Jueckstock, J., Kapravelos, A.: Visible V8: in-browser monitoring of JavaScript in the wild. In: Proceedings of the ACM SIGCOMM Internet Measurement Conference, IMC, pp. 393–405 (2019)
26. Kelley, P.G., et al.: Guess again (and again and again): measuring password strength by simulating password-cracking algorithms. In: Proceedings - IEEE Symposium on Security and Privacy (2012)
27. Laperdrix, P., Rudametkin, W., Baudry, B.: Beauty and the beast: diverting modern web browsers to build unique browser fingerprints. In: 37th IEEE Symposium on Security and Privacy (S&P 2016) (2016)
28. Lerner, A., Simpson, A.K., Kohno, T., Roesner, F.: Internet jones and the raiders of the lost trackers: an archaeological study of web tracking from 1996 to 2016. In: USENIX Security 2016 (2016)
29. Lourenço, A.G., Belo, O.O.: Catching web crawlers in the act. In: Proceedings of the 6th International Conference on Web Engineering, pp. 265–272. ACM (2006)
30. Lu, B., Zhang, X., Ling, Z., Zhang, Y., Lin, Z.: A measurement study of authentication rate-limiting mechanisms of modern websites. In: Proceedings of the 34th Annual Computer Security Applications Conference, ACSAC 2018 (2018)

31. McKenna, S.F.: Detection and classification of Web robots with honeypots. Ph.D. thesis, Naval Postgraduate School, Monterey, California (2016)
32. Melicher, W., et al.: Fast, lean, and accurate: Modeling password guessability using neural networks. In: 25th USENIX Security Symposium (USENIX Security 2016). pp. 175–191 (2016)
33. Mowery, K., Bogenreif, D., Yilek, S., Shacham, H.: Fingerprinting information in JavaScript implementations. In: Wang, H. (ed.) Proceedings of W2SP 2011, IEEE Computer Society, May 2011
34. Mowery, K., Shacham, H.: Pixel Perfect: Fingerprinting Canvas in HTML5. In: Proceedings of W2SP 2012 (2012)
35. Mulazzani, M., et al.: Fast and reliable browser identification with javascript engine fingerprinting. In: Web 2.0 Workshop on Security and Privacy (W2SP), vol. 5 (2013)
36. Nikiforakis, N., Kapravelos, A., Joosen, W., Kruegel, C., Piessens, F., Vigna, G.: Cookieless monster: exploring the ecosystem of web-based device fingerprinting. In: Proceedings of the 2013 IEEE Symposium on Security and Privacy, pp. 541–555 (2013)
37. Nikiforakis, N., et al.: Stranger danger: exploring the ecosystem of ad-based URL shortening services (2014)
38. Olejnik, Ł., Acar, G., Castelluccia, C., Diaz, C.: The leaking battery. In: Data Privacy Management, and Security Assurance (2015)
39. Park, K., Pai, V.S., Lee, K.W., Calo, S.B.: Securing web service by automatic robot detection. In: USENIX Annual Technical Conference, General Track, pp. 255–260 (2006)
40. PhantomJS - Scriptable Headless Browser. http://phantomjs.org/
41. Shekyan, S.: Detecting PhantomJS Based Visitors (2015). https://blog. shapesecurity.com/2015/01/22/detecting-phantomjs-based-visitors/
42. Srinivasan, B., et al.: Exposing search and advertisement abuse tactics and infrastructure of technical support scammers. In: Proceedings of the 2018 World Wide Web Conference (2018)
43. Starov, O., Gill, P., Nikiforakis, N.: Are you sure you want to contact us? Quantifying the leakage of PII via website contact forms. In: Proceedings on Privacy Enhancing Technologies (2016)
44. Starov, O., Nikiforakis, N.: XHOUND: quantifying the fingerprintability of browser extensions. In: 38th IEEE Symposium on Security and Privacy (S&P 2017), San Jose, United States (2017)
45. Tajalizadehkhoob, S., et al.: Herding vulnerable cats: a statistical approach to disentangle joint responsibility for web security in shared hosting. In: Proceedings of the 24th ACM SIGSAC Conference on Computer and Communications Security. ACM (2017)
46. Tan, P.N., Kumar, V.: Discovery of web robot sessions based on their navigational patterns. In: Intelligent Technologies for Information Analysis (2004)
47. Thomas, K., McCoy, D., Grier, C., Kolcz, A., Paxson, V.: Trafficking fraudulent accounts: the role of the underground market in twitter spam and abuse. In: USENIX Security (2013)
48. Van Goethem, T., Piessens, F., Joosen, W., Nikiforakis, N.: Clubbing seals: exploring the ecosystem of third-party security seals. In: Proceedings of the 2014 ACM CCS Conference (2014)
49. Vastel, A., Laperdrix, P., Rudametkin, W., Rouvoy, R.: FP-STALKER: tracking browser fingerprint evolutions. In: 39th IEEE Symposium on Security and Privacy (S&P 2018) (2018)

50. Vastel, A., Rudametkin, W., Rouvoy, R., Blanc, X.: FP-Crawlers: studying the resilience of browser fingerprinting to block crawlers. In: Starov, O., Kapravelos, A., Nikiforakis, N. (eds.) NDSS Workshop on Measurements, Attacks, and Defenses for the Web (MADWeb 2020) (2020)
51. Vissers, T., Van Goethem, T., Joosen, W., Nikiforakis, N.: Maneuvering around clouds: bypassing cloud-based security providers. In: Proceedings of the 22nd ACM CCS Conference (2015)
52. Xie, G., Hang, H., Faloutsos, M.: Scanner hunter: understanding http scanning traffic. In: Proceedings of the 9th ACM Symposium on Information, Computer and Communications Security (2014)

Short Paper - Taming the Shape Shifter: Detecting Anti-fingerprinting Browsers

Babak Amin Azad[1(✉)], Oleksii Starov[2], Pierre Laperdrix[3], and Nick Nikiforakis[1]

[1] Stony Brook University, Stony Brook, USA
baminazad@cs.stonybrook.edu
[2] Palo Alto Networks, Santa Clara, USA
[3] CNRS / Univ. Lille / Inria, Lille, France

Abstract. When it comes to leaked credentials and credit card information, we observe the development and use of anti-fingerprinting browsers by malicious actors. These tools are carefully designed to evade detection, often by mimicking the browsing environment of the victim whose credentials were stolen. Even though these tools are popular in the underground markets, they have not received enough attention by researchers. In this paper, we report on the first evaluation of four underground, commercial, and research anti-fingerprinting browsers and highlight their high success rate in bypassing browser fingerprinting. Despite their success against well-known fingerprinting methods and libraries, we show that even slightest variation in the simulated fingerprint compared to the real ones can give away the presence of anti-fingerprinting tools. As a result, we provide techniques and fingerprint-based signatures that can be used to detect the current generation of anti-fingerprinting browsers.

1   Introduction

Major database hacks and personal information leaks have been the common cyber news headline for the past couple of years. Haveibeenpwned[1], the website that hosts the records of publicly known credential leaks, currently hosts 428 instances of credential leakage from different websites, including some highly popular (e.g. Linkedin and Dropbox). The number of accounts affected by these leaked credentials adds up to over 773 million accounts.

In a similar fashion, the online shopping industry has been the prime target of attackers. In 2019, over 180,000 websites were successfully attacked by Magecart hackers [11]. By implanting malicious JavaScript code on hacked websites, attackers behind these operations steal credit card and payment information of clients upon checkout. According to statistics from the security industry [11], these attacks have so far affected more than 2 million users.

The stolen credentials and credit card information typically end up being sold in bulk in the underground markets [30]. Verification and monetization of

---

[1] https://haveibeenpwned.com/.

© Springer Nature Switzerland AG 2020
C. Maurice et al. (Eds.): DIMVA 2020, LNCS 12223, pp. 160–170, 2020.
https://doi.org/10.1007/978-3-030-52683-2_8

the stolen information at scale requires specific tools. Automation is also a vital part of these malicious operations as the size of the data that needs to be verified and then abused becomes increasingly larger. As a result, malicious actors have built automation tools to speed up this process. The existing anti-bot and fraud detection tools and services heavily rely on browser fingerprinting [13]. In order to bypass these mechanisms, malicious actors use specialized browsers that enable them to easily switch fingerprints or simulate a target browsing environment and evade detection. We assembled our list of anti-fingerprinting browsers by searching the underground markets for the tools that malicious actors use, as well as commercial and research projects that promise to defend against tracking. Success stories (e.g., reaching over 90% success rate in carding attempts) and tutorials on configuring and efficiently using these browsers are widely available on different carding forums [1,2,9,10]. Malicious actors use these forums to trade the stolen credit card information and share their latest tips on successful cashout strategies.

Tools such as AntiDetect [22] and Fraudfox [21] are commonly incorporated to mask the browser fingerprints of attackers and evade detection from tools that look for known good (i.e. belonging to a specific benign user) or known bad (i.e. belonging to a previously seen attacker) fingerprints. These browsers not only enable attackers to switch browser fingerprints, they also give them the ability to mimic a victim's environment, such as, setting their timezone and screen resolution to match the victim when visiting websites to make fraudulent purchases or access the hacked accounts.

Even though these tools are popular among attackers, they have not received the attention they deserve from the research community. In this paper, we study the techniques that these tools incorporate to remain undetected and quantify their effectiveness against state-of-the-art, in browser fingerprinting. After analyzing the fingerprintable surface of these tools, we show that we were able to devise fingerprinting-based signatures for all of them which can be used to uniquely identify them. Our findings can be used by the existing anti-fraud systems to precisely identify the usage of anti-fingerprinting browsers.

2   Background

In a typical case of online fraud, multiple entities are involved. Usually, one party is responsible for stealing credentials, which are then sold in bulk to another party to be monetized [28]. The timeliness of these events is crucial. As the stolen information gets stale, it is more likely for the compromised websites or individual victims to have been informed about their information being stolen and invalidate their credentials. In the mean time, to prevent issues with stolen credentials, merchants who process payment information started to incorporate browser fingerprinting to detect fraudulent and automated browsing activities.

Companies providing fraud detection services commonly use browser-fingerprinting to track users [4,5,7,27]. By collecting information from users' web browsers, these services build browsing profiles of normal users. This information is then used to filter out fraudulent requests.

State-of-the-art browser fingerprinting identifies users by leveraging features such as HTTP headers and available JavaScript APIs [16,24]. The act of fingerprinting transcends the actual browser, enabling the identification of the operating system and the underlying hardware [15]. This is typically achieved based on the characteristics of rendered images within an HTML canvas element [14,25]. Other researchers have focused on other parts of the browsing environment to build more robust fingerprints by extracting the list of available fonts and browser extensions [18,29]. Fingerprintjs2 [32], a well-known browser fingerprinting library, compiles the previously mentioned fingerprinting methods in a JavaScript module that can be integrated with any website to collect browser fingerprints of its visitors. Lastly, behavioral features of the user like the use of clicks or touch can be collected to separate interactive user activity from that of an automated client.

3   Anti-fingerprinting Browsers

To battle fingerprinting, anti-fingerprinting browsers capable of modifying the content of their fingerprint were created. We categorize the browser fingerprint modification schemes into three groups. Each group has its own benefits and drawbacks as we discuss below:

- **JavaScript Injection:** In this method, JavaScript is injected into all webpages loaded by the browser. This way, JavaScript properties and methods are overwritten to send different information to servers. For example, when a script wants to access `navigator.userAgent` or render a canvas image, it will find the newly injected version instead of the default one. The strength of this approach is the ease of deployment and maintainability. However, prior work has shown that these spoofing extensions may not offer the best protection against fingerprinting as they often present incomplete coverage of JavaScript objects and can create impossible configurations [26].
- **Native Spoofing:** Native spoofing modifies the source code of the browser to return modified values. For some attributes, changing the sent value is as simple as rewriting a string but for other methods like canvas fingerprinting, successful modifications require a deeper understanding of a browser's codebase to find the right methods and modify them appropriately. The strength of this solution is that it can be hard to detect as an inspection of the Document Object Model (DOM) is not sufficient to detect traces of spoofing. However, the downside is that the cost of maintenance can be high, requiring a complete rebuild of the browser after each update.
- **Recreating Complete Environments:** This method consists of utilizing a virtualized browsing environment with a desired configuration on top of the host system. The advantage of this method is that the fingerprint presented to servers is genuine as the components truly run on the system. For the same reason, no impossible configurations can result from such an approach. On the downside, this approach requires more system resources compared to a simple browser extension or a modified browser.

In this section, we analyze research, commercial, and underground tools against fingerprinting, in order to understand whether masking the true fingerprint of a device can help bypass current fingerprinting techniques. Next, we list the tools that are included in this study along with the anti-fingerprinting mechanism they use.

AntiDetect and Fraudfox [JavaScript Injection]. AntiDetect is one of the first tools that surfaced online against browser fingerprinting, gaining visibility from a 2015 article [3]. AntiDetect uses JavaScript injection and relies on a browser extension to change the exhibited browser fingerprint. To improve usability, users are presented with an interface where they can choose a profile from a pool of existing browser fingerprint profiles. Fraudfox appeared at approximately the same time as AntiDetect and works in a similar fashion by providing an interface to users for selecting the fingerprint they want to expose [21]. Fraudfox offers the option to modify several attributes separately and also targets advanced techniques, such as, font fingerprinting. It uses a custom Windows XP virtual machine and a tool named *OSfuscate* to change the TCP/IP fingerprint of the system in order to confuse `nmap`-like tools that can identify OSes based on the structure of network packets.

Mimic [Native Spoofing]. Mimic is a modified Chrome browser that uses native spoofing to modify its fingerprint [8]. Users can generate various profiles and activate the desired fingerprinting protection. One particularly interesting feature of Mimic is that it gives users the option to either block, or introduce noise into some fingerprinting-related APIs. In contrast to the previously mentioned underground tools, Mimic takes a different approach and advertises itself as a generic solution against browser fingerprinting that can be used for marketing, journalism, cyber investigation, and even web scraping activities.

Blink [Recreating Complete Environments]. Blink is a moving-target-style defense against browser fingerprinting. Proposed by Laperdrix et al. [23], this tool assembles a set of components at runtime into a virtual machine. Upon each execution, the virtual machine's environment is modified with new configurations (e.g., timezone, available fonts, etc.) in order to generate an organic browser fingerprint. This guarantees that the exhibited fingerprint is coherent compared to the other tools where the artificial combination of browser properties can easily result in impossible configurations.

A full comparison of the tools along with the exact fingerprinting techniques that each of them counters, can be found in Table 1. The main tactic that these tools incorporate against detection is frequent rotation of valid fingerprints. That is, the common elements in browser fingerprints as mentioned both in the literature and popular opensource fingerprinting libraries such as Fingerprintjs2, are configurable.

These values are faked through a large list of valid fingerprints that is either shipped with these browsers or can be easily generated through their interface.

For instance, AntiDetect comes with over 4,000 profiles and Fraudfox includes profiles with 90 user-agents and 5 browsers and 6 operating systems. Moreover, users can choose to add noise to certain APIs such as audio context and the canvas API. This variety makes it hard to derive features from the common fingerprinting libraries to uniquely identify these browsers. Interestingly, Fraudfox has been tested against popular browser fingerprinting tools and the successful rotation of fingerprints and removal of tracking information (e.g., Evercookies [6]) has been verified in the underground carding forums [10].

All of the studied anti-fingerprinting browsers, except Blink, which is discussed separately in Sect. 4, modify or add noise to the existing browser properties. We will discuss in more detail how this type of modification will inherently introduce inconsistencies and demonstrate concrete examples of these inconsistencies and use them to build signatures that uniquely identify these browsers in Sect. 4.

Table 1. Overview of the studied tools with the fingerprinting techniques they counter

Tool	AntiDetect	Fraudfox	Mimic	Blink
Type	Injection	Injection	Native	Recreation
Tested version	7.1	1.5.1	1.4.8	1.0
Number of profiles or components	>4,000	600 fonts, 90 user-agents, 85 plugins, 5 browsers and 6 OS	1,000	2,762 fonts, 39 plugins, 6 browsers and 4 OS
Browser used	Firefox 41-48	Firefox 41	Chrome 61	Latest versions of Chrome and Firefox
Network	-	Proxy through *SocksCap64* + Obfuscation of OS Network packet through *OSfuscate*	Built-in proxy management (HTTP, Socks5)	Built-in support for Tor
User Agent	✔	✔	✔	✔
Language	✔	✔	✔	
Screen	✔	✔	✔	
Navigator	✔	✔	✔	✔
Timezone	✔	✔	✔	✔
Date			✔	
Fonts	✔	✔	✔	✔
Plugins	✔	✔	✔	✔
Media devices			✔	
Canvas	Noise (letters in strings)	Noise (fonts and colors)	Noise (fonts and colors)	Noise (change of OS)
WebGL	Blocked	Blocked	Only vendor and renderer	Noise (change of OS)
WebRTC	✔		Block or fake IP address	
Geolocation	✔		✔	
Hardware Concurrency			✔	

4 Detecting the Anti-fingerprinting Tools

To extract unique characteristics that can be used to uniquely identify each browser, we analyzed each tool using the techniques described by Nikiforakis et al. [26] and Acar et al. [12]. We investigate built-in JavaScript objects, such as, navigator and screen with and without anti-fingerprinting mechanisms, looking for inconsistencies. According to Vastel et al., existing bot detection schemes already use similar techniques to detect the presence of impossible fingerprints [34]. To the best of our knowledge, we are the first to report on the fingerprintability of dedicated anti-fingerprinting tools.

```
navigator.getGamepads.toString.toString()
//Returns "function () { return "function getGamepads() {
    [native code] }";}"
//
//Standard Firefox returns
//"function toString() {
//    [native code]
//}"
```

```
CanvasRenderingContext2D.prototype.__lookupSetter__("
    strokeStyle").toString()
//Returns
//"function (){
//"use strict";
//this.strokeStyle=settings.strokeStyle}"
//
//Standard Firefox returns
//"function set strokeStyle() {
//    [native code]
//}"

canvas = document.createElement("canvas");
canvasContext = canvas.getContext("2d");
canvasContext.fillStyle = "#ff6600";
canvasContext.fillStyle.toString();
//Returns the color set by the user: "#71cda0"
//Standard Firefox returns the color from the script: "#
    ff6600"
```

Listing 1. Detecting JavaScript injection performed by AntiDetect (top) and Fraudfox (bottom)

• **AntiDetect** Since AntiDetect relies on a browser extension, a single line of JavaScript is sufficient to detect injected values. Notably, objects created through JavaScript are easily identifiable as they only contain a toString function. In Listing 1 (top), we can clearly see the getGamepads function written by the developers to modify the returned value as if it was a native one.

Like other tools relying on JavaScript injection, inconsistencies in fingerprints are possible and frequent. One example is when AntiDetect launches a Chrome profile where one can observe the presence of both *webkit* and *moz* prefixed properties which is impossible as these belong to two different rendering engines. Another example is a mismatch between two attributes where the user-agent reports a 64-bit OS and the `navigator.platform` indicates a 32-bit one.

• **Fraudfox** presents the same shortcomings as AntiDetect as it also relies on the same spoofing method. However, one needs to look elsewhere to find traces of JavaScript injection. As shown in Listing 1 (bottom), the developers directly poison the prototype of specific objects. One can also easily find the parameters that are set in the tool's interface like the exact filling color of the canvas API. This could, in fact, act as a long-time identifier if the user always reuses the same profile without regularly updating the canvas color. Finally, Fraudfox has its own set of inconsistencies. For example, Chrome profiles present *moz*-prefixed properties but no *webkit* ones. Mac profiles show *.dll* extension for plugins instead of *.plugin*.

• **Mimic** is harder to detect compared to the two previous solutions because it does not rely on JavaScript injection. However, the browser is still identifiable through some unique inconsistencies that come from its database of fingerprints. When spoofing the WebGL Renderer, Mimic always add the *ANGLE* string in front of every value. However, this string can only be found on Windows as Chrome uses the ANGLE backend on this operating system to translate OpenGL API calls to DirectX. On Linux, plugins with the *.so* extension are visible creating an inconsistency if a Windows or a Mac profile is selected. Finally, Mimic presents an incorrect priority in the HTTP language header. The second language should present a priority of 0.9 ("en-US,en;en;q=0.9") but Mimic returns one of 0.8 ("en-US,en;en;q=0.8"). Changing the priority is easily fixable in the profile database but it shows that the smallest detail can render a tool identifiable.

Focus on Canvas Poisoning. Each tool also has its own canvas poisoning technique, which as we demonstrate is identifiable. Figure 1 illustrates them.

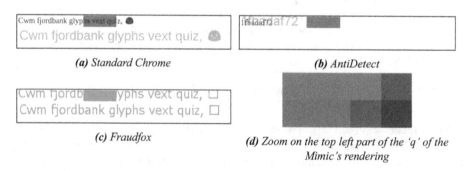

(a) *Standard Chrome*

(b) *AntiDetect*

(c) *Fraudfox*

(d) *Zoom on the top left part of the 'q' of the Mimic's rendering*

Fig. 1. Renderings of the same canvas test

AntiDetect changes the letters of a given string and their position. Fraudfox modifies the colors set by a script. This is directly configurable in the interface of the tool. Moreover, since the tool runs on Windows XP, the OS does not have any fonts that support emojis (presence of a green square at the end of the strings). Mimic is different from the other two as the modification is almost invisible for the user. Mimic introduces a small amount of noise but an in-depth analysis reveals that the transparency of some pixels were changed (on the zoomed-in image, the top half of the orange rectangle is more transparent than the bottom half).

Overall, our findings demonstrate that a combination of several tests is sufficient to precisely identify all evaluated anti-fingerprinting tools. The quirks discovered can be corrected but our results confirm that it is difficult to design an anti-fingerprinting tool that is not detectable. For both JavaScript injection and native spoofing, the smallest oversight can make the user stand out, be marked as malicious and invalidate the offered protection.

Blink and the Recreation of Complete Environments

In this section, we showed how the operators of anti-fraud systems can fingerprint anti-fingerprinting tools, based on the latter's inability of perfectly mimicking a non-native browsing environment. Blink, the research prototype by Laperdrix et al. [23] that we introduced in Sect. 3, sets itself apart from the rest by the fact that it does not attempt to mimick a foreign environment. Instead, Blink assembles a real environment with different components and launches that environment in a virtual machine. As such, none of the techniques presented in this section can be used to detect Blink since there is no mimicking involved and therefore no inconsistencies to be discovered.

Despite Blink's attractiveness for defeating fingerprinting-based, unwanted online tracking (since users can keep changing their fingerprints and therefore break the linking of browser sessions), we argue that Blink's utility is limited for attackers. This is because, an attacker who tries to match the fingerprinting of a victim user, must utilize Blink to recreate the entire browsing environment of their victim. This requires not just the installation of the appropriate software, but even the purchase of the appropriate hardware (e.g. to match the number of threads in the victim's CPU and how the victim's graphics card renders complex 3D scenes). All of this is clearly possible for highly targeted attacks but also highly unlikely for the monetization of credentials, since the investment in assembling the right environment can exceed the profit from the stolen credentials.

5   Related Work

Prior work can be split into the study of underground markets, browser fingerprinting, and bot-based fraud detection.

Singh et al. studied the underground ecosystem of credit card fraud [28]. They describe the different methods that attackers use to steal credit card information. These methods range from POS malware to exploitation of a vulnerability. Given the difficulty and risk associated with monetizing stolen credentials, attackers often resort to selling these illicitly obtained credentials to other attackers specializing in monetization. The authors then go over the existing channels to monetize the cards (e.g. by delivering high-end goods purchased with stolen credentials to unsuspecting users who believe they are working for a shipping company and will then re-ship the goods to another destination [19]). Other works focused on trafficking of fraudulent twitter accounts in the underground markets [31]. Fallmann et al. discussed their finding on probing these markets [17] and Thomas et al. assessed the effect of data breaches on the activities of underground markets [30].

In the realm of browser fingerprinting, researchers keep identifying features that can be extracted from browsers and make browser fingerprints more robust [14,15,18,25,29,33]. As fingerprinting-based fraud detection tools incorporate these features into their techniques, the tools used by attackers must also account for them (such as accounting for canvas-based fingerprinting, as described in Sect. 4).

One of the challenges in the study of JavaScript files and fingerprinting scripts is instrumenting the various API calls and monitoring them. VisibleV8 is a Chromium based browser that is easy to maintain over time and provides the ability to monitor JavaScript API calls [20]. The authors used their customized browser to analyze the prevalence of scripts that query for bot and browser automation artifacts on popular Alexa websites.

6   Conclusion

In this paper, we showed that anti-fingerprinting tools are capable of bypassing the protection of state-of-the-art fingerprinting techniques by masking the components that are queried by fingerprinting libraries. We analyzed their masking techniques (i.e., JavaScript injection, native spoofing, and the recreation of complete environments) and described the process of identifying fingerprinting-based inconsistencies which can be used to identify them and block them. Our analysis showed that all tools that attempt to mimick non-native environments are unique fingerprintable and therefore can be identified by anti-fraud systems, through the use of our proposed fingerprinting vectors. Finally, we discussed the difficulty of fingerprinting tools that are based on the recreation of browsing environments and the reasons why these tools are highly unlikely to be used in generic, non-targeted attacks.

Acknowledgements. We thank the anonymous reviewers for their helpful feedback. This work was partially supported by a gift from Amazon and the National Science Foundation (NSF) under grants CNS-1813974, CNS-1617902, and CMMI-1842020.

References

1. AntiDetect tool, only way to cashout from stolen credit cards (2015). https://www.ehacking.net/2015/03/antidetect-tool-only-way-to-cashout.html
2. Fraudfox makes it easier for thieves to empty bank accounts (2015). https://www.pcworld.com/article/2872372/this-tool-may-make-it-easier-for-thieves-to-empty-bank-accounts.html
3. Post by Brian Krebs on AntiDetect (2015). https://krebsonsecurity.com/tag/antidetect/
4. DataDome: Protect your website from bot traffic (2017). https://datadome.co/
5. Distil Networks: Bot Mitigation & API Security (2017). https://www.distilnetworks.com/
6. Evercookie (2017). https://github.com/samyk/evercookie
7. ShieldSquare: Bot Mitigation & Protection (2017). https://www.shieldsquare.com/
8. Multilogin - The Most Advanced Browser Fingerprinting Protection Ever Created - Enter Mimic (2018). https://multiloginapp.com/advanced-browser-fingerprinting-protection-ever-created-enter-mimic/
9. AntiDetect 7 and FraudFox VM, best carder protection (2019). https://imgur.com/a/ycxFTtz and. https://bazaar.blockstamp.market/listings/view/QmX9VGTz2HziSqL7kjNSGjPe8UHDrdyyxZwXyQbBgTbWcN-antidetect-7-fraudfox-vm-full-version-of-both-applications-best
10. Fraudfox tool in and underground carding forum (2019). https://imgur.com/a/6xmYPgN and. https://www.verifiedcarder.ws/threads/fraudfox-tool-cracked.21485/
11. Magecart Skimmers Spotted on 2M Websites (2019). https://www.darkreading.com/endpoint/magecart-skimmers-spotted-on-2m-websites/d/d-id/1336011
12. Acar, G., et al.: FPDetective: dusting the web for fingerprinters. In: Proceedings of the 2013 ACM SIGSAC Conference on Computer & Communications Security (2013)
13. AminAzad, B., Starov, O., Laperdrix, P., Nikiforakis, N.: Web runer 2049: evaluating third-party anti-bot services. In: DIMVA (2020)
14. Bursztein, E., Malyshev, A., Pietraszek, T., Thomas, K.: Picasso: lightweight device class fingerprinting for web clients. In: Proceedings of the 6th Workshop on Security and Privacy in Smartphones and Mobile Devices (2016)
15. Cao, Y., Li, S., Wijmans, E.: (Cross-)browser fingerprinting via OS and hardware level features. In: NDSS (2017)
16. Eckersley, P.: How unique is your web browser? In: Atallah, M.J., Hopper, N.J. (eds.) PETS 2010. LNCS, vol. 6205, pp. 1–18. Springer, Heidelberg (2010). https://doi.org/10.1007/978-3-642-14527-8_1
17. Fallmann, H., Wondracek, G., Platzer, C.: Covertly probing underground economy marketplaces. In: DIMVA (2010)
18. Fifield, D., Egelman, S.: Fingerprinting web users through font metrics. In: Proceedings of the 19th International Conference on Financial Cryptography and Data Security (2015)
19. Hao, S., et al.: Drops for stuff: an analysis of reshipping mule scams. In: Proceedings of the 22nd ACM Conference on Computer and Communications Security (2015)
20. Jueckstock, J., Kapravelos, A.: Visible V8: in-browser monitoring of JavaScript in the wild. In: Proceedings of the ACM SIGCOMM Internet Measurement Conference, IMC (2019)

21. Kirk, J.: This tool may make it easier for thieves to empty bank accounts. https://www.csoonline.com/article/2871248/fraud-prevention/this-tool-may-make-it-easier-for-thieves-to-empty-bank-accounts.html

22. Krebs, B.: 'AntiDetect' Helps Thieves Hide Digital Fingerprints. https://krebsonsecurity.com/2015/03/antidetect-helps-thieves-hide-digital-fingerprints/

23. Laperdrix, P., Rudametkin, W., Baudry, B.: Mitigating browser fingerprint tracking: multi-level reconfiguration and diversification. In: 10th International Symposium on Software Engineering for Adaptive and Self-Managing Systems (SEAMS 2015) (2015)

24. Laperdrix, P., Rudametkin, W., Baudry, B.: Beauty and the beast: diverting modern web browsers to build unique browser fingerprints. In: 37th IEEE Symposium on Security and Privacy (2016)

25. Mowery, K., Shacham, H.: Pixel perfect: fingerprinting canvas in HTML5. In: Proceedings of W2SP 2012 (2012)

26. Nikiforakis, N., Kapravelos, A., Joosen, W., Kruegel, C., Piessens, F., Vigna, G.: Cookieless monster: exploring the ecosystem of web-based device fingerprinting. In: Proceedings of the 2013 IEEE Symposium on Security and Privacy (2013)

27. PerimeterX: Anti Bot Protection - Protect Against Bot Attacks. https://www.perimeterx.com/

28. Singh, A.: The Underground Ecosystem Of Credit Card Fraud. Black Hat Asia (2015)

29. Starov, O., Nikiforakis, N.: XHOUND: quantifying the fingerprintability of browser extensions. In: 38th IEEE Symposium on Security and Privacy (2017)

30. Thomas, K., et al.: Data breaches, phishing, or malware? Understanding the risks of stolen credentials. In: Proceedings of the 2017 ACM SIGSAC Conference on Computer and Communications Security (2017)

31. Thomas, K., McCoy, D., Grier, C., Kolcz, A., Paxson, V.: Trafficking fraudulent accounts: the role of the underground market in Twitter spam and abuse. In: USENIX Security (2013)

32. Vasilyev, V.: FingerprintJS2: Modern & flexible browser fingerprinting library. https://github.com/Valve/fingerprintjs2

33. Vastel, A., Laperdrix, P., Rudametkin, W., Rouvoy, R.: FP-STALKER: tracking browser fingerprint evolutions. In: 39th IEEE Symposium on Security and Privacy (2018)

34. Vastel, A., Rudametkin, W., Rouvoy, R., Blanc, X.: FP-Crawlers: studying the resilience of browser fingerprinting to block crawlers. In: Starov, O., Kapravelos, A., Nikiforakis, N. (eds.) NDSS Workshop on Measurements, Attacks, and Defenses for the Web (2020)

It Never Rains but It Pours: Analyzing and Detecting Fake Removal Information Advertisement Sites

Takashi Koide[1,2(✉)], Daiki Chiba[1], Mitsuaki Akiyama[1], Katsunari Yoshioka[2], and Tsutomu Matsumoto[2]

[1] NTT Secure Platform Laboratories, Musashino, Japan
takashi.koide.fk@hco.ntt.co.jp
{daiki.chiba,akiyama}@ieee.org
[2] Yokohama National University, Yokohama, Japan
{yoshioka,tsutomu}@ynu.ac.jp

Abstract. Fake antivirus (AV) software is a serious threat on the Internet to make users install malware and expose their personal information. Fake removal information advertisement (FRAD) sites, which introduce fake removal information for cyber threats, have emerged as platforms for distributing fake AV software. Although FRAD sites seriously threaten users who have been suffering from cyber threats and need information for removing them, little attention has been given to revealing these sites. In this paper, we propose a system to automatically crawl the web and identify FRAD sites. To shed light on the pervasiveness of this type of attack, we performed a comprehensive analysis of both passively and actively collected data. Our system collected 2,913 FRAD sites in 31 languages, which have 73.5 million visits per month in total. We show that FRAD sites occupy search results when users search for cyber threats, thus preventing the users from obtaining the correct information.

Keywords: Fake AV software · Social engineering attacks

1 Introduction

Antivirus (AV) software is one of the basic defense strategies for protecting users' devices. The major AV software market was valued at 3,770 million USD in 2018 [12], and attackers focus on the needs of such pervasive AV software to gain financial benefits. Specifically, *fake AV software*, which are rogue applications disguised as legitimate AV software, is used to manipulate users' devices and steal money or sensitive information [2,18]. For example, once fake AV software is installed, the software displays fake virus scan results to get users to purchase additional licenses [4,23].

Fake AV software is a traditional cyber threat that can effectively spread malware and unwanted software on the web [11,22]. To infect users and gain more profit, attackers take advantage of online advertisements that target many people

© Springer Nature Switzerland AG 2020
C. Maurice et al. (Eds.): DIMVA 2020, LNCS 12223, pp. 171–191, 2020.
https://doi.org/10.1007/978-3-030-52683-2_9

to distribute fake AV software [26]. The web pages served by these advertisements typically show fake virus infection alerts or messages claiming the necessity of installing their software. These web pages also attract users with promises of speeding up their machines [24]. Attackers use such social engineering techniques that exploit users' psychological vulnerabilities to lure users to download fake AV software. These web pages are known to be major distribution paths for fake AV software [7,15,27].

In this paper, we focus on new techniques that psychologically encourage users to install fake AV software from the web. Attackers create web pages that introduce fake information for handling specific cyber threats, such as malware infection or visits to malicious web pages, and suggest fake AV software. We call these web pages *fake removal information advertisement (FRAD) sites*, which target users who have already suffered from security problems and which make them victims of another one. For example, users who notice their malware infection try to search for removal information using the malware detection names given by virus scanners, and they reach the FRAD sites from search results. Believing the FRAD information, the users follow the instructions and inadvertently install the suggested fake AV software. Although it is well known that attackers induce users to install fake AV software using scaring or attracting messages–such as fake infection alerts or promises to speed up their machines– little attention has been given to analyzing the FRAD sites.

Here, we propose a system that automatically crawls the web pages and detects FRAD sites. Using the linguistic and visual features of the web pages, we accurately identify FRAD sites with 98.8% true positives and only 3.3% false positives. We used our system for a large-scale collection of FRAD sites and found 2,913 distinct domain names of FRAD sites written in 31 languages. The total user accesses to these FRAD sites was 73.5 million visits per month. We observed that these FRAD sites are not adequately reported by existing blacklists.

To reveal the ecosystem of FRAD sites, we performed a measurement study using both passively collected statistical data on user accesses and actively crawled data. We first investigated the incoming traffic to FRAD sites to determine what types of user behaviors are at risk of reaching FRAD sites. We found that many users not only accessed these sites from search engines directly but also reached FRAD sites from videos or messages posted on social media by attackers' accounts. To determine what kinds of attacks users encounter from FRAD sites, we then analyzed the transferred web pages and downloaded files from the FRAD sites. We confirmed that the FRAD sites led to 76 fake AV software families by directly distributing installers and luring users to payment and distribution sites. Also, we investigated search results for the names of specific cyber threats, and we found that 82.6% of the top 10 search results were occupied by FRAD sites. In other words, search results for information concerning cyber threats are poisoned by FRAD sites, making it difficult for users to obtain correct removal information. To the best of our knowledge, this is the first study that has revealed the prevalence and ecosystem of FRAD sites.

Fig. 1. Overview of fake AV software distribution via FRAD sites. Users that require removal information for cyber threats access FRAD sites via a web search (e.g., search engines or social media) (**❶**). They click on download buttons on the FRAD sites and are navigated to software distribution sites (**❷**). They download fake AV software from these sites (**❷**') or from the FRAD sites (**❸**) directly. Then, they make the damage even worse by installing the fake AV software (**❹**).

In summary, our contributions are as follows:

- We propose a system to crawl the web and detect FRAD sites automatically. By extracting linguistic and visual features from crawled web pages, our system detected FRAD sites with 98.8% true positives and 3.3% false positives.
- We performed a large-scale collection of FRAD sites on the web by leveraging a search engine, which is the most common channel used to reach FRAD sites. Using our system, we discovered 2,913 domain names of FRAD sites written in 31 languages. We found that attackers widely deploy FRAD sites targeting users in various countries to increase the number of page views.
- We conducted a comprehensive measurement study using both passively collected statistics data and actively crawled data to reveal the ecosystem of FRAD sites. Our measurement study also clarified the typical incoming channels employed by users to reach FRAD sites and the types of potential threats directed from the FRAD sites. We also found that it is difficult for users who need removal information for specific cyber threats to reach correct information, because most of the search results concerning cyber threats are poisoned by the FRAD sites.

2   Background

We first consider an attack technique for distributing fake AV software via FRAD sites. The purpose of the FRAD sites is to deceive users who need ways to deal with cyber threats, i.e., malicious acts that damage the users' devices and steal their sensitive information. Examples of cyber threats include malware infection, fraudulent popup messages, and malicious browser extensions. Attackers post multiple entries on FRAD sites that introduce fake threat removal guides, using the names of specific cyber threats, such as malware detection names or the domain names of malicious sites. For instance, there can be more than 15k entries in a single FRAD site, and dozens of new entries are added to the FRAD site every day. When users notice that they have security issues by looking at the results from legitimate virus scanners or from suspicious alert messages on web pages, they search for information to remove them. Users who reach FRAD sites and are deceived by false information install fake AV software, which makes matters worse. We focus on such scams on the web in this paper.

Figure 1 shows an overview of the distribution of fake AV software via FRAD sites. First, users who have security problems reach FRAD sites by searching for the specific names of cyber threats they want to remove (❶). Attackers leverage search engine optimization (SEO) techniques that target specific names of cyber threats to increase the web traffic to FRAD sites. Attackers also post fake videos on YouTube that introduce ways to remove the threats, and they post similar articles on Facebook and other social media to lure users to click on links to FRAD sites. Forum and community sites where anyone can post messages are also used by the attackers in the same manner. Thus, users not only visit FRAD sites from results provided by search engines but also reach FRAD sites through social-media postings and other web pages hit by the search results. The FRAD sites contain detailed fake removal guides for individual threats as well as large buttons or banners to direct users to fake AV software. The FRAD sites usually display the logos of famous security vendors or third-party organizations (e.g., software certification companies) to make them look as if they are legitimate web pages. Users who click on the buttons or banners are navigated to software distribution sites (❷). Most of the software distribution sites use domain names containing the names of the fake AV software and disguise themselves as official sites for legitimate AV software by displaying product information and purchase menus. These sites are also reachable through search engines and even provide customer support such as web chats or toll-free calls. On these web pages, users follow the payment and download instructions and then obtain fake AV software installers (❷'). These installers can also be downloaded from the FRAD sites directly (❸). Users install the fake AV software and thus become victims of other cyber threats (❹).

Some social engineering techniques are already known, such as threatening users using fake infection alerts or attracting them by the prospect of improving computer performance. However, it has not been clarified whether attackers use techniques for distributing fake AV software that exploit the weaknesses of users who have already suffered from cyber threats.

3 Method

In this section, we introduce our system for collecting and detecting FRAD sites on the Internet automatically. The system consists of two steps: web crawling and classification.

3.1 Web Crawling

The implementation of a web crawler that collects and stores browser-level information from web pages is the first step in our system. The requirement of the

Table 1. List of terms for each category; used to check the term's frequency in the title, URL paths, domain names, and text content of a web page.

Category	Example terms
way	"how to", "guide", "solution", "tips", "report", "instruction"
removal	"remove", "get rid of", "uninstall", "delete", "fix", "clean", "kill", "block", "repair", "anti", "entfernen", "eliminar", "verwijderen", "deinstallieren", "desinstalar", "supprimer", "remuovere", "usunac"
problem	"virus", "malware", "spyware", "trojan", "backdoor", "adware", "threat", "infection", "ransom", "error", "pop up", "redirect"
device	"computer", "pc", "windows", "mac", "browser"

crawler is to extract linguistic and image features from a web page rendered by a web browser and to compose a feature vector for the result. To analyze the FRAD sites in detail, we also need to capture the network traffic to and perform browser interactions on the web page. To achieve this, we designed and implemented the crawler using Scrapy[1], which is a web crawling framework for Python, in order to develop functions for monitoring and managing logged data. We used Selenium[2] as the middleware for Scrapy to automate a real web browser. We used Google Chrome as the default web browser for the crawler. To monitor network traffic in detail, we used Chrome DevTools API[3]. This is necessary, because we collect network-level information such as HTTP requests and responses that Selenium API does not handle directly. The collected information–such as screenshots, HTML source codes, and network traffic–are stored to MongoDB. We use those kinds of information for the next step, classification.

3.2 Classification

In the second step, our system extracts features from the information collected from the web pages and identifies FRAD sites using a supervised machine learning approach. In particular, the system analyzes term frequencies in web pages and URLs, the presence of logo images on screenshots, and HTML structures, such as the number of tags, and combines them into a feature vector. We explain the detail of each feature below.

Term Frequencies. To capture the linguistic characteristics of FRAD sites, frequencies of terms are used as a feature. To improve the SEO ranking and ensure an easy web page topic for users to understand, FRAD sites use terms meaning for the removal of cyber threats in the titles, URL paths, domain names, and text content of their web pages. Examples

---

[1] https://scrapy.org/.
[2] https://selenium.dev/.
[3] https://developer.chrome.com/extensions/devtools.

of such titles are *"Remove Trojan.Zerocleare (Virus Removal Guide)"* and *"Remove Magiballs.com (Free Guide)."* The URL paths include forms such as "/2019/12/27/how-to-remove-my-login-hub-virus-removal-guide/" and "/uninstall-nvux-xyz-from-windows-7-8-8-1-10." Examples of domain names are `uninstallmalwarefrompc[.]example` and `virusremovalguide[.]example`. The text content of the web page is written with a summary of the cyber threat and specific removal information for it.

Our key insight is that the FRAD sites must include a phrase composed of the following four categories of terms: *way, removal, problem,* and *device.* Table 1 shows a list of example terms. As the feature vector, we use the number of occurrences of each term category in the following four fields: the title, URL path, domain name, and text content. The terms in the four categories are intended to capture phrases such as *"how to remove Trojan.Zerocleare virus from my PC."* Because the FRAD sites are created in many languages, we leverage machine translation services such as Cloud Translation API[4] and Amazon Translate[5]. We translate the title and text content of the crawled web pages into English and then calculate the frequencies of the terms.

To create the list of terms, we extracted all terms that match each category from the title, URL paths, domain names, and text content of 300 FRAD sites that were randomly selected from our created dataset, as discussed below in Sect. 4. Some domain names include non-English terms in the *removal* category, such as "entfernen" in German and "eliminar" in Spanish. Because these domain names are difficult to translate, we manually obtained such terms as much as possible. To this end, we separated the domain names by "." or "-" and used word segmentation[6] and then searched for the meaning of each extracted word.

Logo Images. We next consider features that specify logo images on the FRAD sites. The FRAD sites include download buttons and software packages that may be shared among multiple FRAD sites. The FRAD sites also display logos of security vendors, operating system (OS) vendors or software certification companies in order to pretend to be legitimate sites. These logos are copied from vendors' sites or used as image files modified from the original images. To find such visual characteristics, our system uses an image matching approach on the basis of our logo image database. Specifically, the system extracts images from `img` tags and crops images for which the area matches `a` or `button` tag elements from screenshots. It calculates the perceptual hash[7] of these images and compares them to the image database. If the target image is more than 85% similar to the image in the database, the system determines it to be a logo image. Three types of images are stored in the database: logos of security vendors or software certification company (19 images), package images of fake AV software (33 images), and images of the download buttons (56 images). We extracted images

---

[4] https://cloud.google.com/translate/.
[5] https://aws.amazon.com/translate/.
[6] http://www.grantjenks.com/docs/wordsegment/.
[7] https://github.com/JohannesBuchner/imagehash.

belonging to the three types from the 300 FRAD sites used in the above. Our system counts the number of images that match each type to create feature vectors.

HTML Structure. Here, we explain the features extracted from the HTML structure that we use for identifying FRAD sites. As with previous works that identify specific types of malicious web pages [7,17], the numbers of `a` and `iframe` tags are important indicators of FRAD sites. Also, FRAD sites often re-use web page templates so that they have similar structures of HTML source codes. In other words, the frequency of HTML tags and combinations of those numbers characterize FRAD sites. To find such features, the system counts the number of appearances of HTML tags. The HTML tags to be counted are the top 30 tags frequently used in the 300 FRAD sites mentioned above.

4   Data Collection

We explain the method used to collect FRAD sites in the wild in order to make the dataset employed to evaluate our classification model. We first collected the names of cyber threats. Then, we searched for and gathered candidates of FRAD sites using the names of those cyber threats. Finally, we manually created a labeled dataset for our evaluation experiment.

4.1   Collecting Cyber Threats

We collected the names of cyber threats to make search queries to find candidate FRAD sites. As described in Sect. 2, FRAD sites prepare many entries that introduce ways of removing specific cyber threats such as malware detection names and malicious domain names. To collect such names efficiently, we crawled the database pages of security vendors (e.g., Symantec Security Center[8]) and a security community site (e.g., malwaretips[.]com) in October 2019. We collected 806 names of threats, including 500 malware detection names, 200 malicious domain names, and 106 popup messages.

4.2   Web Search

We created search queries using the collected names of cyber threats and gathered the URLs of web pages using a search engine. To collect FRAD sites efficiently, we added "how to remove" to the name of the cyber threat to create the search query, instead of searching only for the name of the threat. We found that we can collect more FRAD sites by searching with "how to remove" in our experiment described in Sect. 6.3. To collect search results systematically, we used Microsoft Bing Web Search API[9] and gathered 34k URLs. We chose one URL for each domain name from among the gathered URLs. As a result, we extracted 4,188 URLs with 4,188 unique domain names to crawl.

---

[8] https://www.symantec.com/security-center/a-z.
[9] https://azure.microsoft.com/en-us/services/cognitive-services/.

4.3   Creating the Dataset

We crawled 4,188 web pages using our system and created a labeled dataset. Since there is no existing URL blacklist that accurately identifies FRAD sites, we manually labeled them by analyzing the crawled web pages and actually accessed them as necessary. To efficiently conduct this process, we created a web application that displays screenshots and buttons to choose labels (FRAD and non-FRAD sites). This application extracts information about the crawled web pages from our MongoDB database and generates the web pages for labeling. We implemented it using Node.js and the Express[10] framework. We labeled web pages as FRAD sites if they satisfied following heuristic rules. If not, we labeled the web pages as non-FRAD sites.

   i. We check whether a web page introduces a removal guide for a specific cyber threat. If so, we check rule ii.
  ii. We check whether the web page has visual characteristics specific to FRAD sites, as described in Sect. 3.2. Specifically, we check whether the web page has an image of a fake AV software package or a logo of a security vendor or a software certification company. We also check screenshots of the removal instructions or download buttons, which are often shared with multiple FRAD sites. If the web page has these characteristics, we identify it as an FRAD site. If not, we further check rule iii.
 iii. We confirm that clicking a download button on the web page triggers a download of a fake AV software installer or initiates a web transition to a distribution or payment site for fake AV software. We performed this process by manually accessing the web page and clicking the download button.

From the 15-h labeling process, we obtained 804 web pages of FRAD sites with 804 unique domain names. To create a dataset, we randomly selected 800 web pages from these FRAD sites. We also randomly selected 800 web pages from non-FRAD sites, which are the web pages remaining after excluding the 804 web pages of FRAD sites. Since we collected the non-FRAD sites using the same search queries as for the FRAD sites, they often introduce removal information for cyber threats, details of malware, or introductions to legitimate AV software, just as FRAD sites do. Thus, it is a challenging task to identify FRAD sites accurately from these similar web pages.

5   Evaluation

We next evaluated the detection capability of our system in terms of its capability to classify web pages accurately as FRAD sites or non-FRAD sites. We also conducted an experiment to discover unknown FRAD sites in the wild using the trained classification model.

---

[10] https://expressjs.com/.

5.1   Detection Accuracy

We first evaluated the detection accuracy of our system using the balanced dataset including 800 FRAD sites and 800 non-FRAD sites. We used a random forest classifier as the machine learning algorithm for two-class classification, because we can easily tune it due to the small number of hyper parameters to be considered. We conducted a 10-fold cross validation to determine how accurately our system performed classifications. We found that our system classified web pages with a 98.8% true positive (TP) rate ($= \frac{TP}{TP+FN}$), where FN $=$ false negative, a 3.3% false positive (FP) rate ($= \frac{FP}{FP+TN}$), and with 96.8% precision ($= \frac{TP}{TP+FP}$). The system identified 26 non-FRAD sites as FRAD sites (FPs). Examples include articles from security vendors that introduce malware information, ranking web pages for legitimate AV software, and blog entries that describe correct removal instructions. Five FPs were security vendors' web pages that often appear in search results when searching for removal information for cyber threats. We can therefore reduce FPs by placing the domain names of major security vendors on a whitelist. Examples of false negatives include web pages with domain names that do not include words such as "remove" or "malware." Other false negatives do not contain visual features such as images of fake AV software packages or logos of security vendors.

5.2   Detecting Unknown FRAD Sites

To collect unknown FRAD sites that have not been found in Sect. 5.1, we conducted additional data collection and detection using our classification model, which has high detection accuracy.

Additional Data Collection. We first describe additional data collection to find more FRAD sites in the wild, such as non-English FRAD sites and FRAD sites with content copied from other sites. In the process of creating the dataset described in Sect. 4, we found many FRAD sites written in various languages. Some of them were translated automatically according to the browser's language setting when the web pages were loaded. Some web pages were also written in multiple languages to enable users to switch languages. In addition, we found FRAD sites dedicated to certain languages. In such cases, the domain names contain words in those languages (e.g., "entfernen" in entfernen-spyware[.]example and "eliminar" in eliminarvirus[.]example), as described in Sect. 3.2. We also found that FRAD sites are often copied from other FRAD sites and from legitimate sites that introduce specific malware removal information. These FRAD sites not only use the names of cyber threats extracted from legitimate sites but also copy page titles or entire articles from them. To find such FRAD sites, we collected page titles from legitimate sites (malwaretips[.]com and malwarefixes[.]com) and from the 804 FRAD sites we labeled, which include non-English sites, and we searched for the titles using Bing API. Although it is difficult to create search queries in multiple languages to collect non-English FRAD sites, we can gather them efficiently in this way. We gathered 16k page titles from these web pages and collected 836,731 URLs (111,161 domain names) from these search. We extracted up to three URLs from each domain name and crawled them (120,577 URLs) using our system.

Detection Result. As a result of the classification of additionally crawled web pages, we identified 6,130 URLs as FRAD sites. To find FPs, we manually checked web pages classified as positive in the same way as described in Sect. 4.3. Examples of FPs include the following. Some technical-support scam [14,21] sites were falsely identified as FRAD sites, because they offered support for malware removal and displayed noticeable phone numbers and web-chat support. These FPs are not FRAD sites, however, because they did not lead users to fake AV software but instead are actually malicious web pages themselves, which are listed in VirusTotal[11]. Moreover, our system falsely detected pirate web pages that introduce free downloads of fake AV software. Although such fake AV software is useless and not very well-known, some web pages illegally offered such software. Other FPs include software review and download sites, which distribute fake AV software as well as legitimate software. We also found FPs similar to those described in Sect. 5.1. By excluding these FPs, we finally determined 5,780 URLs (2,109 domain names) as FRAD sites. The precision of this classification result was 94.3%. Although this precision is somewhat less than the results obtained in Sect. 5.1, we accurately identified FRAD sites. The reason for this decrease in detection capability is that we changed the search queries from "how to remove" and the name of threats (used in Sect. 4.2) to page titles of known FRAD sites, so that the types of web pages in the search results were somewhat changed.

Summary of Collected FRAD Sites. Overall, in this paper we have identified 2,913 domain names, including the newly discovered 2,109 domain names, to be FRAD sites. To confirm the FRAD sites already reported by security vendors, we searched for all 2,913 domain names in VirusTotal. Of the total, 32.7% (952 domain names) of the domain names had URLs that had already been detected by one or more vendors. We also found 21.5% (626/2,913) of the domain names had URLs that are sources of detected files. Although some FRAD sites have been detected by a small number of security vendors, most of the FRAD sites we found in this paper have been unreported to date. These FRAD sites are less likely to be filtered out from search results, even if they were reported as malicious. Thus, most of these FRAD sites remain easily accessible to users and remain threatening to them.

---

[11] https://www.virustotal.com.

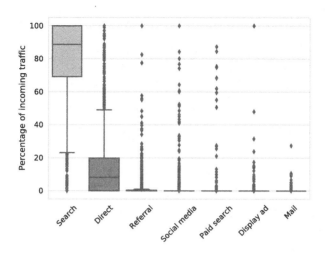

Fig. 2. Percentage of incoming traffic to FRAD sites from each channel.

6 Measurement Study

We measured the ecosystem and risk of FRAD sites using both passively collected statistical data of user accesses and actively crawled data. In the experiment described above, we found FRAD sites using our system and simply checked the detection status for each of them on VirusTotal. Here, we analyze deeply the 2,913 domain names of FRAD sites that we found in Sect. 5 in terms of incoming traffic to those FRAD sites, the distribution of fake AV software from those sites, and poisoned search results that are occupied by FRAD sites.

6.1 Incoming Traffic to FRAD Sites

To find out what browsing behaviors of users are at risk of reaching FRAD sites, we analyzed the incoming channels (i.e., ❶ in Fig. 1 in Sect. 2) of the FRAD sites that we found in Sect. 5. To this end, we need data on the history of user accesses to and traffic volumes of those web pages. Thus, we leveraged the statistical data provided by SimilarWeb[12], which passively observes hundreds of millions of global devices and covers over 220 countries and territories. Using this approach, we collected statistical data from October to December in 2019 that we used in the measurement studies described below.

Overview of Incoming Traffic. We first show an overview of seven types of incoming traffic to FRAD sites. We investigated 1,451 domain names of FRAD sites for which data are available in SimilarWeb (out of 2,913 domain names of the FRAD sites we discovered in this paper). Note that statistical data of web pages with few user accesses are not provided. These FRAD sites have

---
[12] https://www.similarweb.com/.

Table 2. Search queries used by the users to reach FRAD sites.

Category	Search query	#
Cyber threats	how to <remove><threat>	576
	<remove><threat>	438
	<threat>	849
	is <threat> safe ?	27
	what is <threat>	113
	<error>	140
Download	download <software>	421
	crack <software>	101
Fake AV software	<fake AV software>	66
Other	<other>	1,802
Total		4,510

73.5 million visits per month in total. Figure 2 shows the percentage of traffic to the FRAD sites from each incoming channel. The channels consist of seven labels: *Search* (accessed from a search engine), *Direct* (directly accessed by entering URLs in a web browsers), *Referral* (accessed from other web pages), *Social media* (accessed from Social Media), *Paid search* (accessed from keyword advertisements on search engines), *Display ad* (accessed from advertisements on web pages), and *Mail* (accessed from hyperlinks on email). Note that the incoming traffic measured as Mail comes only from web mail. Incoming traffic from email client software or other applications is measured as Direct. The mean values of Search, Direct, Referral, and Social media were 76.7%, 16.5%, 1.7%, and 1.7%, respectively. The value for each of the other three channels is less than 0.6%. Paid search, Display ad, and Mail have few data for further investigation. Also, we only know the amount of incoming traffic that we have shown here from the data of Direct. Therefore, in the following, we analyzed the detail of three channels: Search, Referral, and Social media.

Search. To find out how users reached FRAD sites via search engines, we investigated the statistics of the search queries. We extracted the top 10 English search queries (4,510 unique queries in total) for each FRAD site and categorized them. Table 2 shows the categories and the number of search queries. We found that 47.5% (2,143/4,510) of the search queries were related to the names of specific cyber threats. They included malware detection names (e.g., trojan:win32/bearfoos.a!ml), malicious domain names, and alert dialog messages (e.g., "your computer is infected with dangerous viruses"). Among them, 12.8% (576/4,510) are search queries combining "how to" with words meaning removal (e.g., "remove", "delete") and the names of cyber threats. We found that 9.7% (438/4,510) of the search queries combined words meaning removal with the names of cyber threats. Users also searched for the names of cyber threats alone

Table 3. Top 10 social media that led to FRAD sites.

Social media	# of FRAD sites
Youtube	160
Facebook	111
Reddit	58
Quora	35
Pinterest	22
Pocket	9
Twitter	7
Linkedin	6
Instagram	5

Table 4. Top 10 categories of referral web pages to FRAD sites.

Category of referral web pages	#
Computers electronics and technology	517
Games	29
News and media	25
Science and education	22
Business and consumer services	20
Arts and entertainment	19
Hobbies and leisure	8
Adult	8
Reference materials	7
E-commerce and shopping	6

(18.8%, 849/4,510) of for software or OS error messages (e.g., "MSVCP140.dll missing"). Thus, many users reach FRAD sites by searching for cyber threats and corresponding removal guides. The names of fake AV software were also used as search queries to reach FRAD sites (66/1,802). We found that 11.6% (522/4,510) of the search queries were used to search for downloads of software such as office software or video games and guides of cracking them. Forty percent (1,802/4,510) of the search queries were not included in these categories.

Social Media. We also analyzed incoming traffic from social media. We investigated 167 FRAD sites for which statistical data for queries incoming from social media is available from SimilarWeb. Table 3 shows the top 10 social media that led users to FRAD sites and the number of FRAD sites to which users were redirected from each type of social media. Users visited 95.8% (160/167) of FRAD sites from YouTube and 66.5% (111/167) of those from Facebook. Attackers create social-media accounts for these FRAD sites and post videos or messages to lure users to FRAD sites. These accounts pretended to be official accounts that use the web-site names or domain names of FRAD sites. They introduce removal information for cyber threats in the same way as entries for FRAD sites, and they put hyperlinks leading to FRAD sites in the description of their videos and messages. We found that some accounts post such instruction videos on YouTube several times a day. These videos got as many as 700k views. We also found that attackers created such accounts across multiple social media. In summary, attackers not only optimize search results to lead users directly to FRAD sites, but also they use various social media to increase user accesses to FRAD sites.

Referrals. In addition, we investigated referral traffic that leads users to FRAD sites. In other words, we analyzed the incoming traffic to FRAD sites when users accessed them from other web pages, excluding search engines and social media. We found that users visited 891 web pages belonging to various categories before reaching FRAD sites. Table 4 shows the top 10 SimilarWeb categories of these referral web pages. The most common category of referral web page is Computers Electronics and Technology, which includes forum and community sites such as social.technet.microsoft[.]com., ubuntuforums[.]org, and discussions.apple[.]com. In most cases, attackers abuse these sites, where anyone can post messages, to impersonate good users who introduce removal information for cyber threats with URLs of FRAD sites. The web pages categorized as Games (e.g., steamcommunity[.]com) were used in the same manner. Attackers also posted FRAD sites' URLs in comment sections in articles in News and Media and other categories. In short, attackers leverage popular web pages where they can post comments and hyperlinks to lure users to visit FRAD sites.

6.2   Downloads and Page Transitions from FRAD Sites

To identify threats that occur when users access FRAD sites, we performed an additional crawling experiment. While we simply found FRAD sites using our system in Sect. 5, and we investigated users' incoming traffic to them in Sect. 6.1, the malicious activity derived from them was not revealed by these experiments. Therefore, we actively crawled the FRAD sites and collected installers of fake AV software and their respective distribution sites. To this end, we added a function to the crawler of our system to enable it to detect a download button on an FRAD site and click it. Then we analyzed the downloaded files and transferred the web pages from those FRAD sites.

Collecting File Downloads and Web-Page Transitions. We first describe the details of the new function that enables our crawler to interact with the FRAD sites. The crawler crops images with areas that match the a tag and img tag elements of FRAD sites. If the crawler finds a "download" string in the images using optical character recognition, it clicks on that area. We used two types of UserAgent with different OS (Windows 10 and macOS v10.14). This is because FRAD sites change the fake AV software to be distributed according to the UserAgent's OS, typically Windows or Mac. To collect the URLs of FRAD sites to crawl, we searched for the 2,913 domain names of FRAD sites using Bing API and selected up to three URLs based on the search results for each domain name. The reason for this is that web pages of FRAD sites with the same domain names can lead to different destinations (e.g., different software distribution sites) depending upon their URLs. To find more fake AV software, we collected 8,099 URLs and crawled them twice with two types of UserAgent. As a result, the crawler downloaded 4,548 files with 594 unique MD5 hash values and reached 136 domain names (630 URLs) of web pages from FRAD sites. In the following, we investigated the downloads of fake AV software originating from the FRAD sites (i.e., ❸ in Fig. 1 in Sect. 2), web pages transferred from those sites (i.e., ❷ in Fig. 1), and redirectors that relayed these downloads and web page transitions.

Fake AV Software Downloaded from FRAD Sites. We analyzed the files that our crawler downloaded (see ❸ in Fig. 1) to identify the installers of fake AV software. First, we checked 594 files with unique MD5 hash values on Virus-Total and found that 89 of those files had been detected. To specify fake AV software families from the detected files, we manually analyzed and searched them using their filenames and metadata (e.g., product name, legal copyright, and file description) read by ExifTool[13]. We examined whether the 89 files were related to malware removal, registry fix, or speed up based on the above information and on the software distribution sites that we obtained from the search results. We classified 84 files into 58 unique fake AV software families with different software names. All 58 fake AV software families have software distribution sites reachable from search engines. The software distribution sites profess to be official sites for these fake AV software families. For example, these sites show download and purchase menus and provide customer support such as web chats or toll-free calls. The remaining five detected files were not fake AV software but instead were malware that pretend to be installers of legitimate software, such as music-production software and video games.

To find more fake AV software from the 505 undetected files, we compared their filenames and metadata with those of the classified 58 fake AV software families. As a result of determining files with the same strings as the fake AV software, we additionally found 189 files to be fake AV software. Overall, we found 278 files (31 dmg files and 247 exe files) of the 58 fake AV software families.

Web Pages Transferred from FRAD Sites. We also analyzed the web pages of 136 domain names that our crawler reached after clicking on download buttons (see ❷ in Fig. 1). In the above measurements, we investigated fake AV software directly downloaded from FRAD sites. However, FRAD sites also navigate users to software distribution sites that lure them to purchase and download fake AV software. To find such web pages, we analyzed the crawled data (e.g., screenshots of web pages) and manually classified the malicious web pages. We first checked the 136 domain names on VirusTotal and found that 57 domain names were detected. We then specified the web pages that offered license purchases of known fake AV software or were related to malware removal, registry fixes, and speed-up from the web pages of the 57 detected domain names. We found that 34 domain names were related to distributions of fake AV software, including six domain names of payment sites and 27 domain names of software distribution sites. The payment sites required inputting credit card numbers and personal information to purchase fake AV software. Out of the 27 domain names, we found that 18 domain names were distribution sites for 18 new fake AV software families in addition to the measurements described above, where we found 58 fake AV software families. Thus, we found 76 fake AV software families in total. The detected domain names also included five domain names of FRAD sites that we found in Sect. 5. That is, users may be transferred from one FRAD site to another. We also found malicious web pages that distribute malicious Chrome

---

[13] https://exiftool.org/.

Table 5. The percentage of FRAD sites included in search results.

	Threat name <threat name>	remove <threat name>	how to remove <threat name>
Malware	69.4%	87.9%	87.9%
Domain name	88.5%	93.5%	88.0%
Extension	36.1%	85.1%	87.2%
Total	70.6%	89.7%	87.8%

extensions. We found 14 domain names associated with such threats and four domain names related to distributions of other types of malware.

Redirectors. To reveal the network infrastructure related to the distribution of fake AV software, we investigated the redirectors that relayed the above fake AV software downloads and web page transitions. We analyzed the network traffic that our crawler captured and extracted redirectors for which the effective second-level domains (e2LD; e.g., example.com is a e2LD of www.example.com) are different from those of the source web pages (i.e., the FRAD sites) and destination web pages. We found 169 domain names (38 e2LD names) as redirectors of 1,048 URL redirections associated with fake AV software downloads and web transitions to software distribution sites. Nine of these domain names were known advertising domain names listed in EasyList[14]. In addition, we found a small number of redirectors that were involved in many fake AV software distributions. For example, we found that 76.4% of the URL redirections were associated with just two domain names: safecart[.]com and revenuewire[.]net. These two redirectors navigated to 17 and 14 fake AV software families, respectively. The domain name safecart[.]com not only is a redirector but also is a payment web page that prompts users for their credit card numbers. Some redirectors, such as reimageplus[.]com and paretologic[.]com, which are software distribution sites, navigated to other software distribution sites.

6.3   Search Poisoning

We conducted a further measurement experiment to analyze the percentage of FRAD sites in the search results. In Sect. 6.1, we used statistical data to investigate search queries that users used to reach FRAD sites. Then, we determined the risk of users reaching these FRAD sites by actually searching with those search queries and analyzing the search results. When users search for specific names of cyber threats to find removal information, many FRAD sites prominently show up in search results. To confirm these poisoned search results, we investigated 150 search queries, combining 50 cyber threats and three search patterns. The three search patterns are those that users frequently use, as found

---

[14] https://easylist.to/.

in the measurements in Sect. 6.1: "how to remove" and the name of a cyber threat, "remove" and the name of a cyber threat, and only the name of a cyber threat. We extracted the latest names of cyber threats from public lists: 20 malware detection names from Symantec Security Center and 20 malicious domain names from malwaretips[.]com. Also, we randomly chose 10 malicious browser extensions out of 14 browser extensions that we found in Sect. 6.2. We investigated the top 10 search results for each search query, which are the top result pages from popular search engines such as Google and Bing.

We collected 1,461 web pages from the top 10 search results for each of the 150 search queries in total. By matching the 2,913 domain names of the FRAD sites collected in Sect. 5.2, we found that 1,207 web pages (82.6%) were FRAD sites. Table 5 shows the percentages of FRAD sites included in the search results for each search query and the names of the cyber threats. When we searched for the names of cyber threats with "how to remove" or "remove," the percentages of FRAD sites were 87.8% and 89.7%, respectively. The FRAD sites were also included at a high rate in the results of searching only for the names of cyber threats. In particular, 88.5% of search results for the domain names were FRAD sites. Search results for malicious browser extensions did not include many FRAD sites (36.1%), but there was less useful information available for users to use to remove the threats or determine whether they are malicious. We also found 22 YouTube web pages as search results, with videos and descriptions that introduced FRAD sites. We found that 26.7% (40/150) of the search queries returned search results for which the top 10 web pages were all FRAD sites. In summary, we found that most of the search results were occupied by FRAD sites when users searched for removal information for cyber threats, making it difficult for users to reach correct information.

7 Discussion

Ethical Considerations. We followed research ethics principles and best practices to conduct this study [3]. We analyzed users' behavior to visit FRAD sites using anonymized statistical data on user accesses for this study. We purchased a license to access data that is legally collected based on SimilarWeb's privacy policy. The information extracted from the web pages we crawled is publicly available data. To reduce server load, our experiment that interacted with download buttons was performed only once for each web page that we identified as an FRAD site.

Limitation. Although our system can accurately identify FRAD sites, there are some limitations. Since our system is specialized for collecting and detecting FRAD sites, which are the important platforms used by attackers to distribute fake AV software, detecting software distribution sites is out of scope for this paper. We identified software distribution sites that pretended to be official sites for legitimate AV software on the basis of detection results from VirusTotal and manual analysis. We showed that we can visit various software distribution sites from FRAD sites by clicking on the FRAD sites. We also found that these software distribution sites share common network infrastructures, such as ad networks and redirectors. Thus, further analyses focusing on the web pages arriving from the FRAD sites collected by our system should support efficient collections of software distribution sites.

We then discussed a technique that can be used to evade our classification of FRAD sites. Developers of FRAD sites employ phrases related to the removal information for threats in domain names, URLs, titles, and text contents. This is because they use the topic of the web pages to attract or persuade users. They also place logos of trusted companies to disguise FRAD sites as legitimate sites. A possible evasion technique would be to remove these characteristics that psychologically affect users. However, this also would reduce the interest of users and the usefulness of the FRAD sites to the attackers. In addition, excluding phrases related to malware removal lowers the SEO rankings of FRAD sites and user accesses. Since our system relies on these characteristics to identify FRAD sites, we can accurately detect high-risk FRAD sites that strongly affect the users' psychology.

Since our collection of FRAD sites depends on search engine results, we have not collected all FRAD sites on the Internet. To efficiently collect FRAD sites, we used the names of the cyber threats that are mainly used by attackers to lure users and leverage search engines, which are the most common channel to lead a user to FRAD sites. As a result, our analysis found that FRAD sites are created in many languages and have a large amount of user access. Our system is useful for continuously collecting FRAD sites to create URL blacklists and for analyzing trends for this type of attack.

8   Related Work

We have reviewed related work that investigated the distribution infrastructure for fake AV software and the social engineering techniques attackers use to trick users. Using a combination of unsupervised, graph-based clustering, Cova et al. analyzed the network infrastructure (e.g., domain registration information and IP addresses) of fake AV software distributions to reveal their ecosystem and attack campaigns [2]. Although they investigated the relationship of servers hosting fake AV software, they did not discuss how users access these web pages. Rajab et al. conducted a measurement study that discovered web pages related to the distribution of fake AV software from data collected by Google [18]. They showed the prevalence of fake AV software in malware distributions on the web. Stone-Gross et al. proposed an economic model and estimated attackers' revenue by analyzing back-end servers that attackers used to support fake AV software businesses [23]. They identified the incoming channels that users employ to reach distribution sites, such as landing pages that exploit browsers to redirect users. They also described the social engineering techniques used to install fake AV software using web pages that display fake infection alerts. Although these studies analyzed the infrastructure and traditional distribution techniques for fake AV software–such as drive-by downloads and fake infection alerts–new distribution tactics using FRAD sites have not been revealed. There is also related work that describes case studies of fake AV software distribution from social engineering aspects [1,4–6,8–10,13–16,19–21,25,27–29]. In most studies, they analyzed fake infection alerts via advertisements that threaten or attract users to install fake AV software. However, no previous study has focused on the FRAD sites or analyzed attackers' techniques that exploit the psychological weakness of users who are suffering security problems.

9 Conclusion

We have proposed a system to crawl the web and automatically identify FRAD sites that introduce fake removal information for cyber threats and lure users to fake AV software. Using the proposed system, the first comprehensive measurement study was conducted to disclose the ecosystem of distributing fake AV software via FRAD sites. We have analyzed both passively collected statistical data on user accesses and actively crawled data to clarify users' risky behavior that leads them to reach FRAD sites and which exposes them to attacks navigated from FRAD sites. Our findings emphasize that it is very difficult for users who are suffering from cyber threats to reach correct removal information, because search results related to the specific cyber threats are poisoned by FRAD sites. Our system is useful for search engine providers and security vendors for excluding and blocking FRAD sites.

References

1. Caballero, J., Grier, C., Kreibich, C., Paxson, V.: Measuring pay-per-install: the commoditization of malware distribution. In: USENIX Security Symposium (2011)
2. Cova, M., Leita, C., Thonnard, O., Keromytis, A.D., Dacier, M.: An analysis of rogue AV campaigns. In: Recent Advances in Intrusion Detection, RAID 2010 (2010)
3. Dittrich, D., Kenneally, E.: The Menlo report: ethical principles guiding information and communication technology research. Technical report, U.S. Department of Homeland Security (2012)
4. Grier, C., et al.: Manufacturing compromise: the emergence of exploit-as-a-service. In: The ACM Conference on Computer and Communications Security, CCS 2012, pp. 821–832 (2012)
5. Invernizzi, L., Comparetti, P.M.: Evilseed: A guided approach to finding malicious web pages. In: IEEE Symposium on Security and Privacy, SP 2012 (2012)
6. John, J.P., Yu, F., Xie, Y., Krishnamurthy, A., Abadi, M.: deSEO: Combating search-result poisoning. In: 20th USENIX Security Symposium (2011)
7. Kharraz, A., Robertson, W.K., Kirda, E.: Surveylance: automatically detecting online survey scams. In: IEEE Symposium on Security and Privacy, SP 2018 (2018)
8. Kwon, Y., Saltaformaggio, B., Kim, I.L., Lee, K.H., Zhang, X., Xu, D.: Self destructing exploit executions via input perturbation. In: 24th Annual Network and Distributed System Security Symposium, NDSS (2017)
9. Li, Z., Zhang, K., Xie, Y., Yu, F., Wang, X.: Knowing your enemy: understanding and detecting malicious web advertising. In: The ACM Conference on Computer and Communications Security, CCS 2012, pp. 674–686 (2012)

10. Lu, L., Perdisci, R., Lee, W.: SURF: detecting and measuring search poisoning. In: Proceedings of the 18th ACM Conference on Computer and Communications Security, CCS 2011, pp. 467–476 (2011)
11. Malwarebytes Corporation: 2020 State of Malware Report (2020). https://resources.malwarebytes.com/files/2020/02/2020_State-of-Malware-Report.pdf
12. MarketWatch Inc: Global Antivirus Software Market Report 2019 and Future Opportunity Assessment 2024 (2019). https://www.marketwatch.com/press-release/global-antivirus-software-market-report-2019-and-future-opportunity-assessment-2024-2019-09-30
13. Mekky, H., Torres, R., Zhang, Z., Saha, S., Nucci, A.: Detecting malicious HTTP redirections using trees of user browsing activity. In: 2014 IEEE Conference on Computer Communications, INFOCOM 2014, pp. 1159–1167 (2014)
14. Miramirkhani, N., Starov, O., Nikiforakis, N.: Dial one for scam: a large-scale analysis of technical support scams. In: 24th Annual Network and Distributed System Security Symposium, NDSS (2017)
15. Nelms, T., Perdisci, R., Antonakakis, M., Ahamad, M.: Towards measuring and mitigating social engineering software download attacks. In: 25th USENIX Security Symposium, USENIX Security 16, pp. 773–789 (2016)
16. Nikiforakis, N., et al.: Stranger danger: exploring the ecosystem of ad-based URL shortening services. In: World Wide Web Conference, WWW (2014)
17. Rafique, M.Z., van Goethem, T., Joosen, W., Huygens, C., Nikiforakis, N.: It's free for a reason: exploring the ecosystem of free live streaming services. In: 23rd Annual Network and Distributed System Security Symposium NDSS (2016)
18. Rajab, M.A., Ballard, L., Mavrommatis, P., Provos, N., Zhao, X.: The nocebo effect on the web: an analysis of fake anti-virus distribution. In: 3rd USENIX Workshop on Large-Scale Exploits and Emergent Threats LEET 2010 (2010)
19. Sharif, M., Urakawa, J., Christin, N., Kubota, A., Yamada, A.: Predicting impending exposure to malicious content from user behavior. In: The 2018 ACM SIGSAC Conference on Computer and Communications Security CCS 2018 (2018)
20. Shen, Y., Mariconti, E., Vervier, P., Stringhini, G.: Tiresias: predicting security events through deep learning. In: Proceedings of the 2018 ACM SIGSAC Conference on Computer and Communications Security CCS 2018, pp. 592–605 (2018)
21. Srinivasan, B., et al.: Exposing search and advertisement abuse tactics and infrastructure of technical support scammers. In: Proceedings of the 2018 World Wide Web Conference on World Wide Web, WWW 2018, pp. 319–328 (2018)
22. Stein, E.: Hong Kong Based Malvertiser brokers traffic to fake antivirus scams (2019). https://blog.confiant.com/hong-kong-based-malvertiser-brokers-traffic-to-fake-antivirus-scams-over-100-million-ads-300e251eff06
23. Stone-Gross, B., Abman, R., Kemmerer, R.A., Kruegel, C., Steigerwald, D.G.: The underground economy of fake antivirus software. In: 10th Annual Workshop on the Economics of Information Security WEIS 2011 (2011)
24. Thomas, K., et al.: Investigating commercial pay-per-install and the distribution of unwanted software. In: 25th USENIX Security Symposium USENIX Security 16, pp. 721–739 (2016)
25. Vadrevu, P., Liu, J., Li, B., Rahbarinia, B., Lee, K.H., Perdisci, R.: Enabling reconstruction of attacks on users via efficient browsing snapshots. In: 24th Annual Network and Distributed System Security Symposium NDSS 2017 (2017)
26. Vadrevu, P., Perdisci, R.: What you see is NOT what you get: discovering and tracking social engineering attack campaigns. Proc. Internet Meas. Conf. IMC **2019**, 308–321 (2019)

27. Vissers, T., Joosen, W., Nikiforakis, N.: Parking sensors: analyzing and detecting parked domains. In: Network and Distributed System Security Symposium NDSS (2015)
28. Zhang, J., Yang, C., Xu, Z., Gu, G.: Poisonamplier: a guided approach of discovering compromised websites through reversing search poisoning attacks. In: Research in Attacks, Intrusions, and Defenses, RAID 2012 (2012)
29. Zhang, M., Meng, W., Lee, S., Lee, B., Xing, X.: All your clicks belong to me: investigating click interception on the web. In: 28th USENIX Security Symposium, USENIX Security 2019, pp. 941–957 (2019)

On the Security of Application Installers and Online Software Repositories

Marcus Botacin[1]([✉]), Giovanni Bertão[2], Paulo de Geus[2], André Grégio[1],
Christopher Kruegel[3], and Giovanni Vigna[3]

[1] Federal University of Paraná (UFPR), Curitiba, Brazil
{mfbotacin,gregio}@inf.ufpr.br
[2] University of Campinas (UNICAMP), Campinas, Brazil
{bertao,paulo}@lasca.ic.unicamp.br
[3] University of California Santa Barbara (UCSB), Santa Barbara, USA
{chris,vigna}@ucsb.edu

Abstract. The security of application installers is often overlooked, but the security risks associated to these pieces of code are not negligible. Online public repositories have been one of the most popular ways for end users to obtain software, but there is a lack of systematic security evaluation of popular public repositories. In this paper, we bridge this gap by analyzing five popular software repositories. We focus on their software updating dynamics, as well as the presence of traces of vulnerable and/or trojanized applications among the top-100 most downloaded Windows programs on each of the evaluated repositories. We analyzed 2,935 unique programs collected in a period of 144 consecutive days. Our results show that: (i) the repositories frequently exhibit rank changes due to applications fast climbing toward the first positions; (ii) the repositories often update their payloads, which may cause the distribution of distinct binaries for the same intended application (binaries for the same applications may also be different in each repository); (iii) the installers are composed by multiple components and often download payloads from the Internet to complete their installation steps, posing new risks for users (we demonstrate that some installers are vulnerable to content tampering through man-in-the-middle attacks); (iv) the ever-changing nature of repositories and installers makes them prone to abuse, as we observed that 30% of all applications were reported malicious by at least one AV.

Keywords: Installer · Downloader · Trojan

1 Introduction

Modern operating systems (OS) have been providing more resources to meet users requirements over time. However, the unique needs of an heterogeneous user population can only be fulfilled by third-party software. Whereas Linux-based systems model for obtaining new applications often depends from official distribution repositories [24], MS-Windows based systems do not present any centralized software repository, outsourcing to the users the responsibility for downloading additional programs.

In this scenario, online software repositories have become the *de-facto* standard repository for most users. On the one hand, these repositories are a very practical service, as they group multiple applications in a single place with ranking and searching features. On the other hand, these repositories hardly check binaries' security, neither regarding vulnerabilities nor maliciousness, and their providers often do not take full responsibility for the distributed software. Therefore, the users themselves are responsible for the implications of installing software downloaded from these repositories.

Actually, most users blindly trust the repositories, which makes them vulnerable to exploitable code constructions (e.g., buffer overflows and/or man-in-the-middle attacks) and/or Trojanization attacks, i.e., when malicious code is added to legitimate applications. Trojanization is a common practice among attackers to deceive users into installing their malicious payloads inconspicuously and, when deployed on popular repositories, it might have a large-scale impact if we consider the potential target population of trojanized downloads. Repository Trojanization examples include the cases of the Arch Linux repository [9], the Asus update system [38], and the Android platform [20].

This scenario becomes even worse if we consider that most software repositories are known for appending other components to their distributed applications (e.g., adware), in a process named "bundling" [17]. Software bundling might end up adding vulnerable components to previously safe applications. It might also add tracking capabilities to initially privacy-respecting applications. It also opens to attackers the opportunity of embedding malicious payloads in programs distributed through repositories. Recent cases include `Sourceforge` [34]—accused of distributing malware via bundled binaries [18]—and malicious samples distribution via application installers [28]. Despite all occurrences of trojanized software in popular online software repositories, the academic literature dedicated to investigate this phenomenon is limited, and the few existing work mostly target the Android OS [1, 4, 37], rather than MS-Windows, whose few existing work are still limited in coverage [13]. Therefore, to bridge this gap, we propose to investigate the five more popular online software repositories (according to Alexa [2]), aiming at shedding light on the occurrence of vulnerable constructions and Trojanized applications that actually may infect end users. To do so, we obtained the 100 most-downloaded Windows programs on each of the five chosen repositories for a period of consecutive 144 days (from Feb/2019 until May/2019). We submitted the resulting 2,935 distinct binaries to static and dynamic analysis systems. We also developed a tool to automatically install those programs during their run in the sandbox, which allowed us to observe interactions between the monitored program and the OS.

Our results show that (i) the repositories are very dynamic, presenting frequent rank changes, thus allowing applications to fast climb to the first rank positions; (ii) the repositories often update their payloads, with distinct binaries being distributed over time even for the same applications. We also observed differences in the installers for the same applications distributed by distinct repositories; (iii) the installers are very dynamic, presenting modular constructions and often downloading payloads from the Internet to complement their installation steps. Whereas enabling flexibility, relying on the Internet also poses new risks if security measures are not taken. In this sense, we demonstrate that some installers are vulnerable to content tampering via man-in-the-middle attacks; and finally (iv) all this dynamic characteristic of installers and repositories open space for abuse, with 30% of all applications being reported as malicious by at least one AV.

In summary, our contributions are as follows: (i) We characterize the way in which online software repositories update their application's rankings and binary sharing among distinct installers regarding their interaction with OS components to understand their implementation decisions, scope, and impact on users' devices; (ii) We present statistics about multiple aspects of the installers distributed by popular repositories aiming to support further research work and investigations; (iii) We investigate the interaction between application installers and the OS and evaluate installer's implementation choices; and (iv) We pinpoint behaviors found in installers that are compatible with malicious actions deployed by malware samples, and discuss best practices that could be adopted for the next-generation of non-intrusive application installers.

This paper is organized as follows: In Sect. 2, we present the main characteristics of online software repositories; In Sect. 3, we present the methodology adopted to conduct the performed experiments; In Sect. 4, we present evaluation results regarding the files distributed in online software repositories; In Sect. 5, we discuss our findings, their implications, and open research questions; In Sect. 6, we present related work to better position our developments; we draw our conclusion in Sect. 7.

2   Online Software Repositories

Online software repositories are popular websites: Softpedia ranks first in the Alexa's Shareware website list [2], with million accesses and downloads everyday. Google Chrome ranks third in this repository and accounts for 6M downloads. Microsoft Skype, the 28th, was downloaded 3M times. Other repositories present same magnitude data: Ubit ranks first in the CNET repository and was downloaded 24M times. Therefore, every action in these repositories has potential to affect million users. In this scenario, every small percentage matters in the long-tail.

Table 1 summarizes the diverse operation of the software repositories. It shows who starts the procedure to include a software in the repository (e.g., according to user's requests or to the website managers), who reviews the inclusion request (e.g., website managers), if the rankings are sponsored or not (e.g., if applications can climb ranking positions if they pay for it), on which servers the payloads are stored (e.g., internal repository's servers or developer's servers),

Table 1. Repository Summary. Repositories are diverse in multiple aspects.

Repository	Uploaded by	Reviewed by	Sponsored ranking	Servers	Security checks
FileHorse	Users	Site	✗	Internal/External	✓
Cnet	Users	Site	✓	External*	✓
FileHippo	Site	Site	✗	Internal	✓
SourceForge	Users	✗	✗	Internal	✓
Softpedia	Users	Site	✗	Internal/External	✓

and if the repository checks the distributed binaries (e.g., by performing some type of AV scanning). For most repositories, the process for adding a new software is started by the user filling some form. This will be further reviewed by the website managers. All repositories advertise they assure the software quality, but no guideline is specified for any repository. FileHippo does not accept user requests and its managers decide by themselves which application will be included. In Sourceforge's case, a project can be directly imported from Github. Once a software is included, its download page mentions the software creator, but they do not report who requested the software to be included. Most repositories allow the software to become popular by themselves, according to the number of downloads. CNET is a noticeable exception, allowing developers to sponsor their applications and climb ranking positions. Therefore, the application ranked first in the CNET repository is not necessarily the most popular application among all.

Most payloads are stored on internal repository servers and some repositories also allow users to directly get files from external sources (as an alternative link option). In most cases, the links point to the software creator's page. In CNET's case, they point to a CDN. Requests are performed along with tokens which allow identifying the request origin. In our tests, on the one hand, direct links always resulted in the download of the same updated binaries available in the software creator's page. On the other hand, internal links always served distinct files than the official release (mostly outdated versions). All repositories claim the provided files are security checked. Some of them are backed by popular solutions, such as Avast (FileHippo) and Bitdefender (SourceForge). Despite that, it is not clear to what extent analyses are performed.

3   Methodology

In this section, we describe our methodology for our experiments in collecting and analyzing programs distributed via online software repositories.

Repository Selection and Programs Collection. We selected the five most popular online software repositories according to Alexa score [2]: Softpedia [32], Source Forge [34], CNet [10], File Hippo [11], and File Horse [12]. Our intention was to ensure a broad range of samples and, at the same time, to be able to process all collected data on a daily basis. We developed an automated crawler (using Python's `Scrapy` [29]) to collect programs distributed by the aforementioned repositories. Our crawler operates as follows: (i) it first traverses all application ranking pages enumerating the available software and pages; (ii) it selects the top 100 most downloaded apps in the ranking; (iii) it accesses each selected application page and retrieves the download links; (iv) it downloads the file to our storage. This process was repeated daily for the five selected repositories, for a consecutive period of 144 days (from Feb/2019 until May/2019). Metadata from downloaded files were stored on a `sqlite` database, allowing further queries, such as: (i) what binary hashes were associated to which repositories; (ii) the binary's ranking position on a given day; (iii) the amount of distinct hashes collected under the same program's name in a given repository, among other information presented in Sect. 4.

Automated Application Installation and Analysis. Although some installers enable unattended software installs, most of them requires users to interact with GUIs to proceed with installing steps (Fig. 1). Therefore, to scale analysis of thousand samples, we developed a "clicker", i.e., an installing automation script that simulates user interaction with application installers. More specifically, we developed an `Autoit` [5] script to click the `Next` and `Finish` buttons displayed within graphical windows, allowing installers to proceed without human interaction.

Fig. 1. Automated Installation Example. AutoIT scripts click on the next button until the installation is complete.

We leverage static and dynamic analyses procedures [31] to identify whether an installer was Trojanized with malicious payloads and/or was implemented following bad development practices. To do so, we propose to match behaviors identified in installers to those knowingly exhibited by malware and suspicious software [16]. Our hypothesis is that benign software will exhibit none or few suspicious behaviors. We conducted static analysis procedures based on basic binary inspection—format and library identification, and samples submission to `VirusTotal` [35], to verify if those binaries would be detected by some AV installed on users' devices. The dynamic analysis consisted of running the samples in a virtualized sandbox machine with a malware monitoring system [7] to observe processes creation, filesystem operations, registry key changes, and network traffic. All valid Windows binaries were uploaded to that sandbox, in which each one was installed using our clicker.

Assumptions. The experimental setup described in this section is supported by the following assumptions: (i) Our goal is not to provide an exhaustive analysis of all existing application installers, but a view on the most downloaded (and supposedly most installed) applications; (ii) Since not all websites will be reachable and not all binaries will be available every day, our goal is to provide a long-term view of the evaluated repositories dynamics, instead of a snapshot of a certain day; and (iii) We understand that some installers' operation might be unsuccessful due to the sandbox execution and the clicker stimulation. Thus, our goal is to provide an overview of common practices implemented by the applications installers, avoiding focusing on particular cases.

4   Repositories Evaluation Results

In this section, we present the results obtained from the evaluation of the programs distributed by the five selected online software repositories. Our experiment consisted of the following steps: (i) description of the collected dataset; (ii) evaluation of the content distribution dynamics within the repositories; (iii) drawing a landscape associating installers interaction with operating system internals; (iv) comparing the behavior exhibited by installers of the same software, but distributed by different repositories; (v) investigation for evidences of software trojanization.

4.1   Dataset Description

During the 144 days of collection, we successfully downloaded 46,018 files from the five online software repositories and built a dataset with 2,935 unique files, related to 1,633 distinct programs (Table 2). From those programs, 13 were software intended to remove other applications (uninstallers) and, due to that, they were evaluated separately from the remainder of the dataset samples (considered as "installers").

The number of unique files is greater than that of unique applications because the distributed files vary over time (among distinct repositories as well as within the same repository), and the total number of downloaded files does not correspond to the expected sum of each repository downloads. The reason is that

Table 2. Dataset overview. The number of unique files differs due to changes in distribution over time.

Repository	Programs (#)	Unique Files (#)
FileHorse	82	314
Cnet	118	295
FileHippo	433	906
SourceForge	99	631
Softpedia	901	897
Total	1,633	2,935

Table 3. File sharing among repositories. They usually do not share files for the same programs.

Repositories	Sharing Rate (%)
(Cnet, FileHorse)	48.04
(FileHippo, FileHorse)	17.65
(Cnet, FileHippo)	15.69
(FileHippo, Source Forge)	07.84
(Cnet, Softpedia)	04.90
(Cnet, Source Forge)	03.92
(FileHorse, Softpedia)	00.98
(FileHippo, Softpedia)	00.98

105 (3.6%) files were shared by two (95% of all shared files) or three (5% of all shared files) repositories. In Table 3, we show that most repositories do not share files among themselves even for the same programs, implying that they distribute distinct program versions or installers.

Programs distributed by the repositories are packaged in multiple formats (Table 4). Although Trojanization can be implemented via any packaging type, we focused on binaries with Windows PE file format [25], since they are the prevalent file format in our dataset, and are also self-contained installers, which makes Trojanization easier for attackers. Most PE files present in our dataset are 32-bits, still reflecting the long-term trend of developers that delay the adoption of new programming techniques to native support 64-bit applications, as reported in [36]. Interestingly, some installers are packed with UPX (2.6%) and/or Armadillo (0.6%) so as to compress their payloads. Only 19.3% of the PE installers were crypto-signed.

Table 4. File types distribution.
Self-contained PE files are the prevalent type of program installers.

Type	Format		Prevalence (%)	
Java			0.67	
ISO			1.04	
Compressed	7-zip 0.37	RAR 0.30		
File	XZ 0.37	ZIP 20.47		
Formats	bzip2 0.37	gzip 1.34		
Windows	DOS 0.45	PE 65.63		
Binaries	.Net 0.67	PE+ 0.45		
Other			7.87	

Table 5. Binary file's size distribution.
Small binaries are associated to downloaders and large ones to droppers.

Interval (MB)	Frequency	Binaries (%)
[0.000, 0.400)	93	5.42
[0.400, 1.400)	128	7.46
[1.400, 5.000)	242	14.11
[5.000, 70.000)	619	36.08
[70.000, 150.400)	145	8.45
[150.400, 600.400)	105	6.12
[600.400, 888.000)	16	0.93

The variety of formats distributed by the software repositories affects the installers' file sizes, shown in Table 5. The differences in files sizes is important due to storage issues and because they may reveal implementation strategies behind the installer: smaller binaries usually only implement a client that downloads the actual payload from the Internet (Type I installer); larger binaries embed the payload themselves, dropping them at installation time (Type II installer). Although the first approach enables content creators to keep distributing up-to-date versions of their software, it makes security checking harder, as the distributed content changes very often. In terms of Trojanization, an attacker who controls a Type-I installer might implement a downloader [27], whereas an attacker who controls a Type-II installer might implement a dropper [16].

4.2 Repositories Dynamics

The chances that a malicious actor trojanizes a given repository and the impact that it can cause are strongly tied to the repository's operation dynamics, since more frequent repository updates make it harder to track newly added code. In addition, if it is easier for newly added software to climb the top ranking positions, their infection might become even more impacting. To delve into those dynamics, we evaluated the samples crawled daily from the repositories.

In Fig. 2, we show the number of downloads from each repository along the experiment's period. Overall, all datasets grew almost linearly due to our daily queries to the top-100 ranking positions. Variations were caused due to unreachable servers on a given day, or broken links/Web pages.

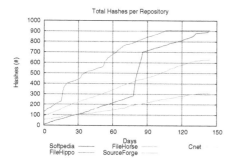

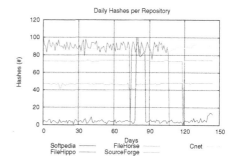

Fig. 2. Accumulative downloads for each software repository.

Fig. 3. Daily Downloads. FileHippo's servers were unreachable in the last week.

In Fig. 3, it is possible to observe that the download of more than 80 unique files (from the top-100) was only accomplished within FileHippo and CNET. The daily number of collected programs was mostly constant, if we consider each repository, with few days presenting peaks or valleys in the crawling process. The observed variations were related to Website updates or unavailability.

Each repository distinguishes itself regarding the samples successfully downloaded, as in the addition of new samples. Figure 4 shows the number of new unique samples (based on the binaries' MD5 hash) added to the repositories daily. We notice that `FileHippo` has many more new additions each day than the other repositories (except for particular peaks in Softpedia, Sourceforge, and CNET). This is caused by the frequent update of the distributed payloads, which indicates that FileHippo is more volatile about the content of its distributed installers (therefore may be riskier for users).

The observed strategy of payload replacement led us to hypothesize that the top-100 programs may also change their ranking positions frequently. To investigate this hypothesis, we measured the fraction of programs whose ranks changed each day. Figure 5 shows the change ratio per repository (we did not show FileHorse's results due to its incipient rank changes of less than 1% in most days), which confirms that almost all programs changed their position on some days. Similar to the aforementioned new hashes' case, we noticed that each repository has distinct ranking dynamics.

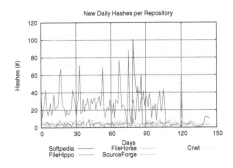

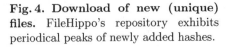

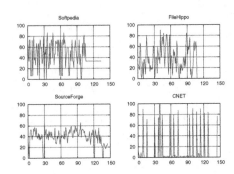

Fig. 4. Download of new (unique) files. FileHippo's repository exhibits periodical peaks of newly added hashes.

Fig. 5. Ranking position changes of the top-100 downloaded programs in each repository, but FileHorse. Observation days vs. applications (#) whose rank changed.

The ever-changing operation of software repositories is highlighted when we limit our analyses to the most downloaded programs. Initially, we believed that their ranking positions would hardly change, given their popularity. In practice, we observed that ranking changes affect even the most downloaded programs, occurring more frequently among the top-5 in all repositories. Understanding the phenomenon of frequent rank changes is important because it shows how quick a new (potentially malicious) software can reach the top of the ranking after its release. It also allows us to evaluate the extent of potential damages according to the number of affected users based on the popularity of programs. To explore this possibility, we measured how many programs change their ranking position at least once within a given repository, and how many positions on average they scale up the rank. Figure 6 shows that most programs change their position at least once (on average, only 12% finished the observed period in the same ranking position). We observed in all repositories' rankings that most programs scaled up few positions. We also observed that more programs increased their ranking instead of having it decreased. It happens due to the repository removing some programs from the top lists to add newer software, thus creating a gap in the former individual ranks while naturally allowing the latter to scale up some positions.

Although most programs does not reach the top of rankings, some of them scaled from the last pages to the first positions. We also observed that this growth occurred in a short period of time (only 4 days for Google Chrome and a month for other programs). The popularity of these programs raise concerns about the potential harm that might be caused if one of them is Trojanized. Highly popular programs, such as Google Chrome, were not expected to be low in the rankings any time. However, in times of Google Chrome version releases, (72.0.3626 in the period [14]), the ranks have to be updated with a new entry for this program. The possibility of changes in the binaries distributed for the same

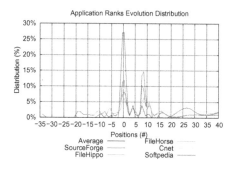

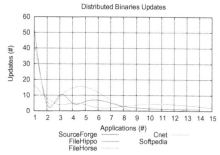

Fig. 6. Distribution of Programs in Ranking Positions. Most programs increase their ranking position (at least once).

Fig. 7. Distributed Binaries Updates. Most programs were updated few times, whereas some others, every week.

application over time also raises security concerns, since Trojanized versions of them could serve as a replacement to the legitimate ones. To evaluate this hypothesis, we measured how many repositories implement this practice and how frequent it is deployed by them. The rate of the software in each repository which had their binaries changed at least once in the observed period indicates that there is Trojanization opportunities for malicious actors: FileHorse (42.74%); FileHippo (30.36%), Sourceforge (29.58%); CNET (11.41%); Softpedia (9.43%). We consider these rates significant as they show that the repositories evolve not only by adding new software entries over time but also by modifying existing ones. The update of the distributed binaries is not homogeneous for all programs. Figure 7 shows the frequency in which each one of the applications have their distributed binaries updated during the observation period. We notice that while most programs are updated only few times—probably due to software updates— the remainder programs are updated very often. Some programs were updated more than 50 times (considering distinct repositories), an update rate greater than one time per week during the observation period. This constant updating routine opens a significant attack opportunity window, since at the time of the security analysis of previously distributed binaries is complete, the repository is already distributing a novel, not-yet-analyzed software version.

Among the programs whose binaries were updated more frequently, we highlight once again the importance of paying attention to the popular applications. For instance, Skype changed six times in FileHippo and seven times in FileHorse from February 13, 2019 to May 15, 2019. Those changes referred to updates either in the software version or in its distributed installer (discussed next in Sect. 4.3).

4.3   Installers' Dynamics

Repositories usually provide program installers, which perform numerous interactions with the underlying OS. For instance, they are responsible for copying contents to the correct directories, setting environment paths, adjusting Registry keys, loading drivers, installing additional services, and so on. The implementation strategies to accomplish those tasks is varied: installers may download payloads and related configuration files from remote servers, or directly extract them from embedded resources; their system configuration changes may affect a single user or the whole system; they may rely on system libraries or install their own ones; they may require privilege escalation or not. All of these actions affect system security, thus we present an overview of which of them were found in the evaluated installers, so as to draw a landscape of installers operations and the associated security risks. From the 1,633 collected programs, we limited our evaluation to the 993 unique binary samples packed as Windows executables (PE file format) that were successfully installed in our sandbox (the unsuccessful ones failed mostly due to corrupted files and/or missing environment variables).

Installers Modularity. We observed that installers present highly modular constructions. 52.62% of them created at least one child process during the installation process (98% of these created only a single process, but we identified one installer that created up to 15 child processes during its operation). Installers rely on child processes for multiple tasks: (i) 13.4% of the installers create new processes to relaunch the program installer with properly defined parameters, with the main installer executable being responsible only for displaying the Graphical User Interface (GUI), which allows users to specify what components will be installed; (ii) 1% of the installers create new processes to launch external tools to extract compressed objects (e.g., unzip); (iii) another 1% of installers rely on child processes to launch downloaders; (iv) 1% use children to launch post-installation procedures, such as opening a browser to display installation messages; and (v) 1% make child processes execute `cmd` or `powershell` scripts for them. The remaining modules invoked by installers were system processes intended to perform generic tasks. A major motivation for installers launching child process is to execute payloads extracted from the main installation binary. This "dropping" strategy was identified in 25.3% of samples. Code 1.1 shows two installers writing their payloads in executable files on disk. Their goal is to distribute multiple components as a single file.

```
1  C:\installer.exe|Write|C:\Users\Win7\AppData\Local\Temp
        \{907A1104-E812-4b5c-959B-E4DAB37A96AB}\vsdrinst64.exe
2  C:\installer.exe|Write|C:\Users\Win7\AppData\Local\Temp
        \{907A1104-E812-4b5c-959B-E4DAB37A96AB}\Install.exe
```

Code 1.1. Dropper Installer. Some Installers drop embedded payloads to disk and launch them as new processes.

Installers might also retrieve payloads from the Internet—10.8% of the evaluated ones exhibited this behavior. On the one hand, downloading payloads from Internet allows installers to retrieve them according to the installation environment (e.g., distinct OS versions), and to install updated versions of all software components. On the other hand, it requires a machine connected to the Internet at the moment of the intended program's install, which makes the installer less self-contained. Code 1.2 illustrates an installer requesting to download a payload from the Internet. This request was encoded to not reveal much information about its content.

```
1  GET 200.143.247.9:80 (et1.zonealarm.com/V1?
2  TW9kdWxlPWluc3RhbGxlch98U2Vzc2lvbj0wYzNjNDA1OD)
```

Code 1.2. Downloader Installer. Some Installers perform (encoded) network requests to retrieve payloads from Internet.

The exhibited behaviors of modularity (many child processes), downloader, and dropper are also reflected in the installers' written files (Table 6). The prevalent file types are libraries, which allow code reuse. Executables are the second most popular ones, since they represent the programs being installed. Temporary files are the third most popular extensions, mostly due to the objects dropped during installation procedures: installers usually drop small pieces of data to files to reconstruct global, complex structures, and the temporary files are used to store binary blobs, raw text, and proprietary structures. We also identified that VPX files—closed source files used by Avast and AVG antiviruses to store malware definitions—are very popular within installers, being used to deploy signature updates. Finally, we observed that some installers write SYS files, which allow them to load kernel drivers and affect the system as a whole.

Table 6. Top-5 file extensions most written by installers.

Extension	DLL	EXE	TMP	VPX	SYS
Files (#)	6,949	1,309	1,302	811	790

Network Usage. Payload downloading enables updated software versions install (e.g., AVs with up-to-date signatures). However, download mechanisms proper deployment may be challenging, resulting in security issues. For instance, flawed cryptography (or the lack of support for encrypted connections) may expose users to payload tampering via Man-In-The-Middle (MITM) attacks [26]. We identified 39 applications that download binaries via HTTP-only connections, as shown in Code 1.3. The list of installers that retrieve payloads via HTTP includes popular programs, such as Avast, BitDefender, AVG, and Kaspersky AVs. The AV's choice for HTTP-only downloads has already been reported in the past [22], but it seems to keep its standard practice status over time.

```
1  GET iavs9x.u.avast.com/iavs9x/
       avast_free_antivirus_setup_online_x64.exe
2  GET download.bitdefender.com/windows/bp/all/avfree_64b.exe
3  GET iavs9x.avg.u.avcdn.net/avg/iavs9x/
       avg_antivirus_free_setup_x64.exe
4  GET dm.kaspersky-labs.com/en/KAV/19.0.0.1088/startup.exe
5  GET download.bullguard.com/BullGuard190AV_x64_190411.exe
```

Code 1.3. Unencrypted Download by Installers. The use of HTTP-only connections may make users vulnerable.

To test whether the installers were actually vulnerable to payload tampering, we performed a MITM against them. Despite the unencrypted payload downloads, all popular installers, including AVs, were not vulnerable to payload tampering, since they are able to realize payload changes through certificates and checksum verification. Other programs, such as the BullGuard backup solution, are vulnerable to this type of attack[1]: its installer downloaded our supplied payload and executed it without any checks. This opens a significant infection vector for the execution of any attacker-supplied code if the installer is executed in a hostile network.

Installation Tracking. Installers also rely on Internet support to track programs' installs. 4% of all installers sent clear tracking data back to their servers during the installation step (Code 1.4). Additional tracking data might be sent after the program runs for the first time (e.g., software that require users registration).

```
1  GET /v1/offer/campaignFilter/?bundleId=UT006&campaignId=5
      b6352b3ce72513ae0a6beef
2  GET sos.adaware.com|/v1/offer/campaignFilter/?bundleId=
      UT006&campaignId=5b6352b3ce72513ae0a6beef
3  GET flow.lavasoft.com|/v1/event-stat?ProductID=IS&Type=
      StubBundleStart
```

Code 1.4. Installation Tracking. Some installers sent back tracking information to notify providers about the installation.

Application installers collect tracking data for many reasons, such as identifying software popularity by keeping track of the number of installations, and displaying targeted ads campaigns. Unfortunately, most installers do not make this user data collection explicit. For instance, the privacy terms for Code 1.4's program installer state that: *"We collect some limited information that your device and browser routinely make available whenever you visit a website or interact with any online service." "We collect this data to improve the overall quality of the online experience, including product monitoring, product improvement, and targeted advertising."* and that *"We may also include offers from third parties as part of the installation process for our Software"*. Besides the claims that the program collects a wide range of data, it is not clear what kind of data is collected during website visits, software execution, and software installation. Moreover, the installation step deserved a single line in the whole privacy term, showing that the impact of software installation is often understated.

Installer's Proxies. To access the Internet, some installers end up performing intrusive system changes. We identified that 5% of all installers changed proxy settings of the whole system. Code 1.5 shows an installer that enabled a proxy by writing to a system's Registry key. While some installers define new proxies, others only remove previously defined proxy settings. Although it may happen

---

[1] We contacted the vendor and disclosed all vulnerability's details so the company could fix it.

with the solely purpose to ensure that the payloads are downloaded from a proper source, it affects all further network requests.

```
214|2019-2-12 C:\Users\Win7\AppData\Local\Temp\BullGuard
    Backup Setup.exe|SetValueKey|HKU\<userid>\Software\
    Microsoft\Windows\CurrentVersion\Internet Settings|
    ProxyEnable|1
```

Code 1.5. Proxy Definition. Some installers change system-wide proxy settings.

Installers Persistence. Installers may change Registry keys to allow binaries to be invoked upon a system reboot. We identified that 1% of them exhibit this behavior. One reason for installers implement persistence is to set the installed program as a background daemon. This task is often performed by security applications' installers, such as AVs (Code 1.6). Another reason for the persistence behavior is because it allows splitting the installation process in multiple steps. This is required when the installation of some components requires rebooting (e.g., to load kernel drivers). Whereas daemons are often set by writing to the AutoRun Registry keys, multi-step installers often implement their own counters, as exemplified in Code 1.7.

```
C:\Users\Win7\AppData\Local\Temp\7zS4DEAD364\Stub.exe|
    SetValueKey|HKU\<userid>\Software\Microsoft\Windows\
    CurrentVersion\RunOnce|PandaRunOnce|
```

Code 1.6. Persistence. Some installers set executable paths in the Registry to be executed after a system reboot.

```
C:\Users\Win7\AppData\Local\Temp\ajAE1E.exe|SetValueKey|
    HKLM\SOFTWARE\Wow6432Node\AVAST Software\Browser|
    installer_run_count|1
```

Code 1.7. Multi-Step Installers. They control how many times they will run.

Affected System Scope. Installers may modify several other Registry keys. In many cases, these modified keys affect the whole system instead of the single user running the installer process. We identified that 56% of all installers affected only the single user who is installing the program (HKCU keys), whereas the remaining 44% also affected machine-wide Registry keys (HKLM).

Application Removal. Most installers do not implement proper cleanup routines after finishing the installation process. Only 33% of all installers dependent on temporary files deleted them before ending their process.

Allowing software to be properly removed is as important as to properly install the application. Unfortunately, not all installers provide adequate mechanisms to remove their installed objects: only 1% of them created an uninstaller object able to be invoked in a standalone fashion, as shown in Code 1.8.

```
1  C:\Users\Win7\AppData\Local\Temp\{907A1104-E812-4b5c-959B-
     E4DAB37A96AB}\Install.exe|Create|C:\Users\Win7\AppData
     \Local\Temp\{907A1104-E812-4b5c-959B-E4DAB37A96AB}\
     Uninst.exe
```

Code 1.8. Uninstaller Definition. Some Installers set uninstallers for the applications.

Identifying whether installers defined an uninstalling routine or not has proven to be a hard task: 1% of the tested programs define uninstalling routines based on specific parameters, as illustrated in Code 1.9.

```
1  C:\Program Files (x86)\GUM5D5C.tmp\fmanUpdate.exe|
     SetValueKey||HKU\<userid>\Software\fman\Update|
     UninstallCmdLine|"C:\Users\Win7\AppData\Local\fman\
     Update\fmanUpdate.exe" /uninstall
```

Code 1.9. Parameter-Based Uninstallers. They define command line parameters for software removal (difficult for users), instead of providing a self-contained uninstaller.

4.4   Comparison of Installers Versions

We identified that distinct binaries have been distributed for the same application over time and across repositories. Understanding the modifications that these binaries underwent might provide important insights to improve installers development and security.

Differences in Installers Within the Same Repository. We first evaluated how the binaries available for the same program and distributed by the same repositories change over time. We initially hypothesized that these binaries could be subject to significant modifications. However, we discovered that the modifications overall are more structural than behavioral, thus suggesting that the differences occur more due to installers evolution than due to other code insertion mechanisms.

In the cases when the installers were effectively modified to embed additional applications, their most prevalent payloads referred to toolbars and browsers add-ons. 1% of all binaries were versions of previous installers modified to include the Google Toolbar, which is often embedded as part of third party extensions within the main application (Code 1.10).

```
1  C:\installer\3rdPartyApp\GoogleToolBar\
     GoogleToolbarInstaller_zh-TW.exe
```

Code 1.10. Google Toolbar. It is embedded as 3rd-party extensions of the main app.

In cases where the installers do not directly perform a toolbar installation, they managed to change the native Internet Explorer configurations to display customized settings, which includes adding new bookmarks and cookies (Code 1.11).

```
1  HKCU\Software\Microsoft\Internet Explorer\LinksBar\
      ItemCache\ToolBar|Add
```

Code 1.11. IE Settings Modification. New bookmarks, cookies, and configurations set in the browser.

Another 1% of all binaries were embedded with advertisement applications instead of toolbars. These applications, known as `adware` (advertisement software), often run in background and keep collecting users information to feed targeted ads campaigns. Code 1.12 shows an adware running from a temporary file dropped by the main installer.

```
1  C:\Users\Win7\AppData\Local\Temp\is-3ACQL.tmp\
      Advertising_english.exe
```

Code 1.12. Adware. The advertisement software is dropped from a file created by the main installer.

Differences in Installers Among the Repositories. The tracking capabilities present in the installers are clearly revealed when we compare installers for the same applications downloaded from distinct repositories. While we were unable to identify any significant difference in the behaviors exhibited by the binaries, we easily noticed their tracking capabilities. Code 1.13 illustrates an excerpt of the installation trace for the same program, but using binaries downloaded from three distinct repositories. We notice that the `UserId` values considered in each installation is different for each binary. We executed many installation attempts and discovered that this number is not randomly generated, but seems to be tied to each binary. We considered this an indication that the installers are able to identify the origin of their installation.

```
1  C:\Setup.exe|SetValueKey|HKCU\Software\Microsoft\Client|
      UserId|{C2CFE0D4-A3A2-4458-A73F-F16F10E4C0D7}
2  C:\Setup.exe|SetValueKey|HKCU\Software\Microsoft\Client|
      UserId|{EA0CB74D-DB5D-40EE-A402-47A97F23904E}
3  C:\Setup.exe|SetValueKey|HKCU\Software\Microsoft\Client|
      UserId|{E81A6607-9EB3-49BA-B354-FA42817594BA}
```

Code 1.13. Tracking IDs of installers of distinct repositories. Each installer presents a distinct tracking ID according the repository from which they were downloaded.

4.5   Trojanization Evidences

The major problem associated with downloading software from third-party repositories is that the downloaded binary may be a Trojanized version of the original software. This type of attack has been becoming popular to the point of some installers explicitly warning users about this possibility, as shown in Fig. 8.

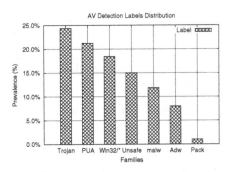

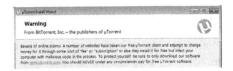

Fig. 8. Security Warning. Trojanization has become popular to the point of some installers warning users about this possibility.

Fig. 9.   AV   Labels   Distribution. Many samples were considered either as malicious or as trojanized.

To verify if Trojanization cases occur in practice, we performed AV scans on all downloaded binaries. We submitted all binaries to VirusTotal [35] and normalized the retrieved labels using AVClass [30]. We discovered that 31% of all binaries were detected by at least one AV. We further investigated the nature of these detection occurrences by inspecting the assigned AV labels, whose distribution is shown in Fig. 9.

The most prevalent detection label is "Trojan", which means that malicious code was inserted into application's native code. This finding shows that, as hypothesized, there is a real risk of application Trojanization in online software repositories. Among the Trojanized programs, we were able to identify 20 distinct families of the `Artemis` malware [33], thus showing that the attackers have been embedding real, harmful malware to the online repositories' distributed programs. Some AVs also detected the adware software embedded in part of the programs as malicious. This type of detection happens because the AV understands that the embodiment of advertising software to the original application implies on privacy leak risks to the user. A smaller part of the samples was detected as malicious due to their innate nature—12 installers were detected as downloaders and two as droppers, since the AVs were unable to distinguish their "legitimate" operation from the same behavior exhibited by malware classified as downloaders or droppers.

The detection of Trojanized apps is not uniform among the AVs, as shown in Fig. 10. Whereas some AVs detected only 3% of all samples reported as Trojanized by at least one AV, other AVs detected more than 60% of all reported samples. This shows that the AVs employ very distinct criteria for detecting Trojanization (e.g., adware inclusion is considered malicious for some but not for others). This highlights the need of checking multiple AVs in addition to the

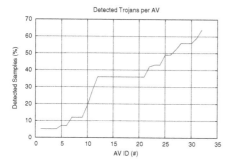

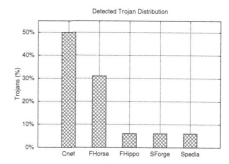

Fig. 10. Trojanized Apps Detection per AV. Distinct AVs present very distinct criteria and thus detection rates.

Fig. 11. Trojanized Apps Detection per Repository. Distinct repositories present very distinct rates.

ones considered in the repository pages, as this AV might have a very lax detection criteria. The detection is also not uniform among the repositories, as shown in Fig. 11. Whereas some repositories accounted for less than 10% of all detected malicious files in the period, CNET accounted for 50% of all samples. Despite that, we cannot claim that the CNET repository is more insecure than the others, as most detection occurrences are due to the repeated upload of the same flagged file. This shows that the evaluation of software repositories should also consider the frequency of upload of malicious files in addition to their occurrence.

5 Discussion

In this section, we revisit and discuss our findings to pinpoint existing gaps in the security of online software repositories and some possible and concrete improvement actions.

Paying Attention to Popular Applications. Although the software repositories may contain thousands of distinct applications, some of them gather more attention than others. Popular applications may be downloaded million times each month, thus presenting a huge potential of damage if they have been Trojanized. Our study showed that some programs are really popular, being present in the top download application rankings of multiple repositories simultaneously. In addition, in some cases, popular applications might quickly achieve the top ranking positions after a short period of time, which shows that the hypothesized popularity and usage broadness occurs in practice. In this scenario, it is essential for the repository administrators (and all security-related players) to pay attention to these programs to prevent trojanization cases, and counter them when they happen. In this sense, we consider that the recent decision of Google of extending its bug bounty program from its own applications to all other ones present in Google Play that have more than 100M installs [6] as a correct and very necessary move. Moreover, we consider that all other good security practices, such as fuzzy testing and audits, should be extended as well. Unfortunately, we are not aware of any kind of similar action regarding the samples provided by popular online Windows application repositories.

Reproducibility of Studies Leveraging Software Repositories. Many studies rely on software repositories as a source of binaries for their evaluation, either to measure bug prevalence in the software engineering context [15, 40], or as a direct source of goodware for balancing malware analysis datasets and/or machine learning training. These studies may be strongly impacted by our findings, since we showed that software repositories are very dynamic. In this scenario, a study conducted with the top applications of one repository might result in completely different conclusions when applied to other repositories. The same effect may happen even within the same repository if the software is collected on different days, as ranks and binary versions change over time. Therefore, reproducibility should be a concern for all researchers whose works rely on software repositories. Researchers need to find ways to make samples and other information available and reproducible, as only stating that the most popular samples from a given repositories were used in their study is not enough information to reproduce their experiments and obtained results in this ever-changing context.

Repositories as Source of Goodware. Binaries downloaded from software repositories are often used for malware classification and/or ground-truth [39]. Our findings also present strong implications to these cases. We showed that Trojanization might affect all repositories, thus even programs downloaded from "official" or popular repositories must be checked by antivirus solutions before being considered clean. Otherwise, the researcher could wrongly consider existing malicious behaviors embedded in the Trojanized application as ground-truth for benign applications. Even worse, one could mistakenly make a machine learning algorithm to learn a set of malicious behaviors as legitimate. Therefore, researchers should not blindly trust software repositories.

Other Repositories Issues. This work investigated the overall impact of using software repositories. Our results can be applied to both end-users downloading applications from these repositories as well as for researchers leveraging these applications as ground-truth for their experiments. However, software repositories present a myriad of applications that deserve special attention. Our goal in this work was not to exhaust the subject, but to give a first step towards a better understanding of characteristics of online repositories. We pinpoint that other repositories aspects might be addressed as future work. In particular, we understand that uninstallers might also be studied, in addition to the installers, since traces of previous applications can also significantly affect systems operations, either regarding continuous privacy leaks or performance degradation.

Limitations and Future Work. Software Repositories are very diverse and popular. Therefore, other repositories than the ones presented here should be studied to present a broader overview of security issues. This additional investigation might raise new hypothesis, such as if less popular repositories are more prone to be Trojanized than the ones here presented. The data collected in our experiments was not enough to cluster the tools used to trojanize the apps in classes. We expect that this task could be done via larger-scale experiments using multiple repositories.

6 Related Work

We here present related work to better position our contributions.

Trojanization is an effective and efficient approach to deliver malicious payloads, and its occurrence in practice presents large-scale implications. Code Trojanization has already been reported in practice in the repository of the Arch Linux distribution [9], in the Asus update platform [38], and even in the Android platform [20]. In the context of this research, we investigate occurrences similar to ones reported for SourceForge, accused of distributing malware among other applications [18]. We believe that Trojanization might become a prevalent problem in future years. Currently, Trojanization occurrence has been already reported even for hardware devices [8].

Software Repositories are very popular among many users as they allow gathering new software pieces in an easy way. Thus, they were studied by many researchers in the software engineering literature [15,40]. These work, however, are more focused on source-code analysis rather than on the binaries distributed to end-users. This type of research was only made popular in recent years due the emergence of application stores for mobile devices, as observed in the rise of many studies targeting the Android platform [1,4,37]. These research work identified phenomena such as the same app being distributed in different packages according the repository [3]. In this work, we extend this type of phenomenon observation to the scenario of online repositories for Windows binaries, whose few existing research work are still limited in coverage (e.g., evaluating less than thousand samples collected on a single day [13]).

Installers & Uninstallers are critical pieces of software for system operation as they perform extensive changes on the system's state. For instance, remaining registry entries after a software removal may cause systems to slowdown [19]. Unfortunately, there are currently a limited number of research work in the literature dedicated to investigate their impact, with most developments focusing on how to perform remote apps installation [41]. The closest work to ours are related to the investigation of the application installation logs on the Android platform [23] and the detection of piracy signs on application installers [21]. We extend these initiatives to investigate the occurrence of Trojanization on application installers.

7 Conclusions

In this paper, we investigated the occurrence of application Trojanization in the binaries distributed by popular Internet software repositories. We crawled the top-100 most downloaded Windows applications of five repositories for 144 days, which allowed us to characterize the dynamic of these repositories' operations. We also investigated the characteristics of the downloaded installers by running them in a sandbox solution instrumented with a clicker for automatic application installation, which allowed us to characterize installer's interactions with the operating systems. Our results show that: (i) the repositories are very dynamic, presenting frequent rank changes, thus allowing applications to fast climb to the first rank positions; (ii) the repositories often update their payloads, with distinct binaries being distributed for the same applications. There are also differences in the binaries for the same applications distributed by distinct repositories; (iii) the installers are very dynamic, presenting modular constructions and often downloading payloads from the Internet to complement their installation steps. Whereas enabling flexibility, this also poses new risks if security measures are not taken. We demonstrate that some installers are vulnerable to content tampering via man-in-the-middle attacks; and (iv) all this dynamic characteristic of installers and repositories open space for abuse, with 30% of all applications being reported as compromised by at least one AV solution. Our results shed light on some drawbacks of relying on software repositories, both by end-users installing these programs in their computers, as well for researchers leveraging these software repositories as ground-truth for their experiments. We also hope that our analysis could motivate other researchers to investigate other software repositories issues and help the community to understand their impact.

Reproducibility. all code developed to support this research work is available at https://github.com/marcusbotacin/Application.Installers.Overview.

Acknowledgments. We thank the anonymous reviewers and the shepherd Pierre Laperdrix for their valuable comments. This project was funded by the Brazilian National Counsel of Technological and Scientific Development (CNPq, PhD Scholarship, process 164745/2017-3) and the Coordination for the Improvement of Higher Education Personnel (CAPES, Project FORTE, Forensics Sciences Program 24/2014, process 23038.007604/2014-69).

References

1. Al-Subaihin, A., et al.: App store mining and analysis. In: DeMobile. ACM (2015)
2. Alexa: Top sites (2019). https://www.alexa.com/topsites
3. Ali, M., Joorabchi, M.E., Mesbah, A.: Same app, different app stores: a comparative study. In: MOBILESoft. IEEE (2017)
4. Allix, K., Bissyandé, T.F., Klein, J., Le Traon, Y.: Androzoo: collecting millions of android apps for the research community. In: MSR. ACM (2016)
5. Auto-it: Auto-it (2019). https://www.autoitscript.com
6. Bacchus, A., Porst, S., Mutchler, P.: Expanding bug bounties on google play. https://security.googleblog.com/2019/08/expanding-bug-bounties-on-google-play.html (2019)
7. Botacin, M.F., de Geus, P.L., Grégio, A.R.A.: The other guys: automated analysis of marginalized malware. J. Comput. Virol. Hack. Tech. **14**(1), 87–98 (2017). https://doi.org/10.1007/s11416-017-0292-8

8. Bronchain, O., Dassy, L., Faust, S., Standaert, F.X.: Implementing trojan-resilient hardware from (mostly) untrusted components designed by colluding manufacturers. In: ASHES. ACM (2018)

9. Cimpanu, C.: Malware found in arch linux aur package repository (2018). https://www.bleepingcomputer.com/news/security/malware-found-in-arch-linux-aur-package-repository/

10. Cnet: Cnet (2019). https://www.cnet.com/

11. FileHippo: Filehippo (2019). https://www.filehippo.com

12. FileHorse: Filehorse (2019). https://www.filehorse.com

13. Geniola, A., Antikainen, M., Aura, T.: Automated analysis of freeware installers promoted by download portals. Comput. Secur. **77**, 209–225 (2018)

14. Google: Release updates from the chrome team (2019). https://chromereleases.googleblog.com/

15. Gousios, G., Kalliamvakou, E., Spinellis, D.: Measuring developer contribution from software repository data. In: MSR. ACM (2008)

16. Grégio, A.R.A., Afonso, V.M., Filho, D.S.F., de Geus, P.L., Jino, M.: Toward a taxonomy of malware behaviors. Comput. J. **58**(10), 2758–2777 (2015)

17. Han, J., Chung, T., Kim, S., Kwon, T.T., Kim, H.C., Choi, Y.: How prevalent is content bundling in bittorrent. In: SIGMETRICS. ACM (2011)

18. Hoffman, C.: Warning: Don't download software from sourceforge if you can help it [updated] (2018). https://www.howtogeek.com/218764/warning-don%E2%80%99t-download-software-from-sourceforge-if-you-can-help-it/

19. Kahvedžić, D., Kechadi, T.: On the persistence of deleted windows registry data structures. In: SAC. ACM (2009)

20. Khandelwal, S.: New malware replaced legit android apps with fake ones on 25 m devices (2019). https://thehackernews.com/2019/07/whatsapp-android-malware.html

21. Kim, D., Kim, Y., Moon, J., Cho, S.J., Woo, J., You, I.: Identifying windows installer package files for detection of pirated software. In: ICIMISUComp (2014)

22. Koret, J., Bachaalany, E.: The Antivirus Hacker's Handbook, 1st edn. Wiley, New York (2015)

23. Lee, J., Lee, Y., Jin, M., Kim, J., Hong, J.: Analysis of application installation logs on android systems. In: SAC 2019. ACM (2019)

24. McNab, N., Bryan, A.: An implementation of the linux software repository model for other operating systems. In: HotSWUp 2009. ACM (2009)

25. Pietrek, M.: Peering inside the PE: a tour of the win32 portable executable file format (1994). https://msdn.microsoft.com/en-us/library/ms809762.aspx

26. Potter, B., Fleck, B.: 802.11 Security. O'Reilly (2002)

27. Rossow, C., Dietrich, C., Bos, H.: Large-scale analysis of malware downloaders. In: Flegel, U., Markatos, E., Robertson, W. (eds.) DIMVA 2012. LNCS, vol. 7591, pp. 42–61. Springer, Heidelberg (2013). https://doi.org/10.1007/978-3-642-37300-8_3

28. Sans: Malware delivered via windows installer files (2018). https://isc.sans.edu/forums/diary/Malware+Delivered+via+Windows+Installer+Files/23349/

29. Scrapy: Scrapy (2019). https://www.scrapy.org

30. Sebastián, M., Rivera, R., Kotzias, P., Caballero, J.: AVCLASS: a tool for massive malware labeling. In: Monrose, F., Dacier, M., Blanc, G., Garcia-Alfaro, J. (eds.) RAID 2016. LNCS, vol. 9854, pp. 230–253. Springer, Cham (2016). https://doi.org/10.1007/978-3-319-45719-2_11

31. Sikorski, M., Honig, A.: Practical Malware Analysis: The Hands-On Guide to Dissecting Malicious Software, 1st edn. No Starch Press, San Francisco (2012)

32. Softpedia: Softpedia (2019). https://www.softpedia.com/
33. Software, E.: Artemis trojan (2013). https://www.enigmasoftware.com/artemistrojan-removal/
34. SourceForge: Sourceforge (2019). https://www.sourceforge.net
35. Total, V.: Virus total (2019). https://www.virustotal.com
36. Vaughan-Nichols, S.J.: Why software development is lagging hardware improvements (2009). https://www.cio.com/article/2431061/from-32-bit-to-64-bit-why-software-development-is-lagging-hardware-improvements.html
37. Wang, H., Li, H., Li, L., Guo, Y., Xu, G.: Why are android apps removed from google play?: A large-scale empirical study. In: MSR. ACM (2018)
38. Whitwam, R.: Asus live update pushed malware to 1 million pcs (2019). https://www.extremetech.com/internet/288283-asus-update-servers-pushed-malware-to-hundreds-of-thousands-of-pcs
39. Willems, C., Freiling, F.C., Holz, T.: Using memory management to detect and extract illegitimate code for malware analysis. In: ACSAC. ACM (2012)
40. Williams, C.C., Hollingsworth, J.K.: Automatic mining of source coderepositories to improve bug finding techniques. IEEE Trans. Software Eng. **31**(6), 466–480 (2005)
41. Zope, M.: Unattended installation and uninstallation of softwares remotely. In: ICWET. ACM (2010)

Detection and Containment

Distributed Heterogeneous N-Variant Execution

Alexios Voulimeneas[1]([✉]), Dokyung Song[1], Fabian Parzefall[1], Yeoul Na[1],
Per Larsen[1], Michael Franz[1], and Stijn Volckaert[2]

[1] Department of Computer Science, University of California, Irvine, USA
{avoulime,dokyungs,fparzefa,yeouln,perl,franz}@uci.edu
[2] Department of Computer Science, imec-DistriNet, KU Leuven, Leuven, Belgium
stijn.volckaert@cs.kuleuven.be

Abstract. N-Variant Execution (NVX) systems utilize artificial diversity techniques to enhance software security. The general idea is to run multiple *different* variants of the same program alongside each other while monitoring their diverging behavior on a malicious input. Existing NVX systems execute diversified program variants on a *single* host. This means the level of inter-variant diversity will be limited to what a single platform can offer, without costly emulation. This paper presents DMON, a novel distributed NVX design that executes native program variants across *multiple* heterogeneous hosts. Our approach greatly increases the level of diversity between the simultaneously running variants that can be supported, encompassing different ISAs and ABIs. Our evaluation shows that DMON can provide comparable performance to traditional, non-distributed NVX systems, while enhancing security.

1 Introduction

Memory errors are a continuous source of software vulnerabilities for C and C++ programs. Attackers and defenders are engaged in an arms race in which the latter keep developing sophisticated defenses while their adversaries create new exploits that bypass these defenses [46]. At present, adversaries rely on intimate knowledge of the target environment to mount code-reuse [7,42,43] or data-oriented attacks [9,22,23] that allow them to take control of the target or leak its sensitive data. While memory safety techniques protect against these threats, many of these techniques have not seen widespread deployment due to performance [34,35] and compatibility problems [44]. Instead, defenders resort to mitigations that have a more reasonable performance impact, e.g., control-flow integrity (CFI) techniques [1,6], automated software diversity techniques [28], or a combination thereof. However, both classes of defenses have a history of known weaknesses: CFI defenses often still leave some leeway to mount control-flow hijacking attacks [11,14,48]. Software diversity techniques have been bypassed using brute-forcing and information leakage attacks, including attacks enabled by micro-architectural side channels [4,18,24,43].

© Springer Nature Switzerland AG 2020
C. Maurice et al. (Eds.): DIMVA 2020, LNCS 12223, pp. 217–237, 2020.
https://doi.org/10.1007/978-3-030-52683-2_11

N-Variant eXecution (NVX) systems amplify the effectiveness of software diversity techniques and increase resilience [3,5,12,20,21,25–27,31,32,36,39,50, 52–55]. An NVX system runs multiple diversified variants of the same program in parallel on the same inputs while monitoring the variants' behavior for divergences. With the right selection of diversity techniques, NVX can make exploitation substantially harder (and, in some cases, provably impossible) as it forces adversaries to simultaneously compromise multiple program variants without causing observable changes in their behavior. Existing NVX systems have been particularly effective at stopping attacks that rely on knowledge of the target's absolute virtual address space layout [5,12,52], as well as attacks that attempt to acquire that knowledge through information leakage [31]. However, these systems are not resilient to Position-Independent Return-Oriented Programming (PIROP) attacks [16] and certain Data-Oriented Programming (DOP) attacks [23], which build on knowledge of the program's internal geometry (e.g., relative data/instruction layouts) and/or data representation. The main reason is that in previous NVX systems all the variants run on the same machine. Thus, the amount of diversity that such systems can achieve is limited to what a single platform can offer, without using costly emulation.

In this paper, we present DMON, an NVX system that leverages the diversity that naturally exists across different platforms, thereby increasing resilience to memory exploits. DMON runs each program variant natively on its own dedicated machine and monitors divergent behavior between these distributed variants by cross-checking them at the system call boundary via a network. To bypass DMON, adversaries would need to develop exploits that work simultaneously against the two or more different Instruction Set Architectures (ISAs) and Application Binary Interfaces (ABIs) for which the program variants are compiled.

Our contributions are as follows:

- We present DMON, the first system that combines ISA and ABI heterogeneity with N-Variant Execution. DMON distributes the execution of a set of variants over a heterogeneous set of physical machines.
- We redefine *semantic equivalence* of system calls in the context of heterogeneous platforms. Based on this definition, we propose Platform-Independent State Canonicalization (PISC), a novel technique that translates system call states in different platforms into platform-independent states.
- We present ways to reduce the performance overheads associated with a distributed NVX system. Our results show that with the proposed performance optimizations, DMON performs on par with traditional `ptrace`-based NVX systems while providing stronger security guarantees.
- We evaluate DMON's security on several server applications and show that DMON makes code-reuse attacks substantially more difficult, and that DMON naturally provides a high degree of structure layout diversity which raises the bar for attacks that rely on consistent structure layout.

2 Background

Researchers in the information security [3,5,12,26,31,36,39,50,52–55] and software reliability communities [20,21,25,27,32,38] have presented over a dozen different NVX systems since 2006. Although serving different purposes, they do have some essential similarities. All systems have the same high-level architecture; two or more software variants execute simultaneously on the same physical machine, while a monitoring component (on that same machine) compares the variants' overall behavior, provides them with identical inputs, and demultiplexes their outputs. Most monitors force the variants to execute in lock-step at the granularity of system calls. Thus, the variants are suspended at every system call entry and exit, and do not proceed until the system call numbers and arguments have been cross-checked across all variants. In addition, the majority of existing NVX systems cross-check behavior and replicate I/O by intercepting the variants' system calls. Most early systems used a dedicated monitoring process that attaches to the variants and intercepts their system calls using the `ptrace` API [5,20,32,39,53]. To avoid the high run-time performance overhead incurred by context switching between a variant process and the monitor process, several teams explored alternative designs that use binary rewriting [21], virtualization features [26], or kernel modules [12,31,52,54] to intercept and cross-check system calls more efficiently, within the variants' processes and address spaces.

2.1 System Calls and I/O Replication

Most NVX systems monitor behavior and replicate I/O at the system call interface. This design lets the system monitor all behavior that can affect the integrity of the OS or other processes, as well as all communication between the variants and external entities. The monitoring and replication must be transparent to the program variants and to the end-user, i.e., no observable functional differences between native execution of a single variant and NVX of multiple variants. To provide this guarantee, most NVX systems designate one variant as the leader, while the others become followers. Whenever the variants attempt an I/O operation, the NVX systems ensure that only the leader variant actually completes the operation, while the followers skip the operation and wait until they receive the I/O results from the monitor.

2.2 ISA and ABI Heterogeneity

An underlying assumption of most NVX systems is that the program variants will behave identically at the system call level when they receive equivalent, benign inputs. This assumption no longer holds in our setting, where variants run on processors with different Instruction Set Architectures (ISAs). Differences in the endianness, register and pointer width, and the available system calls could lead to observable (yet benign) differences in the variants' behavior, which would all cause false alarms in a traditional NVX system. In addition, the Application Binary Interface (ABI) documents rules such as sizes of primitive data types, struct packing, calling conventions, etc. Many of these conventions also affect the program behavior as observed from the system call interface. Therefore, we had to carefully design DMON to tolerate divergences arising from the heterogeneous ISA and ABI setting.

3   Threat Model

Throughout the rest of the paper, we will make the following assumptions about the host system and the attacker. Our assumptions are consistent with related work in this area [52].

Host Defenses. We assume that the standard set of mitigations are in place on any of the physical machines DMON and the variants run on. Specifically, we assume that Data Execution Prevention (DEP) is used, which therefore rules out direct code-injection attacks. Likewise, we assume that all of the host systems have Address Space Layout Randomization (ASLR) enabled. ASLR randomizes the base addresses of the main program executable and shared libraries, as well as the heap, stack, and any other mapped memory regions.

Remote Attacker. We assume that the attacker does not have direct physical access to any of the machines DMON (or the variants) run on. The attacker can only communicate with the protected application running on the leader machine via a remote communication channel such as a network socket. The followers are connected to the leader through a secure private network connection. The adversary can, therefore, not communicate with the follower variants. We also consider attacks on this private connection to be outside the scope of this paper. Because the attacker is remote, we also assume that any run-time secrets embedded into the variants (e.g., randomized base addresses) are not known a priori. The goal of the attacker in this scenario is to take control of the leader variant, e.g., by exploiting a memory-corruption vulnerability. We assume that the protected application has an arbitrary memory read/write vulnerability that the attacker knows how to trigger.

4   DMON Design

DMON orchestrates and supervises the execution of a set of diversified program variants running natively on machines that differ in their instruction set architecture. Like most other NVX systems, DMON uses a leader/follower-model for I/O replication. The designated leader variant is the only variant allowed to perform externally observable I/O operations such as sending or receiving data from a network socket. DMON forces follower variants to skip these I/O operations and instead provides them with the leader's I/O results, thus emulating the original operation unbeknownst to the follower.

Similar to other security-focused NVX systems such as ReMon [52] and MvArmor [26], DMON executes all security sensitive system calls in lock step. Whenever the variants attempt to execute a sensitive system call, DMON ensures

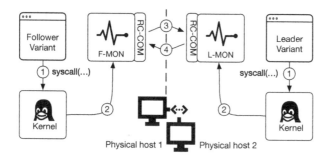

Fig. 1. DMON's basic components and interactions.

that the variants can neither enter the system call routine, nor exit from it until DMON has ensured that all variants have reached equivalent states. We distinguish between the following components of a running DMON system:

1. **Leader Variant.** Only the designated leader variant is allowed to perform externally observable I/O. As in any other NVX system, DMON requires that there is exactly one leader variant.
2. **Follower Variants.** Follower variants skip externally observable I/O operations and use the leader's I/O results instead.
3. **Monitors.** DMON uses two types of monitors: the (single) L-MON monitor supervises the leader variant, while every follower variant is supervised by its own F-MON monitor.
4. **RC-COM.** A reliable communication component used to exchange system call metadata between the monitors. Separating the communication logic into its own layer lets the monitors communicate over a variety of channels.

These components interact whenever the variants execute system calls, as shown in Fig. 1. Whenever a leader or follower variant attempts to enter or exit from a system call (①), the corresponding L-MON or F-MON interrupts and suspends the variant, reads the call number of the interrupted system call, and invokes a specialized handler routine within the monitor process (②), which implements the cross-checking and replication logic for that system call.

The monitors use cross-checking handlers when they interrupt variants upon entering a system call. In F-MON, the cross-checking handler gathers information about the variant's state, sends this information to L-MON (③), and waits for L-MON to confirm that the follower variant is in a state equivalent to the leader variant (④). In L-MON, the cross-checking handler waits for incoming state information from F-MON, compares that state information with the leader variant's state, and informs F-MON about the results of the comparison.

The state information consists of system call numbers and arguments, with the latter often consisting of pointers to complex data structures (e.g., I/O vectors). The cross-checking handlers serialize these corresponding data structures and append the serialized data to the state information, thereby allowing L-MON to check the variant states for deep equivalence (two data structures are deeply equivalent when the raw data they contain is identical, even though the data or the data structures may be stored at different addresses). If the variant states do not match, DMON takes that as a sign of potential compromise and aborts execution to protect the host system.

Naive cross-checking of these variant states triggers false alarms for divergent behavior because the system call interfaces, calling conventions, etc. differ across platforms. DMON transforms system call states to platform-independent states before comparing them, to avoid alarms for the expected platform differences (see Sect. 4.1). If the states match, the cross-checking handler allows the leader variant to proceed and to enter the kernel-space system call routine. The follower variants can also proceed, but may (optionally) see their system call number replaced by that of the sys_getpid routine in case they attempt to perform an externally observable I/O operation. This mechanism for skipping system calls was also used in prior work [39]. The monitors use replication handlers when they interrupt variants that return from a system call. Replication handlers for I/O system calls broadcast the system call results from the leader variant to the followers. Replication handlers for other system calls are generally no-ops.

4.1   Platform-Independent State Canonicalization

In traditional NVX systems, all program variants are compiled for the same target architecture and execute on a single machine. In DMON, on the other hand, individual variants run on different physical machines and thus the variants may target different ISAs/ABIs. Heterogeneous platforms expose different system call interfaces. Without awareness of this heterogeneity, cross-checking at this interface leads to false alarms, where the NVX system detects divergence despite the program behavior being equivalent. We find that the root cause of this type of false alarm is the lack of understanding of *semantic equivalence* of system calls in the presence of heterogeneous platforms. To broaden this understanding, we define *semantic equivalence* of system calls as follows:

Definition 1. *The functionality of a syscall is a transformation of one user-observable system state to the other, which constitutes observable behavior. We do not consider behavior observable if it is only visible through side-channels.*

Definition 2. *Given a syscall (c, p), where c is a vector of configuration parameters and p is a vector of data parameters, a unique c on platform A determines the functionality of the system call, which we denote as $F(p)$. c includes the system call number, as well as any flags, modes, etc. that the syscall accepts as parameters to configure its behavior.*

Definition 3. $F(p)$ *and* $F'(p')$ *are semantically equivalent iff F and F' are mapped to the same system call functionality and parameters p and p' are identical in a serialized form.*

Based on the definition of semantic equivalence, we introduce a technique called platform-independent state canonicalization (PISC), which marshalls syscall states into a canonical syscall state. To do so, DMON internally maintains a canonical representation of system call functionalities and serialization rules. By cross-checking this canonical state, DMON eliminates false positive detections that stem from ABI/ISA heterogeneity.

Semantically equivalent system calls must be mapped to the same canonical system call state. To preserve this property, we define a set of rules that DMON should follow to perform platform-independent state canonicalization (PISC).

Rule 1 - Configuration Constant Canonicalization. According to our definition of semantic equivalence, the configuration parameters of a system call (c) include the system call number, syscall flags and modes, the union of which determines the system call functionality. These constant values can be different across ABIs and platforms. For example, the `sys_read` system call has system call number 0 on x86-64 platforms and 3 on i386 platforms. Directly comparing these constants, as traditional NVX systems do, will cause a false alarm even if they are "semantically" equivalent.

Rule 1 resolves this issue, by translating these configuration parameters to a canonical representation before comparing them. PISC compiles this rule automatically by reading the system call tables on the fly and replace system call numbers, with their corresponding system call name before comparison. For flags, modes and any other configuration constant defined as a macro inside glibc, PISC follows the same principle. This is a fully automated procedure and thus allows DMON to seamlessly extend to additional platforms.

Rule 2 - Struct Layout Canonicalization. Data parameters p of a system call may include some struct type parameters. Determining equivalence of struct type parameters is challenging because C structs are not necessarily bit-for-bit identical across ABIs, even when the arguments are semantically equivalent; different platforms define different packing (i.e., padding) and alignment rules for a data structure. To allow for bitwise comparisons of such structs, PISC canonicalizes structs to an internal "shadow" type that uses fixed size fields and is carefully constructed so it has the same layout across platforms. Again, this procedure is completely automated and thus extensible to new architectures.

Rule 3 - Implicit Parameter Canonicalization. Beyond differences in the syscall numbers for the same system call, heterogeneous-ISA variants may use similar yet different system calls for the same functionality, because not all system calls are available on every platform. According to our definition of semantic equivalence of system calls, such similar system calls represent an equivalent functionality F. Checking equivalence of the data parameters p in this case serves as a key to determine semantic equivalence of these system calls.

x86-64 kernels, for example, implement both `sys_open` and `sys_openat`. ARMv8 kernels, on the other hand, do not implement `sys_open`. ARMv8 variants therefore always use `sys_openat` to open a file. `sys_openat` is similar to `sys_open`, but has an additional argument that can hold the file descriptor of a directory. If the **pathname** argument of the `sys_openat` is relative, then it is interpreted relative to the directory specified in the additional argument. In this concrete example, PISC maps `sys_open` and `sys_openat` to the same system call functionality and it fully resolves equivalence of the data parameters including the directory paths that the variants are trying to access.

4.2 Distributed Monitor Design

Prior work often used a central monitor process which simultaneously supervised all of the variants [5,39,53]. Subsequent research showed that this centralized model was overly focused on simplicity and security at the expense of performance, and suggested various designs in which each variant was supervised by a dedicated monitor instance [21,26,31,52,54,55]. This dedicated monitor instance could be loaded directly into the variants' address spaces, thereby trading off the isolation between the variants and the monitor for reduced variant-monitor communication overhead. DMON combines elements of both designs. Since we run ISA-heterogeneous variants on different machines, we cannot use a central monitor that attaches locally to all variants. Instead, we use a dedicated monitor for each variant and run the monitor on the same machine as the variant it supervises. Our design does, however, enforce strict isolation between the variant and its monitor by running the monitor as a separate process that attaches to the variant using the `ptrace` API.

4.3 Inter-Monitor Communication

F-MON and L-MON communicate whenever the variants execute a system call. This exchange may include system call numbers, serialized system call arguments, system call results, or instructions on how to proceed from a system call entry point (see Sect. 4). In many cases, particularly when the system call being executed is deemed security-sensitive, communication must happen synchronously. For instance, L-MON cannot allow the leader variant to proceed past a system call entry point until all instances of F-MON have serialized the state of their corresponding variant, and until they have sent this state to L-MON. F-MON needs to wait even longer as it cannot allow the follower variants to proceed until L-MON has compared the variant states and it has received L-MON's confirmation that the states match. To achieve good performance, DMON therefore requires a reliable inter-monitor communication channel with minimal latency and high bandwidth. We experimented with various designs of this communication channel and implemented them in our RC-COM, which exposes the inter-monitor communication API to our monitors.

Network Protocol Choice. The most obvious protocol that meets our reliability demands is TCP, which we used as the basis for our first implementation of RC-COM. However, even with extensive tuning, our TCP-based implementation had poor throughput and high latency. As an alternative, we therefore used ENet, a lightweight UDP-based protocol that also offers reliable in-order and error-free data transfer [17]. Besides the networking hardware, the operating system also affects the communication bandwidth and latency. When a network adapter receives a packet, for example, the OS first stores the packet in a kernel-space buffer, before copying it into the receiving application's memory and transferring control to the application. Remote Direct Memory Access (RDMA) avoids these extra copy operations by allowing two communicating peers to read or write directly from or to the other peer's application memory, thus bypassing the kernel's networking stack. We implemented an RDMA-based version of our RC-COM using Mellanox ConnectX 100 gigabit Ethernet interfaces [33] and the Mellanox Messaging Accelerator user-space networking library [29].

4.4   Optimizations

To further improve DMON's performance, we implemented several optimizations that reduce the number of the data packets exchanged by our monitors.

Permissive Filesystem Access. Traditional NVX systems allow one variant to perform *all* I/O operations and then replicate the results to the other variants. Even though this replication mechanism seamlessly provides identical inputs to all variants, it is not always necessary. Specifically, there is no need to replicate read accesses to read-only files that were identical on all physical machines when DMON started, as long as the files have not been modified while DMON was running. We refer to such files as *static files* and designed the replication handlers for read-only operations such as sys_read and sys_fstat so that all variants may (optionally) read static files directly from their local file system, thus bypassing the I/O replication. For this optional optimization, DMON requires that the application's root directory has the same path name on all machines as well as identical content including sub-directories with the exception of executables and shared libraries.

Asynchronous Cross-Checking. Our basic approach described in Sect. 4 adds considerable overhead to every system call invocation as every cross-check happens synchronously and requires at least two network round-trips; one for F-MONs to send the system call states of their supervised variants to L-MON, and one for L-MON to instruct F-MONs on how to proceed (abort or continue execution of the variant). We developed a technique which we call *asynchronous cross-checking* to reduce this overhead. Inspired by previous work [26,52], the idea is to classify system calls into three categories—highly sensitive, moderately sensitive, and non-sensitive—based on the system call number and/or arguments. With asynchronous cross-checking, highly sensitive system calls still execute in lock-step, as before. When F-MON deems a system call moderately sensitive, however, it still sends the system call state information to L-MON, but then immediately resumes execution of the supervised variant without waiting for a reply from L-MON. L-MON eventually receives the state information and may detect a divergence. In that case, L-MON will instruct F-MONs to abort execution through a separate error channel that is used only for this specific purpose. Non-sensitive system calls can execute without any cross-checking.

5   Implementation

We implemented DMON for GNU/Linux. DMON runs natively on the x86-64 and ARMv8 architectures. DMON also has partial support for ARMv7 and i386. Currently, our prototype has 35k lines of C and C++ code and supports variants compiled with the stock versions of gcc and Clang. We do, however, require the variants to link against our patched C library (see *Virtual System Calls* below for details). DMON currently supports 100 system calls. Adding support for additional system calls generally requires a trivial amount of engineering effort (typically less than 10 lines of code), as DMON defines helper macros to replicate and cross-check most types of system call arguments (see Sect. 4.1). Our helper macros resemble those used in ReMon [52], but differ from them as they automatically apply PISC, thus making our macros fully portable. The type of cross-checking depends on the security-sensitivity of the call (see Sect. 4.4).

DMON always cross-checks highly sensitive system calls in lock-step. Moderately sensitive calls are checked asynchronously. Non-sensitive calls are not checked at all. The type of replication depends on the kind of results the system call returns. DMON enforces replication for all I/O operations that are not reads from static files (see Sect. 4.4), and for all system calls that return mutable program state. Read operations from static files execute without replication if the permissive filesystem access optimization is enabled. System calls that must be executed by all variants are not subject to any replication.

Virtual System Calls. On most architectures, Linux loads a Virtual Dynamic Shared Object (VDSO) or vsyscall page into the address spaces of all user-space programs. These executable code pages expose virtual system calls, which allow the program to execute certain system calls (e.g., sys_gettimeofday) without switching into kernel space. Most NVX systems either hide, replace, or disable the VDSO and vsyscall page because virtual system calls are invisible to the monitor. For our prototype, we patched the C library our variants link against so that virtual system calls are disabled.

6   Security Analysis

Scope. NVX systems can prevent usage of *absolute* code addresses by adopting Address Space Partitioning (ASP) [12,31,50] that lays out the variants' code sections to have non-overlapping/disjoint virtual addresses. In this Section, we focus on evaluating the additional security DMON can provide through ISA/ABI-heterogeneity. Specifically, we show the extent to which ISA/ABI-heterogeneity prevents concrete code-reuse and data-only attacks that cannot be easily stopped using existing NVX systems.

Analysis Targets and Configurations. We used four popular server applications—Nginx 1.14.2, Lighttpd 1.4.52, Redis 5.0.1, and ProFTPD 1.3.0—as our analysis targets, which is in line with previous work on security-oriented NVX systems [26,31,52,54]. We evaluated the security of a heterogeneous configuration with one program variant compiled for Intel x86-64 and one for ARMv7.

6.1   Code Layout Diversity

Existing NVX systems that deploy address space partitioning (ASP) can be bypassed using attacks that rely on partial overwrites of code pointers such as return addresses or function pointers [13,16]. The basic idea is to force the program to produce a (number of) legal code pointer(s) at memory locations that the attacker can overwrite. The attacker then overwrites the least significant bits or adds arbitrary offsets to each of these code pointers, and thereby diverts the execution of the program to a series of attacker-chosen gadgets (i.e., instruction sequences ending with indirect branches, such as return instructions). In the PIROP attack, for example, Goktas et al. exploited a vulnerability in the Asterisk communication server that allowed them to produce legal return addresses at an attacker-controlled position on the stack [16]. They then overwrote the least significant byte of each of these return addresses to build a PIROP gadget chain, which they then invoked by exploiting another vulnerability.

These attacks can in principal bypass existing NVX systems because they do not require any information leakage (which the NVX system would detect), and because the same partial pointer overwrites can achieve the same results in each variant. In this section, we show that DMON makes these position-independent code-reuse attacks far more challenging because ISA/ABI-heterogeneity substantially reduces the number of position-independent gadgets available to the attacker.

Position-Independent Gadget Availability.   Position-independent gadgets are instruction sequences that can be *reliably* invoked by patching legal code pointers. We consider two ways to patch legal code pointers. First, an attacker could overwrite an offset variable that is later added to a code pointer in a pointer arithmetic operation. This primitive allows attackers to reliably invoke any gadget, as long as the internal layout of the target binary is known. Second, the attacker could overwrite the least significant bits of a code pointer directly using a memory write vulnerability. This primitive is far less potent than the former, as it allows the attacker to overwrite only the 8 least significant bits (i.e., one byte). Overwriting more than one byte is not possible unless the attacker knows the base address of the target binary because the ASP scheme randomizes all but the 12 least significant bits of each base address.

We compiled a list of the position-independent gadgets in both our x86-64 and ARMv7 binaries as follows. We first collected the addresses of (i) all instructions that immediately follow call instructions, and (ii) all address-taken functions in the program. The former is an approximation of the set of legal return addresses that could exist in the program's address space at any given point during its execution. The latter is the set of other code pointers that could be found in the program's memory. Combined, this list approximates the set of pointers that *could* potentially be patched by attackers to construct position-independent code-reuse payloads. We then used Ropper to generate lists of regular ROP gadgets consisting of 15 instructions or less [40]. This, again, is consistent with related work [16]. Next, we combined the two lists for each binary as follows. For

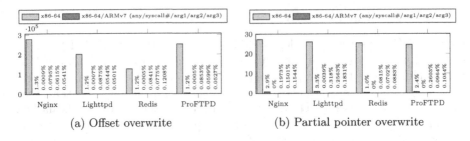

Fig. 2. Number of position-independent code-reuse gadgets.

every code pointer in the first list, we calculated the (i) addresses of all gadgets relative to the pointer, and (ii) absolute addresses of gadgets that only differ from the code pointer in their 8 least significant bits. The former is the set of gadgets reachable through offset overwrites, while the latter is the set of gadgets reachable through partial pointer overwrites.

Next, we correlated the position-independent gadgets found for the x86-64 binary with those found for ARMv7. For each x86-64 gadget, we checked whether there is an ARMv7 gadget that can be reached using the same offset overwrite/partial pointer overwrite. We then eliminated gadgets whose absolute address or offset from the source code pointer is not 4-byte aligned, since code pointers patched in either way would be unaligned on ARMv7 and would trigger an unaligned instruction exception when the gadget is invoked. We collected 2553 code pointers from Nginx, 1988 code pointers from Lighttpd, 1732 code pointers from Redis, and 4514 code pointers from ProFTPD. Figure 2 shows how many gadgets can be reached on average from each code pointer by offset overwrite and partial pointer overwrite attacks. In a traditional NVX system where all variants are compiled for Intel x86-64, all of the gadgets identified in the x86-64 binary would survive. In contrast, in all four of our target programs, and for both code pointer patching strategies, less than 3.3% of the gadgets survive in an NVX configuration with a x86-64 variant and an ARMv7 variant.

Position-Independent Gadget Semantics. The final step of an exploit is often to call a security-sensitive function or a system call with attacker-specified arguments (e.g., `execve` with "`/bin/sh`" as argument for a shell). The ABI-heterogeneity provided by DMON imposes another constraint on chaining gadgets to build such an exploit. Because different architectures have different calling conventions for system calls and subroutines, as shown in Table 1, the attacker should chain a sequence of gadgets that prepare the same set of arguments, but in a different way for each architecture. For example, in an ARMv7 variant, the attacker must use `r7` to prepare a system call number, whereas in a x86-64 variant the same attacker must use `rax`. To show the difficulty of constructing a code-reuse attack that performs one or more system calls and/or subroutine calls, we analyzed the semantics of position-independent gadgets surviving under DMON. Specifically, we looked for gadgets that read a value from memory and write that

Distributed Heterogeneous N-Variant Execution   229

value into the system call number register, or the registers for one of the first
three arguments of a system or function call. As shown in Fig. 2, only a small
fraction of the position-independent gadgets have suitable semantics for argument preparation (see 3rd to 6th bars in the figure). More interestingly, system
call number preparation gadgets are rare compared to other argument preparation gadgets. In a standalone ARMv7 binary of Nginx, Redis, and ProFTPD,
we could not find a single partial-pointer-overwrite based position-independent
gadget which can load a system call number. Obviously then, we also could not
find such gadgets among those that survive across architectures.

Table 1. Comparison of function and syscall conventions.

arch/ABI	syscall#	arg1	arg2	arg3	arg4	arg5	arg6	arg7	result
x86-64	–	rdi	rsi	rdx	rcx	r8	r9	–	rax
arm/EABI	–	r0	r1	r2	r3	Stack	Stack	Stack	r0-r3
x86-64	rax	rdi	rsi	rdx	r10	r8	r9	–	rax
arm/EABI	r7	r0	r1	r2	r3	r4	r5	r6	r0

Table 2. Number of diversified data structures.

	Artificial	DMON	Total
Nginx 1.14.2	53	335	365
Lighttpd 1.4.52	15	95	116
Redis 5.0.1	57	158	209
ProFTPD 1.3.0	23	72	84

6.2 Structure Layout Diversity

Apart from code layout diversity we achieve from ISA-heterogeneity, DMON
naturally provides data structure layout diversity. Due to differences in sizes
of pointers and primitive data types, as well as differences in struct packing
and alignment, data structures rarely have the same sizes and layouts across
platforms. Diversifying structure layouts greatly raises the bar for attacks that
require knowledge about data structure definitions including certain types of
data-only attacks that rely on deterministic placement of structure fields [15,23].

Previous NVX systems could achieve structure layout diversity by artificially
reorganizing structures at compile time. However, in practice, only a limited number of structs can be diversified at compile time. Specifically, it is not safe to
diversify (i) structures used as arguments or return types of external library functions, (ii) structures with an initialization list, (iii) structs cast to different types,
etc. [10,30]. We implemented existing type-based structure layout randomization
techniques [10,30], and we examined struct layouts in a set of server applications
to show how much structure layout diversity DMON can naturally achieve, compared to the number of structures that can be artificially diversified. As shown in
Table 2, our heterogeneous NVX system provides a much higher degree of structure layout diversity than one can achieve using a compiler-based technique.

Case Study: ProFTPD SSL Private Key Leak. Hu et al. demonstrated an information disclosure attack on ProFTPD, in which the attacker locates a base
pointer to an SSL context data structure, and then uses Data-Oriented Programming (DOP) gadgets to traverse through the context and 6 other data

structures, ultimately reaching a private key, which is then leaked to a remote attacker [23]. DMON can prevent this attack because the layouts of the 6 data structures differ across architectures. We examined the relevant data structures in ARMv7 and x86-64 binaries of ProFTPD and found that 4 of the 6 pointer fields that need to be dereferenced in this attack are located at different offsets in the two binaries. A DOP exploit that traverses through the structs therefore cannot simultaneously reach and leak the private key on both platforms without triggering a divergence in DMON.

7   Performance Evaluation

We conducted an extensive performance evaluation of DMON using handwritten microbenchmarks (see Sect. 7.1), as well as popular high-performance server applications (see Sect. 7.2). We tried two different configurations:

The **low-end configuration** had an ARMv8 variant running on a Raspberry Pi 3 Model B board with a quad-core 1.2GHz Broadcom BCM2837 64-bit CPU and 1GB of RAM, running the 64-bit ARM Debian 9 distribution of GNU/Linux, as well as an x86-64 variant running on a desktop machine with a quad-core Intel i5-6500 CPU and 16GB of RAM, running the x86-64 version of Ubuntu 16.04.5 LTS. The machines were connected through a *private* 100 megabit Ethernet connection with approximately 0.5 ms latency.

The **high-end configuration** had an x86-64 variant running on a desktop machine with an octa-core Intel i9-9900K CPU and 32GB of RAM, and an x86-64 variant running on a machine with a quad-core Intel i5-6500 CPU and 16GB of RAM. Both machines ran the x86-64 version of Ubuntu 16.04.5 LTS and were connected using a private 100 gigabit connection between two Mellanox ConnectX Ethernet interface cards. These RDMA-capable cards support the Mellanox Messaging Accelerator, a user-space networking library with low latency.

In both configurations, we ran the leader variant on the slower machine. We evaluated two implementations of RC-COM (see Sect. 4.3) for the low-end configuration. The first implementation, which appears as KTCP in the graphs, uses standard TCP/IP. The second implementation uses the ENet protocol. For the high-end configuration, we additionally evaluated an implementation that leverages the Mellanox Messaging Accelerator. This implementation appears as UTCP (short for user-space TCP) in the graphs. We could not test this UTCP implementation for low-end configuration as it was not supported by our ARMv8 board. Finally, we evaluated the impact of our replication and cross-checking optimizations described in Sect. 4.4. Our Asynchronous Cross-Checking and Permissive Filesystem Access optimizations appear as ACC and PFA respectively in the graphs.

7.1   Microbenchmarks

To measure the overhead introduced by DMON, we designed microbenchmarks to test our optimizations (see Sect. 5). We used the following system calls:

1. **sys_read(STATIC_FILE_FD, buf, 512)** is treated as a moderately sensitive system call. As such, this microbenchmark benefits from our asynchronous cross-checking optimization and skips replication if all optimizations are enabled (see Sect. 4.4).
2. **sys_getcwd(buf, 512)** The results of this system call do not need to be replicated, as long as the current working directory is either the application's root directory, or one of its subdirectories (see Sect. 4.4).
3. **sys_sched_yield()** is a representative of system calls that require neither cross-checking nor replication.

Figure 3(a) shows the execution time under DMON's hign-end configuration relative to the native execution time. We used our UTCP implementation of RC-COM for all experiments, but did run separate tests with and without our permissive file access (PFA) and asynchronous cross-checking (ACC) optimizations. We also measured the execution time without cross-checking and replication (PTRACE). This experiment shows that the `ptrace` API is the main performance bottleneck in our system. Prior work illustrates that replacing `ptrace`-based monitoring by in-process alternatives allows for a much wider range of security-performance trade-offs [26, 52].

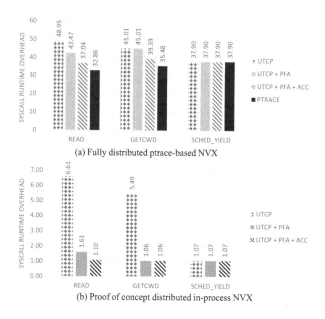

Fig. 3. Microbenchmarks for *high-end* configuration

The results show that the overhead can be attributed to the network communication of our replication and cross-checking mechanisms, and the context switching caused by `ptrace`. PFA reduces the overhead of **read** from 48.95× to

42.47×, but does not affect the other benchmarks. ACC further decreases overhead of `read` and `getcwd`, from 42.47× to 37.04× and from 45.01× to 39.39× respectively. `sched_yield`'s performance is unaffected, since DMON does not perform any cross-checking for this system call. Finally, the rightmost columns in Fig. 3(a) indicate that the context switching overhead of `ptrace` is by far the biggest contributor to DMON's overhead. We hypothesized that monitoring non-sensitive system calls in-process, as was done in prior work [21,38,52], would substantially reduce the context switching overhead, and set up an experiment to confirm this hypothesis. Specifically, we implemented a distributed in-process NVX system using the `syscall_intercept` [45], and evaluated it on the same microbenchmarks we used for the `ptrace`-based prototype. Our in-process prototype implements the optimizations described in Sect. 4.4, but only supports a small set of system calls. Figure 3(b) shows that in-process monitoring reduces the per-system call overhead from 32.86–37.90× to only 6–10% with all optimizations enabled.

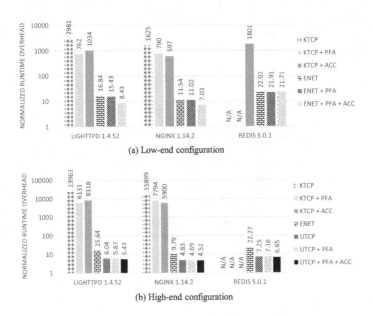

(a) Low-end configuration

(b) High-end configuration

Fig. 4. Server benchmarks in two configurations

7.2   Server Benchmarks

We evaluated DMON on 3 popular server applications—Nginx 1.14.2, Lighttpd 1.4.52 and Redis 5.0.1—that were also used to evaluate prior work [21,26,31,52]. For each of our experiments, we connected a benchmarking client to the leader machine through a 100 megabit Ethernet connection (for our low-end configuration) or a 1 gigabit Ethernet connection (for the high-end configuration). Figure 4 shows our results. We used the `wrk` client to evaluate Nginx and Lighttpd, and the `redis-benchmark` utility to evaluate Redis. We configured `wrk` to repeatedly request the same static 4KB web page for 10 s using 10 parallel connections, and `redis-benchmark` to simulate 50 clients issuing 100,000 requests in total. Running `redis-benchmark` under DMON's slowest configurations would take over a day, so we skipped them and denote it as *N/A* in Fig. 4. The latency on the 100 megabit link was just under 0.5 ms, whereas the latency on the 1 gigabit link was under 0.1 ms. With all of DMON's optimizations enabled, the performance overheads ranged between 7.03× and 21.71× for the low-end configuration, and between 4.52× and 6.65× for the high-end configuration.

7.3 Comparison with Other NVX Systems

We compared the performance of DMON with traditional NVX systems. Thanks to our inter-monitor communication optimizations, DMON achieves similar (or better) performance than traditional single-host NVX systems with `ptrace`-based monitors. Specifically, GHUMVEE (the state of the art `ptrace`-based NVX system) was tested on the same server applications (albeit slightly older versions), and in highly similar conditions, with a 1 gigabit link that had less than 0.1 ms of latency. GHUMVEE's overhead on Lighttpd was 7.0× on a saturated server (vs 5.43× for DMON), and 12.48× for Redis (vs 6.65× for DMON) [52]. Delegating the monitoring of non-sensitive system calls to an in-process monitor would substantially reduce the overhead, as was shown in prior work [21,38,52], as well as in Sect. 7.1. We summarize our findings in Table 3. DMON (IP) refers to our PoC distributed in-process prototype and DMON (CP) refers to our distributed `ptrace`-based implementation. As GHUMVEE was not evaluated on microbenchmarks, and DMON (IP) currently does not support server applications, these numbers are shown as *N/A* in the table.

Table 3. Comparison with other NVX systems.

NVX system	Monitor type	Distributed	Overhead	
			System call	Server apps
GHUMVEE [52]	CP	No	N/A	7.0–12.48×
DMON (CP)	CP	Yes	**32.86–37.90×**	**4.52–6.65×**
Varan [21]	IP	No	36–139%	11–37%
DMON (IP)	IP	Yes	**6–61%**	**N/A**

8 Discussion

Performance Improvements. While developing DMON, we identified a promising path to substantially improve our monitoring performance. We could replace our `ptrace`-based monitoring mechanism with an in-process alternative based on API call interception [21], or hardware-based virtualization extensions [26]. Securing an in-process monitoring design is challenging, however.

Leveraging Hardware Features. A potential advantage of running variants on different architectures is that the NVX system could leverage hardware security features available on one platform to protect software running on other platforms. A hypothetical configuration in which DMON runs one variant on an ARMv8.5-A CPU and one variant on an Intel x86-64 CPU could be used to bring the benefits of memory tagging to Intel x86-64 software.

Micro-Architectural Attacks. While our primary focus was on defending against memory exploits, we believe DMON might also be able to stop certain micro-architectural attacks. Rowhammer attacks in particular would become exceedingly hard to launch against DMON [19,41,49]. To build reliable Rowhammer attacks, the attacker needs to know exactly how the memory controller translates physical memory addresses into DRAM addresses [37,47]. Translation schemes differ greatly across platforms, however, which makes Rowhammer attack payloads non-portable.

9   Related Work

N-Variant eXecution. Inspired by Chen and Avizienis' seminal work on N-Version Programming [2,8], Berger and Zorn proposed a system for probabilistic memory safety that could simultaneously execute identical variants with differently seeded randomizing memory allocators [3]. This system only supported trivial applications, however. Cox et al.'s N-Variant Systems monitored a much wider array of system calls, thus supporting variants of complex applications [12]. Subsequent publications explored consistent delivery of asynchronous signals [5,39], dealing with shared memory [5], thread synchronization [51], or address-dependent behavior [53], and new schemes for generating software variants [26,31,50,54]. Other researchers suggested to use NVX systems for live patch testing [20,21,25,27,32,38].

10   Conclusion

We presented DMON, a novel, distributed N-Variant Execution system that leverages diversity in ISAs and ABIs to protect against memory corruption attacks. To bypass DMON, attackers must provide exploits that simultaneously work on different platforms. DMON's heterogeneous platform setting naturally provides code layout diversity which greatly raises the bar for code-reuse attacks, and it naturally provides a higher level of structure layout diversity than what existing compiler-based techniques can provide. To avoid benign divergences caused by expected cross-platform differences, we propose PISC, a technique that transforms system call states into platform-independent states. Also, we introduce new optimization strategies to alleviate performance issues that are unique to the distributed NVX setting. Our performance evaluation shows that the proposed optimizations, combined with an optimized network protocol, greatly reduce the performance overhead without sacrificing DMON's security.

Acknowledgments. The authors thank Kostis Kaffes, Marios Pomonis, Georgios Detorakis, Lefteris Kokoris-Kogias, Anil Altinay, Mohaned Qunaibit, Paul Kirth, David Gens, Adrian Dabrowski and our reviewers. This material is based upon work partially supported by the Defense Advanced Research Projects Agency under contract FA8750-16-C-0260, by the United States Office of Naval Research under contract N00014-17-1-2782, and by the National Science Foundation under award CNS-161921. Any opinions, findings, and conclusions or recommendations expressed in this material are those of the authors and do not necessarily reflect the views of the Defense Advanced Research Projects Agency or its Contracting Agents, the Office of Naval Research or its Contracting Agents, the National Science Foundation, or any other agency of the U.S. Government.

References

1. Abadi, M., Budiu, M., Erlingsson, U., Ligatti, J.: Control-flow integrity. In: CCS (2005)
2. Avizienis, A.: The N-version approach to fault-tolerant software. IEEE TSE (12), 1491–1501 (1985)
3. Berger, E.D., Zorn, B.G.: Diehard: probabilistic memory safety for unsafe languages. In: PLDI (2006)
4. Bittau, A., Belay, A., Mashtizadeh, A., Mazières, D., Boneh, D.: Hacking blind. In: IEEE S&P (2014)
5. Bruschi, D., Cavallaro, L., Lanzi, A.: Diversified process replicæ for defeating memory error exploits. In: IEEE IPCCC (2007)
6. Burow, N., et al.: Control-flow integrity: precision, security, and performance. ACM Comput. Surv. (CSUR) **50**(1), 16 (2017)
7. Checkoway, S., Davi, L., Dmitrienko, A., Sadeghi, A., Shacham, H., Winandy, M.: Return-oriented programming without returns. In: CCS (2010)
8. Chen, L., Avizienis, A.: N-version programming: a fault-tolerance approach to reliability of software operation. In: FTCS (1978)
9. Chen, S., Xu, J., Sezer, E.C., Gauriar, P., Iyer, R.K.: Non-control-data attacks are realistic threats. In: USENIX Security Symposium (2005)
10. Chen, Z., Han, H.: Attack mitigation by data structure randomization. In: Cuppens, F., Wang, L., Cuppens-Boulahia, N., Tawbi, N., Garcia-Alfaro, J. (eds.) FPS 2016. LNCS, vol. 10128, pp. 85–93. Springer, Cham (2017). https://doi.org/10.1007/978-3-319-51966-1_6
11. Conti, M., et al.: Losing control: on the effectiveness of control-flow integrity under stack attacks. In: CCS (2015)
12. Cox, B., et al.: N-variant systems: a secretless framework for security through diversity. In: USENIX Security Symposium (2006)
13. Durden, T.: Bypassing PaX ASLR protection. Phrack Mag. **11** (2002)
14. Evans, I., et al.: Control jujutsu: on the weaknesses of fine-grained control flow integrity. In: CCS (2015)
15. Gil, R., Okhravi, H., Shrobe, H.: There's a hole in the bottom of the C: on the effectiveness of allocation protection. In: IEEE SecDev (2018)
16. Göktas, E., et al.: Position-independent code reuse: on the effectiveness of ASLR in the absence of information disclosure. In: IEEE EuroS&P (2018)
17. ENet: Reliable UDP networking library. http://enet.bespin.org
18. Gras, B., Razavi, K., Bosman, E., Bos, H., Giuffrida, C.: ASLR on the line: practical cache attacks on the MMU. In: NDSS (2017)

19. Gruss, D., Maurice, C., Mangard, S.: Rowhammer.js: a remote software-induced fault attack in javascript. In: Caballero, J., Zurutuza, U., Rodríguez, R.J. (eds.) DIMVA 2016. LNCS, vol. 9721, pp. 300–321. Springer, Cham (2016). https://doi.org/10.1007/978-3-319-40667-1_15

20. Hosek, P., Cadar, C.: Safe software updates via multi-version execution. In: ICSE (2013)

21. Hosek, P., Cadar, C.: Varan the unbelievable: an efficient n-version execution framework. In: ASPLOS (2015)

22. Hu, H., Chua, Z.L., Adrian, S., Saxena, P., Liang, Z.: Automatic generation of data-oriented exploits. In: USENIX Security Symposium (2015)

23. Hu, H., Shinde, S., Adrian, S., Chua, Z.L., Saxena, P., Liang, Z.: Data-oriented programming: on the expressiveness of non-control data attacks. In: IEEE S&P (2016)

24. Hund, R., Willems, C., Holz, T.: Practical timing side channel attacks against kernel space ASLR. In: IEEE S&P (2013)

25. Kim, D., Kwon, Y., Sumner, W.N., Zhang, X., Xu, D.: Dual execution for on the fly fine grained execution comparison. In: ASPLOS (2015)

26. Koning, K., Bos, H., Giuffrida, C.: Secure and efficient multi-variant execution using hardware-assisted process virtualization. In: DSN (2016)

27. Kwon, Y., et al.: LDX: causality inference by lightweight dual execution. In: ASPLOS (2016)

28. Larsen, P., Homescu, A., Brunthaler, S., Franz, M.: SoK: automated software diversity. In: IEEE S&P (2014)

29. Mellanox's Messaging Accelerator. https://github.com/Mellanox/libvma/

30. Lin, Z., Riley, R.D., Xu, D.: Polymorphing software by randomizing data structure layout. In: Flegel, U., Bruschi, D. (eds.) DIMVA 2009. LNCS, vol. 5587, pp. 107–126. Springer, Heidelberg (2009). https://doi.org/10.1007/978-3-642-02918-9_7

31. Lu, K., Xu, M., Song, C., Kim, T., Lee, W.: Stopping memory disclosures via diversification and replicated execution. In: IEEE TDSC (2018)

32. Maurer, M., Brumley, D.: TACHYON: tandem execution for efficient live patch testing. In: USENIX Security Symposium (2012)

33. Mellanox ConnectX-5 EN Adapter Supporting 100 Gb/s Ethernet

34. Nagarakatte, S., Zhao, J., Martin, M.M., Zdancewic, S.: SoftBound: highly compatible and complete spatial memory safety for C. In: PLDI (2009)

35. Nagarakatte, S., Zhao, J., Martin, M.M., Zdancewic, S.: CETS: compiler enforced temporal safety for C. In: ISMM (2010)

36. Novark, G., Berger, E.D.: DieHarder: securing the heap. In: CCS (2010)

37. Pessl, P., Gruss, D., Maurice, C., Schwarz, M., Mangard, S.: Drama: Exploiting dram addressing for cross-cpu attacks. In: USENIX Security Symposium (2016)

38. Pina, L., Andronidis, A., Hicks, M., Cadar, C.: Mvedsua: higher availability dynamic software updates via multi-version execution. In: ASPLOS (2019)

39. Salamat, B., Jackson, T., Gal, A., Franz, M.: Orchestra: intrusion detection using parallel execution and monitoring of program variants in user-space. In: EuroSys (2009)

40. Schirra, S.: Ropper (2014). https://github.com/sashs/Ropper

41. Seaborn, M., Dullien, T.: Exploiting the dram rowhammer bug to gain kernel privileges. In: BlackHat USA (2015)

42. Shacham, H.: The geometry of innocent flesh on the bone: return-into-libc without function calls (on the x86). In: CCS (2007)

43. Snow, K.Z., Monrose, F., Davi, L., Dmitrienko, A., Liebchen, C., Sadeghi, A.: Just-in-time code reuse: on the effectiveness of fine-grained address space layout randomization. In: IEEE S&P (2013)
44. Song, D., et al.: SoK: sanitizing for security. In: IEEE S&P (2019)
45. System call intercepting library. https://github.com/pmem/syscall_intercept
46. Szekeres, L., Payer, M., Wei, T., Song, D.: SoK: eternal war in memory. In: IEEE S&P (2013)
47. Tatar, A., Giuffrida, C., Bos, H., Razavi, K.: Defeating software mitigations against rowhammer: a surgical precision hammer. In: RAID (2018)
48. van der Veen, V., Andriesse, D., Stamatogiannakis, M., Chen, X., Bos, H., Giuffrida, C.: The dynamics of innocent flesh on the bone: Code reuse ten years later. In: CCS (2017)
49. Van Der Veen, V., et al.: Drammer: deterministic rowhammer attacks on mobile platforms. In: CCS (2016)
50. Volckaert, S., Coppens, B., De Sutter, B.: Cloning your gadgets: complete ROP attack immunity with multi-variant execution. IEEE TDSC **13**(4), 437–450 (2016)
51. Volckaert, S., Coppens, B., De Sutter, B., De Bosschere, K., Larsen, P., Franz, M.: Taming parallelism in a multi-variant execution environment. In: EuroSys (2017)
52. Volckaert, S., et al.: Secure and efficient application monitoring and replication. In: USENIX ATC (2016)
53. Volckaert, S., De Sutter, B., De Baets, T., De Bosschere, K.: GHUMVEE: efficient, effective, and flexible replication. In: FPS (2012)
54. Xu, M., Lu, K., Kim, T., Lee, W.: Bunshin: compositing security mechanisms through diversification. In: USENIX ATC (2017)
55. Österlund, S., Koning, K., Olivier, P., Barbalace, A., Bos, H., Giuffrida, C.: kMVX: detecting kernel information leaks with multi-variant execution. In: ASPLOS (2019)

Sec2graph: Network Attack Detection Based on Novelty Detection on Graph Structured Data

Laetitia Leichtnam[1(✉)], Eric Totel[2], Nicolas Prigent[3], and Ludovic Mé[4]

[1] CentraleSupélec, University of Rennes, IRISA, Rennes, France
`laetitia.leichtnam@centralesupelec.fr`
[2] IMT-Atlantique, IRISA, Cesson-Sévigné, France
[3] LSTI, Saint-Malo, France
[4] Inria, University of Rennes, IRISA, Rennes, France

Abstract. Being able to timely detect new kinds of attacks in highly distributed, heterogeneous and evolving networks without generating too many false alarms is especially challenging. Many researchers proposed various anomaly detection techniques to identify events that are inconsistent with past observations. While supervised learning is often used to that end, security experts generally do not have labeled datasets and labeling their data would be excessively expensive. Unsupervised learning, that does not require labeled data should then be used preferably, even if these approaches have led to less relevant results. We introduce in this paper a unified and unique graph representation called security objects' graphs. This representation mixes and links events of different kinds and allows a rich description of the activities to be analyzed. To detect anomalies in these graphs, we propose an unsupervised learning approach based on auto-encoder. Our hypothesis is that as security objects' graphs bring a rich vision of the normal situation, an auto-encoder is able to build a relevant model of this situation. To validate this hypothesis, we apply our approach to the CICIDS2017 dataset and show that although our approach is unsupervised, its detection results are as good, and even better than those obtained by many supervised approaches.

1 Introduction

Security Operational Centers (SOC) ensure the collection, correlation, and analysis of security events on the perimeter of the organization they are protecting. The SOC must detect and analyze internal and external attacks and respond to intrusions into the information system. This mission is hard because security analysts must supervise numerous highly-distributed and heterogeneous systems using multiple communications protocols that are evolving in time. Furthermore, external threats are increasingly complex and silent.

One of the tracks commonly taken to improve the situation is the detection of anomalies. The term *anomaly* has several definitions. Generally speaking,

C. Maurice et al. (Eds.): DIMVA 2020, LNCS 12223, pp. 238–258, 2020.
https://doi.org/10.1007/978-3-030-52683-2_12

Barnett and Lewis [27] define an anomaly as "observation (or a sub-set of observations) which appears to be inconsistent with the remainder of that set of data". In the security field, the NIST defined anomaly-based detection as "the process of comparing definitions of what activity is considered normal against observed events to identify significant deviation" [30].

Nowadays, learning is often used for anomaly detection.Current anomaly detection techniques often build on supervised learning, which needs labeled data during the learning phase. However, security experts often do not have such labeled datasets of their own logs events and labeling data is very expensive [3]. Unfortunately, unsupervised techniques, which do not require labeled data, are not as good as supervised techniques. Nevertheless, a specific technique of unsupervised anomaly detection called "novelty detection" can be used. This technique is typically used when the quantity of available abnormal data is insufficient to construct explicit models for non-normal classes [26]. This approach is also known as "one-class classification". A model is built to describe the *normal data* injected during the training phase.

In this paper, we propose a unified graph representation of heterogeneous types of network logs. The graph we propose integrates heterogeneous information found in the events of various types of log files at our disposal: TCP, DNS, HTTP, information relative to transferred files, etc. A graph structure is well adapted to encode logical links between all these various types of events. By logical link, we mean common values for given fields in given events, such as those relating to network addresses. Structuring in a single graph heterogeneous information coming from various log files allows the construction of a rich vision of the normal situation from which a machine learning algorithm will be able to build a relevant model of this situation. This model will then allow the identification of abnormal situations.

We also propose a process to efficiently encode this unified graph so that an auto-encoder can learn the normal situation and then detect abnormal activities. The learning phase requires normal traffic data but does not need a labeled dataset. We use CICIDS2017 dataset [31] to evaluate the ability of the learned model to detect anomalies.

Our contributions are, therefore:

- The definition of a security objects' graph built from security events of various types. We mix all this heterogeneous information in a single and unified graph structure.
- A way to efficiently encode this graph into values suited to a machine learning algorithm (e.g., an auto-encoder).
- An auto-encoder that detects anomalies on graph structured data.
- Experimental results on the CICIDS2017 dataset composed of millions of log events that show that, while being unsupervised, our approach brings a significant improvement over supervised baseline algorithms.

This paper is organized as follows: our global approach, named *sec2graph*, is presented in Sect. 2. Anomaly detection results and comparative analysis with other methods are discussed in Sect. 3 and 4. Related work about the use of auto-encoders and the use of graph modeling for anomaly detection are reviewed in Sect. 5. Finally, conclusions are presented in Sect. 6.

2   The Sec2graph Approach

Sec2graph detects abnormal patterns in network traffic. Network event logs are used as an input for the whole process. The three key steps of sec2graph are presented in Fig. 1.

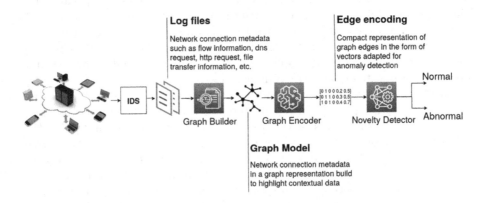

Fig. 1. Overview of the sec2graph workflow

Section 2.1 explains how we build a graph of security objects from the network events; Sect. 2.2 explains how we encode this graph into vectors able to be handled by an auto-encoder; Sect. 2.3 explains how anomalies can be detected by the auto-encoder.

2.1   Building Security Object Graphs from Network Events

In this section, we formally define the graphs we introduce in this paper, and explain how we build them from logs.

A log file can be described as a sequence of n ordered events $\{e_1, e_2, ..., e_n\}$ where e_i is an event resulting from the observation of activity in the network. Each event is made of several fields that differ depending on the semantic of the event itself. Some of these fields are particularly relevant to identify links between events. For each type of event, we identify the most relevant fields to create one or several Security Objects (SOs). A SO is thus a set of attributes, each attribute corresponding to a particular event field.

For example, a network connection leads to four SOs: a source IP Address SO, a destination IP Address SO, a Destination Port SO and a last SO, the NetworkConnection itself that regroups attributes corresponding to the fields we identified as less important to create relations between events. For instance, the payload size attribute is captured as a mere attribute of the `Network Connection` object since there is no reason to believe that two events, having the same payload size, are linked. By contrast, two events for which the same IP addresses appear can be linked with high probability.

For each type of event, we designed a translation into a set of SOs. To keep track of each type of events, links are created between security objects that represent this type. The different type of events considered are network connection, application events (e.g., dns, dhcp, dce/rpc, ftp, http, kerberos, ssh, snmp, smtp,etc.), and information about transferred files and x509 certificates. All of these events are important in the context of intrusion detection because they may contain evidence of compromise. For example, network connection events indicate which devices are communicating and how. This can be useful for detecting port scans, or communications that violate internal security policies. Application events allow the capture of protocol-specific characteristics such as the versions used, thus revealing vulnerabilities. Finally, information about file transfers can be useful as they are a common way to spread viruses, for example by sending executable files.

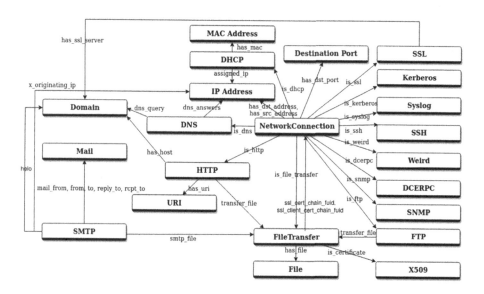

Fig. 2. Complete security objects and relations model representation

The graph model in Fig. 2 shows the different types of SOs (nodes of the graphs) and their semantic links (edges of the graphs). For clarity reason, we have not represented the attributes of the SOs on this figure. Our model is suited to the pieces of information that are representative of network events. It can also evolve easily according to the needs of the analysts. For instance, the X509 object which corresponds to the certificate used during an SSL/TLS session was integrated in a second phase in accordance with the evolution of network communications that are increasingly encrypted.

More formally, our graphs are directed graphs $G = (SO, E)$ with SO being the set of nodes and E being the set of edges. Let $l \in E$ be a link between two nodes a and b. l is defined by the triple (a, b, l_{type}). l_{type} corresponds to the type of the link. For example, for a network connection event, a *NetworkConnection* SO is created and linked to an *IPAddress* SO: this link is of type *has_src_address*. Figure 2 shows the different types of links between SOs. The semantic of these links is derived from the CybOX model [8].

To build the graph, we take as an input a set of network events coming from various log files. From each event, and according to it type, we extract the SOs and the links between them. In other words, we first build a sub-graph representing this event. We then take each SO of the sub-graph. If this SO already exists in the global graph (for instance, a same *IPAddress* was already identified in a previous event), we replace the SO in the new sub-graph by the SO that already exists in the global graph. Therefore, if an event contains an SO that was already found in a previous event, the sub-graph that represents it will be linked to the graph through this SO.

As an example, let's consider three log events extracted from the Zeek [24] analysis of the CICIDS2017 dataset [31]. The three log events represent the same FTP connection analyzes by different modules of the Intrusion Detection System. The first event e_1 is a report on the TCP network connection from the IP address `192.168.10.15` to the IP address `192.168.10.50` on port 21. The second event e_2 gives the details of the FTP reply. The third event e_3 corresponds to file transfer details. A graph for each of these three events is represented on the left hand of Fig. 3. We represent the global graph composed of six SOs and obtained from the three previously described sub-graphs on the right hand of the figure: the first event is colored in blue surrounded by a solid line ($e1$), the second is in red surrounded by a dotted line ($e2$) and the third is in yellow surrounded by a small dotted line ($e3$). e_1 and e_2 shares a reference to the same `NetworkConnection` SO (same uid value) and e_2 and e_3 share the same `FileTransfer` SO (same fluid value). By combining the different log files, the graph makes possible to deduce relationships within different log events and thus to learn more complex patterns.

2.2 Encoding the Graph for Machine Learning

The second step of sec2graph transforms the graph we computed in a structure that can be processed efficiently by a machine learning algorithm. To the best of our knowledge, there does not exist a method to encode multi-attributes and heterogeneous graphs that would be considered as generically efficient. For example, an adjacency matrix is inefficient for large graphs. It also carries no information on nodes and edges. In our case, the encoding method must encode both the structure of the graph (i.e., the relations between the nodes) and the specific information associated with the nodes and the edges. Moreover, the result of the encoding should be of reasonable size while it should contain enough information to detect anomalies. Since there does not exist a single best method to encode our graph, we had to design one tailored to our specific case. ion on

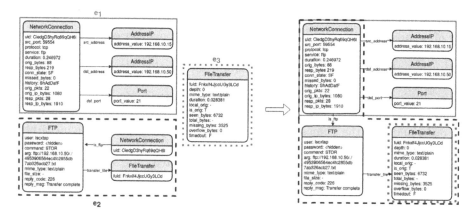

Fig. 3. (**left**) Building of sub-graphs from three events, (**right**) Complete graph issued from three events

a new port. When a collection of similar data instances behave anomalously with respect to the entire dataset, the group of data instances is considered as a collective anomaly. For example, a deny of service can be considered as a collective anomaly. Contextual anomalies or conditional anomalies, are events considered as anomalous depending on the context in which they are found, for example, specific attack on vulnerable version of services or vulnerable network device.

We are looking for anomalies. A given SO can be linked to several events, normal or abnormal. An edge, on the other hand, is only related to the event that led to its construction. Therefore, the anomaly is not carried by the node (an IP address or a port are not abnormal per se) but by the edges that link the SOs together. Consequently, we have chosen to encode our graph by encoding each of its edges. To preserve the context of the event related to this edge, we have chosen the following pieces of information to encode an edge: the type of the edge, information about the source node and the destination node, information about the neighborhood of the source node and information about the neighborhood of the destination node. It should be mentioned that, by construction, a security event cannot be represented by a sub-graph with a diameter greater than three. Indeed, the translation method that we defined to convert events to sub-graph never produces a sub-graph that has a path between two nodes made of more than three edges.

In our graph, there are different kinds of attributes with categorical (version numbers, protocol types, etc.) or continuous (essentially size or duration) values. Anomaly detection requires to encode these two types of attributes in a unified way (see Sect. 2.3). Therefore, categories must be determined for each attribute, even for continuous ones.

Determining Categories. For each *categorical attribute*, we count the number of occurrences of each category, for example, the number of times the value 'tcp' appears for the attribute 'protocol'. For single-value attributes such as port_value, the number of occurrences is by construction always equal to one, since we create only one `Port` SO for this port number. In this type of cases, single-value attributes are distinguished by counting the number of edges of the node carrying this single value attribute. In both cases, we sort them in descending order and keep the N most represented categories that account cumulatively for 90% of the total number of occurrences or number of edges. If more than 20 categories remain, we only keep the 20 most represented categories. It should be noted that we choose the value 20 according to an analysis we performed on the CICIDS2017 dataset [31] that showed that considering more than 20 categories for an attribute does not improve detection.

To translate *continuous attributes* into categories, considering intervals (e.g. [0:10[, [10:20[, etc.) is not an option because this would not take into account the statistical distribution of values and would not be useful for the auto-encoder. Therefore, we categorize the continuous data according to the distribution of the attribute values since our data samples do not necessarily follow a usual probability law, but a law whose density function is a mixed density. To do that, we use the classical Gaussian Mixture Model (GMM), assuming that the values of the attributes follow a mixture of a finite number of Gaussian distributions. It has been shown that GMM gives a good approximation of densities [15]. Furthermore, this technique has already been used for anomaly detection [7].

Two methods exist to infer the Gaussian equation and classify the data. The first one, the expectation-maximization algorithm (EM), is the fastest algorithm for learning mixture models but it requires to define the number of Gaussian components to infer [10]. The second one uses the variational inference algorithm [5]. It does not require to define the number of components but it requires hyperparameters that might need experimental tuning via cross-validation. We choose the first technique to control the number of Gaussian and hence control the number of dimensions of our vector as we will associate one dimension to one component. The number of Gaussian distributions is determined by the classical Bayes Information Criterion (BIC). This consists of successively calculating mixtures of Gaussian in increasing numbers and choose the one with the lowest BIC. In practice, we do not mix more than eight Gaussian, because we found in our data set that the BIC is never smaller. The result is a mixture of no more than eight Gaussian, which brings us down to a case with no more than eight categories.

Encoding Attributes Using Categories. Once we have determined all the categories for our dataset, we can encode the nodes as a binary vector. We proceed as follows.

To fit the auto-encoder, all entries need to be the same size. For each node and each attribute, we distinguish three cases: either the node has the attribute and its value corresponds to one of the categories of the attribute, or the node has the attribute but its value does not correspond to one of the categories, or the node does not have the attribute given its type (for instance, it is an IPAddress node and therefore does not have the port_value attribute). The one-hot-encoding technique is used. For each node of the graph, we build a binary vector x of size $N + 1$, N corresponding to the number of categories. Each bit of this vector corresponds to a given category and is thus set to one if the attribute value of the nodes is of this category. It is set to zero otherwise. One last bit with the value 0 is added to this vector to represent the category "other". In the second case, each bit is assigned the value 0 and one last bit is added to '1' for the "other" category. Finally, in the last case, i.e., if the encoded attributes are not related to the type of the node, all the bits are assigned the value 0. This method makes it possible to encode uniformly all the nodes whatever there type. We build a vector for each attribute then we concatenate all these vectors into a binary vector corresponding to the encoding of our node.

Encoding the Structure of the Graph. The encoding of the attributes presented above is relative to the information contained in the nodes' attributes. Our representation also takes into account the structure of the graph and the types of the edges. To this end, we encode an edge as a vector resulting of the concatenation of information on (a) the type of this edge, (b) the attributes of its source node, (c) the attributes of its destination node, (d) information about the neighborhood of its source node and (e) information about the neighborhood of its destination:

- (a): there are 18 types of edges. For each edge, we encode its type using the same one-hot encoding technique that we use to encode the node's attributes.
- (b) and (c): We encode the attributes of the source node and destination node as previously described.
- (d) and (e): for each source node and destination node, we select randomly 10.000 neighbors and compute the mean of their encoding vector. We choose 10.000 nodes because this allows us to reduce the computational complexity and we have determined that the mean does not change significantly above this threshold.

Considering that a l edge between s and d is of type l_{type}, as well as that the s node has $N(s)$ neighbors and the d node has $N(d)$ neighbors, we randomly select 10,000 nodes in $N(s)$ and $N(d)$ to constitute a representative sample of the neighborhood $N(s)_{sample}$ and $N(d)_{sample}$. It should be noted that we already have the encoding of each of these nodes in the form of a binary vector each having the same size.

We define $mean(\overrightarrow{enc}_{N(s)_{sample}})$ and $mean(\overrightarrow{enc}_{N(d)_{sample}})$ as the bit-wise average of the vectors encoding each node of $N(s)_{sample}$ and $N(d)_{sample}$ respectively. It should be noted that, at this point, the vector is made of continuous values between 1 and 0 for the encoding of the neighbors. We thus obtain a compact representation of the neighborhood of the node that is sufficient for the processing of the graph and to detect anomalies. In this compact representation, each element of each vector takes a value between 0 and 1, but each element corresponds to a category of a certain attribute. Therefore, this vector of values between 0 and 1 gives an idea of the distribution of the categories in the considered neighborhood.

2.3 Novelty Detection with an Auto-Encoder

We use an auto-encoder for novelty detection as already proposed by [2, 4, 6, 22, 29] in the security field where novelty is viewed as an anomaly that may be generated by an attack. An auto-encoder [19] learns a representation (encoding) of a set of pieces of data, typically for dimensional reduction. To do so, it learns a function that sets the outputs of the network to be equal to its inputs. It is made of two parts : an encoder and a decoder. The encoder compresses the input data into a low-dimensional representation, and the decoder generates a representation that is as close as possible to its original input from the reduced encoding.

The inputs to our auto-encoder consist of the vectors whose construction was explained in Sect. 2.2. Recall that these vectors encode the following information: edge type, source node attributes, destination node attributes, source node neighborhood attributes, and destination node neighborhood attributes. The first three pieces of information are encoded by binary vectors while the last two are encoded by vectors whose components are continuous values between 0 and 1 (see 2.2). In a similar case, Bastos et al. [9] showed that it was desirable to have a single encoding function (which makes it possible to take into account possible correlations between the different types of encoding) and a decoding function specific to each type of information (binary vs. between 0 and 1) or specific to each piece of information.

Our auto-encoder, therefore, has five outputs and uses two types of loss functions: binary cross-entropy, that is suited to binary values, and mean-square error, that is suited to continuous values. The result is made of five error values between 0 and 1. To determine whether there is an anomaly, we calculate an overall error which is the sum of these five errors and raise an anomaly alert if it reaches a certain threshold. This threshold is set experimentally (see 3.2). Of course, the lower it is, the more alerts we have and the greater the risk of false positives. The analyst sets the threshold value according to his or her monitoring context by lowering the value if it is more important for the analyst not to miss any attacks than to have a large number of false positives.

3 Implementation and Experimental Results

This section details our implementation choices, experiments, and analysis. We first describe the technologies used, the dataset and the evaluation criteria in Sect. 3.1. We then carefully choose a threshold value in Sect. 3.2. Finally, we dive into the results obtained by deploying the sec2graph approach compared to other approaches based on anomaly detection in Sect. 3.3.

3.1   Experimental Setup

Dataset. We choose to use the CICIDS2017 dataset [31] that is made of five pcap and csv files encompassing more than two million network sessions. This dataset was generated at the Canadian Cybersecurity Institute at the University of New Brunswick and contains five days (Monday to Friday) of mixed traffic, benign and attacks such as DoS, DDoS, BruteForce, XSS, SQL injection, infiltration, port scan, and botnet activities.

Normal traffic was generated using the CIC-B-Profile [31] system, that can reproduce the behavior of 25 users using various protocols (FTP, SSH, HTTP, HTTPS and SMTP). Attacks were executed using classic tools such as Metasploit and Nmap. This dataset is labeled, i.e., we know when attacks occur and when the traffic is normal. For example, the traffic captured on Monday is entirely normal. According to [13], the CICIDS2017 dataset is the most recent one that models a complete network configuration with components such as firewalls, routers, modems, and a variety of operating systems such as Windows, Ubuntu Linux or Macintosh and that has been used in several studies. The protocols in the capture (e.g., HTTP, HTTPS, FTP, SSH) are representative of protocols used in a real network and a variety of common attacks are covered. The data set is also labeled, allowing us to quantify the effectiveness of our method. To generate log files from the capture files, we used the Zeek IDS tool (formerly Bro) that can generate network and application logs such as connections, http communications or file transfers. The default configuration for the Zeek IDS was applied.

Implementation Details and Configuration. We chose the Python language and we use a Gremlin API [28] for the construction of the graph from the events logs and the manipulation of this graph. Indeed, the gremlin language is particularly well adapted to the construction and manipulation of graphs. Besides, we used the Python language for the implementation of the auto-encoder based on the Keras library.

We used a Janusgraph database with an external index backend, Elasticsearch, and a Cassandra storage backend to store the graph data. We choose these technologies for scalability as they are adapted to large graph databases. Experiments were performed on a Debian 9 machine with 64 GB RAM.

The structure of our auto-encoder is depicted in Fig. 4. The sizes of both the input layer and the output layers ($18 + 4 * 360 = 1458$ neurons) come from the sizes of our vectors (recall that the output should be equal to the output). The auto-encoder counts five hidden layers: the diversity of the SOs in the graph leads to very diverse encoding and thus this number of hidden layers is suited for learning complex relations between the different bits of the vectors. The intermediate layer between the encoder and the decoder has a size of 80: the input vectors are indeed sparse, thus we choose a little number of neurons for this layer. The number of neurons in each layer and the number of hidden layers was determined by experimentation, trying different values looking for a minimum value for the reconstruction error. We choose a number of epochs (the number of iteration of the forward and backpropagation phase) of 20 as experiments show

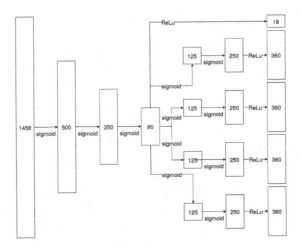

Fig. 4. Structure of the auto-encoder

that the reconstruction error did not decrease significantly for a larger number of epochs. We choose the Adam optimizer with a learning rate of 0.001 to back-propagate the reconstruction error as it is well-adapted when more than one hidden layer is used.

To train our auto-encoder, we used during a first phase (learning phase), the data captured on Monday as it is entirely normal. This data is split in a training set and a validation set with a validation split of 0.1. This allows to validate the model on unseen data and thus prevent overfitting. Depending on the various parameters we have, the learning phases took about an hour. In the second phase (anomaly detection phase), we used the whole dataset (Monday to Friday) to evaluate the detection capacity of our approach.

Evaluation Criteria. Our approach seeks to identify anomalies related to links between objects. Classical approaches seek to identify anomalies relating to events. Although our ultimate goal remains to present the anomalous edges to the analyst, in this section, to compare ourselves to the classical approaches, we determine from the anomalous edges we find in the graph the events that gave birth to them. We consider as abnormal any event whose representation contains at least one abnormal edge.

All the results presented in this section are related to events. These are processed in one-hour shifts. For each time slot, we build a graph, then the vectors to enter into the auto-encoder and finally we evaluate the novelty of each vector.

In addition to the number of true positives (TP), false positives (FP), true negatives (TN) and false negatives (FN), we evaluate our results through the following standard metrics: Precision, Recall, F1-score, False Positive Rate (FPR) and Accuracy. The Precision gives the ratio of real anomalous events among all the events declared as anomalous. The Recall gives the proportion of events correctly detected as anomalous among all the really anomalous events. The F1-Score is the harmonic mean of the Precision and Recall. The FPR is the proportion of events for which an anomaly has wrongly been emitted and the accuracy is the number of events correctly classified (as anomaly or as normal events) divided by the total number of events. Formally, these criteria can be defined as follows:

$$Precision = \frac{TP}{TP+FP}; Recall = \frac{TP}{TP+FN}; FPR = \frac{FP}{FP+TN};$$
$$Accuracy = \frac{TP+TN}{TP+FN+TN+FP}; F1_{score} = \frac{2*Precision*Recall}{Precision+Recall}$$

3.2 Defining an Optimal Threshold for Detection

In this section, we present the experiments conducted to determine the threshold value to be used. As noted above, the analyst sets this threshold value according to his or her supervisory context, lowering the threshold value if it is more important for the analyst not to miss any attacks than to have to eliminate a large number of false positives.

We determine the value of the threshold as follows: first, we consider all the events of Monday, a day without attacks. With this data, we determine the rate of false positives according to the detection threshold. We obviously want the lowest possible false-positive rate. The curve in Fig. 5 shows the evolution of the FPR as a function of the detection threshold. A threshold of 0.003 gives us an FPR of 0.031. In the figure, for threshold values on the right of the value of 0.003, the FPR decreases weakly, while for threshold values on the left, it strongly increases.

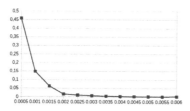

Fig. 5. False Positive Rate (FPR) according to the value of the detection threshold on Monday data (normal events).

We conclude that a threshold higher than 0.003 should be retained. To determine the value of this threshold more precisely, we need to consider the different types of attacks in our dataset and determine the value that allows the most efficient detection of these attacks. For this purpose, we consider the time slots during which each attack occurs. For example, the FTP Patator attack takes place on Tuesday from 9:20 to 10:20, so we consider the data between 9:00 and 11:00. During these time slots in which the attacks take place, we want the maximum number of events belonging to the attacks to be detected as anomalies while keeping the number of false positives as low as possible. In other words, we naturally want to maximize precision and recall. Figure 6 gives the values of recall and precision as a function of the detection threshold for the different types of attacks in the CICIDS2017 dataset. We varied this threshold over the entire range for which this variation has a significant impact on recall and precision.

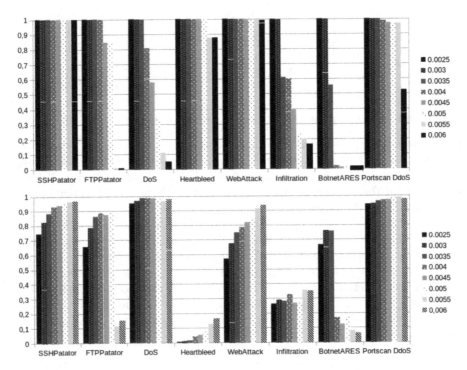

Fig. 6. Values of Recall (top figure) and Precision (bottom figure) for the range of variation of the threshold leading to a significant evolution of these values.

On the diagram at the top of the figure, it can be seen that a quasi-optimal recall can be obtained (between 0.993 and 1) for a threshold value of 0.003. On the diagram of the bottom of the figure, we also see that for this threshold value, the precision is between 0.675 and 0.967, except for the Heartbleed attack (0.012) and the infiltration attack (0.287). However, increasing the threshold further does not significantly increase the precision, but does significantly decrease the recall for infiltration and botnet. We, therefore, conclude that we can retain a threshold value of 0.003.

The two cases of low precision, i.e., Heartbleed and infiltration can be explained differently. In the case of Heartbleed, the low precision is explained by the silent nature of this attack. Indeed, if we detect 100% of the events related to the attack for a threshold of 0.003, this represents only eight network connections compared to almost 93.000 network connections that took place during the attack. While the FPR is consistent with other slots in our dataset, the 93.000

normal network connections lead to 681 false positives and thus decrease the precision. In the case of the infiltration attack, the low accuracy is explained by an abnormally large number of false positives. The infiltration attack is indeed followed by a portscan performed by the victim of the infiltration. The perturbation being massive, it impacts the neighborhood of the events linked to the scan. This leads to considering a large amount of this neighborhood abnormal, even for normal events, leading to a high rate of false positive.

3.3 Comparison with Other Anomaly Detection Algorithms on the Same Dataset

To compare our results with the state of the art, we have taken the results of three studies on attack detection that use the same dataset as we do, the CICIDS2017

Table 1. Comparison of False Positive Rate (FPR), Recall, Precision, Accuracy, and F1-score results (in %) for supervised and semi-supervised approaches of literature and sec2graph. The values in brackets are worse than those obtained with sec2graph. The rank indicates the ranking of sec2graph in relation to other approaches.

Evaluation criteria	FPR	Recall	Precision	Accuracy	F1-score
Better if	Smaller	Greater	Greater	Greater	Greater
Algorithm					
KNN [31]	–	(96)	96	–	96
RF [31]	–	(97)	98	–	97
ID3 [31]	–	(98)	98	–	98
Adaboost [31]	–	(84)	(77)	–	(77)
MLP [31]	–	(83)	(77)	–	(76)
NaiveBayes [31]	–	(84)	(88)	–	(84)
QDA [31]	–	(88)	97	–	(92)
DecisionTree + Rules [1]	1.145	(94.475)	–	(96.665)	–
WISARD [1]	2.865	(48.175)	–	(72.655)	–
Forest PA [1]	(3.550)	(92.920)	–	(94.685)	–
J48consolidated [1]	(6.645)	(92.020)	–	(92.688)	–
LIBSVM	(5.130)	(54.595)	–	(74.733)	–
FURIA [1]	(3.165)	(90.500)	–	(93.668)	–
REP Tree [1]	(4.835)	(91.640)	–	(93.403)	–
NaiveBayes [1]	(33.455)	(82.510)	–	(74.528)	–
Jrip [1]	(4.470)	(93.400)	–	(94.465)	–
J48 [1]	(5.040)	(91.990)	–	(93.475)	–
SU-IDS (0.5% supervised) [22]	(5)	(93.68)	–	(93.68)	
Mean result	6,50	86,34	90,14	88.88	88,57
sec2graph (threshold 0.003)	3.125	99.910	88.872	97.481	94.069
Rank	3/11	1/18	5/7	1/11	4/7

dataset[1]. These studies are the only three that present results according to all or part of the criteria we have defined above and the comparison is therefore possible.

Sharafaldin *et al.* [31] compares the results of seven supervised classical machine learning algorithms applied on this dataset: K-Nearest Neighbors (KNN), Random Forest (RF), ID3, Adaboost, Multilayer perceptron (MLP), Naive-Bayes (NB) and Quadratic Discriminant Analysis (QDA), that are all supervised machine learning algorithms. Ahmim *et al.* [1] compare the results of twelve classical or more recent classification algorithms: DecisionTree and rules, WISARD, Forest PA, J48 consolidated, LibSVM, FURIA, REP Tree, Naive-Bayes, Jrip, J48, MLP, and RandomForest. Since the latter two algorithms were used in both studies, only the best results were retained in the comparison. Min *et al.* [22] propose a semi-supervised method SU-IDS based on an auto-encoder and a classification method. The SU-IDS experiments were carried out with a variable number (from 0.5% to 100%) of labeled data. To compare our proposal to a method close to an unsupervised model, we have chosen to use the results of the tests carried out on a sample with 0.1% of labeled data.

All these algorithms were tested starting from a dataset containing 80 features selected according to their relevance for the detection of attacks using the CICFlowMeter tool [31]. In the case of the first seven algorithms listed above, the authors trained their algorithms on a specifically chosen subset of the 80 attributes using a Random Forest Regressor. These attributes were chosen because they were most likely to help detect the attacks in the dataset and thus improved the performance of the algorithms for these specific types of attacks. In our case, we used all the features contained in Zeek event logs without making a prior selection according to their relevance for observing attacks. Our objective is to measure the ability of the auto-encoder to choose the most relevant features to represent a normal behavior in our dataset without targeting specific types of attack.

Table 1 provides a comparison of the classical learning machine algorithms listed above against our approach sec2graph with the optimal value previously determined for the detection threshold. Results of the different algorithms come directly from the original papers and parameters of the algorithms can be assumed to have been optimized to produce the best possible results.

The values in this table show that, although being an *unsupervised* approach, sec2graph achieves performances at worst slightly below the average of those obtained by the *supervised* approaches it is compared to. Given the strategy we have adopted to set the detection threshold, we achieve the best performance in terms of recall, with 99.91% of attack events correctly marked as abnormal (all attacks tested generate marked events). Nevertheless, sec2graph's ranking remains close to the average in terms of precision, which means that the analyst

---

[1] Another study was published very recently [11] that deals with the 2018 version of the CICIDS data. These data are richer in terms of protocols but different in terms of attacks. While we cannot compare our proposal to this study, we have a work in progress in this direction.

will not be drowned by false positives: 88.872% of alerts are indeed true positives. Moreover, we did not select attributes according to the type of attacks we want to detect, allowing us to adapt to new kinds of attacks.

4   Discussion

While CICIDS2017 is arguably one of the most realistic and reasonably large datasets, it contains numerous attacks that impact the total volume of network communications. We trained our model only with the normal traffic on Monday because the dataset on other days contains far too many attack sessions. While the hypothesis of a learning dataset without attacks is strong, it is realistic to think that attacks can be very limited in some real-life network traffic samples. Auto-encoders also learn a general model, not taking into account particular cases such as these attacks. Future work on a learning dataset with a low attack proportion would allow to validate this hypothesis.

As discussed in Sect. 3.2, some attacks such as Infiltration are well detected but also induce many false positives. Indeed, in this very case, nodes identified as abnormal impact the calculation on their normal neighboring nodes, making them look abnormal. Refining the method to calculate the reconstruction error could reduce this effect. More generally, incorrectly labelling 3% of all the events as abnormal (see FPR in Table 1 is way too high. However, the graph approach allows the analyst to take into account a large number of events at once. Moreover, the use of an auto-encoder allows a better interpretation of the results. During our analysis, we defined a reconstruction error corresponding to the sum of the reconstruction errors, but it is possible to obtain the detail of the values expected by the model and thus better interpret the results.

We tested our algorithm on data where normal traffic does not evolve while in a real environment network activities, devices and behaviors change over time. Since auto-encoders allow for iterative learning, it is possible to use new data to evolve the model and learn new behaviors. This can be used to eliminate recurring false positives or to track the evolution of network activities.

To cope with new type of data or new networks, changing the number of layers and neurons of the auto-encoder is needed. Thus, we cannot directly transfer the learning result to a new context. However, study of the FPR (see Sect. 3.2) allows to adjust the parameters and choose a threshold for reconstruction error. Diverse network communications and complexity require a larger number of neurons for learning while a simple network on which actions are not very diversified requires to decrease the number of neurons to avoid overfitting.

5   Related Work

In this section, we position our work in relation to similar approaches in the literature. To our best knowledge, at the time of writing, none of these approaches has sought to detect anomalies on graphs using auto-encoders. Here, we position our work, firstly with respect to pieces of work that relied on graphs for anomaly detection, and secondly with respect to pieces of work that used auto-encoders for anomaly detection.

5.1   Using Graph Structures for Anomaly Detection

In the field of intrusion anomaly, graph structures have often been used. Hercule [25] represents inter-log similarities within a graph of log events. In this representation, a node represents a log event and an edge represents a predefined similarity relationship between two logs events. Clustering techniques are then applied to the graph to identify the set of events related to a given attack. Strictly speaking, there is no anomaly detection but the identification of information related to a known attack occurrence identified thanks to a compromise indicator. Experiments on APT attacks shows that the system performs well in this task (accuracy of 88% on average), and once the events related to the attack have been identified, it allows forensic analysis of the attack.

Other work relates to forensic analysis and exploits graph structures. For example, King and Chen [16], as well as Goel et al. [14], propose to reconstruct a chain of events in a dependency graph to explain an attack. In [21], Milajerdi et al. use audit logs to reconstruct the history of attacks using traces from common Advanced Persistent Threat (APT) attacks. Kobayashi et al. [17] use syslog events to infer causality between security system events. These proposals are however limited since they only consider one type of event format. Xu et al. [32] represent, as a graph, the causal dependency among system events.

Other works use graphs to detect attacks and more precisely to detect botnets [12,18,23]. They use network-related data to build topological graphs with nodes representing hosts and links representing network communication between them. They then use clustering, PageRank algorithm or statistical-based mining techniques on graphs to identify abnormal network traffic based. While having similar objective, we do not limit to botnet detection. Furthermore, in addition to the fact that we process our graphs with an auto-encoder for anomaly detection, our dataset is richer since not limited to netflow data. This rich data also allows us to take into account the global context in which the attacks occur.

Finally, Log2vec [20] detects user's malicious behavior based on a clustering algorithm applied to relations among user's operations. Log2vec represents user's actions with small graphs and embeds them in a vector by using a random-based walk algorithm. By contrast, we represent all network events in one big graph and detect anomalies that occur on multiple devices by multiple attackers.

5.2   Using Auto-Encoders for Anomaly Detection

Several pieces of work already used auto-encoders for anomaly detection [2,4,6, 22,29], among which only [6,29] proposes unsupervised approaches.

The authors of [6] use two types of auto-encoders namely, stochastic denoising auto-encoder and deep auto-encoder, to detect anomaly in the NSL-KDD dataset. The experiments conducted by the authors show that their model achieves an F1-score score respectively of 89.5% and 89,3%, a recall of 87.9%

and 83.1% and a precision of 91.2% and 96.5%. However, the dataset used contains redundant data that can distort the results obtained by learning machine algorithms. In our study, we used the CICIDS2017 dataset that addresses the problems posed by the NSL-KDD dataset and we were able to obtain better results thanks to our graph representation of SOs.

The authors of [22] propose to remedy the problems of data with little or no security label by proposing an unsupervised and semi-supervised approach. The idea is to use an auto-encoder in association with a classification algorithm for the semi-supervised approach. The latter is then trained on a restricted portion of labeled data. In the unsupervised approach, the auto-encoder is used alone. The study was carried out on the NSL-KDD and CICIDS2017 datasets. The results are good only in the semi-supervised approach, even if the unsupervised approach seems to isolate some attacks. In our work, on the CICIDS2017 data and with an unsupervised approach, we obtain better detection results, especially for false positives. Our graph approach handles heterogeneous types of events and links between these events, allowing us to detect anomalies without using a supervised algorithm.

In [29], the authors propose to use an auto-encoder to detect intrusion on IoT radio networks. The approach is based on the monitoring of the communication activities generated by the connected objects. The radio-activities patterns are then encoded in features specific to the IoT domain and normal activities are then learned with the auto-encoder to detect anomalies in a second phase. Similarly, Kitsune [33] is an auto-encoder-based NIDS capable of extracting features and creating a dynamically unsupervised learning model that has been tested for IoT devices. These methods are specific to the considered context but proposes, as in our case, an unsupervised intrusion detection system to detect anomalies with the help of an auto-encoder.

The other studies mentioned at the beginning of this paragraph [2, 4] add a supervised layer to the unsupervised output of the auto-encoder. The general idea is to use the auto-encoder to identify normal traffic almost certainly. Traffic that is not considered normal by the auto-encoder is then provided to a supervised classification device, trained on data labeled to identify attacks. We differ from this work since we refuse to label data, contenting ourselves with learning attack-free data. Indeed, in a production environment, the data is much too voluminous to be possible to label them. Moreover, the experimental results obtained by these other studies are based on data that are different from ours. It is therefore difficult if not impossible to compare these experimental results with ours.

6   Conclusion and Future Work

We proposed in this paper a graph representation of security events that underlines the relationship between them. We also proposed an unsupervised technique built on an auto-encoder to efficiently detect anomalies on this graph representation. This approach can be applied to any data set without prior data labeling.

Using the CICIDS2017 dataset, we have shown that the use of graph structures to represent security data coupled with an auto-encoder gives results that are as good as or better than the supervised machine learning methods.

We are currently conducting new experiments with a wider neighborhood in the encoding of the graph to evaluate the potential improvement of intrusion detection and reduction of the number of false positives. To further improve our detection results, we plan to use another kind of auto-encoder (LSTM auto-encoder) to take temporal links between events into account in addition to logical links that we already take into account. As these improvements should lead to an increased duration of this learning phase, we will investigate a reduction of the size of the encoding of the nodes by using entity embedding instead of one-hot encoding. Another area for improvement is related to the usability and interpretability of results by a security analyst. Here, the idea is to present to the analyst a graphical view of the detected anomalies, based on the SOs graphs that we have defined. We want to provide to the analyst the subsets of the edges of this graph that have been detected as abnormal, as well as of course the SOs linked by these edges. We believe that this would help the analyst eliminating false positives or reconstructing global attack scenarios.

References

1. Ahmim, A., Maglaras, L., Ferrag, M.A., Derdour, M., Janicke, H.: A novel hierarchical intrusion detection system based on decision tree and rules-based models. In: 15th International Conference on Distributed Computing in Sensor Systems (DCOSS) (2019)
2. Al-Qatf, M., Lasheng, Y., Al-Habib, M., Al-Sabahi, K.: Deep learning approach combining sparse autoencoder with SVM for network intrusion detection. IEEE Access **6**, 52843–52856 (2018)
3. Anagnostopoulos, C.: Weakly supervised learning: how to engineer labels for machine learning in cyber-security. Data Sci. Cyber-Secur., 195–226 (2018)
4. Andresini, G., Appice, A., Di Mauro, N., Loglisci, C., Malerba, D.: Exploiting the auto-encoder residual error for intrusion detection. In: IEEE European Symposium on Security and Privacy Workshops (EuroS&PW) (2019)
5. Attias, H.: A variational baysian framework for graphical models. In: Advances in Neural Information Processing Systems (2000)
6. Aygun, R.C., Yavuz, A.G.: Network anomaly detection with stochastically improved autoencoder based models. In: IEEE 4th International Conference on Cyber Security and Cloud Computing (CSCloud) (2017)
7. Bahrololum, M., Khaleghi, M.: Anomaly intrusion detection system using hierarchical gaussian mixture model. Int. J. Comput. Sci. Netw. Secur. **8**(8), 264–271 (2008)
8. Barnum, S., Martin, R., Worrell, B., Kirillov, I.: The cybox language specification draft. The MITRE Corporation (2012)
9. Bastos, I.L., Melo, V.H., Gonçalves, G.R., Schwartz, W.R.: Mora: A generative approach to extract spatiotemporal information applied to gesture recognition. In: 15th IEEE International Conference on Advanced Video and Signal Based Surveillance (AVSS) (2018)

10. Dempster, A.P., Laird, N.M., Rubin, D.B.: Maximum likelihood from incomplete data via the EM algorithm. J. Roy. Stat. Soc. Ser. B (Methodol.) **39**(1), 1–22 (1977)

11. Ferrag, M.A., Maglaras, L., Moschoyiannis, S., Janicke, H.: Deep learning for cyber security intrusion detection: approaches, datasets, and comparative study. J. Inf. Secur. Appl. **50**, 102419 (2020)

12. François, J., Wang, S., State, R., Engel, T.: BotTrack: tracking botnets using Net-Flow and PageRank. In: Domingo-Pascual, J., Manzoni, P., Palazzo, S., Pont, A., Scoglio, C. (eds.) NETWORKING 2011. LNCS, vol. 6640, pp. 1–14. Springer, Heidelberg (2011). https://doi.org/10.1007/978-3-642-20757-0_1

13. Gharib, A., Sharafaldin, I., Lashkari, A.H., Ghorbani, A.A.: An evaluation framework for intrusion detection dataset. In: International Conference on Information Science and Security (ICISS) (2016)

14. Goel, A., Po, K., Farhadi, K., Li, Z., De Lara, E.: The taser intrusion recovery system. In: ACM SIGOPS Operating Systems Review (2005)

15. Goodfellow, I., Bengio, Y., Courville, A.: Deep Learning. MIT Press, Cambridge (2016)

16. King, S.T., Chen, P.M.: Backtracking intrusions. In: ACM SIGOPS Operating Systems Review (2003)

17. Kobayashi, S., Otomo, K., Fukuda, K., Esaki, H.: Mining causality of network events in log data. IEEE Trans. Netw. Serv. Manag. **15**(1), 53–67 (2017)

18. Lagraa, S., François, J., Lahmadi, A., Miner, M., Hammerschmidt, C., State, R.: Botgm: unsupervised graph mining to detect botnets in traffic flows. In: 1st Cyber Security in Networking Conference (CSNet) (2017)

19. Le Cun, Y., Fogelman-Soulié, F.: Modèles connexionnistes de l'apprentissage. Intellectica (1987)

20. Liu, F., Wen, Y., Zhang, D., Jiang, X., Xing, X., Meng, D.: Log2vec: a heterogeneous graph embedding based approach for detecting cyber threats within enterprise. In: Proceedings of the ACM SIGSAC Conference on Computer and Communications Security (2019)

21. Milajerdi, S.M., Gjomemo, R., Eshete, B., Sekar, R., Venkatakrishnan, V.: Holmes: real-time apt detection through correlation of suspicious information flows. In: IEEE Symposium on Security and Privacy (SP) (2019)

22. Min, E., Long, J., Liu, Q., Cui, J., Cai, Z., Ma, J.: SU-IDS: a semi-supervised and unsupervised framework for network intrusion detection. In: Sun, X., Pan, Z., Bertino, E. (eds.) ICCCS 2018. LNCS, vol. 11065, pp. 322–334. Springer, Cham (2018). https://doi.org/10.1007/978-3-030-00012-7_30

23. Nagaraja, S., Mittal, P., Hong, C.Y., Caesar, M., Borisov, N.: Botgrep: finding P2P bots with structured graph analysis. In: USENIX security symposium (2010)

24. Paxson, V.: Bro: a system for detecting network intruders in real-time. Comput. Netw. **31**, 2435–2463 (1999)

25. Pei, K., et al.: Hercule: attack story reconstruction via community discovery on correlated log graph. In: Proceedings of the 32th Annual Conference on Computer Security Applications (2016)

26. Pimentel, M.A., Clifton, D.A., Clifton, L., Tarassenko, L.: A review of novelty detection. Signal Process. **99**, 215–249 (2014)

27. Pincus, R.: Barnett, V., and Lewis, T.: Outliers in statistical data.J. Wiley & Sons 1994, XVII. 582 pp.,£ 49.95. Biometrical J. **37**(2), 256 (1995)

28. Rodriguez, M.A.: The gremlin graph traversal machine and language. In: Proceedings of the 15th Symposium on Database Programming Languages (2015)

29. Roux, J., Alata, E., Auriol, G., Kaâniche, M., Nicomette, V., Cayre, R.: Radiot: Iadio communications intrusion detection for IoT-a protocol independent approach. In: IEEE 17th International Symposium on Network Computing and Applications (NCA) (2018)
30. Scarfone, K., Mell, P.: Guide to intrusion detection and prevention systems (IDPS). Technical Report, National Institute of Standards and Technology (2012)
31. Sharafaldin, I., Lashkari, A.H., Ghorbani, A.A.: Toward generating a new intrusion detection dataset and intrusion traffic characterization. In: ICISSP (2018)
32. Xu, Z., et al.: High fidelity data reduction for big data security dependency analyses. In: ACM SIGSAC Conference on Computer and Communications Security (2016)
33. Yisroel, M., Tomer, D., Yuval, E., Asaf, S.: Kitsune: an ensemble of autoencoders for online network intrusion detection. In: Network and Distributed System Security Symposium (NDSS) (2018)

Efficient Context-Sensitive CFI Enforcement Through a Hardware Monitor

Sadullah Canakci(✉), Leila Delshadtehrani, Boyou Zhou, Ajay Joshi,
and Manuel Egele

Boston University, Boston, MA 02215, USA
{scanakci,delshad,bobzhou,joshi,megele}@bu.edu

Abstract. Recent works on Control-Flow Integrity (CFI) have mainly focused on Context-Sensitive CFI policies to provide higher security guarantees. They utilize a debugging hardware feature in modern Intel CPUs, *Processor Trace* (PT), to efficiently collect runtime contextual information. These PT-based CFI mechanisms offload the processing of the collected PT trace and CFI enforcement onto idle cores. However, a processor does not always have idle cores due to the commonly-used multi-threaded applications such as web browsers. In fact, dedicating one or more cores for CFI enforcement reduces the number of available cores for running user programs. Our evaluation with a state-of-the-art CFI mechanism (μCFI) shows that the performance overhead of a CFI mechanism can substantially increase (up to 652% on a single-core processor) when there is no idle core for CFI enforcement. To improve the performance of μCFI, we propose to leverage a hardware monitor that unlike PT does not incur trace processing overhead. We show that the hardware monitor can be used to efficiently collect program traces (<1% overhead) in their original forms and apply μCFI. We prototype the hardware-monitor based μCFI on a single-core RISC-V processor. Our analysis show that hardware-monitor based μCFI incurs, on average, 43% (up to 277%) performance overhead.

Keywords: CFI · Hardware monitor · Processor trace

1 Introduction and Motivation

With the introduction of Data Execution Prevention (DEP) [8], attackers changed their focus from code injection to code-reuse attacks such as Return-Oriented Programming (ROP) [35] and Jump-Oriented Programming (JOP) [12]. Control-Flow Integrity (CFI) [7] is a security defense that aims to prevent these attacks by drastically reducing the allowed code targets for each *Indirect Control-Flow Transfers* (ICTs). Most CFI mechanisms consist of two phases [10]: an analysis phase and an enforcement phase. The analysis phase generates a statically constructed Control-Flow Graph (CFG), which approximates the allowed

© Springer Nature Switzerland AG 2020
C. Maurice et al. (Eds.): DIMVA 2020, LNCS 12223, pp. 259–279, 2020.
https://doi.org/10.1007/978-3-030-52683-2_13

code targets for each control-flow transfer. The enforcement phase ensures that all the executed control-flow transfers follow valid paths in the CFG.

The success of a CFI mechanism mainly relies on two metrics: performance and security. Recent works focus on *context-sensitive CFI* [20,24,27,28] to provide stronger security guarantees than traditional context-insensitive CFI [42,43]. Context-sensitive CFI mechanisms refine the CFG with additional contextual information. Unfortunately, introducing contextual information requires additional processing time during the enforcement phase; thus, it increases the overall performance overhead of the CFI mechanisms [20,21].

For efficient context-sensitive CFI enforcement, researchers have repurposed an already deployed hardware feature in modern Intel CPUs, *Processor Trace* (PT) [34]. PT has been designed for **offline** debugging and failure diagnosis by capturing runtime target and timing information of ICT instructions (`ret` and indirect `jmp/call`) [32]. Although several works [15,26,38] used PT in its intended direction, recent works leveraged PT to efficiently collect contextual information for **online** CFI enforcement [20,21,24,29].

Using PT for CFI enforcement is practical since it already exists in the commodity hardware. However, PT is not an optimal hardware feature for CFI enforcement. Although PT efficiently collects traces (<3% overhead [29]) in the form of encoded *packets* at the hardware level, the decoding of these packets (*trace processing*) performed with a software-level decoder is significantly slower than the trace collection [21,24,29]. Unfortunately, any PT-based CFI mechanism requires this inefficient trace processing prior to validating ICT targets at enforcement phase. To avoid the additional performance overhead, existing PT-based CFI mechanisms [20,21,24,29] offload the trace processing and ICT validation onto idle cores[1]. However, commonly used applications (such as web browsers/servers and games) are multi-threaded; thus, the processor will not always have idle cores available for CFI enforcement. In fact, dedicating one or more cores for CFI enforcement reduces the number of available cores for running user applications.

In Fig. 1, we show the performance impact of the number of cores on CFI enforcement by using a state-of-the-art PT-based approach (μCFI [24]) for SPEC2006 benchmark suite [23]. The details of the experimental setup are provided in Sect. 4. We evaluate PT-based μCFI using four configurations: single-core (1-Core), two-core (2-Core), three-core (3-Core), and eight-core (8-Core). 8-Core and 3-Core configurations incur similar performance overheads since μCFI enforcement uses two additional idle cores (one for ICT validation and one for trace processing). 2-Core and 1-Core results clearly show that PT-based μCFI significantly impacts the performance of benchmarks if the processor does not have any idle cores. On average, the performance overhead of μCFI increases from 23% to 42% from 3-Core to 1-Core. Note that the benchmarks generating more packets show higher degradation in performance since trace processing requires more CPU time for these benchmarks. In the worst case, μCFI incurs

---

[1] Throughout the paper, a "core" refers to a logical core.

652% overhead on 1-Core for `h264ref`, which is significantly higher than 3-Core overhead (372%).

Based on the insights gained from our measurements, efficient context-sensitive CFI policies should be enforced through a hardware feature which efficiently collects contextual information without requiring trace processing. We show that a programmable hardware monitor (PHMon [19]) with fine-grained configuration capabilities can be used to efficiently implement a state-of-the-art context-sensitive CFI mechanism (μCFI [24]) to defend against forward-edge attacks. PHMon incurs only 1% trace collection overhead when collecting the contextual information. Moreover, PHMon does not require trace processing during CFI enforcement as opposed to PT. In addition, we integrate a hardware-based shadow stack [19] into PHMon-based μCFI to protect backward-edges as well.

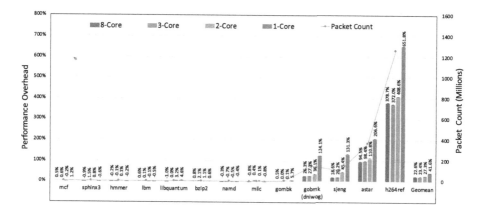

Fig. 1. Performance overhead (left y-axis) of PT-based μCFI for varying number of cores and the packet count (right y-axis) for various SPEC2006 benchmarks. (The depicted performance overhead of some of the benchmarks differs from those reported in the original work [24]. Section 4.1 provides an explanation for this performance variation.)

To evaluate our work, we implement a prototype of PHMon-based μCFI interfaced with the RISC-V Rocket core [9] on an FPGA. We choose the RISC-V Rocket core since its open-source nature allows us to evaluate our mechanism using an actual implementation rather than merely a simulation. In summary, we make the following contributions:

- We show that the performance impact of the trace processing on CFI becomes substantial if a processor does not have idle cores dedicated to software-level decoding. According to our measurements, a state-of-the-art CFI mechanism (μCFI) incurs up to 652% overhead on a single-core processor.
- Based on the insights gained from our measurements, we propose to implement μCFI through a hardware monitor (PHMon [19]), which unlike PT does not incur trace processing overhead.

- We evaluate PHMon-based μCFI on a single-core RISC-V processor. We demonstrate that PHMon can efficiently collect traces in their original forms with only 1% trace collection overhead on average. PHMon-based μCFI incurs 43% performance overhead, on average, to secure forward-edges.
- We show that PHMon-based μCFI is compatible with backward-edge CFI solutions by integrating a shadow stack based on a prior work [19]. Integrating shadow stack minimally affects the performance overhead (<1% additional overhead) and allows us to secure both forward and backward edges.

The rest of the paper is organized as follows. Section 2 provides background. Section 3 describes our design and implementation. Section 4 provides our evaluation. We discuss our implementation choices in Sect. 5 and present related work in Sect. 6. Finally, Sect. 7 concludes our work.

2   Background

In this section, we provide the background on Intel PT [32], PHMon [19], and μCFI [24].

2.1   Intel PT

PT is a debugging hardware feature in modern Intel CPUs [34]. PT collects Change of Flow Instructions (CoFIs) that cannot be derived statically. Specifically, PT generates three types of packets while encoding the CoFIs: (1) TNT packets to record 1-bit taken or non-taken information for each conditional branch (i.e., jcc), (2) TIP packets to record the target addresses of indirect branches (i.e., indirect jmp/call and ret), and (3) FUP packets for the source addresses of signals and interrupts. PT uses an efficient encoding mechanism while collecting the traces of a program. A software decoder can reconstruct the control-flow of the program using the program binary and the PT packets recorded during the execution. To reduce the number of generated packets, PT can be configured to specify the address range, privilege level, and CR3 (page table pointer) value to be monitored.

2.2   PHMon

PHMon [19] is a parallel decoupled monitor interfaced with the RISC-V Rocket processor [9] via Rocket Custom Coprocessor (RoCC). A user can configure PHMon through its software API and monitor the execution of processes. In Fig. 2, we present a simplified overview of PHMon. As the processor executes instructions, PHMon receives the architectural state of the processor for the monitored program in the form of a commit log from the writeback stage of the pipeline. The commit log includes the instruction (inst), the PC (pc_src), the next PC (pc_dst), memory/register address used in the instruction (addr), and the data accessed by the instruction (data). Note that unlike PT, PHMon collects these fields in their original forms and does not require software-decoding.

The incoming commit log is then provided to the Matching Units (MUs). Each MU applies a set of distinct monitoring rules defined via the software interface of PHMon. The MU checks the commit log to detect the matches based on these rules. For instance, a user can set an MU to detect specific instructions (e.g., `ret`, `jalr`) or instructions at specific PC values. Upon detecting a match, an MU sends a matching packet to the Action Unit (AU). The AU consists of a queue, Config Units (CFUs), an Arithmetic and Logical Unit (ALU), a local Register File, and a Control Unit. The AU stores the incoming matching packets in the queue. Each MU is associated with a CFU, where the user-defined instructions are stored for the corresponding match. The AU executes these user-defined instructions through either hardware operations (i.e., ALU or memory read/write operations) or an interrupt handled by the Operating System (OS) running on the RISC-V core.

2.3 μCFI

Although context-sensitive CFI policies significantly reduce the allowed code targets for each ICT, most of them [20,27,40] are unable to provide a unique valid target for each ICT. As an example, we provide a code snippet (inspired by the original work [24]) in Listing 1.1. In this example, the value of the function pointer (`func_ptr`) is specified by a variable `uid` that indexes into the array `func_ptr_arr`. Since the index value (`uid`) is non-constant and resolves at run-time, most context-sensitive CFI policies identify all array elements (`A`, `B`, and `C`) as valid targets. On the contrary, μCFI [24] (a state-of-the-art context-sensitive CFI) ensures that each ICT instruction has one Unique Code Target (UCT) at each step of the program execution. μCFI achieves the UCT property by identifying *constraining data* (c-data) from the program source code and using c-data as context when enforcing CFI. c-data refers to any non-constant operand (`uid`

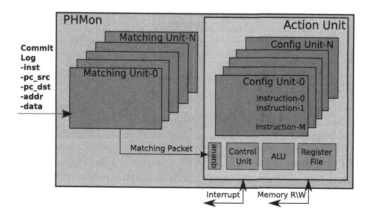

Fig. 2. A simplified overview of the PHMon [19] architecture: PHMon receives a commit log from a processor. It processes the commit log based on the user-defined rules and performs the follow-up operations such as an interrupt.

in the example) of a *sensitive instruction*, where an instruction is considered sensitive if it is involved in a function pointer calculation (line 3–4 in the example). For efficient CFI enforcement, µCFI uses PT when collecting c-data and ICT targets.

```
1  void A(); void B(); void C();
2  void handleReq(int uid) {
3     void (*func_ptr_arr[3])() = {&A, &B, &C};
4     void (*func_ptr)() = func_ptr_arr[uid];
5     (*func_ptr)();
6  }
```

Listing 1.1. Code snippet for describing µCFI.

In Fig. 3, we present the overview of µCFI enforcement using PT (PT-based µCFI). µCFI consists of a compiler (µCFI-compiler) and a dynamic monitor (µCFI-monitor). The µCFI-compiler instruments the program source to identify c-data and generates an instrumented binary. During the execution of the instrumented binary, PT writes the encoded traces into its trace buffer. When the trace buffer reaches capacity, the kernel driver (PT-Driver) copies the trace buffer into a kernel buffer. µCFI-monitor obtains the encoded PT trace of the instrumented program from the kernel buffer by signaling PT-Driver, decodes the PT trace in its trace decoder unit, and validates the ICT targets in the points-to analyzer unit.

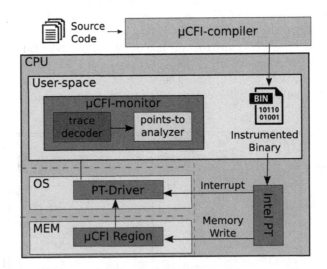

Fig. 3. µCFI [24] **design overview:** µCFI consists of two components: a compiler (µCFI-compiler) that instruments the program to identify c-data, and a runtime monitor (µCFI-monitor) to validate ICTs.

To guarantee the protection of forward-edges, μCFI-monitor requires collecting c-data, the target of indirect `calls`[2], and the target of sensitive `rets` from the instrumented program. Note that μCFI-monitor requires the target value of some of the returns (only sensitive ones) for forward-edge protection since they are involved in the function pointer calculation. More specifically, a return is "sensitive" if its corresponding function contains at least one sensitive instruction. For backward-edge protection, the μCFI-compiler instruments the program to implement a software-based shadow stack based on a prior work [16].

3   PHMon-Based μCFI

PHMon-based μCFI is a hardware-assisted context-sensitive CFI enforcement. There are two main advantages of leveraging PHMon when enforcing μCFI. First, PHMon collects the program traces in their original forms. Therefore, it does not introduce trace processing overhead when enforcing CFI. Second, PHMon offers a variety of configuration capabilities. This feature allows PHMon to easily collect both contextual data and ICT targets.

3.1   Design

In Fig. 4, we show the overview of μCFI enforcement using PHMon (PHMon-based μCFI). First, we explain how we leverage PHMon to protect forward-edges. As a first step, we compile a program with a modified version of the μCFI-compiler (detailed in Sect. 3.2) and generate the instrumented binary. Prior to the execution of this binary, PHMon is programmed to collect the required information (i.e., c-data, the target of indirect calls, and the target of sensitive returns) for μCFI enforcement. While the processor executes the binary, PHMon collects the commit log through RoCC. Then, PHMon applies the user-defined monitoring rules to the commit log to determine if the commit log includes any information for μCFI enforcement. PHMon writes the collected information from the binary into a trace buffer depicted as μCFI Region in Fig. 4. Whenever the trace buffer becomes full, PHMon raises an interrupt. Our kernel module (PHMon-Driver) copies the collected trace buffer to a kernel buffer and informs the OS such that the OS can resume the execution of the instrumented binary. The PHMon-Driver is also in charge of providing the collected traces to the μCFI-monitor as the μCFI-monitor performs the enforcement of the ICT instructions.

We protect backward-edges by implementing a shadow stack. Delshadtehrani et al. [19] already showed that PHMon can be used to implement a shadow stack (PHMon-based shadow stack). Instead of implementing a software-only shadow stack like PT-based μCFI, we implement PHMon-based shadow stack in our prototype for completeness. We program PHMon to validate the return targets by monitoring `call/ret` instructions (details provided in Sect. 3.2). In

---

[2] Since the current μCFI implementation does not protect indirect `jmps`, μCFI-compiler converts each indirect `jmp` to a conditional branch.

case of a `call` instruction, PHMon stores the new return address in a shared memory space (Shadow Stack in Fig. 4). Whenever the function returns, PHMon compares the return address with the one stored in the Shadow Stack to validate the return target.

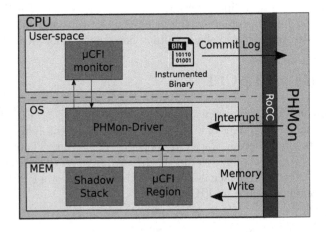

Fig. 4. Design Overview of PHMon-based μCFI: PHMon writes the collected program traces into μCFI Region and Shadow Stack in memory for forward-edge protection and backward-edge protection, respectively. μCFI-monitor fetches the traces via PHMon-Driver and enforces CFI.

One of the main differences between protecting forward and backward edges is the enforcement mechanism. For forward-edge protection, PT-based μCFI stores the collected packets in trace buffers and provides the buffer content to the software monitor by raising an interrupt. We keep our PHMon-based μCFI implementation similar to PT-based μCFI to fairly represent the architectural benefit of using PHMon. Specifically, PHMon stores the necessary information in a memory buffer and provides this information to the software monitor by triggering an interrupt. Here, we use PHMon as a trace collection mechanism (similar to PT) by leaving the ICT validation to the software monitor. For a shadow stack, PHMon validates the ICT targets at the hardware level by using a sequence of ALU instructions. Therefore, PHMon validates the ICT targets without requiring a software monitor. Note that we implement the shadow stack to show that our PHMon-based protection mechanism for forward edges is compatible with a backward-edge protection mechanism. The performance benefit of this work arises from the forward-edge protection mechanism.

3.2   Implementation

To enforce μCFI using PHMon, we applied changes to both the μCFI-compiler and μCFI-monitor. We used the same front-end IR-level instrumentation (LLVM

3.6) used by the original μCFI-compiler [2]. This front-end instrumentation is in charge of identifying c-data. We used our RISC-V back-end instrumentation to collect c-data, indirect call targets, and sensitive return targets (detailed later in this section) using PHMon. At the release of LLVM 3.6, RISC-V was not a supported architecture. Therefore, we used a newer version (LLVM 7.0) for the back-end instrumentation. We removed the code that implements the trace decoder unit (color-coded with red in Fig. 3) from the μCFI-monitor since PHMon does not perform any encoding while collecting the traces from the binary. We applied the necessary changes to allow the μCFI monitor to communicate with the PHMon-Driver. We used LLVM 7.0 to cross-compile the μCFI-monitor [3] for RISC-V. Overall, we aim to minimize the software-level implementation differences between PT-based μCFI and PHMon-based μCFI, so that we can fairly represent the architectural benefit of using PHMon.

We slightly modified the Linux kernel to support PHMon-based μCFI. Since the frequent suspension of the protected program increases the performance overhead, μCFI suspends the protected program only at security-sensitive system calls to validate the target of the collected ICTs. Similar to many prior works [13,20,24,40], we modify our kernel to suspend the execution of the protected program at the following security-sensitive system calls: mmap, mremap, remap_file_pages, mprotect, execve, execveat, sendmsg, sendmmsg, sendto, and write.

As we explained in Sect. 2.2, PHMon maintains the incoming match packets in a queue prior to executing the user-defined instructions stored in the CFU. When the queue gets full, an obvious option for PHMon [19] is to stall the fetch stage of the Rocket core's pipeline until PHMon processes all the packets waiting in the queue. However, this is not the proper way of handling the queue problem for PHMon-based μCFI since match packets frequently require an action that should be processed by the processor, i.e., interrupt. Instead of stalling the processor, we modified PHMon to raise an interrupt handled by the OS whenever the queue becomes full. We then perform busy-waiting in the interrupt handler until all the match packets in the queue are processed. To provide full protection against control-flow attacks, in addition to leveraging PHMon for forward-edge protection (PHMon-based μCFI), we also use it for backward-edge protection (PHMon-based shadow stack). In total, we program 5 MUs to simultaneously implement PHMon-based μCFI and PHMon-based shadow stack. In the rest of this section, we explain about programming PHMon for forward-edge as well as backward-edge protection.

Programming PHMon for Forward-Edge Protection: For μCFI forward-edge protection, we use three MUs: one MU for indirect calls, one MU for sensitive returns, and one MU for c-data collection. We use two registers from the Register File of PHMon to store the base address and the current pointer of μCFI Region.

Indirect Calls: To collect indirect call targets with PHMon, we replace each indirect call in the program with an indirect jump to a special function (ICF as shown in Listing 1.2). The ICF loads the indirect call target into a temporary register (t1) from a fixed memory address, and jumps to the target address stored in t1. To obtain the target address during the instrumented binary execution, we use one MU which compares the pc_src of the collected commit log with the PC value of the load instruction (0x104b4 in Listing 1.2) in the ICF. This PC value can be statically obtained by disassembling the binary. Whenever PHMon detects a match, it writes the content of data field of the commit log (this field holds the t1 value) to the trace buffer allocated for μCFI.

Sensitive Returns: As explained in Sect. 2, the target address of each sensitive return is required by the μCFI-monitor for forward-edge protection. To obtain the target values for sensitive returns, we insert a mv t1,ra instruction before each sensitive return instruction in the application. This instruction copies the return address value to the temporary register t1. PHMon can then simply collect the value of t1. To do this, we use one MU to detect the execution of the mv t1,ra instruction. Whenever the inst value in the incoming commit log matches with the machine code of the mv t1,ra, PHMon writes the content of data field of the commit log (t1 in this case) into the trace buffer allocated for μCFI.

c-data Collection: To collect c-data, we instrument the program to call a special write_cdata function as shown in Listing 1.3. The program calls the write_cdata function to send c-data to the μCFI-monitor. The write_cdata loads the value of c-data into a temporary register (t1) from a fixed memory address, and immediately returns. We program one MU to monitor the ld instruction in the write_cdata. The MU compares the pc_src value of the incoming commit logs with the PC value of the ld instruction (0x104bc in Listing 1.3). Whenever PHMon detects a match, PHMon writes the content of data field (t1 in this case) into the trace buffer allocated for μCFI.

```
1 #load indirect call target to t1
2 <ICF>:
3     104b4:   ld   t1,-728(gp)
4     104b8:   jr   t1
```

```
1 #load c-data value into t1
2 <write_cdata>:
3     104bc:   ld   t1,-720(gp)
4     104c0:   ret
```

Listing 1.2. RISC-V assembly code of the function ICF

Listing 1.3. RISC-V assembly code of the function write_cdata

Programming PHMon for Backward-Edge Protection: We implement a shadow stack (similar to original work [19]) using PHMon to demonstrate the compatibility of PHMon-based μCFI with backward-edge CFI mechanisms. We use one MU to monitor calls and one MU to monitor returns. We use two registers from the Register File of PHMon to store the base address of the Shadow Stack and the Shadow Stack pointer. We program PHMon to write the original return addresses into a trace buffer (Shadow Stack in Fig. 4) when a call instruction is executed. Upon a return instruction, PHMon pops a value from the shadow stack and compares it with the current return value. PHMon performs the comparison directly on hardware using its ALU unit. In case of a mismatch, PHMon raises an interrupt and the OS terminates the process.

Table 1. Microarchitectural details of Intel processor, Rocket core and PHMon.

Intel(R) Core(TM) i7-8700 CPU @ 3.20 GHz	
Pipeline	Out-of-order
L1 instruction cache	32 KB, 8-way set-associative
L1 data cache	32 KB, 8-way set-associative
L2 cache	256 KB, 4-way set-associative
L3 cache	12 MB, 16-way set-associative
Rocket Core @ 25 MHz	
Pipeline	6-stage, in-order
L1 I cache	16 KB, 4-way set-associative
L1 D cache	16 KB, 4-way set-associative
Register file	31 entries, 64-bit
PHMon	
MUs	5
Local Register File	6 entries, 64-bit
Match Queue	1,024 entries, 129-bit
Action Config Table	16 entries

4   Evaluation

We evaluated our PHMon-based μCFI system to answer the following questions:

(1) What is the execution time overhead of our source code instrumentation to leverage PHMon?

(2) How much overhead does PHMon incur to collect the program traces?

(3) How much overhead does PHMon-based μCFI incur when protecting forward edges only?

(4) What is the performance degradation of integrating a backward-edge CFI mechanism into PHMon-based μCFI?

4.1   Evaluation Framework

To evaluate the performance of PT-based μCFI for systems with varying core numbers, we used an Intel(R) Core(TM) i7-8700 CPU @ 3.20 GHz machine running Ubuntu 16.04. The microarchitectural details are provided in Table 1. We run PT-based μCFI on four different configurations; 1-Core, 2-Core, 3-Core, and

8-Core. As discussed in Sect. 1, in Fig. 1, we reported the performance overhead of μCFI for these four configurations. In addition, we reported the packet count collected by PT for enforcing μCFI. We used the open-source μCFI-monitor [3], μCFI-compiler [2], and μCFI-kernel [4][3] repositories. By using these three repositories with no modifications, we successfully reproduced the results (within 1% standard deviation) reported in the original work [24] on an 8-Core processor. However, we observed that μCFI-kernel does not suspend the execution of the protected program for three of the security-sensitive system calls (mremap, remap_file_pages, and write) reported in the paper [24]. Hence, we modified μCFI-kernel to include these missing system calls. This modification lead to higher performance overhead of some benchmarks (i.e., +9% for sjeng, +84% for astar, and +234% for h264ref) compared to the overheads reported in the original work [24]. In our analysis, we ran each benchmark three times and calculated the average (geometric mean) overhead. The standard deviation in our measurements is less than 1%. We also provide the error bars for each benchmark in Fig. 1.

To measure the PHMon-based μCFI performance overhead, we compared PHMon-based μCFI with the baseline implementation of the Rocket processor. The microarchitectural parameters of Rocket core and PHMon are listed in Table 1. For both experiments, Rocket core includes a 16K L1 instruction cache and a 16K L1 data cache without an L2 or an L3 cache[4]. Due to the limitation of our FPGA-base evaluation platform, we could run Rocket core with maximum frequency of 25 MHz for both experiments. We modified the open-source PHMon architecture [1] interfaced with the 6-stage in-order RISC-V Rocket processor [9] via RoCC interface. PHMon-based μCFI is prototyped on a Xilinx Zynq Zedboard [33], running a modified version of RISC-V Linux (v4.20) kernel. For both experiments, i.e., the baseline and PHMon-based μCFI, we setup the Rocket processor with the same configurations including a 16K L1 instruction and data cache. We performed each experiment three times and calculated the average value. All standard deviations were below 1%. To show the stability of our measurements, we include the error bars as well (both in Fig. 5 and 6).

During development, we observed that the μCFI-monitor validates the traces much slower than PHMon's trace collection speed. Hence, the collected traces accumulated in the kernel. Due to the limited available memory in our evaluation framework, the accumulated traces eventually resulted in an out of memory situation for some of the benchmarks. To circumvent this issue when we reach the memory limit, PHMon-Driver suspends the protected program until all the collected traces are processed by the μCFI-monitor. Note that this increases the duration that we suspend the process and potentially increases the performance overhead of PHMon-based μCFI. In an evaluation framework with more available memory, PHMon-based μCFI could outperform our current prototype.

---

[3] μCFI-kernel is the modified Linux kernel which supports μCFI.

[4] At time of our evaluation, Rocket core was not supporting L2 and L3 cache.

4.2   Evaluation Benchmarks

We calculated the runtime overhead of PT-based μCFI (Fig. 1) for C/C++ applications using the 'test' workload of SPEC2006 benchmark suite [23]. We could not obtain results (similar to original work [24]) for gcc, dealII, povray, omnetpp and xalancbmk since PT loses packets at the hardware level, which manifests as a segmentation fault in the μCFI-monitor. Additionally, in our evaluation framework, soplex caused a segmentation fault in the μCFI-monitor. We did not include perlbench in our evaluation since this benchmark frequently uses the fork system call. The heavy usage of fork puts more pressure on a single-core compared to an 8-Core; hence, using this benchmark in our evaluation framework misrepresents the performance impact of the trace processing for μCFI enforcement. Note that we represent the dniwog input as a separate data point for gobmk since its packet number is drastically higher than the remaining data points.

To evaluate PHMon-based μCFI on a Rocket processor, we used 8 out of 12 benchmarks which successfully run with PT-based μCFI. Unfortunately, we could not run lbm, namd, and gobmk with a PHMon-based μCFI due to RISC-V cross-compilation errors using LLVM 7.0. We could not run mcf and perlbench due to the limited memory on our FPGA. Similarly, sjeng was also too large for our FPGA. However, by reducing the value of TTSize (which controls the size of one of the hashtables in sjeng) to 3000 in sjeng's source code, we were able to run it with PHMon-based μCFI. For a fair evaluation, we also report the overhead of PT-based μCFI for sjeng using TTSize=3000 in Fig. 6.

4.3   Evaluation Results

Figure 5 depicts the performance impact of the source code instrumentation to collect program traces (instrumentation overhead) using PHMon. We measured the instrumentation overhead of the benchmarks by comparing the execution time of a baseline program with the instrumented program for μCFI enforcement. Our results demonstrate that the code instrumentation (Instru in Fig. 5), including our RISC-V back-end passes to transfer c-data and ICT targets to the μCFI-monitor, incurs very low performance overhead (1.7% on average). Note that the instrumentation overhead is higher (peak 5%) for the benchmarks generating more packets such as sjeng, astar, and h264ref.

To demonstrate that PHMon can efficiently collect contextual information, we measured the trace collection overhead of PHMon (TC in Fig. 5). To do this, we ran the instrumented benchmarks under the monitoring of PHMon without μCFI enforcement. Whenever the trace buffer of PHMon became full, PHMon triggered an interrupt and returned from the interrupt handler without processing the trace buffers. Note that Instru+TC overhead also includes the instrumentation overhead. Our results show that PHMon can efficiently collect program traces (<1% overhead on average and 4% peak). Note that PHMon's trace collection overhead is maximum of 4% even for benchmarks generating more packets such as sjeng, astar, and h264ref.

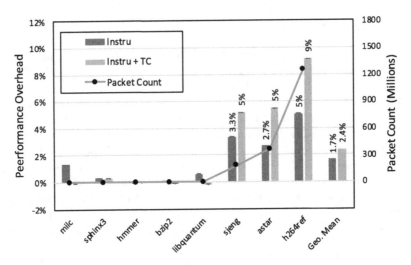

Fig. 5. Performance overhead (left y-axis) of the instrumented binary (`Instru`) and trace collection (`TC`) overhead of PHMon. We use the right y-axis to show the packet count for each benchmark.

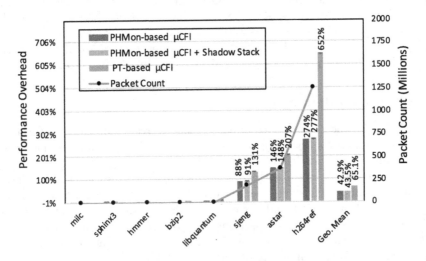

Fig. 6. Performance overhead of PHMon-based μCFI, PHMon-based μCFI + Shadow Stack, and PT-based μCFI. We use the right y-axis for providing the packet count for each benchmark.

Using Fig. 6, we first depict the performance overhead of PHMon-based μCFI and PT-based μCFI when protecting only the forward-edges. Both PHMon-based and PT-based μCFI perform efficiently for benchmarks such as `milc`, `sphinx3`, `hmmer`, `bzip2`, and `libquantum` that generate fewer packets. PHMon-based μCFI introduces 88%, 146%, and 274% overhead for packet-intensive sjeng, astar, and h264ref benchmarks, respectively. For these benchmarks, PT-based μCFI results in 131%, 207%, and 652% performance overhead, respectively. Since PHMon-based μCFI does not incur trace processing overhead, its performance bottleneck mainly arises from the ICT validation performed by the μCFI-monitor. For PT-based μCFI, there is an additional trace processing overhead prior to ICT validation.

In Fig. 6, we also show the full PHMon-based CFI protection overhead. The full protection secures forward-edges and backward-edges with PHMon-based μCFI and PHMon-based shadow stack, respectively. Adding the shadow stack increases the performance overhead of PHMon-based μCFI by less than 1% on average (peak 3%) and allows us to fully protect the programs against control-flow hijacking attacks.

The original work [19] reports the power and area overhead of PHMon with varying number of MUs. Based on those results, PHMon-based μCFI using three MUs incurs 6.5% power and 15.1% area overhead. The full protection requires five MUs, which results in 9.2% power and 18.4% area overhead.

5   Discussion

In this section, we discuss some of our design choices when implementing μCFI using PHMon. We specifically discuss aspects of our source code instrumentation (Sect. 3.2) to protect forward-edges.

When enforcing μCFI using PHMon, we aim to minimize the software-level implementation differences with the original PT-based μCFI work so that we can fairly represent the architectural benefit of using PHMon. Therefore, similar to PT-based μCFI, we collected indirect call targets by redirecting the control-flow to the special function (ICF as shown in Listing 1.2). We initially aimed to replace indirect calls with direct calls to ICF similar to PT-based μCFI targeting x86_64. Unfortunately, direct calls in RISC-V can target a limited range (± 1 MiB) since the offset is encoded into the operand of the instruction and that operand is only 20 bits. Therefore, we could not replace each indirect call with a direct call in RISC-V, especially for benchmarks with bigger code size, and had to use indirect jumps instead. Unfortunately, we do not provide additional checks to ensure that these indirect jumps are not subverted by an attacker at run-time. However, we could easily avoid these indirect jumps in the binary by instrumenting the code with "custom" instructions. The RISC-V ISA allows adding a custom ISA extension. We could insert a custom instruction that stores the target address of an indirect call in a register before each indirect call instruction. This way, we could obtain indirect call targets without redirecting indirect calls to the ICF using indirect jumps. We redirect indirect calls to ICF using indirect jumps instead of inserting custom instructions to have a similar implementation with PT-based μCFI.

We collect c-data by monitoring the ld instruction at a fixed address (see Listing 1.3). We obtain the PC value of ld instruction using a static analysis. Our design choice aligns with PT-based μCFI which generates packets only for fixed addresses. To minimize the software-level implementation differences, we implement PHMon-based μCFI in a similar way. Unfortunately, this design choice can result in some portability issues. For instance, it can cause problems with randomization mechanisms like ASLR. In fact, this issue could also easily be addressed by inserting a custom instruction that will help us store the constraining data in a register. This way, we could program PHMon to monitor the custom instruction rather than a specific program counter. Since the instruction machine code is the same regardless of the program layout, μCFI enforcement would be more portable than our current implementation.

We insert `mv t1,ra` instruction before each sensitive return to collect the return value using PHMon. We choose the `mv t1,ra` instruction since none of the SPEC2006 benchmarks contains it when compiled without our back-end pass. We acknowledge that the proper way to collect sensitive return values would be to insert a custom instruction before each sensitive return. For instance, the custom instruction could store the return value in a register. We could program PHMon to monitor this custom instruction and write the content of the register value into memory. This way, we could ensure that the original program does not contain the inserted instruction unless it enforces μCFI.

6 Related Work

Our PHMon-based μCFI approach is closely related to works which use hardware support for CFI enforcement. We divide these hardware mechanisms into two categories: the ones already deployed in modern processors, and the new hardware designs proposed for future deployment.

6.1 Reusing Deployed Hardware Features

CFI mechanisms that rely on existing hardware features are practical since they can be readily deployed on commodity hardware. Unfortunately, existing hardware features have several drawbacks since the hardware features are not designed with security in mind. Specifically, CFIMon [42] utilizes Branch Trace Store (BTS) [34] to enforce CFI. However, BTS incurs high performance overheads ($20\times$–$40\times$) [40]. To reduce the overhead, several works [13,31,40] use Last Branch Record (LBR) [34] for CFI enforcement. LBR can record the last N executed branches where N can be 4, 8, 16, or 32 depending on the processor model. For instance, kBouncer [31] aims to protect backward-edges from ROP attacks using LBR. kBouncer checks the control flow of the program whenever the program makes a security sensitive system call. ROPecker [13] extended kBouncer's approach by emulating the potential program execution with the help of a statically generated ROP gadget database. The key idea is to detect ROP gadgets which can possibly be stitched together towards a malicious purpose. Due to LBR's branch recording capacity, kBouncer and ROPecker are shown to be vulnerable to history flushing attacks [11]. This attack initially cleanses any evidence of the ROP attack in the short-term history and then creates a view of history that the defense will not classify as an attack. Another LBR-based CFI mechanism (PathArmor [40]) raises the bar for history flushing attacks thanks to its context-sensitive CFI policy. PathArmor uses LBR to record the last 16 indirect branches and direct calls as the context. Unfortunately, PathArmor checks less than 0.1% of total returns on NGINX [21] for backward-edge protection because of the LBR's limited trace recording capability.

CFIGuard [41] overcomes the limited size of LBR by combining it with the Performance Monitoring Unit. CFIGuard raises an interrupt whenever LBR buffer is full. However, triggering an interrupt every 16 branches can significantly increase the performance overhead, especially for CPU-intensive applications. OS-CFI [28] implements an origin sensitive context-sensitive CFI mechanism to reduce the attack surface for C-style indirect calls and C++ virtual calls. For the former, the origin is the most recently updated code location. For the latter, the origin refers to code location where receiving object's constructor is called. OS-CFI uses Intel MPX for efficiently storing and retrieving the origin of the code pointers. OS-CFI uses inline reference monitors to collect and maintain the contextual information. Since these monitors extensively use memory to store the temporary data for searching hash table, they are vulnerable to race conditions for a short interval. To protect the integrity of inline reference monitors, OS-CFI utilizes the transactional memory (Intel TSX). LMP [25] uses MPX for protecting backward-edges by implementing a shadow stack via program source instrumentation. Unfortunately, Intel MPX is not adopted by industry widely due to the considerable performance overhead and compatibility issues [30]. MPX is not available on future Intel processors [5].

Several researchers also leverage Intel PT for CFI enforcement. PT can record higher number of indirect branches than LBR, which allows researchers to enforce more precise CFI mechanisms. For instance, PT-CFI [22] enforces backward-edge CFI by implementing a shadow stack for the COTS binaries based on the PT traces. Griffin [21] implements three different CFI policies over unmodified binaries and shows the tradeoff between precision and performance. Also, Griffin shows the performance impact of the number of kernel threads on the speed of buffer trace processing and CFI enforcement, which goes up from ~%8 to ~%19 on NGINX as we increase the number of threads from one to six. FlowGuard [29] attempts to minimize the performance overhead of PT with its fuzzing-assisted approach. The key idea is to collect program traces prior to the program execution by using a fuzzer and minimize the overhead of expensive software-level decoding of PT. Dynamic analysis-based approaches [20,24] increase the precision of CFI by obtaining additional information from the program at runtime, but at the expense of introducing higher performance overhead. More specifically, PITTYPAT [20] implements a path-sensitive CFI policy, which verifies the whole executed control path of the program. μCFI uses constraining data to provide unique code target for each ICT.

PHMon-based μCFI enforces CFI without weakening any security guarantees. As opposed to PT-based μCFI, PHMon-based μCFI can collect the original form of the data and does not require software-level decoding of collected information when validating control-flows. Also, PHMon-based μCFI is not vulnerable to history flushing attacks as opposed to LBR-based CFI mechanisms.

6.2 New Hardware Designs

Several works propose new hardware designs to enforce CFI. For instance, HAFIX [17] proposes a fine-grained backward-edge CFI system which confines function returns to active call sites. It assigns unique labels to each function by instrumenting the program source with compiler support and enforces the CFI policy directly on hardware for efficiency. Unfortunately, recent work shows that HAFIX is vulnerable to Back-Call-Site attack [39] and cannot fully protect backward-edges. Also, it is vulnerable to any forward-edge attacks. HCFI [14] can fully protect backward-edges by implementing a shadow stack. Additionally, it implements the forward-edge CFI policy discussed by Abadi et al. [7]. Similar to HAFIX, HCFI also modifies the ISA and introduces new instructions to provide CFI capability to the core. Sullivan et al. [37] enhance HAFIX by supporting forward edge protection. Although both Sullivan et al. [37] and HCFI implement efficient forward-edge CFI policies directly on hardware, unlike μCFI, they are still unable to provide a unique target for each ICT and cannot fully protect against forward edge attacks. Intel announced its hardware support for CFI in the form of CET [6]. CET offers strong backward-edge protection with a shadow stack. Unfortunately, the forward-edge policy protection (i.e., Indirect branch tracking) is coarse-grained and vulnerable to advanced attacks such as JOP [12] and COOP [36]. Nile [18] and PHMon [19] offer full protection against backward-edge attacks by implementing a shadow stack with less than 2% performance overhead. However, these two works cannot protect against forward-edge attacks. This work complements PHMon by offering forward-edge protection.

7   Conclusion

In this work, we show that the hardware features originally designed for debugging on Intel processors are not efficient when used for enforcing CFI. Specifically, Intel PT-based CFI mechanisms put high pressure onto idle cores in processor since they require expensive software-level decoding prior to ICT enforcement. All of these PT-based mechanisms assume that idle cores are readily available for CFI enforcement, which is not necessarily the case considering the multithreaded nature of common applications. We evaluate the performance impact of the trace processing on PT-based CFI enforcement and show that a state-of-the-art CFI mechanism (μCFI) incurs up to 652% overhead on a single-core compared to 372% overhead on a 3-Core processor. When enforcing CFI, we leverage a programmable hardware monitor (PHMon) which does not introduce trace processing overhead unlike PT. Our PHMon-based μCFI mechanism incurs 43% performance overhead, on average, to secure forward edges. We also integrate a hardware-based shadow stack to fully secure the program including backward-edges. Adding the shadow stack increases the performance overhead of PHMon-based μCFI by less than 1% on average.

Acknowledgements. This work was supported in part by NSF SaTC Award 1916393 and Google Faculty Research Award.

References

1. bu-icsg. https://github.com/bu-icsg/PHMon. Accessed 10 Feb 2020
2. uCFI-GATech. github.com/uCFI-GATech/ucfi-compiler/commit/6502e1c. Accessed 10 Feb 2020
3. uCFI-GATech. github.com/uCFI-GATech/ucfi-monitor/commit/8787121. Accessed 10 Feb 2020
4. uCFI-GATech. github.com/uCFI-GATech/ucfi-kernel/commit/08a15f7. Accessed 10 Feb 2020
5. Intel memory protection extensions (2013). https://software.intel.com/en-us/articles/introduction-to-intel-memory-protection-extensions
6. Intel control-flow enforcement technology (2019). https://software.intel.com/sites/default/files/managed/4d/2a/control-flow-enforcement-technology-preview.pdf. Accessed 10 Feb 2020
7. Abadi, M., Budiu, M., Erlingsson, Ú., Ligatti, J.: Control-flow integrity principles, implementations, and applications. ACM Trans. Inf. Syst. Secur. (TISSEC) **13**(1), 1–40 (2009)
8. Andersen, S.: Changes to functionality in Microsoft windows XP service pack 2 part 3: memory protection technologies (2004)
9. Asanović, K., et al.: The rocket chip generator. Technical report, EECS Department, UC Berkeley (2016)
10. Burow, N., et al.: Control-flow integrity: precision, security, and performance. ACM Comput. Surv. (CSUR) **50**(1), 1–33 (2017)
11. Carlini, N., Wagner, D.: ROP is still dangerous: breaking modern defenses. In: Proceedings of the USENIX Security Symposium (2014)
12. Checkoway, S., Davi, L., Dmitrienko, A., Sadeghi, A.R., Shacham, H., Winandy, M.: Return-oriented programming without returns. In: Proceedings of the Conference on Computer and Communications Security, CCS (2010)
13. Cheng, Y., Zhou, Z., Miao, Y., Ding, X., Deng, H.R.: ROPecker: a generic and practical approach for defending against ROP attacks. In: Symposium on Network and Distributed System Security, NDSS (2014)
14. Christoulakis, N., Christou, G., Athanasopoulos, E., Ioannidis, S.: HCFI: hardware-enforced control-flow integrity. In: Proceedings of the Sixth Conference on Data and Application Security and Privacy, CODASPY (2016)
15. Cui, W., et al.: REPT: reverse debugging of failures in deployed software. In: Proceedings of the USENIX Symposium on Operating Systems Design and Implementation, OSDI (2018)
16. Dang, T.H., Maniatis, P., Wagner, D.: The performance cost of shadow stacks and stack canaries. In: Proceedings of the ACM Symposium on Information, Computer and Communications Security, ASIA CCS (2015)
17. Davi, L., et al.: HAFIX: hardware-assisted flow integrity extension. In: Proceedings of the Design Automation Conference, DAC (2015)
18. Delshadtehrani, L., Eldridge, S., Canakci, S., Egele, M., Joshi, A.: Nile: a programmable monitoring coprocessor. IEEE Comput. Archit. Lett. **17**(1), 92–95 (2018)

19. Delshadtehrani, L., Canakci, S., Zhou, B., Eldridge, S., Joshi, A., Egele, M.: Phmon: a programmable hardware monitor and its security use cases. In: Proceedings of the USENIX Security Symposium (2020)

20. Ding, R., Qian, C., Song, C., Harris, B., Kim, T., Lee, W.: Efficient protection of path-sensitive control security. In: Proceedings of the USENIX Security Symposium (2017)

21. Ge, X., Cui, W., Jaeger, T.: Griffin: guarding control flows using intel processor trace. In: Proceedings of the International Conference on Architectural Support for Programming Languages and Operating Systems, ASPLOS (2017)

22. Gu, Y., Zhao, Q., Zhang, Y., Lin, Z.: PT-CFI: transparent backward-edge control flow violation detection using intel processor trace. In: Proceedings of the Conference on Data and Application Security and Privacy, CODASPY (2017)

23. Henning, J.L.: SPEC CPU2006 benchmark descriptions. ACM SIGARCH Comput. Archit. News **34**(4), 1–17 (2006)

24. Hu, H., et al.: Enforcing unique code target property for control-flow integrity. In: Proceedings of the Conference on Computer and Communications Security, CCS (2018)

25. Huang, W., Huang, Z., Miyani, D., Lie, D.: LMP: light-weighted memory protection with hardware assistance. In: Proceedings of the Annual Conference on Computer Security Applications, ACSAC (2016)

26. Kasikci, B., Schubert, B., Pereira, C., Pokam, G., Candea, G.: Failure sketching: a technique for automated root cause diagnosis of in-production failures. In: Proceedings of the Symposium on Operating Systems Principles, SOSP (2015)

27. Khandaker, M., Naser, A., Liu, W., Wang, Z., Zhou, Y., Cheng, Y.: Adaptive call-site sensitive control flow integrity. In: Proceedings of the European Symposium on Security and Privacy, EuroS&P (2019)

28. Khandaker, M.R., Liu, W., Naser, A., Wang, Z., Yang, J.: Origin-sensitive control flow integrity. In: Proceedings of the USENIX Security Symposium (2019)

29. Liu, Y., Shi, P., Wang, X., Chen, H., Zang, B., Guan, H.: Transparent and efficient CFI enforcement with intel processor trace. In: Proceedings of the International Symposium on High Performance Computer Architecture (HPCA), HPCA (2017)

30. Oleksenko, O., Kuvaiskii, D., Bhatotia, P., Felber, P., Fetzer, C.: Intel MPX explained: a cross-layer analysis of the intel MPX system stack. Proc. ACM Meas. Anal. Comput. Syst. **2**(2), 1–30 (2018)

31. Pappas, V., Polychronakis, M., Keromytis, A.D.: Transparent ROP exploit mitigation using indirect branch tracing. In: Proceedings of the USENIX Security Symposium (2013)

32. Reinders, J.: Processor tracing, June 2017. https://software.intel.com/en-us/blogs/2013/09/18/processor-tracing

33. Digilent's ZedBoard Zynq FPGA (2017). http://www.digilentinc.com/Products/Detail.cfm?Prod=ZEDBOARD/. Accessed 10 Feb 2020

34. Intel Corporation: Intel 64 and IA-32 architectures software developer's manual. System Programming Guide, vol. 3 (3A, 3B, 3C & 3D) (2016)

35. Roemer, R., Buchanan, E., Shacham, H., Savage, S.: Return-oriented programming: systems, languages, and applications. ACM Trans. Inf. Syst. Secur. (TISSEC) **15**(1), 1–34 (2012)

36. Schuster, F., Tendyck, T., Liebchen, C., Davi, L., Sadeghi, A.R., Holz, T.: Counterfeit object-oriented programming: on the difficulty of preventing code reuse attacks in C++ applications. In: Proceedings of the Symposium on Security and Privacy, S&P (2015)

37. Sullivan, D., Arias, O., Davi, L., Larsen, P., Sadeghi, A., Jin, Y.: Strategy without tactics: policy-agnostic hardware-enhanced control-flow integrity. In: Proceedings of the Design Automation Conference, DAC (2016)

38. Thalheim, J., Bhatotia, P., Fetzer, C.: Inspector: data provenance using intel processor trace (PT). In: International Conference on Distributed Computing Systems (ICDCS) (2016)

39. Theodorides, M., Wagner, D.: Breaking active-set backward-edge CFI. In: International Symposium on Hardware Oriented Security and Trust, HOST (2017)

40. van der Veen, V., et al.: Practical context-sensitive CFI. In: Proceedings of the Conference on Computer and Communications Security, CCS (2015)

41. Yuan, P., Zeng, Q., Ding, X.: Hardware-assisted fine-grained code-reuse attack detection. In: Proceedings of the International Symposium on Research in Attacks, Intrusions, and Defenses, RAID (2015)

42. Xia, Y., Liu, Y., Chen, H., Zang, B.: CFIMon: detecting violation of control flow integrity using performance counters. In: IEEE/IFIP International Conference on Dependable Systems and Networks, DSN (2012)

43. Zhang, M., Sekar, R.: Control flow integrity for COTS binaries. In: Proceedings of the USENIX Security Symposium (2013)

Author Index

Printed in the United States
By Bookmasters